The History of English
in a Social Context

Trends in Linguistics
Studies and Monographs 129

Editor
Werner Winter

Mouton de Gruyter
Berlin · New York

The History of English in a Social Context

A Contribution to Historical Sociolinguistics

edited by
Dieter Kastovsky
Arthur Mettinger

Mouton de Gruyter
Berlin · New York   2000

Mouton de Gruyter (formerly Mouton, The Hague)
is a Division of Walter de Gruyter GmbH & Co. KG, Berlin.

☉ Printed on acid-free paper which falls within the guidelines
of the ANSI to ensure permanence and durability.

Die Deutsche Bibliothek − *CIP-Einheitsaufnahme*

> The history of English in a social context : a contribution to
> historical sociolinguistics / ed. by Dieter Kastovsky ; Arthur
> Mettinger. − Berlin ; New York : Mouton de Gruyter, 2000
>   (Trends in linguistics : Studies and monographs ; 129)
> ISBN 3-11-016707-7

© Copyright 2000 by Walter de Gruyter GmbH & Co. KG, 10785 Berlin
All rights reserved, including those of translation into foreign languages. No part of this book may be reproduced or transmitted in any form or by any means, electronic or mechanical, including photocopy, recording or any information storage and retrieval system, without permission in writing from the publisher.
Printing & Binding: Hubert & Co, Göttingen.
Cover design: Christopher Schneider, Berlin.
Printed in Germany.

Introduction

Dieter Kastovsky and Arthur Mettinger

Since the work of Labov in the sixties and seventies (cf. Labov 1966, 1972a, 1972b), it has been generally accepted that linguistic change is inextricably connected with synchronic variation, variation which involves space (diatopic variation), social strata, gender (diastratic variation), text type and type of discourse as well as subject matter (diaphasic variation)[1], and possibly a number of additional factors. The tools of modern sociolinguistics, whose objective is the study of these variations, involve primarily quantitative, i.e. statistical analyses of large amounts of data, which are the basis for further, qualitative assessments relating to the direction of the change in question as it is reflected by the variation observed. These methods were developed in connection with investigations of the contemporary language, where data were much more readily available than for historical periods of a language. In this way it became possible to plot the progress of an ongoing change (such as the spread of rhoticity in New York, or the propagation of various vowel shifts in the U.S.) through the various strata of a speech community on the basis of directly observable data, which were usually gathered through elicitation (unfortunately involving what came to be called the "observer's paradox", cf. Tieken-Boon van Ostade's paper in this volume). It was only with the advent of machine-readable historical corpora such as the *Diachronic part of the Helsinki Corpus of English texts* in the eighties and the numerous other historical corpora, which have been compiled since then, that systematic studies in historical sociolinguistics could be undertaken along the same lines. As the references in the articles contained in this volume show, it was – and still is – the group of scholars working with Matti Rissanen in Helsinki, who provided the groundwork for this new direction – historical sociolinguistics within the framework of variationist theory –, but as the range of contributors to this volume also shows, this direction has in the meantime been taken up in many other places. It was this development which had prompted the editors to devote their 1997 conference in Tulln (September 11-14, 1997) to *The history of English in a social context* (for short *HESCO*), after the previous conference had focused on *Language contact in the history of English* (*LACHE* 1994, cf. Kastovsky and Mettinger ((eds.) 2000)). It just so happened that right before the Tulln conference, the 4th ESSE conference took place in Debrecen, Hungary (September 5-9, 1997), where Terttu Nevalainen and Ingrid Tieken-Boon van Ostade organised a workshop on historical sociolinguistics, in which also some participants of the Tulln conference took part. In view of this topical and personal overlap, the editors decided to select papers from both the Tulln conference and the ESSE workshop for the present publication. All the papers contained in this volume were substantially revised and brought up to date in 1999. The papers by Norman Blake, Christiane Dalton-Puffer, Roberta Facchinetti, Gabriella Mazzon, Anneli Meurman-Solin, Robert McColl Millar, Stephen Nagle, Arja Nurmi, Clausdirk Pollner, Ute Smit come from the Tulln conference, those by Silvia Bruti, Roderick W. McConchie, Margaret Sönmez and Ingrid Tieken-Boon van Ostade from the ESSE workshop, and the papers by Jonathan Culpeper and Merja Kytö and Terttu Nevalainen and Helena Raumolin-Brunberg are expanded combinations of their papers presented at both occasions.

The papers included in this volume cover a wide range of topics (forms of address, spelling and pronunciation, lexis, language attitudes, auxiliaries), periods (Middle English, Early Modern English, Modern English) and varieties of English (British English, American English, Scots, South African English) and thus provide a multifaceted illustration of the questions dealt with in historical sociolinguistics and the various methodologies applied to answer them. The majority of the papers deals with the Early Modern English period (Blake; Bruti; Culpeper and Kytö; McConchie; Meurman-Solin; Nurmi; Sönmez), which is not surprising in view of the fact that this period is one of the major centres of interest of the

Helsinki research group, cf. also Kastovsky ((ed.) 1994)). But there are also papers on Middle English (Mazzon), and the nineteenth and twentieth centuries (Facchinetti; McColl Millar; Nagle, Fain, and Sanders; Pollner; Smit).

Although all papers in one way or another also address theoretical and methodological problems beside actual changes going on in the period of time investigated, with some papers theoretical aspects are more in the foreground than in others. This is, e.g., the case with Tieken-Boon van Ostade's "Sociohistorical linguistics and the observer's paradox". It is well known from work with informants that the presence of an observer influences their behaviour and thus might skew the results. In work with historical texts it is generally assumed, however, that one need not reckon with this observer's paradox, because the texts we are dealing with have come into being without any such observer or interviewer. Tieken-Boon van Ostade, however, warns us that this may well be a fallacy, since even those records which we think come closest to unmonitored spoken language may have been subject to conscious or unconscious editing and do not represent actual, unmonitored spoken language. Thus, letters were often read publicly, and also followed certain stylistic conventions, by which the letter-writer would have been constrained not to use his real vernacular as might have been the case in face-to-face conversation. And the same holds for reported conversation, since conversation was also subject to certain stylistic conventions. Thus, according to Tieken-Boon van Ostade, the historical sociolinguist has to reckon with the observer's paradox as much as the modern sociolinguist does, except that in this case it is the consciously or subconsciously applied degree of formality which causes the paradox and has therefore to be taken into consideration.

Another programmatic paper is Culpeper and Kytö's "Gender voices in the spoken interaction of the past: a pilot study based on Early Modern English trial proceedings". The authors investigate different approaches to the relationship between language and gender and conclude that the most popular one, the variationist approach based purely on token frequencies, may lead to wrong results, if status, role and speech situation are not also taken into consideration.

They show that the linguistic differences in the behaviour of women as compared to men in court trials are not just a reflection of gender differences as such, but also due to different speech styles used in the exchanges between judges and witnesses, women usually resorting to narratives, whereas men are more often subject to cross examination. This, in turn, seems to be the result of different expectations on the part of the judges, prosecutors and scribes with regard to the roles the different genders are supposed to play in a court trial.

Nevalainen and Raumolin-Brunberg's "The changing role of London on the linguistic map of Tudor and Stuart England" is also concerned with more general questions. One aspect is the embedding of individual changes into more general, global tendencies, which might be regarded as "drifts" (cf. Sapir 1921), or as "typological changes", as has been advocated by one of the editors in several publications (cf. Kastovsky 1992, 1994, 1998, 1999). The other major theoretical problem discussed is the wave model of linguistic change as an explanation of how a change gets propagated through a speech community, viz. by moving through neighbouring dialects. This model seems to be contradicted by many changes having taken place in London in the period in question. These usually started out in the North, then were taken up in London (more or less successfully for the time being), but not necessarily in the Midlands, e.g. in East Anglia (especially Norwich). The changes involved concern subject-verb agreement, the relative pronouns *the which* vs. *which*, subject pronoun *ye* vs. *you*, the emergence of *its*, the prop-word *one*, and indefinite compound pronouns. The authors systematically compare the development in the North, in East Anglia (Norwich) and London, and show that one of the major factors is the large-scale immigration into London from the North, which makes London a dialectally – and also socially – mixed area. It is the interaction of this dialect mixture and the social structure of the capital which is responsible for the development of these features, and this development is far more complex than would have been the case in a basically monodialectal society as, e.g., Norwich. Thus, these examples in no way refute the wave model of the spread of linguistic change, but they do point towards important modifications of this model.

Two papers deal with forms of address, Mazzon's on "Social relations and forms of address in the *Canterbury Tales*", and Bruti's on "Address pronouns in Shakespeare's English: a re-appraisal in terms of markedness". Mazzon shows that the choice between T and V address pronouns in the *Canterbury Tales* is not merely connected to the social relationship between the interlocutors, their state of mind, or some affective undertone, but that it can also be very consciously manipulated as an additional politeness strategy fulfilling some "face-work" in the interchange, as has been noticed before in the works of Shakespeare. Similar conclusions are reached by Bruti, who demonstrates that the choice of T and V pronouns in Shakespeare is more complex than so far assumed, because there are additional pragmatic aspects to be considered, e.g. the question, in which situation which pronoun is more marked than the other. And this may change from situation to situation, even with the same interlocutors, which makes it possible that a pronoun switch can take place both from social/emotional remoteness to closeness, but also from closeness to remoteness. This means that pronoun markedness is not absolute but context-dependent.

Norman Blake's "*Excellent* in Shakespeare" is an in-depth study of this adjective and related adverbs and nouns, claiming that this word-family had a "two-edged pragmatic use", which, depending on the context, could be positive, ironic, or negative, the latter use on the whole disregarded in the dictionaries, because they tend to neglect pragmatic aspects. Another lexical study is McConchie's "Fashionable idiolects? The use of the negative prefix *dis-* 1520-1620", which concentrates on *dis*-neologisms in medical terminology. McConchie questions the assumption, based on the *OED* listings of *dis*-formations, that this pattern was particularly productive in the circle around the Sidney family and expanded from there, because there are many *dis*-formations not listed in the *OED*, which occur in writings of people not connected with Sidney. Consequently, Sidney may not necessarily have acted as the starting-point of a fashion, the fashion might have had a broader basis.

Three papers are devoted to graphemic-phonological aspects of linguistic change and the sociolinguistic factors involved. Sönmez's "Perceived and real differences between men's and women's spellings of the early to mid seventeenth century" takes up the claim that throughout the history of English men have always been better spellers than women. She first addresses the methodological problem of how to measure the quality of spelling when one has to compare different texts (belonging to different text types) of different lengths by different people, and then discusses the spelling of two contemporaries, Lady Brilliana Harley and the Duke of Newcastle. She concludes that judgements like the above are questionable in a situation where there is a lot of variation, and where phonetic spellings interfere with beginning standardisation. In any case, the empirical comparison does not confirm the assumption of unequal spelling performance. Meurman-Solin's "On the conditioning of geographical and social distance in language variation and change in Renaissance Scots" investigates how incipient phonetic changes are reflected by the geographical, but also socially conditioned distribution of spelling variants. Especially important is the question whether the spread of a particular spelling at the same time reflects the spread of a phonetic change (i.e. constitutes a phonetic spelling), or is conditioned by a prestige spelling becoming the norm, but without being accompanied by the phonetic change in question. This cannot always be determined unambiguously. Finally, Dalton-Puffer's paper "Is there a social element in English word-stress? Explorations into a non-categorical treatment of English stress: a long-term view" takes up the frequently discussed nature of the Modern English stress system and its development from an exclusively Germanic system to a Romance dominated (or possibly mixed) one. Starting from the observation that since the beginning of the inroad of French and Latin loans in Middle English there has always been stress variation, a canonical treatment based on syllable weight, which takes the Romance stress assignment from left to right as basic, is unsatisfactory, since it does not account for this variation. Instead she proposes a number of rivalling principles for stress assignment, whose hierarchy might be influenced also by pragmatic and sociolinguistic factors (e.g. level of education).

Two studies deal with auxiliaries. Facchinetti ("The modal verb *shall* between grammar and usage in the nineteenth century") bases her investigation on data collected from *The Times* and *The Sunday Times* (articles dealing with the Irish Question in the nineteenth century) and compares this actual usage with the prescriptive statements in contemporary grammars. It turns out that the grammatical rules are largely, but by no means universally, followed; on the other hand, the criticism of deviant Irish usage found in the same grammars is not corroborated – it is also clearly found in texts of British English provenience. The rise of periphrastic *do* in Early Modern English has for a long time been a favourite topic of historical English linguistics, and is also addressed in this volume, viz. in Nurmi's paper "The rise and regulation of periphrastic *do* in negative declarative sentences: a sociolinguistic study". The study is based on the *Corpus of Early English Correspondences*, recently compiled under the direction of Terttu Nevalainen and Helena Raumolin-Brunberg, which will certainly become a very important research tool in the future because of the relative closeness of the texts to spoken language (*pace* Tieken-Boon van Ostade). Nurmi shows that the rise of *do* in negative-declarative sentences is strongly influenced by text type (genre), as it is in affirmative sentences, but not by sociolinguistic factors, at least in the sixteenth century, in contradistinction to affirmative *do*. In the seventeenth century, however, the use of *do* in negative declarative sentences proves to be increasingly subject to sociolinguistic factors, especially gender: it seems that women were leading this change and its implementation.

Sociolinguistics is not only concerned with variation and its conditioning factors; another important domain is attitudes towards variation and varieties, since these may also play an important role in determining the speed and the direction of linguistic change. This is the topic of three papers, two dealing with Scots, one dealing with South African English (the latter with an admixture of "political correctness"). McColl Millar ("Covert and overt language attitudes to the Scots tongue expressed in the *Statistical accounts of Scotland*") discusses the status accorded to Scots as compared to Standard English in these surveys from the 1790s, the 1830s/1840s and from the 1940s on. He correlates these assessments with extralinguistic developments in science, economy, politics and demonstrates that language attitudes were shaped by these to a considerable extent. Pollner's "Shibboleth's galore: the treatment of Irish and Scottish English in histories of the English language" shows that until fairly recently these varieties of English were either hardly discussed at all, or discussed with gross misconceptions in histories of the English language. This is even true of fairly recent, mainly popular publications. Finally, Smit's "Ethnolinguistic identity as a common denominator: a socio-historical investigation of the lexical items for 'people' in South African English", more precisely lexical items referring to people living in South Africa, deals with the influence of political changes in the country on the lexicon. The study is based on a combination of structural and prototype semantics and shows that – due to the recent political changes – the original major subdivision of the lexical set 'people in South Africa' into WHITE – NON-WHITE based on "ethnolinguistic identity" with the parameters RACE and LANGUAGE is gradually being replaced by a classification based on the parameter AREA.

This brings us to the last paper, which also discusses a change in progress, viz. Nagle, Fain, and Sanders's "The influence of political correctness on lexical and grammatical change in late-twentieth-century English". The authors discuss the history of political correctness, primarily in the U.S., but also in Europe, and its influence on various domains of the language. While lexical innovations ("euphemisms") and pronoun agreement phenomena are generally regarded as the major exponents of this movement, the effect of political correctness on noun phrase structure – an increase of postpositional modification instead of the standard adjective–noun structure (*disabled people > people with disabilities*) seems to be new, and is to our knowledge pointed out for the first time in this paper.

Since the majority of the papers in this volume go back to papers presented at the HESCO conference in Tulln 1997, we would first of all like to acknowledge our debt of gratitude to the benefactors who made this conference a most enjoyable occasion for the conference organisers, but hopefully also for the conference participants.

First and foremost, our thanks go to the Bundesminister für Wissenschaft und Forschung, Herrn Dr. Caspar Einem, and the Landeshauptmann of Niederösterreich, Herrn Dr. Erwin Pröll, both for accepting the patronage of the conference and for subsidising it substantially. We also gratefully acknowledge the assistance of the Österreichische Nationalbank and the I. Österreichische Sparkasse. And we would also like to thank the Mayor and the Town Councillor for Cultural Affairs of Tulln for the hospitality extended to the conference in the form of a memorable reception. Thanks also again go the staff of the Hotel Rossmühle, our venue, and in particular to its chef for the delicious meals we were served. And, as always, the conference secretary, Frau Christine Klein, was the real conference organiser, because whatever worked smoothly was her doing, and whatever went wrong was our responsibility.

The editors would also like to thank Werner Winter for accepting this volume into his series *Trends in Linguistics. Studies and Monographs*. Finally we are also grateful for the editorial help provided by Dr. Gunther Kaltenböck, but above all we would like to say "thank you" to Ms. Anna-Maria Adaktylos, linguist and computer freak, who did a great job with the final editing and the preparation of the camera-ready manuscript. Her zest and eagerness immensely helped us to keep to the tight schedule set up by the publishers; editors don't normally like to have someone breathing down their neck, but she did it efficiently – and pleasantly.

Notes

1. The terms "diatopic, diastratic, diaphasic variation" are taken over from Coseriu, cf. e.g. Coseriu (1970); Coseriu and Geckeler (1981).

References

Coseriu, Eugenio
    1970   *Einführung in die strukturelle Betrachtung des Wortschatzes.* (Tübinger Beiträge zur Linguistik 14). Tübingen: Narr.

Coseriu, Eugenio and Horst Geckeler
    1981   *Trends in structural semantics.* (Tübinger Beiträge zur Linguistik 158.) Tübingen: Narr.

Hogg, Richard and Linda van Bergen (eds.)
    1998   *Historical linguistics 1995: selected papers from the XIIth international Conference on Historical Linguistics, Manchester 1995. Volume 2: Germanic linguistics.* (Current Issues in Linguistic Theory 162). Amsterdam/Philadelphia: Benjamins.

Kastovsky, Dieter
    1992   Typological reorientation as a result of level interaction: the case of English morphology. In: Günter Kellermann and Michael D. Morrissey (eds.), 411-428.
    1994   Typological differences between English and German morphology and their causes. In: Toril Swan, Endre Mørk and Olaf Jansen Westvik (eds.), 135-157.
    1998   Morphological restructuring: the case of Old English and Middle English verbs. In: Richard Hogg and Linda van Bergen (eds.), 131-147.
    1999   On writing a history of English: the "local" and the "global". *The European English Messenger* 8/1: 13-15.

Kastovsky, Dieter (ed.)
    1994   *Studies in Early Modern English.* (Topics in English Linguistics 13.) Berlin/New York: Mouton de Gruyter.

Kastovsky, Dieter and Arthur Mettinger (eds.)
    2000   *Language contact in the history of English.* (Studies in English Medieval Language and Literature.) Frankfurt (Main)/Vienna: Lang.

Kellermann, Günter and Michael D. Morrissey (eds.)
    1992   *Diachrony within synchrony: language history and cognition.* (Duisburger Arbeiten zur Sprach- und Kulturwissenschaft 14.) Frankfurt (Main): Lang.

Labov, William
    1966   *The social stratification of English in New York City.* Washington, DC: Centre for Applied Linguistics.
    1972a   *Sociolinguistic patterns.* Philadelphia, PA: University of Pennsylvania Press.

1972b   *Language in the Inner City: studies in the Black English vernacular.* Philadelphia, PA: University of Pennsylvania Press.

OED
1979   *The compact edition of the Oxford English dictionary.* London: Book Club Associates.

Sapir, Edward
1921   *Language: an introduction to the study of speech.* New York: Harcourt, Brace and Company.

Swan, Toril, Endre Mørk and Olaf Jansen Westvik (eds.)
1994   *Language change and language structure: older Germanic languages in a comparative perspective.* (Trends in Linguistics. Studies and Monographs 73.) Berlin: Mouton de Gruyter.

Contents

Norman Blake
Excellent in Shakespeare 1

Silvia Bruti
Address pronouns in Shakespeare's English:
a re-appraisal in terms of markedness 25

Jonathan Culpeper and Merja Kytö
Gender voices in the spoken interaction of the past:
a pilot study based on Early Modern English trial proceedings 53

Christiane Dalton-Puffer
Is there a social element in English word-stress?
Explorations into a non-categorial treatment of English stress:
a long-term view 91

Roberta Facchinetti
The modal verb *shall* between grammar and usage in the
nineteenth century 115

Gabriella Mazzon
Social relations and forms of address in the *Canterbury Tales* 135

Robert McColl Millar (with the assistance of Dauvit Horsbroch)
Covert and overt language attitudes to the Scots tongue
expressed in the *Statistical accounts of Scotland* 169

Roderick W. McConchie
Fashionable idiolects?
The use of the negative prefix *dis-* 1520-1620 199

Anneli Meurman-Solin
On the conditioning of geographical and social distance in language variation and change in Renaissance Scots 227

Stephen J. Nagle, Margaret A. Fain, and Sara L. Sanders
The influence of political correctness on lexical and grammatical change in late-twentieth-century English 257

Terttu Nevalainen and Helena Raumolin-Brunberg
The changing role of London on the linguistic map of Tudor and Stuart England 279

Arja Nurmi
The rise and regulation of periphrastic *do* in negative declarative sentences: a sociolinguistic study 339

Clausdirk Pollner
Shibboleths galore: the treatment of Irish and Scottish English in histories of the English language 363

Ute Smit
Ethnolinguistic identity as common denominator: a socio-historical investigation of the lexical items for 'people' in South African English 377

Margaret J.-M. Sönmez
Perceived and real differences between men's and women's spellings of the early to mid-seventeenth century 405

Ingrid Tieken-Boon van Ostade
Sociohistorical linguistics and the observer's paradox 441

Index of subjects 463

Index of authors 477

Excellent in Shakespeare

Norman Blake

1. Introduction

1.1. When I chanced to look up the word *excellent* in a quotation from Shakespeare in the *Oxford English Dictionary* (*OED*), I discovered the following position. Under **Excellent B.** *adj.* there are three meanings. The first, now obsolete and merged with sense 3, is 'preeminent, superior, supreme' and is found both "**a.** in favourable sense" from 1382 to 1744 and "**b.** in bad or neutral sense" from 1588 to 1818. The earliest examples of the bad or neutral sense are from Shakespeare. The "neutral" sense is difficult to grasp, but the "bad" sense arises when *excellent* occurs with a noun which has an unfavourable moral implication. Quotations in the *OED* for this bad sense include *A very excellent piece of villainy* (*Titus Andronicus* 2.3.7)[1] and *Excellent falsehood* (*Antony and Cleopatra* 1.1.42). It is this association of *excellent* with *villainy* and *falsehood* which gives it the "bad" sense, though the meaning 'preeminent, superior, supreme' fits as well here as it does with the "favourable" sense. The second meaning in *OED* is also obsolete and lasted from c.1400 to 1702 with the sense 'Excelling in rank or dignity; exalted, highly honourable' and has three uses: the first is the major meaning with dates as already given; the second is as a title from 1611 to 1634 only; and the third is 'Assuming superiority, haughty, 'superior',' with a single quotation from c.1430. *OED*'s third and current meaning is 'an emphatic expression of praise or approval, ... Extremely good' which is found from 1604 onwards. Once again Shakespeare provides the early examples such as *an excellent song* (*Othello* 2.3.69) and *an excellent place* (*Troilus and Cressida* 1.2.177). These entries suggest that *excellent* has had an interesting history which saw it as usually expressing something pre-eminently good in all sorts of contexts, but with a period in which it could also be used to express something reprehensible or bad. It also seems as though Shakespeare played a crucial role in this development and this may indicate that in the light of his work as a dramatist the use of *excellent* has something to do with pragmatics. So first it may be helpful to review other words related to *excellent* and what other dictionaries record for *excellent* and related words.

OED recognises that *excellent* can be used as an adverb as well as an adjective with the meaning 'excellently', though this usage survived only from 1483 to 1756. As an adverb it can be used with verbs, adjectives, and other adverbs. In the latter two instances it acts as an intensifier. *OED* notes without comment that the adverbs it can be used with include both *well* and *ill*, so the "bad" sense of the adjective appears to extend to its adverbial usage. *OED* gives three meanings for the adverb *excellently*. The first occurs in a single quotation from 1340 meaning 'So as to surpass (others)'. The second, 'In an unusual degree; exceedingly, superlatively, surpassingly', occurs in three grammatical environments "**a.** with verbs (*obs.*); **b.** with adjs.: now only in good sense (with mixed notion of sense 3); **c.** with adv. *well* (*arch.*)". A Shakespeare quotation (*Much Ado about Nothing* 3.4.21) occurs only under sense **a**. Finally, the third meaning 'Extremely well' occurs with quotations from 1527, but none from Shakespeare are given. *OED* records the rare form *excellentness* from 1569 to 1775, but not from Shakespeare. It records both *excellence* and *excellency* as nouns, though the meanings overlap. For *excellence* it records the following meanings. The first is 'The state or fact of excelling; the possession chiefly of good qualities in an eminent or unusual degree; surpassing merit, skill, virtue, worth, etc.; dignity, eminence'. The use of the word "chiefly" indicates that it may have a bad sense, though this is not given a separate sub-category and the good sense is evidently the most common in *OED*'s opinion. There are two quotations from Shakespeare, the first from *Henry V*: *Hath got the voice of hell for excellence* (2.2.110) and the second from *Hamlet*: *of what excellence Laertes is* (5.2.107). The first of these quotations may be regarded as having the bad sense of *excellence* since it is linked to *hell*. The second meaning is 'That in which a person or thing excels: an excellent feature or quality' with one quotation from *Twelfth Night*: *thy excellence in a galliard* (1.3.115). The third meaning, "**a.** An excellent personality. **b.** As a title of honour", existed from 1447-1790 and has been replaced by *excellency*. There are no quotations for this sense from Shakespeare. *Excellency* has most of the same meanings as *excellence*, but *OED* gives no quotations from Shakespeare.

1.2. Schmidt and Sarrazin ((eds.)) 1902) define **Excellent** adj. as 'highly praiseworthy, eminent' and gives numerous quotations, and then adds "In a bad sense" with quotations from *Antony and Cleopatra, King Lear, Richard III* and *Titus Andronicus*, with the first and last of these being those quoted in *OED*. In these quotations *excellent* is linked with words like *tyrant, falsehood* and *foppery*, which is why they are said to have a bad sense. As an adverb it is glossed 'well, in a high degree, eminently' with numerous quotations. **Excellently** has two meanings: "1) eminently, extremely well; 2) in a high degree'. **Excellence** is given four meanings: '1) the state of possessing good qualities in an eminent degree; 2) high degree, uncommon manner; 3) any laudable quality; 4) a title of honour given a) to kings, b) to princes of the royal house'. **Excellency** is glossed as 'high quality, eminence'. Only for *excellent* is there any suggestion in Schmidt and Sarrazin ((eds.) 1902) that there could be a bad sense of the word. Onions ((ed.) 1919) defines **excellent** adj. as 'surpassing, exceptionally great, exceeding (used in a bad sense)' and gives the quotations from *Titus Andronicus* and *Antony and Cleopatra* found in *OED* and Schmidt and Sarrazin ((eds.) 1902) and the one from *Richard III* found in Schmidt and Sarrazin ((eds.) 1902). There is little substantial difference in Onions and Eagleson ((eds.) 1986). Since Onions ((ed.) 1919) claims to record only unusual senses, this does not mean that the word had only this bad sense. Onions notes that *excellent* can also be used as an adverb. The adverb **excellently** is given with the sense 'exceedingly', but neither *excellence* nor *excellency* is included. But this and the other dictionaries tend to regard the bad, which presumably include ironic, senses as somewhat unusual and give the same quotations to justify their definition of this usage. In other words, most commentators see *excellent* as having an inherently good sense, though it could occasionally be employed with words with an unfavourable sense which gives it a "bad" sense itself. This bad sense is rarely thought to extend to nouns or adverbs formed from the same root.

1.3. Before considering the use of the word in Shakespeare in detail, it might be sensible to consider how the word *excellent* and its related words are treated in the *Middle English Dictionary* (*MED*), since it is a word borrowed into English during that period. *MED* records *excellent* as an adjective in four senses:

> **1.** Of qualities: outstanding, surpassing, supreme; unexcelled, surpassing (beauty, wisdom, courage, mercy, etc.); great (renown); supreme (glory).
> **2.** Of persons and gods: outstanding, of high rank, noble, illustrious, glorious; excellent (poet), worthy (knight), (person) of high rank, illustrious (ruler), glorious (divinity).
> **3.** Of things and actions: good, excellent, noble, refined; excellent, superior, or refined in quality or character; good or refined (way of doing something); precious (stone); majestic (mountain).
> **4.** Great or extreme (effort, hardship, suffering, poverty).

These definitions suggest only favourable senses for the word and this view is reinforced by the fact that the majority of the quotations are religious or biblical. Only one quotation, from the *Canterbury Tales*, may suggest that there was some ambivalence in the concept 'excellent'. In the Merchant's Tale when May decides to take pity on Damian, for pity is found freely in noble hearts, the narrator comments:

> *Heere may ye se how excellent franchise*
> *In wommen is whan they hem narwe ayyse.* (5: 743-744 [E1987-1988]).[2]

MED records *excellent* as an adverb once, but *excellentli* several times with the meanings '(a) In an unusual or conspicuous degree or manner; greatly, highly, surpassingly; (to praise) highly; (b) extremely (difficult, severe)'. Most quotations are religious, though a few are courtly. It records *excellencie* only twice meaning 'High rank or station', but *excellence* occurs frequently. Its meanings are:

1. Superiority, greatness, distinction (in a certain respect): distinction or eminence (in ability, artistry), refinement (in manners), excellence (of character), greatness or culmination (of fame or reputation) prominence (of birth or wealth), distinction or dignity (of old age), excellence (of a jewel).
2. Outstanding or supreme quality: greatness, prominence, distinction, illustriousness (in some unspecified respect, often to be gathered from the context); esp. integrity or refinement of character.
3. Your (high) excellence.

There are rather more secular quotations under this lemma than for *excellent*, especially in the works of Chaucer, Gower, and even Lydgate, though there is no suggestion from the editors that any quotation is anything other than laudatory. However, some ambiguity may again be traced in a quotation from the *Canterbury Tales* where the Sergeant of the Law is described in the General Prologue as:

A sergeaunt of the lawe waar and wys
That often hadde been at the Parvys
Ther was also, ful ryche of excellence. (1: 311-13 [A309-11])

In view of the Sergeant's acquisitive abilities, the word *excellence* linked with *ryche* is often understood to have at least an ironic edge to it. But in the Middle English period, the evidence of *MED* is that *excellent* and associated words were essentially complimentary and often had a religious implication of moral value. Some indication that this was not universal is provided by the *Canterbury Tales*, where perhaps the tone of colloquial banter and light entertainment may have permitted a less high tone for these words. But it would be difficult to suggest anything other than the beginnings of a different pragmatic use of *excellent/excellence* at this time.

2. Number of examples of *excellent* in Shakespeare

Let us turn now to the examples in Shakespeare. I will first review the number of occurrences of these words found in the plays and poems with the proviso that only examples found in Wells and Taylor ((eds.) 1988) are included in the figures.[3]

excellent			
Comedies	Histories	Tragedies	Poems
Total 56	Total 23	Total 42	Total 2
Temp. 3,	*John* 0,	*T&C* 3,	*Son.* 1,
TG 2,	*R2* 0,	*Cor.* 2,	*PP* 1,
MWW 4,	*1H4* 2,	*Tit.* 1,	others 0.
MM 1,	*2H4* 8,	*R&J* 2,	
Errors 1,	*H5* 7,	*Timon* 5,	
Ado 12,	*1H6* 1,	*Ham.* 10,	
LLL 3,	*2H6* 1,	*Lear* 2,	
MND 2,	*3H6* 0,	*Oth.* 5,	
MV 1,	*R3* 2,	*A&C* 6,	
AYLI 5,	*H8* 2.	*Cymb.* 2,	
Shrew 4,		*Per.* 4.	
AWEW 2,			
TN 15,			
WT 1.			

These crude figures reveal several things immediately. The word *excellent* occurs most frequently in absolute terms in the comedies, followed closely by the tragedies. The histories have far fewer examples and the poems almost none. In relative terms, the comedies and tragedies have 3.8 examples per play, whereas the histories have only 2.3 per play. The histories are the only group with plays without a single example, though there are many poems which have no examples as well. The scarcity of examples in the poems is surprising in view of the courtly nature of some of these poems, and the same might be said of some of the histories. The word occurs frequently in a small number of plays, *Much Ado about Nothing* and *Twelfth Night* among the comedies, *The Second Part of King Henry IV* and *Henry V* among the histories, and *Hamlet* among the tragedies. There ought to be some reason for this grouping which we shall need to enquire into. Its frequency in the comedies is at first glance surprising in view of the laudatory nature which it is said to have.

The frequency of the other words linked with *excellent* should also be noted:

excellently

Comedies	Histories	Tragedies	Poems
Total 5	Total 0.	Total 1	Total 0.
(*Ado* 1, *AWEW* 1, *TN* 3).		(*T&C* 1).	

excellence/excellency

Comedies	Histories	Tragedies	Poems
Total 8	Total 9	Total 4	Total 2
(*MWW* 2, *MM* 1, *Ado* 2, *TN* 2, *WT* 1).	(*John* 2, *H5* 1, *1H6* 2, *2H6* 3, *H8* 1).	(*Ham.* 3, *Cymb.* 1).	(*Son.* 2).

These figures are hardly surprising in view of the earlier ones except for the large number of examples of *excellence/excellency* in the histories. These are to be explained simply because in those plays *excellence* is used as a title for royalty or nobles.

3. Data on all examples of *excellent* etc. found in Shakespeare's works

3.1. In a few moments I will examine the examples in the plays in which these words occur most frequently in detail, but before them I give a list of all examples found in Wells and Taylor ((eds.) 1988). The columns are organised as follows: 1. Play title in italics and line reference; 2. speaker, with name as given in Wells and Taylor ((eds.) 1988); 3. addressee (as far as that can be determined) or *alone* or *aside* as found in Wells and Taylor ((eds.) 1988); 4. the grammatical category of *excellent* and *excellently* (though this item is not found for *excellence/excellency*); and 5. the context. The context consists usually of two elements: first, the word(s) in inverted commas which *excellent* depends upon grammatically, and second, a subjective assessment of the pragmatics of the word in bold distinguished by one of the following one-word categories: **amazement, approval, hyperbole, irony, neutral, scorn,** or **wit**.

excellent

title line	speaker	addressee	grammatical category	context
The Tempest				
3.2.111	Trinculo	Stefano	interj.	**approval**
3.3.38-39	Alonso	Gonzalo	intens.	"dumb discourse" **amazement**
4.1.242	Stefano	Trinculo	adj.	"pass of pate" **scorn**
Two Gentlemen of Verona				
2.1.89	Speed	*aside*	adj.	"motion" **scorn**
2.1.131	Speed	*aside*	adj.	"device" **scorn**
Merry Wives of Windsor				
2.2.217-218	Ford	Sir John	adj.	"breeding" **irony**
3.1.91	Caius	Host	interj.	**approval**
3.3.58	Sir John	Ms. Ford	adj.	"motion" **hyperbole**
4.4.69	Ford	Evans	adj.	"That" **approval**
Measure for Measure				
2.2.109	Isabella	Angelo	adj.	"have a giant's strength" **scorn**
Comedy of Errors				
3.1.110	Antipholus	Balthasar of Ephesus	adj.	"wench of discourse" **irony**
Much Ado About Nothing				
1.1.50	Beatrice	Messenger	adj.	"stomach" **wit**
2.1.6	Beatrice	Leonato	adj	"man" **wit**
2.1.112	Ursula	Antonio (masked)	adj.	"wit" **irony**
2.1.304	Beatrice	Don Pedro	adj.	"husbands" **wit**
2.1.329	Don Pedro	Leonato	adj.	"wife" **approval**
2.3.33	Benedick	*alone*	adj.	"musician" **wit**
2.3.87	Don Pedro	Balthasar	adj.	"music" **approval**
2.3.154	Don Pedro	Claudio	intens.	"sweet lady" **approval**
3.1.89	Ursula	Hero	adj.	"wit" **approval**
3.1.98	Hero	Ursula	intens.	"good name" **approval**

3.4.21	Margaret	Hero	adj.	"fashion" **approval**
3.4.58	Hero	Beatrice	adj.	"perfume" **approval**

Love's Labour's Lost

1.2.166	Armado	*alone*	adj.	"strength" **hyperbole**
4.3.330	Biron	lords	adv.	"proves" **hyperbole**
5.1.131	Mote	Holofernes	adj.	"device" **irony**

Midsummer Night's Dream

3.2.248	Helena	Lysander	interj.	**amazement**
5.1.215	Theseus	Hippolyta	adj.	"men" **irony**

Merchant of Venice

4.1.243	Shylock	Portia (disguised)	intens.	"young man" **approval**

As You Like It

1.2.112	Le Beau	Rosalind	adj.	"growth" **approval**
1.2.174	Orlando	Rosalind/Celia	adj.	"ladies" **hyperbole**
1.2.202	Roslaind	Celia	intens.	"young man" **approval**
3.4.10	Celia	Rosalind	adj.	"colour" **irony**
5.1.26	Touchstone	William	intens.	"good answer" **irony**

The Taming of the Shrew

Int.1.65	Lord	Huntsmen	adj.	"pastime" **approval**
Int.1.67	Lord	Player	adv.	"didst it" **approval**
1.1.251	Sly	Lady	adj.	"piece of work" **irony**
1.2.280	Grumio/ Biondello	Tranio	adj.	"motion" **approval**

Alls Well That Ends Well

1.1.26	Lafeu	Countess	adj.	"He" (Gerard) **approval**
3.6.49	Paroles	Dumaine	adj.	"command" **irony**

Twelfth Night

1.3.93	Sir Toby	Sir Andrew	adj.	"head of hair" **irony**
1.3.98	Sir Toby	Sir Andrew	interj.	**irony**
1.3.127	Sir Toby	Sir Andrew	adj.	"constitution of thy leg" **irony**
1.3.137	Sir Toby	Sir Andrew	interj.	**irony**
2.1.10	Sebastian	Antonio	adj.	"touch of modesty" **approval**
2.3.18	Sir Andrew	Sir Toby	adj.	"breast" **hyperbole**

2.3.28	Sir Andrew	Feste	interj.	**hyperbole**
2.3.44	Sir Andrew	Feste	intens.	"good, i'faith" **hyperbole**
2.3.156	Sir Toby	Maria	interj.	**approval**
2.5.108	Sir Toby	Fabian	adj.	"wench" **approval**
2.5.125	Fabian	Sir Toby	adj.	"cur" **scorn**
2.5.125	Sir Toby	Maria	adj.	"devil of wit" **approval**
3.1.83	Viola [Cesario]	Olivia	intens.	"accomplished lady" **hyperbole**
3.2.21	Fabian	Sir Andrew	adj.	"jests" **irony**
5.1.22	Orsino	Feste	adj.	"this" **approval**

Winter's Tale

4.4.423	Polixenes	Perdita	adj.	"fresh piece of witchcraft" **scorn**

The First Part of King Henry IV

2.4.18	Hotspur	*alone*	adj.	"plot" **approval**
2.5.394	Hostess	company	adj.	"sport, i'faith" **approval**

The Second Part of King Henry IV

2.2.28	Poins	Prince Harry	intens.	"good thing" **approval**
2.4.18	1. Drawer	2. Drawer	adj.	"stratagem" **approval**
2.4.21	Ms. Quickly	Doll Tearsheet	intens.	"good temperality" **approval**
3.2.79	Bardolph	Shallow	adj.	"thing" **hyperbole**
3.2.106	Shallow	Sir John	interj.	"i'faith" **approval**
4.2.98	Sir John	*alone*	adj.	"wit" **wit**
4.2.99	Sir John	*alone*	adj.	"sherry" **wit**
4.2.116	Sir John	*alone*	adj.	"endeavour of drinking" **wit**

Henry V

3.4.56	Alice	Katherine	interj.	**approval** (?French)
3.6.3	Fluellen	Gower	adj.	"services" **approval**
3.6.11	Fluellen	Gower	adj.	"discipline" **approval**
3.6.35	Fluellen	Pistol	adj.	"description" **approval**
3.6.35	Fluellen	Pistol	adj.	"moral" **approval**
3.7.3	Orleans	Constable	adj.	"armour" **approval**
3.7.26	Constable	Bourbon	adj.	"horse" **irony**

Excellent *in Shakespeare* 11

The First Part of King Henry VI				
1.3.89	Charles	Joan	adj.	"Pucelle" **approval**
The Second Part of King Henry VI				
3.1.230	Q. Margaret	Lords	adj.	"it" (snake) **scorn**
Richard III				
1.4.154	2. Murderer	1. Murderer	adj.	"device" **irony**
4.4.53	Q. Margaret	Duchess York	intens.	"grand tyrant" **scorn**
King Henry VIII (All for Love)				
2.4.44	Q. Katherine	K. Henry	adj.	"wit" **approval**
4.2.62	Griffith	Q. Katherine	adj.	"other" (Oxford) **approval**
Troilus and Cressida				
1.2.177	Pandarus	Cressida	adj.	"place" **approval**
1.3.164	Ulysses	Greeks	interj.	(reporting Achilles) **scorn**
1.3.169	Ulysses	Greeks	interj.	(reporting Achilles) **scorn**
Coriolanus				
1.3.91	Valeria	Virgilia	adj.	"news" **approval**
4.5.172	2. Servingman	Servingmen	adj.	"our general" **approval**
Titus Andronicus				
2.3.7	Aaron	*alone*	adj.	"piece of villainy" **scorn**
Romeo and Juliet				
1.2.50	Romeo	Benvolio	adj.	"plantain leaf" **wit**
2.2.13	Fr. Laurence	*alone*	adj.	"virtues" **approval**
Timon of Athens				
1.1.29	Poet	Painter	adv.	"comes off" **approval**
3.3.27	Servant	*alone*	interj.	**scorn**
4.3.215	Apemantus	Timon	adj.	"it" (vicious strain) **scorn**
5.1.19	Painter	Poet	adj.	"piece" **approval**
5.1.30	Timon	*aside*	adj.	"workman" **scorn**
Hamlet				
1.2.139	Hamlet	*alone*	adj.	"a king" **approval**
2.2.113	Polonium/ Hamlet's letter	Claudius	adj.	"white bosom" **hyperbole**
2.2.176 [2x]	Hamlet	Polonium	intens.	"e. e. well" **irony**

2.2.226	Hamet	Rosencrantz/ Guildenstern	intens.	"good friends" **irony**
2.2.301	Hamlet	Rosencrantz/ Guildenstern	adj.	"canopy of air" **irony**
2.2.442	Hamlet	Player	adj.	"play" **approval**
3.2.90	Hamlet	Claudius	interj.	"i'faith" **irony**
3.2.356	Hamlet	Rosencrantz/ Guildenstern	adj.	"voice" **irony**
5.1.181	Hamlet	Horatio	adj.	"fancy" **approval**
King Lear				
1.2.116	Edmond	*alone*	adj.	"foppery" **scorn**
5.3.248	Lear	court	adj.	"thing" **approval**
Othello				
2.1.178	Iago	*aside*	adj.	"curtsy" **scorn**
2.3.69	Cassio	Iago	adj.	"song" **approval**
2.3.109	Gentleman	Cassio	intens.	"well" **irony**
3.3.91	Othello	Iago	adj.	"wretch" **approval**
4.1.207	Othello	Iago	intens.	"good" **approval**
Antony and Cleopatra				
1.1.42	Cleopatra	*aside*	adj.	"falsehood" **scorn**
1.2.22	Charmian	Soothsayer	interj.	"fortune" **wit**
1.2.28	Charmian	Soothsayer	adj.	**irony**
1.3.79	Cleopatra	Antony	adj.	"dissembling" **scorn**
3.2.14	Agrippa	Enobarbus	adj.	"praises" **irony**
3.3.25	Charmian	Cleopatra	interj.	**irony**
Cymbeline				
2.3.16	Cloten	musicians	intens.	"good-conceited thing" **wit**
5.6.198	Giacomo	Cymbeline	interj.	**scorn**
Pericles				
sc.7.106	Simonidea	Pericles	adj.	"knights of Tyre" **approval**
sc.7.107	Simonides	Pericles	adj.	"measures" **approval**
sc.15.91	Dionyza	Marina	adj.	"complexion" **approval**
sc.16.45	Boult	Bawd	intens.	"good clothes" **scorn**
The Sonnets				
38.3	*Thine own sweet argument, too excellent For every vulgar paper to rehearse?*			

Excellent *in Shakespeare* 13

The Passionate Pilgrim				
7.18	Was this a lover or a lecher whether,			
	Bad in the best, though excellent in neither?			

Excellently				
Much Ado about Nothing				
3.4.12	Margaret	Hero	adv.	"like" **approval**
Alls Well That Ends Well				
4.3.215	1. Dumaine	*aside*	interj.	**irony**
Twelfth Night				
1.5.166	Viola [Cesario]	Olivia	intens.	"well penned" **hyperbole**
1.5.226	Viola [Cesario]	Olivia	intens.	"done" **hyperbole**
3.4.185	Sir Toby	Maria	intens.	"ignorant" **scorn**
Troilus and Cressida				
4.1.25	Aeneas	Diomede	adv.	"kill" **wit**

excellence/excellency				
Merry Wives of Windsor				
2.2.233	Ford	Sir John		"e. of her honour" **hyperbole**
3.3.167	Ms. Page	Ms. Ford		"double e." **approval**
Measure for Measure				
1.1.37	Duke	Angelo		"her [Nature's] e." **approval**
Much Ado about Nothing				
2.3.45	Don Pedro	Balthasar		"witness still of e." **approval**
3.1.99	Ursula	Hero		"His e. did earn it" **approval**
Twelfth Night				
1.3.115	Sir Toby	Sir Andrew		"e. in a galliard" **irony**
2.3.145	Maria	Sir Toby		"crammed with e." **scorn**
Winter's Tale				
5.3.30	Paulina	Polixenes		"our carver's e." **wit**
King John				
2.1.440	Citizen	King John		"a fair divided e." **approval**
4.3.66	Salisbury	Pembroke/Bigot		"his breathless e." **approval**
Henry V				
2.2.110	King Harry	Scrope		"voice in hell for e." **scorn**
The First Part of King Henry VI				
5.1.4	Gloucester	King Henry		**title**
5.6.94	Winchester	Richard of York		**title**

The Second Part of King Henry VI			
1.1.3	Suffolk	King Henry	**title**
1.1.159	Gloucester	Cardinal Beaufort	**title**
1.3.122	Q. Margaret	Gloucester	**title**
King Henry VIII (All for Love)			
2.2.33	Norfolk	Suffolk	"e. that angels love" **approval**
Hamlet			
4.7.104	Claudius	Laertes	"praise your e." **approval**
5.2.107	Osric	Hamlet	"of what e. Laertes is" **approval**
Cymbeline			
1.6.45	Giacomo	Innogen	"to such neat e. opposed" **approval**
The Sonnets			
94.8	*Others but stewards of their excellence*		
105.6	*Still constant in a wondrous excellence.*		

3.2. From the above lists, it is clear that *excellence/excellency* are less likely to be used outside the normal sense of approval that one associates with words of this type. However, even allowing for the fact that the pragmatic descriptions are both subjective and very broad, the evidence suggests that both *excellent* and *excellently* were used much more frequently in less favourable senses than the dictionaries would have us to believe. What I have described as **approval** or even **neutral** might perhaps be regarded as the equivalent of 'good' in the dictionaries. But the number of examples with either of these descriptions is quite outweighed by those which are described as having **amazement, irony** or **scorn**. Even those which are categorised as **approval** are not as straightforward as that description might imply. For example, at *Othello* 2.3.69 Cassio exclaims *Fore God, an excellent song*, which I have marked as **approval**, which seems appropriate. But we have to understand that Cassio is already well under the influence of drink and that this exclamation is that of an inebriated man. It can hardly be understood as a normal kind of approval. Equally, at *Othello* 4.1.207, Othello exclaims *Excellent good*. But he is here approving the murder of Cassio and so the approval he gives is to an evil deed. One might in the dictionary terms describe this as "in a bad sense". In other plays, the approval may be ironic, though it is sometimes difficult to tell. At the start of *Timon of Athens,* several artists and artisans gather before

Timon's door to seek his patronage and to get his money. To that extent they are in competition with one another. So when the Poet praises the Painter's picture by saying *That comes off well and excellent* (1.1.29), he may mean it ironically and one could certainly imagine productions which made this clear. The pragmatic descriptions I have given need to be read as very general and, if anything, I have underestimated the examples which could be regarded as scornful or ironic.

3.3. I have followed the Wells and Taylor ((eds.) 1988) edition in indicating asides. A feature of the lists is how many examples are said to be asides or are delivered in monologues. This itself suggests that editors often take a word like *excellent* as a sign that the speaker is making some less than complimentary comment about others. Not all editors indicate that Cleopatra's *Excellent falsehood* (1.1.42) is an aside as Wells and Taylor ((eds.) 1988) do. It is this editorial decision which has led me to allocate it the category **scorn.** If it were said to Antony, I would probably have described it as **irony**. There are other examples which are very similar to this one, and it is interesting that editors tend to treat this word as more ambiguous than dictionary makers.

3.4. There is some evidence that the words *excellent/excellently* may have been fashionable in their less favourable senses. This can be seen both by the words with which they are used and by the speakers and, to some extent, the addressees involved. The first thing to notice is that there are very few words with a favourable moral sense acting as the head to the adjective *excellent*. To link it with a word like *virtue*, which was common in an earlier period, as in Friar Laurence's *many virtues excellent* (*Romeo and Juliet* 2.2.13), is uncommon in Shakespeare. There are, however, examples where the type of moral and religious approval found in Middle English do occur, but they are in a very clear minority. Much more common are words like *motion* and *device*, and the latter word almost always has a bad or at least a harmful meaning, for most devices are designed to inflict some pain on the people who will suffer it. Even when *excellent* is linked with a word like *wench*, one tends to assume that the latter word gives the former one a rather different gloss than would be the case if it had been linked with *lady*. At the very least, it suggests that *excellent* was often used by many as a vogue word expressing general approval, rather like *nice* today, but without any of the finer moral and religious associations it had had. The same is true when it is linked with a word like *sport* which suggests something racy and possibly vulgar. The sense that these words may be somewhat extravagant is created by their frequent association with intensifiers like *most* and *very* as well as with other asseverations like *i'faith* or just *faith*.

3.5. In the plays, *excellent/excellently* tend to be associated with a certain group of characters or even with an individual character and they are found rarely if at all in other characters. They also tend to occur in blocks in the plays, as if one character had suddenly decided to exploit a fashionable word or had sparked off its use by other characters in the same scene. They tend not to be used by the most elevated characters in the plays. The histories are here very significant. The words may be used by some of the comic or less elevated characters, but they are rarely, if ever, used by the more noble characters. No English king uses either of these two words, and when Queen Margaret uses *excellent* in *Richard III* it is to shock and to make her point as forcefully as possible. She had described Richard as *hell-hound*, *dog* and *foul defacer of God's handiwork*, so that her further elaboration of him as *That excellent grand tyrant of the earth* (4.4.53) only adds a further insulting description. Its rare use in the histories makes its use here all the more powerful. In the tragedies, these words serve to highlight evil and unhappiness, but they are not common except in *Hamlet*. In the comedies, it is interesting to note that these words are not used much by the fools; in these plays, they are uttered more often by the fashionable, the braggarts and the pretentious.

4. Analysis of those plays with most examples

4.1. It is time now to consider those plays which have the most examples of *excellent, excellently* and *excellence/excellency*. In *Much*

Ado about Nothing, they are found most often on the lips of the female characters and it is noticeable that none occurs after Act 3 Scene 4. It is about that place in the play when things begin to get nasty as the plot by Don John starts to develop. The words are mostly bunched together in four scenes (2.1, 2.3, 3.1, and 3.4) with a single example in 1.1. These are scenes in which wit, fashion, and clothes are very much to the fore. This is one reason why they occur so frequently in the mouths of the female characters. It is noticeable that they are not spoken by the comic characters like Dogberry or by the wicked characters like Don John. They are perhaps too ephemeral and light for such characters. The only character who does use them outside this circle of the fashionable is Don Pedro himself, who is represented as generally sober and mature, though he is willing to indulge in the stratagem to entrap Beatrice and Benedick into marriage. The nouns associated with *excellent* fit into a pattern of witty praise, for they include *stomach, husband, wife, lady, music, good name, perfume* and *wit*; *excellently* describes *tire*, and *excellence/excellency* the qualities of humility and Beatrice herself. Words which are found otherwise in praise of the qualities of different characters include *good, great, noble(st), valiant* and *exceeding*. Though some of these may also be intended ironically, mostly they have a much less ambiguous feel to them than the group of *excellent* words.

Twelfth Night follows much the same pattern, though with some interesting modifications. Once again, these words are largely confined to certain characters, especially the circle which includes Sir Toby and Sir Andrew. The latter clearly understands *excellent* to be fashionable and exploits it in this way because he has picked it up from Sir Toby. Although he means the word to express general approbation, his primary intention is to appear fashionable, which is why I have characterised his examples as hyperbole in the lists above. The words fall into the same category as Viola's single example of *excellently* when as Cesario she tries to flatter Olivia by indulging in a highly inflated and fashionable language. Sir Toby uses all three words as though they are fashionable, but always with an edge of irony, not to say scorn. It is difficult to decide which is the more appropriate description, though there seems little doubt that mostly the words express his contempt for Sir Andrew and all his examples might have been more appropriately categorised as scorn. Maria and Fabian have picked the words up from Sir Toby and exploit the words to express their own contempt for Sir Andrew and hatred of Malvolio. Sebastian uses *excellent* in a good sense, as does Orsino in praise of Feste's wit, which perhaps gives it a more fashionable and playful feel. The word is never spoken by Olivia, Malvolio, or indeed by Viola when she is not disguised as Cesario. It is also never used by Feste, the fool. Once again, the words which express approval without the same ambiguity as *excellent(ly)* include *good, great, noble, discreet, gracious, valiant,* and *sweet.* There seems little doubt that in the comedies the words linked with *excellent* were part of fashionable and witty talk, which could be used ironically as well.

4.2. In the histories, these words occur most often in *The Second Part of King Henry IV* and *Henry V.* In *The Second Part of King Henry IV,* it is part of the vocabulary of lower-class people, on the one hand, and of Falstaff and Shallow, on the other. For the former group and Shallow, it shows that they have picked up some fashionable words. Possibly Poins, when he says to Prince Harry *faith, let it be an excellent good thing*, intends the expression to have a mocking tone. Other lower-class people use it unthinkingly as a mark of approval, which suggests it had become a colloquialism among that section of the community. Some editions of the play have a further example by Doll Tearsheet, which is not in Wells and Taylor ((eds.) 1988). None of these words is ever spoken by the noble characters, who prefer the words of approval which have been isolated in the comedies. In *Henry V, excellent* is used by the French nobles and Alice, and by Fluellen. Fluellen's examples all occur in one scene and could suggest that he has just picked up a word which he uses briefly before discarding it. Alice's example may well be in French as many editors assume, though the Wells and Taylor ((eds.) 1988) presentation suggests otherwise. It occurs in the language of Orléans and the Constable in the pre-battle scene and this may be deliberate in helping to create that sense of fashionable arrogance which the

French nobles show. In this respect, the French are distinguished from the English, who are humbler and down to earth. The example by the Constable is clearly scornful since everyone wishes to poke fun at Bourbon (other editions have this as the Dauphin) and the rest of the sentence makes the scorn even clearer: *Indeed, my lord, it is a most absolute and excellent horse* (3.7.25-26). The use of *most absolute* with *excellent* suggests the latter is meant scornfully, for the exaggeration is marked. The example earlier in the scene where Orléans praises the Constable's armour may also be ironic, since the French nobles are clearly competing over how good their equipment is and they are trying to score off one another. The words which express goodness without the ambiguity of these words are those which we have already noted for the comedies – words such as *good, great, valiant, noble, glorious, kind,* and *fair*.

4.3. *Hamlet* is somewhat remarkable in that Hamlet initiates all of the examples of *excellent*, though one (2.2.113) is actually quoted from his letter by Polonium. However, it may be noted that in the second quarto Osric uses the expression *most excellent differences* (5.2), though this is not included in the Wells and Taylor ((eds.) 1988) edition and it is difficult to be certain that it is genuine. What may also be noted is that Hamlet does not use *excellence/excellency*, though one or other of these words is used by Claudius and Osric. This difference suggests that *excellent* and *excellently*, the latter of which does not occur in *Hamlet*, have a different pragmatic use and tone than *excellence/excellency*. Here the significant factor in Hamlet's usage is to whom the word *excellent* is addressed. In his monologue (1.2.139) and in his speeches to the Player (2.2.442) and to Horatio (5.1.181) he uses *excellent* in a straight manner where the word has a sense of high approval. In his letter to Ophelia which Polonium reads, it is intended to be hyperbolical, though that may be a deliberate stratagem to deceive others. To those who he suspects of trying to trap him and are real or potential enemies, Polonium, Claudius and Rosencrantz and Guildenstern, he exploits the word as a device to cloak his real feelings. It becomes a tool in his overall strategy of deception, because it can be taken two ways by those to whom it is addressed. Hamlet also uses *excellent* in all three grammatical categories, adjective, adverb, and intensifier, though the adjectival form occurs only when the word is unambiguously complimentary. When characters in the play wish to find a word to imply goodness, those they choose include the ones we have already noted. When Laertes, for example, wishes to praise his sister, in her deranged state, he says *Dear maid, kind sister, sweet Ophelia* (4.5.159). He and other characters avoid *excellent*, because of its pragmatic associations.

I have not considered the examples in the poems which are very few, but it is possible that the few there are should be understood in a different way from the straight interpretation. The quotation from *The Passionate Pilgrim* certainly seems ambiguous, since it occurs with words like *lover, lecher, bad, best*, and it does not strike one as being highly commendatory. The example in *The Sonnets* is more difficult and needs looking at in more detail. As far as I am aware, the use of the word has never been discussed in this passage.

5. Conclusion

I have not in this paper treated the verb *excel* with the adjective, adverb, and noun forms. The reason for this is that it is difficult to make the verb have the same pragmatic force as the other grammatical categories. Certainly in Shakespeare's works the verb *excel* mainly occurs in the sense 'surpass, achieve excellence in' and tends to have a neutral sense. Even when it is found in what might be considered a negative context, because the implication that someone or something excels in some aspect of evil, it is difficult to determine how far the verb itself participates in that negative quality. Thus when Paroles in *Alls Well That Ends Well* 4.3.290-291 says *He excels his brother for a coward, yet his brother is reputed one of the best that is*, the implication of *excel* does not seem to have the same force as the many examples of *excellent* that have been considered. But the verb mostly occurs in a neutral or complimentary context. Its inclusion would have added little to the discussion here.

There seems to me to be no doubt that, despite what the dictionaries say, the different words associated with *excellent* had a two-edged pragmatic use in Shakespeare. One might assume that this came in part from the occurrence of *excellent* as an expletive, where expressions like *Excellent, i'faith* could easily adopt a tone of ironic praise. From there it would not be hard to understand that *excellent* could adopt an ambiguous sense, which may well colloquially have become the dominant one for a time. Throughout history words which have a sense of high approval can easily tip over into irony, as is true of words today like *wonderful* or even *great*. Dictionary makers have been too ready to take *excellent* and its linked words at face value, partly perhaps because of their origins and partly because of their use today. It may well be that at a colloquial level for a couple of hundred years in the early modern period it was more frequently used in a derogatory fashion than otherwise. This development never seems to have affected *excellence/excellency* and was less marked with the verb *excel*, and it could well be that it was these forms which helped to pull it back from its colloquial usage. However, one should not overlook the exhaustion which tends to affect vogue words so that they drop out of the colloquial field, and in the case of *excellent* the demands for propriety from the eighteenth century onwards may also have been influential. It has not been possible to trace the development of these words in other authors, and that is a necessary next step to confirm what I have done here. This article may be considered another small piece in building up an understanding of the pragmatics of Early Modern English, which as a topic has attracted considerable interest recently.

Notes

1. The following abbreviations from Shakespeare's plays are used: *Temp.*: *The Tempest*; *TG*: *Two Gentleman of Verona*; *MWW*: *Merry Wives of Windsor*; *MM*: *Measure for Measure*; *Error*: *Comedy of Errors*; *Ado*: *Much Ado about nothing*; *LLL*: *Love's Labour's Lost*; *MND*: *Midsummer Night's Dream*; *MV*:

Merchant of Venice; *AYLI*: *As You Like It*; *Shrew*: *The Taming of the Shrew*; *AWEW*: *Alls Wells that Ends Well*; *TN*: *Twelfth Night*; *WT*: *Winter's Tale*; *John*: *King John*; *R2*: *Richard II*; *1H4*: *The First Part of King Henry IV*; *2H4*: *The Second Part of King Henry IV*; *H5*: *Henry V*; *1H6*: *The First Part of King Henry VI*; *2H6*: *The Second Part of King Henry VI*; *3H6*: *The Third Part of King Henry VI*; *R3*: *Richard III*; *H8*: *King Henry VIII (All for Love)*; *T&C*: *Troilus and Cressida*; *Cor.*: *Coriolanus*; *Tit.*: *Titus Andronicus*; *R&J*: *Romeo and Juliet*; *Timon*: *Timon of Athens*; *Ham.*: *Hamlet*; *Lear*: *King Lear*; *Oth.*: *Othello*; *A&C*: *Antony and Cleopatra*; *Cymb.*: *Cymbeline*; *Per.*: *Pericles*. The poems with abbreviated forms are *Son.*: *The Sonnets* and *PP*: *The Passionate Pilgrim*. All quotations and line references are to Wells and Taylor ((eds.) 1988). The names of the characters and the stage directions given in this edition are followed so that there may be some discrepancy between the figures and names given below and those found in other editions.
2. Quotations from the poem are taken from Blake ((ed.) 1980). The lineation is from this edition, though the more traditional lineation is given afterwards in square brackets.
3. Many editors include one more example in *Hamlet* and one more in *The First Part of King Henry IV* than Wells and Taylor ((eds.) 1988).

References

Blake, Norman F. (ed.)
    1980   *Geoffrey Chaucer, The Canterbury Tales edited from the Hengwrt manuscript*. London: Arnold.
Kurath, Hans et al. (eds.)
    1954-   *Middle English dictionary*. Ann Arbor, MI: University of Michigan Press.
Murray, James A. H.; Robert W. Burchfield et al. (eds.)
    1933, 1972-1986 *The Oxford English dictionary*. 17 vols. Oxford: Clarendon.
Onions, Charles T. (ed.)
    1919   *A Shakespeare glossary*. (2nd edition.) Oxford: Clarendon.
Onions, Charles T. and Robert D. Eagleson (eds.)
    1986   *A Shakespeare glossary*. (3rd, revised edition.) Oxford: Clarendon.

Schmidt, Alexander and Gregor Sarrazin (eds.)
    1902   *Shakespeare-Lexikon. A complete dictionary of all the English words, phrases and constructions in the works of the poet.* (3rd, revised edition.) Berlin: Reimer.

Wells, Stanley and Gary Taylor (eds.)
    1988   *William Shakespeare, complete works, compact edition.* Oxford: Clarendon.

Address pronouns in Shakespeare's English: a re-appraisal in terms of markedness

Silvia Bruti

1. Introduction

1.1. In this paper I will analyse the use of second person pronouns (sometimes together with terms of address) in Shakespeare's Early Modern English.[1] The period in which Shakespeare lived and wrote for the theatre was one of great change for the language, which was no longer Middle English, not yet Modern English, and was thus defined as Early Modern English in order to underline its temporary state (Abbott 1925; Frank 1989: 211-236; Mazzon 1995: 40-41).

My analysis will be confined to the investigation of second-person pronouns. This topic has been extensively analysed by scholars (Brown and Gilman 1960; Finkenstaedt 1963; Mulholland 1967; Quirk 1971; Barber [1981] 1987; Eagleson 1971; Reploge [1973] 1987; Salmon 1987a, b), but not from a wider pragmatic perspective. My hope is that the analysis of forms of personal reference within the full context of situation and together with their accompanying epithets will offer a re-appraisal of the distinction between marked and unmarked uses across various social groups.

In my discussion of the *thou/you* alternation I will identify some criteria of use, but my results will be far from statistical accuracy because of the limited scope of my analysis, which concentrates on examples drawn from a limited textual universe instead of on a large corpus of data. By adopting a perspective which integrates textual analysis with some basic sociolinguistic notions I aim to achieve some qualitative results.

Although we will see that unmarked terms have a wider distribution than marked ones (see sections 3.4. and 3.5.), frequency alone does not explain the concept of markedness. Quantitative results are in fact neither necessary nor sufficient to establish which pronoun is marked and which unmarked. What I would like to point out is that despite the wide recourse to *you* in many different contexts, there are nonetheless situations in which it turns out to be the least natural choice. I will try to account for such cases by adopting the notion of "markedness reversal" (Shapiro 1983). As I will show, it is not so much a question of frequency, as rather a situationally bound or situationally determined selection which establishes which option is natural or unnatural along a sliding scale of possibilities.

1.2. My choice fell on a group of plays, the so-called *Falstaff plays*[2], because they portray a gallery of characters belonging to different social ranks, each of which has its own distinctive idiom (Brook 1976; Hussey 1982; Blake 1989). I will endeavour to show how the dynamics of personal relationships develops along the diachronic axis, i.e. the evolutionary dimension of the plot, and how therefore pronoun selection can become a strategic instrument of characterisation in the hands of a skilful playwright. The dramatic medium itself required a reduction of the complexity of personal relationships to some easily perceivable information placed at crucial nodes. The choice of pronouns was indeed one of the effective markers of social interactions and attitudes. Since Shakespeare's audience was quite alert to detect a whole range of dramatic stylistic features (such as allusions, puns, intertextual references, and many others), the shades of meaning enclosed in such uses must have had a strong message for it.

When using drama as the source providing material for sociolinguistic analysis it is necessary to consider both its fictional status and literary quality and consequently to be aware of the differences between this framework and that of a natural conversation. Despite this, drama presents a remarkable number of interactions and displays an extensive collection of social types – prototypical characters. On the other hand, legal reports and meeting records, two of the other sources of data for Early Modern English, offer access to authentic everyday interactions, yet they delineate a rather limited range of situations and make use of a restricted technical vocabulary.

2. Pronouns in Early Modern English

2.1. Processes in the use of pronominal forms exhibit degrees of deference or social distance which vary from one language to another in terms of their grammatical scope and range of variation. Alternation of reference items to communicate social meanings may centre around one grammatical category (such as, for instance, person, as in the case of *thou/you*), a combination of categories (such as both number and person), classes or types of pronouns (such as personal or demonstrative pronouns), or a combination of types of pronoun with pronominal categories (for instance, alternation between a personal pronoun in the second person and a third-person reflexive pronoun) (Head 1978: 155). Second person pronouns have in many languages two different forms whose semantics is regulated by the relationships between speaker and hearer. Brown and Gilman (1960) equate this dichotomy to the alternation between T and V pronouns, where the initials stand for the Latin pronouns employed to designate second-person singular, *tu* and *vos*, which correspond to Early Modern English *thou* and *ye*. Second person pronouns necessarily encode social relationships: the same pronoun can be symmetrically and bi-directionally employed when speakers are on the same level (and consider themselves so), or different speakers may have recourse to non-reciprocal forms when their relationship is asymmetrical and unilateral.

2.2. For many scholars the semantic variables of power and solidarity can account for pronoun fluctuation[3], but my point here is that social standing was not the only influential constraint on alternation. Quite the contrary, we must take into consideration the conventional meanings associated with varying degrees of emotional proximity and familiarity. So the generalising rule that the pronoun *you* was used to convey social distance or respect, whereas *thou* was employed to address lower social ranks or inferiors, expressing respectively contempt or familiarity within the family (e.g., from parents to children), does not account for those cases in which *thou* was used to express temporary feelings of either distance or proximity.

The characteristic state of fluctuation in the English language is not biuniquely related to shifts in social status: many switches actually occur within the same situation of utterance and with the same speaker. This leads to formulating a hypothesis: fluctuation might have been a signal of a shift in register and style, a means to indicate a changed emotional attitude and, more generally, a transitory arousal of affective attitudes (Brown and Gilman 1960; Barber 1987; Salmon 1987a: 59; Eagleson 1971: 142).

3. Markedness

3.1. Terminology

In the literature concerning pronoun alternation the notion of markedness is frequently referred to. Yet my impression is that it is a rather limited notion of markedness, which only partially identifies specific parameters for the assignment of markedness values. To put it differently, the term has not been technically used, and it is usually meant to signal an outstanding, complex, or rather unusual stylistic feature.

What I would like to do here is to further specify the relevant and discourse-specific parameters for markedness values of second person pronouns and eventually re-appraise the notion of markedness itself.

3.2. Thou *as a marked option*

Many scholars have tried to settle the problem of variation by resorting to the marked–unmarked distinction (McIntosh 1963; McIntosh and Williamson 1963; Mulholland 1967; Quirk 1971;

Eagleson 1971; Reploge 1987).[4] For them the polarity corresponds to the idea that *thou* could be employed as a marker of a whole range of strong feelings, whereas *you* represented a more neutral form of reference. This distinction also gives evidence of the spreading supremacy of *you* over *thou*, which finally resulted in the latter pronoun being phagocytised. In other words, *you* became the *passe-partout* form and *thou* began to be more and more deeply connoted with additional overtones. So, by the end of the sixteenth century, the use of *you* was firmly established also among the serving classes at the expenses of *thou*, which was left the narrow area of special uses in political or religious quarrels (Finkenstaedt 1963; Brown and Gilman 1960; Wales 1983: 219).[5]

This pre-theoretical notion of markedness, however, is hardly adequate: the alleged neutrality of *you* should be supported with specific evidence of the variables which determine the choice of a marked option, especially within the speech of a single speaker. In my opinion to claim unmarkedness for the *passe-partout you* is oversimplistic[6], especially for the instances of isolated *you*. I am thus proposing to redefine markedness and observe the direction of switch between *you* and *thou*. I would like to demonstrate through examples that it is possible to move from social/emotional remoteness to closeness, but also, contrary to the above-mentioned theoretical premises, the other way round. Consequently, in certain contexts where *thou* has been extensively used, the switch to *you* may represent a significant deviance, and therefore constitutes a case of "marked" *you*.

3.3. *The pronoun + term-of-address unit*

Another point is that most of the analyses, although extremely specific, do not describe the wider linguistic domain in which the pronoun occurs. Address pronouns are in fact accompanied by terms of address, epithets, ritual formulas (Brown and Gilman 1989; Nevalainen and Raumolin-Brunberg 1995; Nevalainen 1996; Raumolin-Brunberg 1996; Nevala 1998), which all convey the speaker's attitude towards his co-speakers, the situation, and the message itself.

My proposal is that the semantic and pragmatic meanings of most of the occurrences of *thou* and *you* may often be confirmed or disconfirmed by the accompanying epithets. For this reason I will consider the reciprocal influences that terms of address and pronouns exert on each other.[7]

3.4. Parameters for markedness value

The notion of markedness was developed into a complete theory by the linguists of the Prague school (among many contributions see Jakobson 1962; Greenberg 1966; Shapiro 1983). It was devised in the field of phonological studies, but it was later applied to morphology and semantics as well.

Among theorists Greenberg was the one who systematised a set of criteria for the assessment of markedness values.

Among them there are:
1) Universal implication law: "if a language has the item A, then it necessarily has also item B, but not vice versa. A is the marked element, B the unmarked one".
2) Zero expression: the unmarked term usually shows zero inflection in comparison with the marked element.
3) Neutralisation/*par excellence* expression: the unmarked choice usually stands for the generic category or the specific opposite item of the marked category.
4) Syncretism: subdistinctions within the unmarked category are syncretised, that is, lost or not developed, in the marked category.
5) Distribution: the unmarked option is supposed to have a wider distribution than the marked one.

3.5. Markedness parameters and the thou/you alternation

In the following I will investigate if the above-mentioned parameters may apply to the *thou/you* distinction, and if they do not, what else may account for their difference in use.

As for the "universal implication law" the *thou/you* distinction seems to be relevant. It has in fact been shown that any language which has the *thou* pronoun has necessarily also the *you* pronoun, but not vice versa (Head 1978).

Aspect 2) of Greenberg's characterisation is difficult to evaluate because of the complexity of the phonological and morphological variations from Middle to Modern English. *Thou* was the subject case, whereas *you* was the accusative form of *ye*. But since case function could be expressed by word order since Middle English times, case endings in pronouns were superfluous, and each form could easily be substituted with another (Görlach 1991: 85).[8] Phonological and sociolinguistic factors seem to have been responsible for a phenomenon of convergence: from the fifteenth century *ye* and *you* shared the same weakly stressed form [jə]. This effect, associated with redundant case endings, generated confusing generalisations (Görlach (1991) suggests that this could be partly influenced by the reverse vowel pattern in *thou/thee*; see also Mausch (1993)). All these adjustments led first to the disappearance of *ye* (around 1600) and then, with the restriction of the use of *thou*, to a reduction from a four- to a one-item system.

Aspect 3) appears on the contrary quite acceptable. We can in fact acknowledge that *you* may represent the generic category, which is confirmed by its widening distribution (see aspect 5)), and also, up to a point, that it may stand for the specific opposite of the marked category. This is what we label as the *passe-partout* use of *you* (see section 2.2.). The alternation was not to last very long, because the contrast between polite and intimate address was in the process of being obliterated and *you* could eventually cover all the circumstances of use (Wales 1983: 17 and 123). Consequently, the encoding of social relationships had to be entrusted to other linguistic means (O'Donnell and Todd 1990: 24; Dunkling 1990: 19-20).

Before this systemic change took place, *you* forms had already spread down the social scale, especially because they belonged to an elevated variety of English, which the lower ranks tried to reproduce. The result was that the occurrences of *you* were not all expressions of polite address, but on the contrary also included cases of middle-rank or popular uses. It is therefore perfectly legitimate to claim that the "neutralisation" parameter applies, or that *you* was in this sense the unmarked or neutralised form. These instances are illustrated in (1).

(1) Fal. *Ha! A bastard son of the King's? And art thou Poins his brother?*
Prince. *Why, thou globe of sinful continents, what a life dost thou lead!*
Fal. *A better than thou – I am a gentleman, thou art a drawer.*
Prince. *Very true, sir, and I come to draw you out by the ears. ...*
Fal. *Thou whoreson mad compound of majesty, by this light flesh and corrupt blood,* [leaning his hand upon Doll], *thou art welcome. ...*
Prince. *You whoreson candle-mine you, how vilely did you speak of me even now, before this honest, virtuous, civil gentlewoman! ...*
Fal. *Didst thou hear me?*
Prince. *Yea, and you knew me, as you did when you ran away by Gad's Hill; you knew I was at your back, and spoke it on purpose to try my patience.*
(*2HIV*, II, iv, 280-305)

In example (1) we can identify different specimens of *you*. The Falstaff–prince relationship is reciprocal and friendly, and *thou* is their mutual form of address. Sometimes they engage in verbal fights which result in sequels of terrible abuses. The terms of address clearly conform to the expression of such heightened emotions.

In this extract Falstaff consistently uses *thou*, whereas the prince oscillates between the two forms. The first time he employs *you* is for stylistic reasons: he somehow wants to ridicule Falstaff and therefore speaks in a formal register, with a mock polite intent which is responsible for the temporary switch to *you* (cf. Barber (1987: 171); see also Kopytko (1995: 538) for a discussion of the relationship between irony and politeness).

In the second and third turn the prince still applies *you*, although it is no longer an ironical *you*. There is in fact no peculiar element which favours this interpretation, but there are a few hateful epithets to confirm his resentment towards Falstaff. It is self-evident that here *you* is neither polite nor ironical, but it fits in a sequence of bitter reproach. What I am basically suggesting is that in this case *you* is a neutral form and the semantic load and connotations are carried by the term of address: for this reason it is acceptable to consider *you* as impartial and dispassionate, in that it delegates the semantic and pragmatic functions to the accompanying epithets.

Another case is for instance the mixture of pronouns employed by Doll Tearsheet towards Falstaff and the way she tends to use *you* with both approbating and offensive terms (see (2), which shows a neutral *you* + epithets).

(2) Doll. *Ah, you sweet little rogue, you! Alas, poor ape, how thou sweat'st! Come, let me wipe thy face. Come on, you whoreson chops! Ah, rogue, i'faith, I love thee. Thou art as valorous as Hector of Troy, worth nine Agamemnon, and ten times better than the Nine Worthies. Ah, villain!*

(*2HIV*, II, iv, 213-218)

It is the nature of epithets which specifies over time the meaning of pronoun forms. Those instances of *you* which occur with either offensive or appreciating terms take on the meaning encoded by the epithets themselves. In example (2) *sweet* and *little* mitigate the negative meaning of *rogue* and turn it into a positive evaluation. Similarly, later on Doll calls Falstaff *whoreson Bartholomew boar pig* (line 227) but does not fail to add the adjectives *little* and *tidy*.

Parameter 4) is again difficult to assess: the distinction among direct and oblique cases was almost equally blurred by the time Shakespeare wrote, so we can find *you* for *ye* and vice versa, or *thee* for *thou*.

The last aspect, i.e., text frequency, is highly relevant for a discussion of the *thou/you* alternation. Generally speaking it is true that *you* had a wider distribution, especially because it was applicable in a larger variety of contexts and also because it gradually assimilated *thou*.

It is perhaps worth noting one additional point concerning Shakespearean English. According to some statistics the occurrences of *thou* outnumber – in some plays – those of *you* (if we keep the instances of singular *you* distinct from those of plural *you*). Barber (1987) argues that it cannot be claimed that in the Shakespeare canon *you* was the usual form and *thou* the occasional variant. He in fact recognises that shifts occur frequently also among members of the same status group, but also admits that drama reproduces a magnified image of real-life interactions, because of its density of intense conflicts and its frequency of one-to-one confrontations (Barber 1987: 177).

On the whole, the notion of markedness seems to be applicable to pronoun fluctuation, but with some reservations. *Thou* and *you* do not represent the extremes of a polar opposition, but rather two items on a "sliding scale" (Wales 1983: 116). It is therefore necessary to identify more specific criteria responsible for pronoun selection on the gradient of markedness.

3.6. Criteria for pronoun selection

3.6.1. Evidence on pronoun use shows that membership in a specific social status group is not in itself a sufficient requirement to adequately describe pronoun selection. If it had simply been a socially conditioned use, as is the case with many other sociolinguistic phenomena of style-shifting and code-switching, alternation would not have occurred in those situations in which both the locutor and the interlocutor are invariable. But this was in fact a rather frequent case in Shakespearean English. Thus pronoun switch seems to be related to many different variables, such as "changes in the situational contexts of speech events, the social characteristics of participants, and the varying purposes of exchanges in speech" (Milroy 1992: 43). Since the social criterion alone did not prove useful to account for such complex phenomena, I chose to integrate it with some other variables and I selected two main parameters whose point of intersection can in most cases account for pronominal selection: the axis of social distance and the axis of emotional attitude.

The first feature may change over a gradient of positions which vary from the upper ranks of society, i.e., kings and nobles, to the lowest social groups. It is important to consider not only the locutor's own social standing (absolute social rank), but also the distance between his social place and that of his interlocutor, a sort of relative social rank.

	Social distance	
	Address to	
Inferiors	Equals	Superiors
←		→
Thou	*(y/t)*	*You*

Figure 1. The axis of social distance

As figure 1 sketchily shows, along this scale *thou* and *you* are the most natural options to address respectively inferiors and superiors; address to equals depends on the social standing of the interlocutors, so it is usually *you* for the upper classes and *thou* for the lower classes.

	Emotional attitude	
anger/contempt	indifference/neutrality	familiarity/intimacy
←		→
Thou	*You*	*Thou*

Figure 2. The axis of emotional attitude

The axis of emotional attitude (figure 2) represents the locutor's affective disposition towards his interlocutor. Here again we move from the pole of open hostility to that of emotional closeness (friendship and love).[9]

3.6.2. It is important to make it clear that a marked choice on one axis may be exactly the opposite on the other. For this reason evaluation of markedness values must take into account both parameters.

The following example may clarify the importance of both of them. In the meeting between King Henry V and his wife-to-be Katherine of France (in *Henry V*) the exchange proceeds symmetrically, with a turn allocated to Henry, and the following to Katherine.[10] According to the above-mentioned criteria, we can predict which form is the most suitable and unmarked. The social-distance requirement is here the following: the two characters are socially equals and belong to the upper rank, so the normal, unmarked option would be reciprocal *you*. Along the axis of emotional vicinity a sudden intense feeling might justify a switch to *thou*.

(3) 1a K. Hen. *Fair Katherine and most fair,*
       Will you vouchsafe to teach a soldier terms
       Such as will enter at a lady's ear
       And plead his love-suit to her gentle heart?
    1b Kath. *Your majesty shall not mock at me; I cannot speak your England.*
    2a K. Hen. *O fair Katherine! If you will love me soundly with your French heart, I will be glad to hear you confess it brokenly with your English tongue. Do you like me, Kate?*
    2b Kath. *Pardonnez-moi, I cannot tell wat is "like me".*
    3a K. Hen. *An angel is like you, Kate, and you are like an angel.*
    3b Kath. *Que dit-il? Que je suis semblable à les anges?* ...
    4a K. Hen. *I said so, dear Katherine, and I must not blush to affirm it.*

4b Kath. *O bon Dieu! Les langues des hommes sont pleines de tromperies. ...*
6a K. Hen. *The princess is the better Englishwoman. I'faith, Kate, my wooing is fit for thy understanding; I am glad thou canst speak no better English; for if thou couldst, thou wouldst find me such a plain king that thou wouldst think I had sold my farm to buy my crown. I know no ways to mince it in love, but directly to say, "I love you": then if you urge me farther than to say, "Do you in faith?" I wear out my suit. Give me your answer; i'faith, do: and so clap hands and a bargain. How say you, lady?*
6b Kath. *Sauf votre honneur, me understand well.*
7a K. Hen. *Marry, if you would put me to verses, or to dance for your sake, Kate, why you undid me: for the one, I have neither words nor measure, and for the other, I have strength in measure, yet a reasonable measure in strength. ... If thou canst love a fellow of this temper, Kate, whose face is not worth sun-burning, that never looks in his glass for love of any thing he sees there, let thine eye be thy cook. I speak to thee plain soldier: if thou canst love me for this take me; if not, to say to thee that I shall die, is true; but for thy love, by the lord, no; yet I love thee too. And while thou livest, dear Kate, take a fellow of plain and uncoined constancy, for he perforce must do thee right; ... If thou would have such a one, take me; and take me, take a soldier; take a soldier, take a king. And what sayst thou then to my love? Speak, my fair, and fairly, I pray thee.*
7b Kath. *Is it possible dat I sould love de enemy of France?*
8a K. Hen. *No; it is not possible you should love the enemy of France, Kate; but, in loving me, you should love the friend of France, for I love France so well that I will not part with a village of it; I will have it all*

mine: and Kate, when France is mine and I am yours, then yours is France and you are mine. ...
9b Kath. *Sauf votre honneur, le Français que vous parlez il est meilleur que l'Anglais lequel je parle.*
10a K. Hen. *No, faith, is't not, Kate; but thy speaking of my tongue, and I thine, most truly-falsely, must needs be granted to be much at one. But, Kate, dost thou understand thus much English? Canst thou love me?*
10b Kath. *I cannot tell.*

What we actually find in the extract is slightly different. Henry starts with a solemn style and addresses Katherine with *you* (numbers (1a)-(4a) in example (3)), which is the most neutral/unmarked option on the axis of social distance. Yet a radical change along the axis of emotional attitude drives him to switch to *thou* in number (6a): in other words, through his courtship he feels authorised to presume an increased level of intimacy. *Thou* is explicitly confirmed and reinforced by a series of appreciating epithets, such as *fair and most fair*, *gentle heart* and later on *dear Kate* and *my fair*. The princess's coldness (her deferential politeness in number (6b) only partially disguises her uncooperative answer) exerts a retroactive influence over Henry's discursive choices and induces him to switch back to *you* (number (8a): she has just called him *the enemy of France*).[11] This latter instance of *you* greatly differs from those employed at the beginning. The use of *you* may thus serve as a strategy for expressing varying degrees of distance from the interlocutor on the axis of emotional attitude, which is here also a situational prime requirement. This "distancing" *you* is a case of markedness reversal (cf. Shapiro 1983; Merlini Barbaresi 1996): on the axis of social distance *you* would be the most natural option as the form of address used by nobles among themselves, but it turns into the marked option on the axis of emotional attitude, where it signals a loss in terms of intimacy.

3.6.3. According to figure 3, there are two possible cases of markedness reversal: the one we have just described, which is theoretically more complicated, and that of the unmarked *you* which turns into the marked *thou* along a different axis.

Figure 3. Markedness reversals

But this latter example coincides with the general accepted rule of use for Early Modern English pronouns: a switch to *thou* could signal the intention of insulting the interlocutor, when addressing social equals or superiors, or the expression of some intimate feelings, such as friendship or love. An instance of the first case is the speech of King Henry V to Lord Scroop, one of his traitors, in which the king replaces the usual *you* with *thou* (*Henry V*, II, ii, 94-99). The switch to a *thou* which indicates love is illustrated in Falstaff's suiting letter to the *merry wives*. He begins with *you*, but at the end of the letter, when he feels sure that his love will be reciprocated, he turns to *thou* (*Merry Wives of Windsor*, II, i, 4-19)).

Before drawing some conclusions I would like to observe another instance of markedness reversal.

(4) a. Fal. *Now Hal, what time of day is it, lad?*
Prince. *Thou art so fat-witted with drinking of old sack, and unbuttoning thee after supper, and sleeping upon benches after noon, that thou has forgotten to demand that truly which thou wouldst truly know. What a devil hast thou to do with the time of the day?*
...
Fal. *Marry then sweet wag, hen thou art King let not us that are squires of the night's body be called thieves of the day's beauty: let us be Diana's foresters, gentlemen of the shade, minions of the moon. ...*
Prince. *Thou sayst well, and it holds well too, for the fortune of us that are the moon's men doth ebb and*

flow like the sea, being governed as the sea is, by the moon.

(*1HIV* I, ii, 1-34)

b. Fal. *But as the devil would have it, three misbegotten knaves in Kendal green came at my back and let drive at me, for it was so dark, Hal, that thou couldst not see thy hand.*
Prince. *These lies are like their father that begets them, gross as a mountain, open, palpable. Why, thou clay-brained guts, thou knotty-pated fool, thou whoreson obscene tallow-catch, –*
Fal. *What, are thou mad? Art thou mad?*
Is not the truth the truth? (II, iv, 216-225)

c. Prince. *Why, Percy I kill'd myself, and saw thee dead.*
Fal. *Didst thou? Lord, Lord, how this world is given to lying! I grant you I was down, and out of breath, and so was he, but we rose both at an instant, and fought a long hour by Shrewsbury clock. ...*
Lanc. *This is the strangest tale that ever I heard.*
Prince. *This is the strangest fellow, brother John.*
  Come, bring your luggage nobly on your back.
  [Aside to Falstaff] *For my part, if a lie may do thee grace,*
  I'll gild it with the happiest terms I have.

(*1HIV* V, iv, 143-157)

The relationship between Prince Hal (the future Henry V) and Falstaff unrolls over two plays. It is at first a close friendship, and it is therefore codified by a reciprocal *thou* of intimacy (as can be seen in examples (4a) and (4b)).[12] The same pronoun form is the most frequently found also in verbal fights, where abusive language is hugely employed (cf. example (4b)). In *Henry IV Part One* Hal is even willing to justify Falstaff in front of his brother Lancaster (cf. example (4c)).

(4) d. Prince and Poins [coming forward] *Anon, anon, Sir.*
Fal.   *Ha! A bastard son of the King's? And art not thou Poins his brother?*
Prince. *Why, thou globe of sinful continents, what a life dost thou lead!*
Fal.   *A better than thou – I am a gentleman, thou art a drawer.*
Prince. *Very true, sir, and I come to draw you out by the ears.*
   [After in the same scene]
Peto. *The King your father is at Westminster,*
   And there are twenty weak and wearied posts
   Come from the north; and as I came along
   I met and overtook a dozen captains,
   Bareheaded, sweating, knocking at the taverns,
   And asking every one for Sir John Falstaff.
Prince. *By heaven, Poins, I feel me much to blame,*
   So idly to profane the precious time ...
   Give me my sword and cloak. Falstaff, goodnight.
            (*2HIV* II, iv, 279-363)

(4) e. Fal. *God save thy Grace, King Hal, my royal Hal!*
Pist. *The heavens thee guard and keep, most royal imp of fame!*
Fal.   *God save thee, my sweet boy!*
King. *My Lord Chief Justice, speak to that vain man.*
Ch. Jus. *Have you your wits? Know you what 'tis you speak?*
Fal.   *My King! My Jove! I speak to thee, my heart!*
King. *I know thee not, old man. Fall to thy prayers.*
   How ill white hairs becomes a fool and jester!
   I have long dreamt of such a kind of man,
   So surfeit-swell'd, so old, and so profane;
   But being awak'd I do despise my dream.
   Make less thy body hence, and more thy grace;
   Leave gormandizing; know the grave doth gape

> *For thee thrice wider than for other men.*
> *Reply not to me with a fool-borne jest;*
> *Presume not that I am the thing I was;*
> *For God doth know, so shall the world perceive,*
> *That I have turn'ed away my former self;*
> *So will I those that kept me company.*
> *When thou dost hear I am as I have been,*
> *Approach me, and thou shalt be as thou wast,*
> *The tutor and feeder of my riots.*
> *Till then I banish thee, on pain of death,*
> *As I have done the rest of my misleaders,*
> *Not to come near our person by ten mile.*
> *For competence of life I will allow you,*
> *That lack of means enforce you not to evils;*
> *And as we hear you do reform yourselves,*
> *We will, according to your strengths and qualities,*
> *Give you advancement.* [To the Lord Chief Justice]
> *Be it your charge, my lord,*
> *To see perform'd the tenor of my word.*
> (*2HIV*, V, v, 41-71)

In *Henry IV Part Two* the tone radically changes because Hal undergoes a process of growth and maturation which gradually estranges him from Falstaff. In example (4d), in fact, Hal ridicules his friend by using a formal style and reverential form of address with a clear ironic intent (it is an isolated instance of *you*, triggered off by Falstaff's own statement *I am a gentleman*). At the end of the passage, when Hal has already been informed that he is needed at court, he briefly and coldly greets Falstaff and calls him by surname.[13]

In example (4e) Hal has become King and Falstaff approaches in order to congratulate him. His mistake is that he presumes an unchanged attitude on the part of the former prince. Yet he knows he should be more deferential than he was. This state of attitudinal uncertainty is clearly reflected in his incoherent choice of terms of address: *thy Grace, my royal Hal*. But camaraderie prevails over honour and deference, for Falstaff chooses the usual friendly tone. The King's reaction effectively displays itself in a first attempt to delegate the matter to the Lord Chief Justice (it should be noticed that here the King refers to a present interlocutor with a third person pronoun, i.e., as if he were a side-participant or a bystander; cf. the distancing effect of third-person pronouns in Head (1978: 168); and for a description of conversational roles see Goffman 1981; Clark 1987; Anderson 1991 and 1993). Then Henry faces Falstaff directly and harshly reproaches him for his sinful life, but still uses the familiar pronoun. A gradual step towards the rejection is signalled by the use of *pluralis maiestatis* to refer to himself (Finkenstaedt 1963; Head 1978): the King hereby clarifies that he is no longer the merry companion he was and strongly asserts his royal authority. This enables him to switch to the final *you*, which ratifies the separation of the two old friends.

On the axis of social distance we have seen that the unmarked option between Henry and Falstaff would be *thou* as an index of friendship among peers. Here the pronoun *you* accomplishes the function of a markedness reversal in that it signals their lost intimacy and an important political change (Falstaff is excluded from the sphere of political power). But in this case the nuances of meaning enclosed in the alternation are even more complicated, because the two axes intersect. The same *thou* employed at the beginning is a marked form on the axis of emotional attitude, because it is emotionally connoted with contempt in the King's reproach, but dissolves at the end into a neutral, unmarked *you* because the King no longer cares about him. Falstaff does not perceive the polysemy of the same pronoun form along the two axes and selects the interpretation he habitually attaches to *thou*, that is the most natural/unmarked option on the axis of social distance. He is totally unaware that this instance of *thou* could be understood at the same time as a negative pole on the axis of emotional closeness (expressing scorn), or even as a negative pole on the axis of distance, if we interpret it as the display of a sense of superiority on the part of the speaker (cf. Elam (ed.) 1986: 199-200).

4. Conclusions

What I have tried to do in this paper is to show the subtle nuances of meaning to be perceived in the use of the pronoun plus term-of-address group in Shakespearean English as a reflection of the dynamics of personal relationships, so relevant in dramatic texts. In drama, in fact, states of affairs constantly change, and speakers' relations evolve over time. Person deixis is one of the instruments which have to convey such situational and interactional variations.

When I set out to explore the rules of use I came across the notion of markedness, which has been largely used in literature, although in most cases rather inadequately. So I tried to establish patterns which can be used as criteria for markedness evaluation. I identified two main axes responsible for pronoun selection, but the most natural option on one axis may turn into the most marked on the other – a phenomenon referred to as markedness reversal. I hope to have shown that markedness is a gradual concept and may be evaluated from different perspectives.

Notes

1. I would like to thank Terttu Nevalainen, chairperson of the ESSE seminar on Historical Sociolinguistics, who read my paper and suggested many improvements.
2. They include *Henry IV Part One*, *Henry IV Part Two*, *Henry V*, and *The Merry Wives of Windsor* hereafter abbreviated respectively as follows: *1HIV*, *2HIV*, *HV* and *MWW*. The quotations are based on the Arden edition of these plays.
3. The introduction of the dimension of solidarity is scarcely effective in accounting for all the instances of non-reciprocal dyads. Wales (1983) tries to settle the problem by adding the parameter of nearness/distance, which explains the adoption of intimate address within small groups of people but still does not explain the persistence of non-reciprocal uses. For a detailed account of the fundamental dimensions that influence language use see Spencer-Oatey (1996).

4. I have not here reported about the stylistic answer to alternation, which considers pronoun fluctuation functional to meter (Quirk 1971), or collocational constraints (Mulholland 1967).
5. The Quakers adopted *thou* as the pronominal form which was nearer to the original Biblical spirit. This choice was confirmed by the abolition of titles as a democratic practice. So *thou* was meant to level all relationships, but it was negatively sanctioned outside their community. In the eighteenth century *you* had already lost its elevated social meaning, so the Quakers had no longer good grounds for avoiding it. In the nineteenth century *thou* still survived in the countryside (especially in Lancashire, Yorkshire, and Somerset), and in literature, where it signalled either rusticity, low education, or sentimental and anachronistic behaviour (Finkenstaedt 1963: 174-213). Besides, in poetry it was employed in addresses to the dead, to God, or in exhortations, that is whenever the addressee could not reply.
6. Barber (1987: 171) anticipates that *you* may be employed as mock-polite or ironical pronoun form, and that it may be followed by a switch back to a more normal *thou*. Kielkiewicz-Janowiak (1994) suggests that it is at least risky to dismiss the issue of fluctuation with the markedness justification.
7. In this respect Brown and Gilman in a later study (1989) consider politeness phenomena in some Shakespearean plays and include terms of address as a cardinal form of encoding social attitudes and a fundamental linguistic factor of variation. As Mazzon accurately points out (1995), Brown and Gilman (1989) fail to relate social distance to pronoun fluctuation, because as the pronoun is an obligatory grammatical category, they state that its contribution in terms of politeness is irrelevant.
8. Yet Görlach's thesis does not hold for possessives, which continued to be fully functional.
9. It is important to notice that the two axes code different types of information: social distance is a more stable feature, and when it varies it is necessary to redefine the social roles of the interactants. The axis of emotional attitude is on the contrary responsible for changeable dispositions, a sort of emotional barometer for each situation.
10. I have identified adjacency pairs with the same number and used (a) for the first pair part and (b) for the second.
11. In King Henry's turns there are several instances of *passe-partout you*, i.e. occurrences where this pronoun does not seem to have a significant meaning.
12. The choice of pronoun forms among equals largely depends on social rank: in *Henry IV Part One* Prince Hal equates himself to the *coney-catching rascals* of the Boar Head's tavern, whose life style he closely follows.

13. This strategy may be employed when a speaker wishes to alter the distance from the addressee. This shift can be a "social accelerator" in either positive or negative polarities (Brown and Levinson 1987; Nevalainen and Raumolin-Brunberg 1995: 589).

References

Abbott, Edwin A.
    [1870] 1925 *A Shakespearian grammar*. London: Macmillan.
Anderson, Laurie
    1991 What's in a name? Vocatives and participant referentials in multiparty conversation. *Textus* 4: 171-216.
    1993 Address terms in dramatic dialogue: selective mimesis, perceived deviance and audience response. In: Grazia Caliumi (ed.), 393-407.
Barber, Charles L.
    [1981] 1987 "You" and "thou" in Shakespeare's *Richard III*. *Leeds Studies in English* 12: 273-289. Reprinted in: Vivian Salmon and Edwina Burness (eds.), 163-177.
Baugh, Albert C.
    1953 *A history of the English language*. London: Routledge and Kegan Paul.
Bazzanella, Carla (ed.)
    1996 *Repetiton in dialogue: Beiträge zur Dialogforschung*. Tübingen: Niemeyer.
Blake, Norman F.
    1989 *The language of Shakespeare*. London: Macmillan.
Brook, George L.
    1976 *The language of Shakespeare*. London: Deutsch.
Brown, Roger and Albert Gilman
    1960 The pronouns of power and solidarity. In: Thomas A. Sebeok (ed.), 253-276.
    1989 Politeness theory and Shakespeare's four major tragedies. *Language in Society* 18: 159-212.
Brown, Penelope and Stephen Levinson
    1987 *Politeness: some universals in language usage*. Cambridge: Cambridge University Press.
Caliumi, Grazia (ed.)
    1993 *Shakespeare e la sua eredità*. Parma: Zara.

Clark, Herbert H.
1987 Four dimensions of language use. In: Jef Verschueren and Marcella Bertuccelli Papi (eds.), 9-25.
Drew, Paul and Anthony Wooton (eds.)
1988 *Erving Goffman: exploring the interaction order.* Boston, MA: Northeastern University Press.
Dunkling, Leslie
1990 *A dictionary of epithets and terms of address.* London/New York: Routledge.
Eagleson, Robert D.
[1971] 1987 Propertied as all the tuned spheres: aspects of Shakespeare's language. *The Teaching of English* 20: 4-15. Reprinted in: Vivian Salmon and Edwina Burness (eds.).
Elam, Keir (ed.)
1986 *La grande festa del linguaggio.* Bologna: Il Mulino.
Ervin-Tripp, Susan
[1972] 1986 On sociolinguistic rules: alternation and co-occurrence. In: John J. Gumperz and Dell Hymes (eds.), 213-250.
Finkenstaedt, Thomas
1963 *You und Thou. Studien zur Anrede im Englischen (mit einem Exkurs über die Anrede im Deutschen).* Berlin: de Gruyter.
Frank, Thomas
1989 *Introduzione allo studio della lingua inglese.* Bologna: Il Mulino.
Giacalone Ramat, Anna, Onofrio Carruba, and Giuliano Bernini (eds.)
1987 *Papers from the 7th International Conference on Historical Linguistics.* Amsterdam/Philadelphia: Benjamins.
Gillet, Peter J.
[1974] 1987 Me, U, and non-U: class connotations of two Shakespeare idioms, *Shakespeare Quarterly* 25: 297-309. Reprinted in: Vivian Salmon and Edwina Burness (eds.), 117-129.
Görlach, Manfred
1991 *Introduction to Early Modern English.* Cambridge: Cambridge University Press.
Greenberg, Joseph H.
1966 *Language universals.* The Hague: Mouton.
Greenberg, Joseph H. (ed.)
1978 *Universals of human language, Volume 3: Word structure.* Stanford: Stanford University Press.
Gumperz, John J. and Dell Hymes (eds.)
1986 *Directions in sociolinguistics: the ethnography of communication.* (2nd edition.) Oxford/Cambridge, MA: Blackwell.

Head, Brian F.
1978 Respect degrees in pronominal reference. In: Joseph H. Greenberg (ed.), 151-211.
Hickey, Raymond, Merja Kytö, Ian Lancashire, and Matti Rissanen (eds.)
1996 *Proceedings from the Second Diachronic Corpora Workshop.* Amsterdam/Atlanta, GA: Rodopi.
Humphreys, Arthur Raleigh (ed.)
1991 *King Henry IV part two.* London/New York: Routledge.
1992 *King Henry IV part one.* London/New York: Routledge.
Hussey, S. S.
1982 *The literary language of Shakespeare.* London: Longman.
Jakobson, Roman
1962 *Selected writings I and II.* The Hague: Mouton.
Jucker, Andreas H. (ed.)
1995 *Historical pragmatics.* Amsterdam/Philadelphia: Benjamins.
Kennedy, Arthur G.
1915 *The pronoun of address in English literature of the thirteenth century.* California: Stanford University Press.
Kielkiewicz-Janowiak, Agnieszka
1994 Sociolinguistics and the computer: pronominal address in Shakespeare. *Studia Anglica Posnaniensia* 29: 49-56.
Kopytko, Roman
1995 Linguistic politeness strategies in Shakespeare's plays. In: Andreas H. Jucker (ed.), 515-540.
Levinson, Stephen
1988 Putting linguistics on a proper footing: explorations in Goffman's concepts of participation. In: Paul Drew and Anthony Wooton (eds.), 161-227.
Machan, Tim William and Charles T. Scott (eds.)
1992 *English in its social context: essays in historical sociolinguistics.* New York/Oxford: Oxford University Press.
Malsch, Derry L.
1987 The grammaticalization of social relationship: the origin of number to encode deference. In: Anna Giacalone Ramat, Onofrio Carruba, and Giuliano Bernini (eds.), 407-418.
Mausch, Hanna
1993 Democratic *you* and paradigm. *Studia Anglica Posnaniensia* 25-27: 143-153.

Mazzon, Gabriella
1992   Shakespearean *thou* and *you* revisited, or socio-affective networks on stage. In: Carmela Nocera Avila, Nicola Pantaleo, and Domenico Pezzini (eds), 123-136.
Mazzon, Gabriella
1995   Pronouns and terms of address in Shakespearean English: a socio-affective marking system of transition. *Views* 4: 20-42.
McIntosh, Angus
1963   *As You Like It*: a grammatical clue to character. *Review of English Literature* 4: 68-81.
McIntosh, Angus and Colin Williamson
1963   *King Lear*, Act I, Scene i: a stylistic note. *Review of English Studies* 14: 54-58.
Merlini Barbaresi, Lavinia
1988   *Markedness in English discourse: a semiotic approach*. Parma: Zara.
1996   Repetiton in dialogue. In: Carla Bazzanella (ed.), 104-118.
Millward, Celia M.
[1966] 1987   Pronominal case in Shakespearean imperatives. *Language* 42: 10-17. Reprinted in: Vivian Salmon and Edwina Burness (eds.), 301-307.
Milroy, James
1992   *Linguistic variation and change (on the historical sociolinguistics of English)*. (Language in Society 19.) Oxford/ Cambridge, MA: Blackwell.
Muir, Kenneth and Samuel Schoenbaum (eds.)
1971   *A new companion to Shakespeare studies*. Cambridge: Cambridge University Press.
Mulholland, Joan
1967   "Thou" and "You" in Shakespeare: a study in the second person pronoun. *English Studies* 48: 34-43.
Nevala, Minna
1998   *By him that loves you*: address forms in letters written to 16th-century social aspirers. In: Antoinette Renouf (ed.), 147-157.
Nevalainen, Terttu
1996   Ongoing work on the Corpus of Early English Correspondence. In: Raymond Hickey et al. (eds.), 81-90.
Nevalainen, Terttu and Helena Raumolin-Brunberg
1995   Constraints on politeness. The pragmatics of address formulae in Early English Correspondence. In: Andreas H. Jucker (ed.), 541-601.

Nocera Avila, Carmela, Nicola Pantaleo, and Domenico Pezzini (eds.)
    1992   *Early Modern English: trends, forms and texts.* Papers read at the IV National Conference of History of English, Catania, 2-3 May 1991. Bari: Schena.

O'Donnell, W. R. and Loreto Todd
    1980   *Variety in contemporary English.* London: Allen and Unwin.

Oliver, Harol James (ed.)
    1993   *The Merry Wives of Windsor.* London/New York: Routledge.

Quirk, Randolph
    1971   Shakespeare and the English language. In: Kenneth Muir and Samuel Schoenbaum (eds.), 67-82.

Raumolin-Brunberg, Helena
    1996   Incorporating sociolinguistic information into a diachronic corpus of English. In: Raymond Hickey et al. (eds.), 105-117.

Renouf, Antoinette (ed.)
    1998   *Explorations in corpus linguistics.* (Language and Computers Studies in Practical Linguistics 23.) Amsterdam/Atlanta, GA: Rodopi.

Reploge, Carol
    [1973] 1987   Shakespeare's salutations: a study in stylistic etiquette. *Studies in Philology* 70: 172-186. Reprinted in: Vivian Salmon and Edwina Burness (eds.), 101-115.

Salmon, Vivian
    [1967] 1987a   Elizabethan colloquial English in the Falstaff plays. *Leeds Studies in English* (New series.): 37-70. Reprinted in: Vivian Salmon and Edwina Burness (eds.), 37-70.
    [1970] 1987b   Some functions of Shakespearian word-formation. *Shakespeare Survey* 23: 13-26. Reprinted in: Vivian Salmon and Edwina Burness (eds.), 193-206.
    [1965] 1987c   Sentence structure in colloquial Shakespearean English. *Transactions of the Philological Society*: 105-140. Reprinted in: Vivian Salmon and Edwina Burness (eds.), 265-300.

Salmon, Vivian and Edwina Burness (eds.)
    1987   *A reader in the language of Shakespearean drama.* Amsterdam/ Philadelphia: Benjamins.

Sebeok, Thomas A. (ed.)
    1960   *Style in Language.* Cambridge, MA: MIT Press.

Shapiro, Michael
    1983   *The sense of grammar: language as semiotics.* Bloomington: Indiana University Press.

Spencer-Oatey, Helen
    1996   Reconsidering power and distance. *Journal of Pragmatics* 26: 1-24.
Verschueren, Jef
    1987   The pragmatic perspective. In: Jef Verschueren and Marcella Bertuccelli Papi (eds.), 3-8.
Verschueren, Jef and Marcella Bertuccelli Papi (eds.)
    1987   *The pragmatic perspective*. Amsterdam/Philadelphia: Benjamins.
Wales, Kathleen
    1983   *Thou* and *you* in early modern English: Brown and Gilman reappraised. *Studia Linguistica* 37: 107-125.
Walter, John H. (ed.)
    1993   *King Henry V*. London/New York: Routledge.
Williams, Joseph M.
    1992   "O! When Degree is Shak'd": sixteenth-century anticipations of some modern attitudes toward usage. In: Tim William Machan and Charles T. Scott (eds.), 69-101.

Gender voices in the spoken interaction of the past: a pilot study based on Early Modern English trial proceedings[1]

Jonathan Culpeper and Merja Kytö

1. Introduction

1.1. Speech and gender studies

The bulk of research carried out over the last few decades relating in some way to issues of language and gender has focussed on features of speech. Many well-known studies have considered phonological variables, such as the presence or absence of postvocalic *r* (Labov 1972) or whether the suffix *-ing* is pronounced /ɪn/ or /ɪŋ/ (Trudgill 1974). Other studies have examined lexical, grammatical, and pragmatic phenomena that are highly typical of speech. For example, R. Lakoff (1975) included the following features in her discussion of what characterises "women's language": tag questions, hedges, exaggerated politeness, "empty" adjectives (that convey an emotional reaction as opposed to information), mild expletives, and direct quotations (instead of paraphrase).[2] More recent studies have been particularly concerned with conversational interaction, and have drawn upon concepts from discourse analysis and conversation analysis (e.g. Coates and Cameron (eds.) 1989: 61-174; Crawford 1995).

Clearly, adding a diachronic dimension to this research presents some data problems, since speech – prior to the relatively recent advent of the tape recorder – is only preserved in writing. Records of women's speech from earlier periods are scanty. As a result, much historical work relating to gender issues uses non-speech-based data.

Some researchers have utilised corpora containing a variety of text-types, mostly of non-speech-based character. Kytö (1993) looked at the third person singular inflections -*s* and -*th* in the Early Modern English period, using texts from the *Helsinki Corpus* and a supplementary corpus of Early American English. Similarly, Meurman-Solin (1993: 161-162) examined a range of texts for older Scots, noting that women retain certain Scottish spellings longer than men. In particular, personal correspondence, where the language is private and informal, has been seen as a data source where the "voice" of the writer might be heard. Correspondence also has the advantage that it is sometimes possible to reconstruct the "social network" a particular writer belonged to. Studies have focussed on both British and Scottish English. For example, Romaine (1982: 167-170) considers relativisation strategies in letters written by men and women to Mary Queen of Scots. Regarding British English, the *Corpus of Early English Correspondence* (see Nevalainen and Raumolin-Brunberg (eds.) 1996) is a notable data source. For example, Nevalainen (1996: 77-91) reports three case studies examining competing lexical and grammatical variants and their correlation with gender in the data provided by this corpus.

Whilst personal correspondence is a source which has yielded valuable research data, it is very different from the kind of material used in twentieth-century studies. In particular, it does not involve face-to-face interaction. In this paper we set out to study the supposedly authentic spoken interactions of male and female witnesses recorded in trial proceedings from late seventeenth-century England.

1.2. Approaches to language and gender issues

Broadly speaking, issues of language and gender have been approached from three directions:

1.2.1. Variationist

Researchers in the tradition of Labov have treated gender as one dimension of variation. Their work has been characterised by a focus on linguistic variants, usually a single phoneme, morpheme or lexical item, and by quantification (e.g. Labov 1966, 1972; Trudgill 1972, 1974; Cheshire 1982). The major finding claimed for this research is that women, regardless of their social characteristics, use more standard forms of the language than men, and that women are generally innovators in linguistic change (e.g. Trudgill 1983; Labov 1990, 1994). The explanation for this finding put forward by Labov and Trudgill relates to women's social role; for example, women's lack of opportunity to pursue social status through work in the same way as men and thus their reliance on the "symbolic status" of language rather than economic status, and their particular responsibility for transmitting speech to children and thus their sensitivity to correctness. However, this finding has not gone unchallenged. L. Milroy (1980), for example, did not find the expected correlation in her Belfast data. In particular, the explanations put forward for this finding have been hotly debated (see Coates and Cameron ((eds.) 1989) for an incisive critique).

1.2.2. Speech style

R. Lakoff's *Language and women's place* (1975) (originally published in 1973) has been instrumental in giving rising to a vast number of studies aiming to reveal a particular speech style for women.[3] Lakoff's work has been criticised on a number of counts, not the least because the features she claims to be typical of "women's language" (see, for example, the list of features given above) are not empirically derived, but seem to reflect linguistic stereotypes (Cameron 1992: 42-54). This lack of empiricism gave rise to many quantitative studies designed to establish whether there where "real" differences between men's and women's language (e.g. Crosby and Nyquist 1977; Dubois and Crouch 1975; Shimanoff 1977; Steckler and Cooper 1980). However, these studies have been beset with methodological problems, including the difficulty (impossibility?) of isolating the variable of "sex" (understood as a biologically determined category) from other variables such as status, and the difficulty in selecting samples of men and women who are comparable in terms of social background. Furthermore, some empirical studies have tended to focus on matters of form, and pay insufficient attention to function and context (we will return to this particular issue in our discussion of hedges below). After more than 20 years of research, the "sex difference" question is still open (Crawford 1995: 26-29), though most sociolinguists acknowledge that differences do exist. As with the variationist approach, explanations for claimed differences have been particularly controversial. There are two main explanations which reflect different views of women in society: the "dominance" view (e.g. R. Lakoff 1975) sees differences as a reflection of men's dominance and women's subordination, the "difference" view (e.g. Jones 1980) sees differences as a reflection of the idea that men and women belong to different subcultures (see Cameron 1992: 74-78 for a discussion of some of the issues).

1.2.3. Constructionist

Both the "variationist" and the "speech style" approaches outlined above have tended to focus on individual speech features and treat them as relatively static in meaning. The more recent "constructionist" approach (e.g. Hall and Bucholtz 1995, Crawford 1995) takes a more "holistic" view of language, typically focussing on spoken interactions, their function and their social context, and drawing analytical and theoretical input from the fields of discourse analysis and the ethnography of speaking. Whereas both the "variationist" and the "speech style" approaches tend to see gender as a relatively static property of the individual and a relatively clear-cut concept (sex as a binary biological category),[4] the "constructionist" view emphasises gender as a dynamic social construct. Gender is not viewed as an attribute of an individual, but "a way of making sense of transactions" (Crawford 1995: 12). Language is not merely a reflection of gender, but a way of shaping it.

Needless to say, this brief outline of three approaches is very much a simplification. The approaches are not mutually exclusive. Nor do descriptions of the approaches capture all aspects of similarity or difference, and they may well overlook issues considered crucial by other researchers. However, they do provide a useful way of placing historical work on language and gender, and of placing our own study.

1.3. Historical work: taking it further

It is worth noting that in the traditional view (e.g. Trudgill 1978) sociolinguistics is often taken to be the variationist approach. Historical sociolinguistics, where gender has been discussed, is to date solidly within this tradition.[5] Given that in the Early Modern period and before there was no clear "standard" language, it is difficult to assess the twentieth century finding that women use more standard language than men. Thus, typically historical studies have addressed the issue of whether women have been linguistic innovators (see the historical studies mentioned above). This particular research question raises an interesting data issue. Where is the locus of linguistic change? J. Milroy (1992) argues that it is in speaker interaction. He stresses the importance of "conversational repair":

> It is in these listener-oriented functions, rather than in message-oriented functions, that structural and phonetic changes are negotiated between speakers, and it is these functions of speech (and not the message oriented function) that makes change possible (and not necessarily dysfunctional) in the basic structural parts of language. Message-oriented discourse, on the contrary, is likely to resist change, and it is a truism that the most context-independent channel (the writing system) is very slow to admit phonological and morphological changes (J. Milroy 1992: 75).

If this is so, then historical studies looking for speaker innovation might have missed some important aspects as a result of the kind of data they used.

We take the broader view of sociolinguistics that the variationist approach is just one approach within sociolinguistics, and that "any research which improves our understanding of language and society and the relationship between the two can be called 'sociolinguistic'" (Coates 1989: 63). The starting point for our study was to separate our data set of courtroom witnesses' speech according to sex. As ours is an exploratory study designed to raise issues rather than come up with conclusive answers, we decided to investigate a wide range of linguistic features in our data, including discourse acts, single lexical items acting as hedges, the third-person-singular morphological markings, and periphrastic *do*. This list includes features that have been typically studied within each of the three approaches outlined above. We also paid particular attention to the function of linguistic features and to their context. It is unfortunate that O'Barr and Atkins (1980), a study which considered courtroom witnesses and gender in the present-day, does not consider the linguistic context of witnesses' speech. We examine the speech of the judges and the effect that this might have on the witnesses. Since our concerns are quite "holistic", our approach bears some similarities to the constructionist approach. However, we shall also attempt to illuminate some interpretative consequences for the other approaches.

The remainder of this paper falls into four parts. In section 2., we describe our data. In section 3., we consider overall speech volume and various discoursal acts, and relate them in particular to the role the witnesses play in the courtroom. In section 4., we examine hedges, a feature which R. Lakoff (1975) claims to be part of "women's language". In section 5., we investigate the third-person-singular morphological markings and periphrastic *do*, grammatical features which have been discussed within a number of variationist studies.

2. Data

Our data are drawn from a corpus of "spoken" dialogues from the Early Modern English period, containing text types such as witness depositions, parliamentary debates, drama, and prose fiction.[6] By focussing on one text type – trial proceedings – which involves one kind of speech event and also a relatively formalised speech event, we hope to be better able to understand, within the scope of this pilot study, the dynamics of the discourse and possible implications for gender.

A particular issue for our data is the possible interference from the scribe, who (as far as we know) invariably was male. Modern studies must also be aware of interpretative issues relating to data collection. After all, any kind of transcription is an interpretation of the primary data. However, the situation in the seventeenth-century was that the court scribe would attempt to convert one medium (speech) into another (writing) in real-time, and from those notes attempt at a later point in time to reconstruct the record of the trial.[7] Clearly, there is a lot of scope for bias. In addition, some court records, particularly if the accused had been a well-known public figure, would receive extensive editing by the Chancellery.[8]

The material included in this pilot study is drawn from the four trials listed in table 1.

Table 1. The trial texts used in our study[9]

Text	Trial/ Printed
The Tryals of Robert Green, Henry Berry & Lawrence Hill	1679/ 1679
The Trial of the Lady Alice Lisle	1685/ 1730
The Tryal of Charles Lord Mohun	1692/ 1693
The Trial of Haagen Swendsen	1702/ 1777 (= 1742)

The fact that these trials cluster within a 23-year period results from the fact that no women appear in the earlier trial proceedings in the corpus.[10] This, in fact, suits our purpose, since we are not here concerned with language change within our data set. Originally, these trial proceedings amounted to some 40,000 words. From this we extracted all interactions which involved female witnesses. In total this amounted to 18 witnesses who made 253 speech contributions or turns. We then attempted to form a matching data set by taking interactions that involved male witnesses up to a total of 18 witnesses and 253 turns. Of course, selecting even an approximately matching set is difficult, not least of all because the social background of men and women at that time was so very different. We employed two criteria for selection: 1) we tried to select a similar number of male witnesses from each trial, and 2) we tried to select a range of male witnesses that broadly reflected the social status range of female witnesses (we do not attempt to match individual with individual, but to match the overall range). In addition to the witnesses' speech, we also extracted the utterances of judges, attorneys, recorders and other representatives of the legal profession into two files, one containing the utterances addressed to the female witnesses we had selected and the other those addressed to male witnesses we had selected. The four files, stripped of all other text except the utterances (i.e. any non-speech, such as the scribe's contextual comments), total some 25,000 words (see table 2).

Table 2. The number of words in the data set

Female witnesses	9,170 words
Male witnesses	7,330 words
Judges addressing female witnesses	3,360 words
Judges addressing male witnesses	4,770 words
Total	24,630 words

Setting up these files was not an unproblematic task. We tried to extract relatively whole interactions. Thus, typically, an extract would begin at the point where a witness was sworn in, and end at the point where their cross-examination would finish. However, this was not always possible to achieve. The following problems arose when we tried to 1) produce a matching data set of male witnesses, and 2) separate the judges from the witnesses:
1. One issue that arose was what constituted a "turn". Mr. James Dunne, one of the witnesses in Lady Alice Lisle's trial, is repeatedly given the opportunity to speak, but 11 times he chooses to be silent. Do these constitute turns? In our view, they do.

2. Occasionally, a witness of the wrong sex would crop up in a particular interaction (for example, when a judge has a brief side interaction with another witness), so this witness's speech and the judge's interaction with that witness would be deleted.
3. Sometimes the accused would cross-examine a witness through a judge. So, for example, the accused would address a question to the judge which was intended for the witness. Often the judge would straightforwardly relay (basically through repetition) the question to the witness, whilst at other times the witness would reply without waiting for the judge to repeat the question. Such dialogue functioning as examination belongs, we think, in the non-witness files, although it is rather odd because it emanates from the accused.

3. Discoursal aspects

3.1. Speech volume

For the twentieth century, researchers appear to disagree about whether men or women contribute most to interaction (see the references given in Thorne, Kramarae, and Henley ((eds.) 1983: 279-281)). Holmes, however, argues convincingly that the discrepancies arise because of the differing contexts and purposes of talk (Holmes 1992: 132). For public and formal contexts, Holmes cites numerous studies which demonstrate that in general men have longer turns, and argues that contributing talk in these contexts is status-enhancing (Holmes 1992: 132-135).

Who has longer turns in our data set, male or female witnesses? In terms of words, female witnesses say considerably more than male: 9,170 words as opposed to 7,330 words (see table 2 above). Why might this be? Holmes reminds us that in a situation like an interview it is the interviewee, the relatively powerless participant, who contributes most talk, and a cooperative interviewee "is one who contributes plenty of talk" (Holmes 1995: 33-34). This may also apply to the courtroom, where one might expect a cooperative witness to provide a full answer to questions. Can we then assume that female witnesses are generally more cooperative? An explanatory hypothesis might be that this is because of the relative lack of power of women. In the sharply patriarchal society of the seventeenth century, women were generally denied power and assumed to be subordinate to men, "whose authority was sustained informally through culture, custom and differences in education, and more formally through the law" (Amussen 1988: 3). Thus, female witnesses might have cooperated more in providing required talk, because they felt they had to. (Certainly, the most uncooperative witness in our data – Dunne in the trial of Lady Lisle – uses silence 11 times, in order not to answer questions put to him by Judge Jeffreys. In fact, one of Dunne's courtroom silences was extraordinarily long. A contextual comment in the trial record tells us that "he paused for half a quarter of an Hour".) However, these interpretations for the relatively large quantity of female witness speech are premature. The evidence is flimsy, since words can also be used strategically to fudge issues, to evade questions, and so on. We need to look more closely at how the discourse is working.

3.2. Elicitations

Questioning is central to courtroom discourse, not only in terms of frequency, but also as a way of controlling the discourse (Harris 1984). A question not only requires a response, but requires a relevant response: it delimits what can be said. We devised a broad categorisation to investigate how the witnesses' discourse is controlled by the judges, and, in particular, how they elicit information. Of course, any categorisation which is based at least in part on functional phenomena is going to be problematic. There are problems to do with identifying watertight criteria, with the segmentation of the data, and with coping with ambiguity and indeterminacy. We are aware of these problems. Nevertheless, with our broad brushstrokes we hope to provide some insights.

Our four "elicitation" types were data-generated.[11] In turn, we will describe each elicitation type and discuss the quantitative results given in table 3.

Table 3. Elicitations in the judges' speech

Elicitation type	Judges addressing female witnesses	Judges addressing male witnesses
Prompters	24 (60%)	16 (40%)
Relatively open questions	19 (36%)	34 (64%)
Relatively closed questions	188 (52%)	172 (48%)
Challenging statements or rhetorical questions	17 (47%)	19 (53%)

3.2.1. Prompters

The most common prompters consist of a command (employing an imperative verb) to start speaking at some length (usually across a number of turns) on a specific topic, for example:

(1)[12] a. *Acquaint my Lords where it was, and in what manner you found them.*
    b. *Give an account of what was after the buying the ring.*
    c. *Prithee, tell us the story of it.*

Many such prompters occur immediately after a witness is sworn in. A few questions have a similar function:

(2) a. *Do you know anything of Mr.* Swendsen?
    b. *What do you know concerning Mrs.* Rawlins *being taken away?*
    c. *What can you say concerning* Hill, *that he was out after eight a clock that night?*

There are two examples, both from Judge Jeffreys in the Lady Lisle trial, which are similar, except that the witness has to infer the relevant topic:

(3) a. *What have you to say for yourself?*
    b. *Well, what do you know?*

Some prompters require the witness to react to some particular information:

(4) a. *What say you to this, Mrs.* Rawlins?
    b. *Mr.* Swendsen, *What do you answer to the evidence?*
    c. *What say you,* Barter, *to that? Well, Woman, what say you?*

Within this category we have also included commands to continue speaking on a current topic. The examples are:

(5) a. *What then?*
    b. *Well, what can you say more?*
    c. *Well, and what then?*
    d. *Well, what did you do then?*
    e. *Well, Sir, go on.*
    f. *Well now go on.*
    g. *Well, go on, and speak aloud.*
    h. *Go on.*

Prompters play a key role in initiating and developing the crime narrative. For example (see also example (13)):

(6) Mr. Att. Gen. *Mrs.* Bracegirdle, *Pray give my Lords an Account of the whole of your Knowledge of the Attempt that was made upon you in* Dury Lane, *and what followed upon it.*
    Mrs. Bracegirdle. *My Lord, I was in* Prince's Street *at supper at Mr.* Page's, *and at ten a Clock at night,*

> *Mr.* Page *went Home with me; and coming down* Drury Lane, *there stood a Coach by my Lord* Craven's *Door, and the Boot of the Coach was down, and a great many men stood by it; and just as I came to the Place where the Coach stood, two Soldiers came and pulled me from Mr.* Page, *and four or five more came up to them, and they knocked my Mother down almost, for my Mother and my Brother were with me.*
>
> (MOHUN BRACEGIRDLE)

Our quantitative work, though the figures are fairly low, suggests that judges use prompters more frequently with female witnesses. Female witnesses seem to be required to perform a rather different role from the male witnesses, namely, that of providing crime narrative.

3.2.2. Relatively open questions

These require from the witness a relatively expansive response, and the response could take place over a number of turns.[13] Typically, such questions seek explanation of some specific issue. Examples include:

(7) a. *Why so?*
 b. *Now I would know what that business was?*
 c. *What kind of a Man was he?*
 d. *How came you there?*
 e. *What was the Reason why you were conducted into another Room, and not where they were?*
 f. *What did he do then?*
 g. *How came you to be released?*

Our quantitative work, and again the figures are low, indicates that such relatively open questions are used more frequently by judges examining male witnesses. It seems that male witnesses are more likely to be subjected to some of the more probing questions of cross-examination, questions which typically attempt to reveal motive.

3.2.3. Relatively closed questions

These include "yes/no" questions and questions that seek very specific information, such as a date or the name of a place or person. The examples below are taken from a single extract but with the witnesses' speech deleted, leaving just the relatively closed questions of the judges.

(8) Mr. Soll. Gen. *Were you one of the Bailiffs that Arrested Mrs.* Busby *and Mrs.* Rawlins?
L. C. J. Holt. *Who employed you?* ...
L. C. J. Holt. *Were you at Mr.* Hartwell's *House?*
L. C. J. Holt. *What Day of the Week was this?*
Mr. Soll. Gen. *Had you seen Mr.* Swendsen *before that Morning?*
L. C. J. Holt. *What did they do in* Stretton-Grounds?
Counsel. *Was it the Prisoner at the Bar?*
L. C. J. Holt. *You were eating Steaks, you say, at the* Vine-Tavern; *Was she there then?*
L. C. J. Holt. *What, before you went in?*
L. C. J. Holt. *Did you see Mrs.* Rawlins *there?*
Mr. Soll. Gen. *When* Hartwell *took away this Gentlewoman, did she go away quietly, or did Mrs.* Busby *and she make an Outcry?*
L. C. J. Holt. *Where was it you first saw Mr.* Swendsen?
L. C. J. Holt. *When was it you saw him there?*
L. C. J. Holt. *Where was it he gave you the Pot of Drink?*
L. C. J. Holt. *How many were there in Company there?*
(SWENDSEN WAKEMAN)

In our quantitative work, such questions are distributed fairly evenly between judges' speech to male witnesses and the judges' speech to female witnesses.

3.2.4. Challenging statements or rhetorical questions

These refute the evidence given in the witness's preceding turn, and are often followed by a defense from the witness. Thus Mary Tilden's evidence is refuted three times in the extract below:

(9) Mr. Justice Jones. *When were you out of Town?*
Mary Tilden. *In October.*
Mr. Justice Dolben. *Nay, now, Mistris, you have spoil'd all; for in* October *this business was done.*
Mr. Justice Jones. *You have undone the man, instead of saving him.*
Mary Tilden. *Why, my Lord, I only mistook the Month.*
L. C. J. *You Woman (speaking to Mrs.* Broadstreet*) what Month was it you were out of Town?*
Broadstreet. *In* September.
L. C. J. *'Tis apparent you consider not what you say, or you come hither to say any thing will serve the turn.*
Mary Tilden. *No, I do not, for I was out of Town in* September, *came to Town the latter end of* September.

(GREEN TILDEN)

These challenging phenomena are rather few. In fact, they cluster solely in three particularly heated cross-examinations: Judge Jeffreys and Dunne (in the trial of Lady Lisle), Judge Jeffreys and Lady Lisle, and the cross-examination of Mary Tilden in the trial of Green, Berry, and Hill.

Our work on elicitation types indicates that the judges do not treat the male and female witnesses in exactly the same way, but tend to allot them different conversational roles. Women are more likely to be required to give crime narrative; men are more likely to be cross-examined about motive. These differing roles might also explain why overall female witnesses speak more than male: giving crime narrative requires a considerable amount of talk (see example (6)).

4. Hedges

Hedges play a central role in the interpersonal dynamics of interactive discourse. They have a pragmatic function: they tell us about the relationship between a message and its context. In a courtroom situation, for example, they might provide linguistic means by which witnesses can try to evade awkward questions or, by contrast, emphasise their commitment to their evidence. G. Lakoff, whose seminal work on semantic criteria and fuzzy logic might be seen as a starting point for any discussion of hedges, referred to hedges as "words whose meaning implicitly involves fuzziness – words whose job is to make things fuzzier or less fuzzy" (G. Lakoff 1972: 195). For instance, the hedges are underlined in the following constructed examples:

(10) a. I think *it's* sort of *good*
b. I'm sure *it's* really *good*

The hedges increase fuzziness in the first sentence, whereas they decrease fuzziness in the second. Note that this is a broad definition of hedges, and is the one which we will follow here. Later researchers have seen hedges or "down-toners" as increasers of fuzziness, and have called decreasers of fuzziness "boosters", "emphatics", or "amplifiers". It should also be noted that we include in our discussion of hedges phenomena that other researchers have called "pragmatic particles" or "discourse markers". Modern-day examples include *you know*, *I mean*, and *well*.

Since R. Lakoff (1975) put forward the idea that hedges are a part of "women's language", a number of researchers have undertaken empirical studies on hedges (e.g. Crosby and Nyquist 1977;

McMillan et al. 1977; O'Barr and Atkins 1980). Later work has pointed out that in this work there has been an over-reliance on form, and insufficient attention has been given to function and context (Cameron, McAlinden, and O'Leary 1989; Holmes 1984, 1992, 1995). In particular, whether one labels a certain form as having a downtoning function or a boosting function is very much dependent on the context. Holmes's (1995: 92-95) discussion of *I think* makes this especially clear. Most researchers, including R. Lakoff (1975: 54), have treated *I think* as a clear-cut example of a word which always has a downtoning function. Holmes argues that it can have a boosting function, as in the following examples:

(11) Male committee convenor in radio interview:
Personally I think you can't sustain that position for long
Female member of a lobby group in radio interview:
I think Mrs McDonald would agree with me (where interviewer has suggested she wouldn't)
(Holmes 1995: 95)

Here "I think" boosts a disagreeing proposition. It explicitly puts the weight of the high-status participants behind what they say.

The need to pay attention to function and context is even more important in historical texts, for the obvious reason that we cannot transpose our modern-day assumptions about hedges and their functions.[14] As a first step, we aimed to quantify the numbers of hedges (i.e. lexical items or expressions with *either* a downtoning *or* a boosting function) according to type of speaker and addressee (i.e. female witness, male witness, judge to female witness, judge to male witness).[15] Table 4 lists the top-dozen most frequent hedges found in our data. To take account of the imbalances in the quantity of speech produced by the various speaker types (see table 2), the density of occurrence (per 1,000 words) was calculated for each hedge across the four speaker types. The list is organised in the decreasing order of frequency.

Table 4. Hedges (the density of occurrence is counted per 1,000 words)

	Female witnesses	Male witnesses	Judges to female witnesses	Judges to male witnesses	Total
very	29	18	3	4	54
	3.2	2.5	0.9	0.8	2.2
about	12	21	0	0	33
	1.3	2.9	–	–	1.3
some	7	17	2	5	31
	0.8	2.3	0.6	1.1	1.3
well	3	5	10	11	29
	0.3	0.7	3.0	2.3	1.2
so	5	8	1	16	30
	0.5	1.1	0.3	3.4	1.2
modals	7	3	2	7	19
	0.8	0.4	0.6	0.7	0.8
sure	3	4	5	4	16
	0.3	0.5	1.5	0.8	0.6
I think	3	6	3	1	13
	0.3	0.8	0.9	0.2	0.5
I believe	4	8	0	1	13
	0.4	1.1	–	0.2	0.5
I suppose	6	2	0	1	9
	0.7	0.3	–	0.2	0.4
Why	4	2	0	1	7
	0.4	0.3	–	0.2	0.3
at all	2	4	0	1	7
	0.2	0.5	–	0.2	0.3
	85	98	26	52	261
	9.3	13.4	7.7	10.9	10.6

The totals show that the distribution of hedges is not completely even. Male witnesses use significantly more hedges than female (a density of 9.3 for women compared to 13.4 for men).[16] As far as the judges are concerned, our figures suggest that judges use more hedges when addressing male witnesses than when addressing female witnesses, though this is mostly due to one hedge – *so*. On the face of it, this would seem to fly in the face of R. Lakoff's (1975) notion that hedges are part of a "women's language".[17] It also appears to contradict O'Barr and Atkins's (1980: 96) results, based on a study of contemporary trial data, which are consistent with R.

Lakoff. However, O'Barr and Atkins stress the variability of their data (though they note that they were able "to find *more* women toward the high end of the continuum" (O'Barr and Atkins 1980: 102), i.e. more women who made great use of hedges), and go on to argue that variability correlates with the varying power of their witnesses. They conclude that "powerless language" is a better term for the phenomena that R. Lakoff describes, and that women tend to speak this language more, because they tend to occupy relatively powerless social positions (O'Barr and Atkins 1980: 104). In order to begin to explain the results for our data, we need to look closely at the individual hedges in the table. It is true that the figures for individual hedges are not high, but we note that in O'Barr and Atkins's (1980) study, which is frequently cited, they considered a total of six witnesses whose frequencies for hedges vary from zero to 19, whereas we consider 32 witnesses whose frequencies for hedges vary from zero to 29.

If we focus on the higher densities of occurrence, male witnesses use the hedges *about, some, so, I think*, and *I believe* more than twice as often as the female witnesses. Consider the following example:

(12) L. C. J. Holt. *Where did Mrs.* Baynton *lodge?*
Mr. Blake. *In the opposite Room against the Gentleman.*
L. C. J. Holt. *How long time?* – Mr. Blake. *About Seven Months.*
Counsel. *How long was Mrs.* Baynton *gone from your House before this Matter happened?*
Mr. Blake. *About Five or Six Weeks.*
L. C. J. Holt. *How long before Michaelmas?*
Mr. Blake. *I cannot certainly tell; but I believe much about that Time.*

(SWENDSEN BLAKE)

Note that all the hedges in example (12) have a downtoning function, as indeed does *not certainly* in the final turn. *About* is being used to add fuzziness to an assertion about the specific span of time that has elapsed between the witnesses' "now" and the commencement of Mrs. Baynton's lodging. Given the failings of human memory and the specificity of the assertion, it is not surprising that a hedge is used. Also, remember the situation: this is a formal hearing before a judge; the witness is formally committed to saying the truth, and there are legal punishments for not doing so. Thus, there are powerful social reasons why one would not want to overstate something. On the other hand, if one sounds too vague, one might be deemed not to have answered the judge's question. This happens to Mr. Blake when he answers *About Five or Six Weeks*. The judge tries to elicit a more exact answer, forcing Mr. Blake to state explicitly his complete lack of certainty. We have not space to comment in detail on *some* and *I think*, but can say that *some* is used in a fairly similar way to *about* and *I think* is used in an almost identical way to *I believe*.[18] All our examples of *about*, *some*, *I believe*, and *I think* had a downtoning function. This is perhaps not surprising: unlike Holmes's examples, witnesses of either sex in these data are not in a position to wield power, but are in a position of relative powerlessness.

Female witnesses make great use of the word *very*, in all cases with a boosting function. This is contrary to R. Lakoff who hints that she would not associate *very* with "women's language" (1975: 54-55). This particular hedge occurred with great frequency in the Early Modern English period. Culpeper and Kytö (1999) found it to be by far the most frequent hedge in their data, consisting of trial proceedings, witness depositions, drama, and prose. For our data set, the example below is highly typical:

(13)   Mr. Soll. Gen. *Pray call to mind what Time it was that you first gave Notice to her that she should not continue in your Lodgings.*
        Mrs. Nightingale. *When I first mistrusted her, I gave Notice of it in my Family ... But before that, she came to me, and told me, and said, Mrs. Nightingale, I have received a Letter from my sister* Baynton *in the Country, which informs me, that the Trustees will agree, and so I design to return when my Month is*

> up, for this Town is <u>very</u> chargeable. <u>Very</u> well, said
> I, for I expect some Ladies <u>very</u> shortly. I went down
> to my Family, and express'd my Joy to them, and
> said I was <u>very</u> glad Mrs. Baynton *had prevented me*
> (LISLE NIGHTINGALE)

Firstly, it should be noted that the witness is asked to discourse on a particular topic, or, in other words, to provide crime narrative. The majority of instances of *very* occur in such crime narrative. Here the witness is not asked for specific information, as in the case of the male witness above (see example (12)), and thus this particular need for downtoning seems less important. Crime narrative is also less interactive than cross-examination, and hedges tend to be more frequent in interactive speech (Biber 1988). Secondly, it is clear that the witness's account contains speech report, both direct and indirect. Of course, this raises the issue of who says these words. Given the fact that the events in question took place some time ago,[19] it seems unlikely that they are verbatim report. Moreover, it is well known, at least for contemporary texts, that direct speech does not necessarily aim for verbatim report (see, for example, Tannen 1989; Fludernik 1993: 409ff.), but often functions to dramatise a text, and hence, for example, the frequent use of direct speech in tabloid newspapers (Semino, Short, and Culpeper 1997). This particular function of direct speech may also help explain the frequent use of *very* as a booster. Holmes argues that "Boosters or lexical items which express certainty or conviction ... may function mainly to express the speaker's attitude to the addressee rather than to the proposition being asserted" (Holmes 1984: 49), and that boosters might serve "a facilitative positive politeness function, by expressing solidarity with the addressee" (Holmes 1984: 59). One way Holmes (1984) suggests this can be done is by supporting the conversation of another speaker. We would like to argue that the high density of *very* in female witnesses' speech may be because they feel compelled to provide convincing and pleasing crime narrative: narrative that is going to please the conversational requirements exacted by the judges.

Before we conclude this section, we will briefly consider hedges in the judges' speech. It seems to be the case that *so* is used much more frequently by the judges to male witnesses than female (the density in speech to female witnesses is 0.3 and in speech to male witnesses it is 3.4). However, this result is misleading: 15 of the 16 instances are used by the notorious Lord Chief Justice Jeffreys, in his attempts to bludgeon Dunne (a prime witness) into answering his questions. It has been suggested in the literature that hedges can be indicative of a highly involved style (e.g. Chafe 1982). Jeffreys's anger is palpable in example (14).

(14) L. C. J. *Jesus God! Was there ever such a Fellow in the World as thou art? ... And wilt thou hazard so dear and precious a thing for a Lye, and an unprofitable Lye too? Thou Wretch! all the Mountains and Hills in the World heaped upon one another, will not cover thee from the Vengeance of the great God for this Transgression of false Witness-bearing: What hopes can there be for so profligate a Villain as thou art, that so impudently stands in open defiance of the Omnipresence, Omniscience and Justice of God, by persisting in so palpable a Lye? I therefore require it of you, in his Name, to tell me the Truth.*

(LISLE DUNNE)

The hedge which is used most frequently by the judges to witnesses of either sex is *well*. *Well* plays a key role in managing discourse. Clearly, the judges are empowered to control the courtroom discourse, and they often use *well*, for example, to signal that a new speaker should speak, to signal that a current speaker should continue speaking, and/or to express a negative attitude towards what a speaker has just said. It is also worth noting that it is used slightly more often when addressing female witnesses than when addressing male witnesses. This might be explained by noticing that *well* often functions as part of a prompter, as in example (15) (see also example (5)):

(15)   *Then Mrs.* Broadstreet *was examined.*
       Mr. Justice Jones. *Well, Woman, what say you?*
       Broadstreet. *We came to Town upon a Monday,* Michaelmas *day was the Sunday following;*
                                                  (GREEN BROADSTREET)

The hedge *sure* appears almost twice as frequently in the judges' speech to female witnesses than it does in the judges speech to male witnesses (though we need to be cautious here, because our raw frequencies are very low). It occurs repeatedly in the phrase *are you sure ...?*, as in example (16):

(16)   Mr. Sol. G. *In what Clothes was he then?*
       E. Curtis, *The same Clothes that he hath now.*
       Mr. Just. Wild, *Are you sure they are the same Clothes?*
       E. Curtis, *Yes.*
                                                  (GREEN CURTIS)

One might speculate that this is because a woman's word was not perceived to be as reliable as a man's. However, we clearly need more data to substantiate this. Indeed, there are many other variables affecting perceived witness reliability. Obviously, whether you were a witness for the prosecution or defence played a part. Also, your religion was crucial. Once Mary Tilden (in the trial of Green, Berry, and Hill) is found to be a Catholic, the judges dismiss her evidence with sneering remarks:

(17)   L. C. J. *You may say anything to a Heretick for a Papist.*
       L. C. J. *They have a general Answer for all Questions.*

Our work on hedges reinforces some of the tentative ideas we presented in our discussion of elicitation types. The overall quantitative difference in the number of hedges used by male witnesses and the number of hedges used by female and our microanalyses of the hedges supports the notion that male witnesses are subjected to the heat of cross-examination more than female witnesses, who are pressured into producing crime narrative which will satisfy the judges.

5. Two morpho-syntactic features

5.1. The third-person singular endings

Labov, referring to phonological changes, is clear that in most of the research he has conducted over the decades women were found to be linguistic innovators (Labov 1994: 156). A number of sociolinguists have also considered the issue of innovation and gender in a historical context.[20] In particular, the role of sex as a variable in the use of the third-person singular endings -*th* and -*s* has been commented on in recent research. Judging from the results obtained in the study of personal writing such as diaries and correspondence, women have been seen to promote the rising -*s* ending (e.g. Kytö 1993: 128-129; Nevalainen 1996: 84). By the end of the seventeenth century, -*s* had already superseded -*th* in most contexts. -*th* lingered on in highly formal contexts, and with the forms *doth, hath* and *saith*, in particular (we omit the zero forms from this discussion). It seems that the change in the pronunciation of the ending took place even earlier: judging by the evidence found in early grammars, the ending -*s* had taken over in spoken language as early as the 1640s (Holmqvist 1922; Jespersen 1942, VI: 14-23; Stein 1987).

The -*th* ending should thus hardly appear in our data, given its disappearance from speech some 40 years before our data were recorded. Moreover, we should bear in mind that if these inflections were essentially written phenomena at this time, then they may reflect the usage of the scribes, who, as far as we know, were male. The issue then is whether the scribe attributes a particular inflection more often to one type of speaker than another type. Table 5 shows our results for verbs other than *do, have*, and *say*.

Table 5. The third-person present singular: -th vs. -s
 (the density of occurrence is counted per 1,000 words)

Lexical verbs (other than *say, do* and *have*)	-th	-s
Female witnesses	7 (0.8)	7 (0.8)
Male witnesses	0	3 (0.4)
Judges addressing female witnesses	0	6 (1.8)
Judges addressing male witnesses	0	24 (5.0)
	7 (0.3)	40 (1.6)

There are seven instances of the *-th* ending and they are all found in women's utterances. On closer inspection, it turns out that they all appear in one trial, that of Lord Mohun from 1692. One of the instances with the ending *-s* in this category occurs in Lord Mohun's trial; the other instances spread across the texts. This pattern is repeated for the verbs *do, have,* and *say*:

Table 6. The third-person present singular inflections for *do, have,* and *say*
 (the density of occurrence is counted per 1,000 words)

	do		have		say	
	-th	-s	-th	-s	-th	-s
Female witnesses	0	1	3	8	30	6
	–	0.1	0.3	0.9	3.3	0.7
Male witnesses	0	3	0	2	8	3
	–	0.4	–	0.3	1.1	0.4
Judges addressing female witnesses	0	1	2	3	2	1
	–	0.3	0.6	0.9	0.6	0.3
Judges addressing male witnesses	0	4	2	2	0	2
	–	0.8	0.4	0.4	–	0.4
	0	9	7	15	40	12
	–	0.4	0.3	0.6	1.6	0.5

The use of *saith* stands out, accounting for 40 instances of *say* out of the 52 recorded with either the *-th* or *-s* endings. Of the 40 instances, 30 occur in female witnesses' speech, again all in Lord Mohun's trial. As for the male witnesses, seven out of the eight instances recorded come, similarly, from Lord Mohun's trial, though all in all, the density of occurrence remains lower than that obtained for women's speech, that is, 1.1 as against 3.3. No instances of the form *doth* were recorded. *Hath* was more frequent (but much less frequent than *saith*): seven instances with *hath* were found as against 15 with *has*. The three instances of *hath* found in witnesses' speech occur in women's production (one in Mohun's trial and two in Green, Berry, and Hill's).

The occurrence of the receding form in female witnesses' speech in Mohun's trial is perhaps puzzling. One might hypothesise that if the *-th* ending was felt to be archaic and highly formal, it might be the case that scribes were couching female-witness speech in a more archaic way for some reason; or that they reacted by way of "hyper-adaptation", representing female-witness speech in excessively polite terms. However, a closer look at the examples reveals another possible explanation. As pointed out above, compared with men's style, female witnesses testify in a more narrative style. The form *saith* occurs precisely in these "pools" of narration. The 30 instances of *saith* found in Lord Mohun's trial in women's speech belong all to this category (see example (18)).

(18)   Mrs. Browne. *My Lord* Mohun *said, he protected her, for if it had not been for him, the* Mob *had torn her in pieces; but if they had a mind to carry her off, they could easily have suppressed the* Mob, *for they had six or seven Pistols in the Coach: But* <u>saith</u> *my Lord,* I had no design upon her my self, but only to serve my Friend. *So* <u>saith</u> *Mr. Hill,* I shall light upon this Mountford. *Why, said I, what hurt hath Mr.* Mountford *done you?* <u>Saith</u> *he,* I have been Abused, and I will have my Revenge. *So I went and told Mrs.* Mountford *of it. About half an Hour after, or more, Mr.* Mountford *came down, and when he came down, I saw him a little before he came to them, and went to him, and would have fain have spoke to him, but he would not stay to let me speak what I had to say to him, but going on, presently he met my Lord* Mohun. <u>Saith</u> *he,* Your Humble Servant, my Lord. <u>Saith</u> *my Lord again,* Your Servant Mr. Mountford. <u>Saith</u> *my Lord,* I have a great Respect for you, Mr. Mountford,

and would have no Difference between us; but there is a thing fallen out between Mr. Hill and Mrs. Bracegirdle. *Saith Mr.* Mountford, My Lord, has my Wife disobliged your Lordship? if she has, she shall ask your Pardon; ...

(MOHUN BROWNE)

The use of *says* in these contexts is not excluded (see example (19)), where both *says* and *saith* occur in a narrow context), but the old form seems to be preferred.

(19)   Sandys. *I Dined with my Lord* Mohun *and Captain* Hill, *at the* Three Tuns *in* Shandois-street, *and there arose a Discourse about Mrs.* Bracegirdle *and* Hill, *and my Lord* Mohun *asked me, if I thought* Mountford *had lay with her or no. I said I could not tell; presently after says my Lord* Mohun, *it will cost* Hill *50 Guineas this Design. Saith Mr.* Hill, *if the Villain offers to resist, I will Stab him; saith my Lord* Mohun, *I will stand by my Friend.*

(MOHUN SANDYS)

Clearly, it can be said that our study of the third-person-present-singular inflections has drawn something of a blank, since the distribution of *-th* could largely reflect the idiosyncrasies of the scribe or scribes who recorded Lord Mohun's trial. However, it is worth noting that at least here it provides further evidence that women tend to present crime narrative. It also acts as an important reminder that our data contain various discourse levels: the scribe reports the witness who in turn may report someone else. Teasing these levels apart is an important issue for any exploration of speaker "voice". The use of the *-th* inflection in Mohun helps signal that the reporting verb belongs to a different discourse level from the reported speech.

5.2. Periphrastic do *in affirmative contexts*

A feature that has been shown to be associated with the oral mode, in particular, is the use of the so-called periphrastic *do* in affirmative contexts (see example (20)) (e.g. Rissanen 1991). Regarding our period, the use had already been in decline for some time; it met a dramatic decrease in its frequency by the end of the seventeenth century, first, as it seems, in speech-based texts (see Rissanen 1991: 329).

(20) L. C. J. *When was this?*
 Bedlow. *It was in October last, about the beginning, or the latter end of September.*
 L. C. J. *Well, Sir, go on.*
 Bedlow. *I did adhere to them all along, for I had a mind to discover two Years ago, but was prevented; and I only drill'd them on, to know the Party, that I might prevent them. But they would never discover the Party.*
 (GREEN BEDLOW)

We considered the distribution of periphrastic *do* in affirmative contexts across our four speaker types (see table 7).

Table 7. Periphrastic *do* in affirmative contexts
(the density of occurrence is counted per 1,000 words)

Periphrastic *do*		
Female witnesses	13	1.4
Male witnesses	15	2.0
Judges addressing female witnesses	3	0.9
Judges addressing male witnesses	10	2.1

Looking first at witnesses, male witnesses use periphrastic *do* slightly more often than female. If periphrastic *do* in affirmative contexts is taken to express emphasis and other related phenomena (Rissanen 1991), this may be evidence that male witnesses are more emphatic than female. This could be related to the idea that male witnesses are subjected more to the heat of cross-examination.

As for judges, those addressing male witnesses use periphrastic *do* more frequently. The examination of James Dunne in Lady Lisle's trial stands out as a case in point: 9 out of the 10 instances produced by the judges addressing male witnesses are from Lord Chief Justice Jeffreys' speech. Dunne himself also uses periphrastic *do* five times. We might point out that our data from Lady Alice Lisle's trial provide eight out of the 15 instances attested in male witnesses' utterances. No instances are recorded in the latest of the four trials included in this survey, Swendsen's trial from 1702.

Once again, our evidence here is consistent with the notion that male witnesses are engaged in a rather different conversational role, that of participant in cross-examination, from female witnesses, who tend to give crime narrative.

6. Concluding observations

In our study, we have approached the topic of language and gender broadly: we have examined aspects of language typically favoured by three different approaches to language and gender. We have attempted to avoid preconceptions, and we have tried to take account of function and context. Whilst the frequencies of individual features in our study are low, it does seem to be the case that sets of features are pointing in the same direction, namely, that the female witnesses in our data are constructed by the male judges (and possibly the male scribes) more as crime-narrative givers than are the male witnesses, who are more involved in intense cross-examination. We have also suggested that women may feel compelled to cooperate in this role because of their relatively powerless state. If we are right that conversational role is the key to our data, this raises issues for other approaches to language and gender. A narrowly conceived variationist approach or speech-style approach to this kind of interactional data could easily have made the mistake of finding particular linguistic features characteristic of women speakers.

An important limitation of our study is lack of data. Though we started with a set of texts totalling 40,000 words, this amount was reduced by nearly a half after we had extracted the non-speech material from the source texts. We should point out that we did a good deal of checking on a number of other linguistic aspects, but, unfortunately, the material did not yield a sufficient number of examples. Among these features were the use of the progressive form, contractions, simple verb in negative and interrogative contexts, relative pronouns, the use of *shall* and *will*, multiple negation, and the use of the second person pronouns *you* and *thou*. Of course, it is worth emphasising that if it is the case that men and women speak differently in some ways, they speak similarly in a lot more ways. In future work, we also need to consider other contextual factors more closely, notably, the effect of whether the witness is also the accused and of whether the witness is a witness for the prosecution or defence[21].

Notes

1. We are deeply indebted to Jane Sunderland and Sally Johnson for commenting on early drafts of this paper. Needless to say, remaining errors and infelicities are ours.
2. R. Lakoff's list of features also includes particular types of intonation (e.g. a rising intonation in a declarative context), hypercorrect grammar and pronunciation, and the idea that women are poor joke tellers. Obviously, matters of intonation and pronunciation are aspects of speech. Joke telling is very much an activity that takes place in speech.
3. Much less work has focussed specifically on a speech style for men. See Johnson and Meinhof (1997) for a notable exception.
4. In fact, whilst many studies in the variationist or speech-style paradigms have claimed just to consider sex, they often touch on issues of gender in their explanatory discussions or even assume that gender will somehow correlate with sex (see, for example, Nevalainen 1996: 77-91).
5. Outside this paradigm there has been a wide scattering of etymological studies with a particular emphasis on sexism in language. For example, Wescott (1974) traces the etymology of *woman* and *man*; Stannard (1977) looks at the history of naming conventions; Kelly (1969) examines semantic change in the word *bitch*; Meredith (1930) considers examples of the "feminine" suffix *-ess*.

6. A full description of this corpus is given in Culpeper and Kytö (1997).
7. It seems that court scribes often developed their own systems of short-hand. More formalised systems did not develop until the eighteenth century.
8. Jardine's ((ed.) 1832) general introduction to criminal trials and his notes to particular trials provide useful background to both the practices of the Early Modern English courtroom and the problems with surviving records.
9. The trial of Green, Berry, and Hill and the trial of Lord Mohun have been taken from original imprints that came out during the year of the trial or soon after. As no contemporary record of Lady Alice Lisle's trial survives, this text was drawn from Hargrave's second edition of *A complete collection of state-trials* which came out in 1730, 45 years after the trial took place. Our copy of the trial of Haagen Swendsen (which was not included in Hargrave's second edition) is drawn from Hargrave's fourth edition, identical to the third edition from 1742. We still hope to procure an earlier version of this text.
10. We are not in a position to say whether it was generally the case that trial records from earlier periods contained no or few women. Women do appear in the witchcraft trials of earlier periods, but the documents of these trials are usually in the form of witness depositions (i.e. they do not contain the direct speech we seek to analyse in this paper).
11. Holmes (1992) studies elicitation types. We have not adopted her categorisation scheme (comprising supportive, critical, and antagonistic elicitations), because 1) it pertains to a very different situation, namely, seminar discussions, and 2) it is not entirely clear how one distinguishes between her elicitation types.
12. The example numbers in this paper refer to individual examples or, as here, to a group of examples.
13. Clearly then, the nature of a response was an important factor in determining the elicitation type.
14. See Culpeper and Kytö (1999) for a general exploration of hedges in the Early Modern English period.
15. We made a decision, like many other studies, to concentrate on words and expressions. We generated a list of forms to search for from three sources: 1) Nikula (1996), who draws up a list of contemporary hedges taken from 20,480 words of tape-recorded informal impromptu conversation, 2) Stoffel (1901), who conducts a historical survey of what he calls "intensives" and "downtoners", and 3) our own readings of data in the corpus. In total we searched for approximately 80 forms.
16. Statistically this result appears to be highly significant: with chi-square, $p < 0.001$, $df = 33$. However, some expected values were less than 5, so chi-square may not be valid.

17. Of course, it should be remembered that our figures include hedges with a boosting function. R. Lakoff had also considered some intensifiers, such as *so*, as features of "women's language" (R. Lakoff 1975: 54).
18. We cannot confidently comment on *so* here. In many contexts, *so* appears ambiguous between being an intensifier and having the sense 'thus'. No clear pattern emerges from so few examples (8 for male witnesses, 5 for female). Clearly, *so* could benefit from individual study. R. Lakoff also recognised the difficulties of commenting on *so* (R. Lakoff 1975: 14-15, footnote), but does say that it is more frequent in "women's language" (R. Lakoff 1975: 54). On the face of it, our data would not support this.
19. Asked how long ago these events happened, Mrs. Nightingale says, "I can't prefix the time". If she cannot remember when the event occurred, it seems unlikely that she would remember the exact words which were said. Judging from other dates given in the trial, the event to which she refers must have happened somewhere between three weeks to two months before the trial.
20. It should be noted that not all researchers have argued that women are linguistic innovators. Jespersen (1922) is perhaps the most well-known writer to argue that women are more conservative than men.
21. In practice, most recorded witnesses are witnesses for the prosecution.

References

Amussen, Susan D.
    1988   *An ordered society: gender and class in Early Modern England.* Oxford: Blackwell.

Biber, Douglas
    1988   *Variation across speech and writing.* Cambridge: Cambridge University Press.

Cameron, Deborah
    1992   *Feminism and linguistic theory.* (2nd edition.) London: Macmillan.

Chafe, Wallace
    1982   Integration and involvement in speaking, writing, and oral literature. In: Deborah Tannen (ed.), 35-54.

Cheshire, Jenny
    1982   *Variation in an English dialect: a sociolinguistic study.* Cambridge: Cambridge University Press.

Coates, Jennifer
    1989   Introduction. In: Jennifer Coates and Deborah Cameron (eds.), 63-73.

Coates, Jennifer and Deborah Cameron (eds.)
1989   *Women in their speech communities.* Harlow: Longman.
Crawford, Mary
1995   *Talking difference: on gender and language.* London/New Delhi: Sage.
Crosby, Faye and Linda Nyquist
1977   The female register: an empirical study of Lakoff's hypotheses. *Language in Society* 6: 313-322.
Culpeper, Jonathan and Merja Kytö
1997   Towards a corpus of dialogues, 1550-1750. In: Heinrich Ramisch and Kenneth Wynne (eds.), 60-73.
1999   Modifying pragmatic force: hedges in a corpus of Early Modern English dialogues. In: Andreas H. Jucker, Gerd Fritz, and Franz Lebsanft (eds.), 293-312.
Dubois, Betty Lou and Isabel Crouch
1975   The question of tag questions in women's speech: they don't really use more of them, do they? *Language in Society* 4: 289-294.
Fludernik, Monika
1993   *The fictions of language and the languages of fiction.* London: Routledge.
Hall, Kira and Mary Bucholtz
1995   *Gender articulated: language and the socially constructed self.* New York/London: Routledge.
Hargrave, Francis (ed.)
1730   *A Complete Collection of State-Trials and Proceedings for High-Treason, and Other Crimes and Misdemeanours; from the Reign of King Richard II. to the End of the Reign of King George I.* (2nd edition.) London: Printed for J. Walthoe Sen. Etc.
Harris, Sandra
1984   Questions as a mode of control in magistrates' courts. *International Journal of the Sociology of Language* 49: 5-27.
The Helsinki Corpus of English Texts [diachronic part]
1991   Helsinki: The Department of English, University of Helsinki.
Holmes, Janet
1984   Hedging your bets and sitting on the fence: some evidence for hedges as support structures. *Te Reo* 27: 47-62.
1992   Women's talk in public contexts. *Discourse and Society* 3(2): 131-150.
1995   *Women, men and politeness.* London/New York: Longman.

Holmqvist, Erik
  1922   *On the history of the English present inflections, particularly* -th *and* -s. Heidelberg: Carl Winter's Universitätsbuchhandlung.
Jardine, David (ed.)
  1832   *Criminal trials,* Volume 1. (The Library of Entertaining Knowledge.) London: Knight.
Jespersen, Otto
  1922   *Language: its nature, development and origin.* London: Allen and Unwin.
  1942   *A Modern English grammar on historical principles.* Part VI: *Morphology.* Copenhagen: Munksgaard.
Johnson, Sally A. and Ulrike Meinhof (eds.)
  1997   *Language and masculinity.* Oxford: Blackwell.
Jones, Deborah
  1980   Gossip: notes on women's oral culture. In: Chris Kramarae (ed.), 193-198.
Jucker, Andreas H., Gerd Fritz, and Franz Lebsanft (eds.)
  1999   *Historical dialogue analysis.* (Pragmatics and Beyond: New Series 66.) Amsterdam/Philadelphia: Benjamins.
Kastovsky, Dieter (ed.)
  1991   *Historical English syntax.* (Topics in English Linguistics 2.) Berlin/New York: Mouton de Gruyter.
Keenan, Elinor O. and Dina Bennet (eds.)
  1977   *Discourse across time and space.* Los Angeles: University of California.
Kelly, Edward H.
  1969   A 'bitch' by any other name is less poetic. *Word Study* 45: 1-4.
Kramarae, Chris (ed.)
  1980   *The voices and words of women and men.* Oxford: Pergamon Press.
Kytö, Merja
  1993   Third-person present singular verb inflection in early British and American English. *Language Variation and Change* 5: 113-139.
Labov, William
  1966   *The social stratification of English in New York City.* Washington, DC: Centre for Applied Linguistics.
  1972   *Sociolinguistic patterns.* Philadephia, PA: University of Pennsylvania Press.
  1990   The intersection of sex and social class in the course of linguistic change. *Language Variation and Change* 2: 205-254.
  1994   *Principles of linguistic change.* Volume 1: *Internal factors.* (Language in Society 20.) Oxford: Blackwell.

Lakoff, George
1972 Hedges: a study in meaning criteria and the logic of fuzzy concepts. *Papers from the Eighth Regional Meeting of the Chicago Linguistic Society*: 183-228.
Lakoff, Robin
1975 *Language and woman's place*. New York: Harper and Row.
McConnell-Ginet, Sally, Ruth Borker, and Nelly Furman (eds.)
1980 *Women and language in literature and society*. New York: Praeger.
McMillan, Julie R., Kay A. Clifton, Diane McGrath, and Wanda Gale
1977 Woman's language: uncertainty or interpersonal sensitivity and emotionality? *Sex Roles* 3(6): 545-559.
Meredith, Mamie
1930 "Doctoresses", "authoresses", and others. *American Speech* 5: 476-481.
Meurman-Solin, Anneli
1993 *Variation and change in Early Scottish prose: studies based on the Helsinki Corpus of Older Scots*. (Annales Academiae Scientiarum Fennicae, Dissertationes Humanarum Litterarum 65.) Helsinki: Suomalainen Tiedeakatemia.
Milroy, James
1992 A social model for the interpretation of language change. In: Matti Rissanen et al. (eds.), 72-91.
Milroy, Lesley
1980 *Language and social networks*. Baltimore: University Park Press.
Nevalainen, Terttu
1996 Gender difference. In: Terttu Nevalainen and Helena Raumolin-Brunberg (eds.), 77-91.
Nevalainen, Terttu and Helena Raumolin-Brunberg (eds.)
1996 *Sociolinguistics and language history: studies based on the Corpus of Early English Correspondence*. (Language and Computers: Studies in Practical Linguistics 15.) Amsterdam/ Atlanta, GA: Rodopi.
Nikula, Tarja
1996 *Pragmatic force modifiers: A study in interlanguage pragmatics*. Jyväskylä: University of Jyväskylä.
O'Barr, William M. and Bowman K. Atkins
1980 "Women's language" or "powerless language"? In: Sally McConnell-Ginet, Ruth Borker, and Nelly Furman (eds.), 93-110.

Ramisch, Heinrich and Kenneth Wynne (eds.)
1997   *Language in time and space: Studies in honour of Wolfgang Viereck on the occasion of his 60th birthday* (Zeitschrift für Dialektologie und Linguistik: Beihefte, Heft 97.) Stuttgart: Franz Steiner Verlag.

Rissanen, Matti
1991   Spoken language and the history of *do*-periphrasis. In: Dieter Kastovsky (ed.), 321-342.

Rissanen, Matti, Ossi Ihalainen, Terttu Nevalainen, and Irma Taavitsainen (eds.)
1992   *History of Englishes: new methods and interpretations in historical linguistics.* (Topics in English Linguistics 10.) Berlin/ New York: Mouton de Gruyter.

Romaine, Suzanne
1982   *Socio-historical linguistics: its status and methodology.* (Cambridge Studies in Linguistics 34.) Cambridge: Cambridge University Press.

Semino, Elena, Mick Short, and Jonathan Culpeper
1997   Using a corpus to test a model of speech and thought presentation. *Poetics* 25: 17-43.

Shimanoff, Susan B.
1977   Investigating politeness. In: Elinor O. Keenan and Dina Bennet (eds.), 213-241.

Stannard, Una
1977   *Mrs. Man.* San Francisco: Germain Books.

Steckler, Nicole A. and William E. Cooper
1980   Sex differences in color naming of unisex apparel. *Anthropological Linguistics* 22: 373-381.

Stein, Dieter
1987   At the crossroads of philology, linguistics and semiotics: notes on the replacement of *th* by *s* in the third person singular in English. *English Studies* 68: 406-431.

Stoffel, Cornelius
1901   *Intensives and down-toners: a study in English adverbs.* Heidelberg: Carl Winter's Universitätsbuchhandlung.

Tannen, Deborah
1989   *Repetition, dialogue and imagery in conversational discourse.* Cambridge: Cambridge University Press.

Tannen, Deborah (ed.)
1982   *Spoken and written language: exploring orality and literature.* Norwood, NJ: Ablex.

Thorne, Barrie, Chris Kramarae, and Nancy Henley (eds.)
1983   *Language, gender and society.* Rowley, MA: Newbury House.

Trudgill, Peter
1972 Sex, covert prestige and linguistic change in the urban British English of Norwich. *Language in Society* 1: 179-195.
1974 *The social differentiation of English in Norwich.* Cambridge: Cambridge University Press.
1978 Introduction: Sociolinguistics and sociolinguistics. In: Peter Trudgill (ed.), 1-18.
1983 *On dialect: social and geographical perspectives.* Oxford: Basil Blackwell.

Trudgill, Peter (ed.)
1978 *Sociolinguistic patterns in British English.* London: Arnold.

Wescott, Roger W.
1974 Women, wife-men, and sexist bias. *Verbatim: The Language Quarterly* 1 (2): 1.

Is there a social element in English word-stress? Explorations into a non-categorical treatment of English stress: a long-term view

Christiane Dalton-Puffer

1. Introduction

Considering the amount of research on English carried out over the last decades, it is surprising how little has been reported on the topic of stress variation. Variationist studies in phonetics and phonology have focused very much on segmental variation, while phonological theory development has given a good deal of attention to suprasegmentals but has tended to totally disregard the issue of variation. The present contribution is an attempt at a fresh start on both accounts and pursues two aims. The first is to present some evidence on word-stress variation in English which shows this to be an area with considerable variation within the standard variety. The second aim is to put forward some ideas on how this fact may reflect back on the way we approach English word-stress theoretically.

The first section of the paper, then, examines synchronic and diachronic evidence on the variability of English word-stress, including a pilot study carried out by a questionnaire. The second (and longer) part of the paper presents some suggestions on how the empirical evidence might inform our way of dealing with the grammar of word-stress. It is important to stress at this early point that this contribution has been written from the vantage point of non-autonomous linguistics. That is to say, it has been conceived in an understanding that language cannot be disconnected from other parts of reality and cannot be fully understood if it is taken to be a system which is totally independent of its users.

2. Evidence for word-stress variation: synchronic and diachronic

The simplest way of accessing the topic of synchronic word-stress variation is to check standard reference works for the pronunciation of English such as Daniel Jones' (1963) *English pronouncing dictionary* (*EPD*) or John Wells' (1990) *Pronunciation dictionary*. Indeed both of them contain a considerable number of items with more than one stress-variant. Mathesius says that 27% of Daniel Jones's (1963) *EPD* entries have alternative pronunciations (Mathesius 1934: 409-410; quoted in Minkova 1997: 136 fn. 3) and Wells is currently replicating his speaker survey for a new edition of his *Pronunciation dictionary*. This lexicographic practice in reference works codifying the standard can only be taken as a result of the dictionary makers' awareness of widespread variation even within those instances of language use identified as "standard".

Another indication for the variability of English word-stress is the fact that so-called "naïve" speakers of the language possess a strong awareness of the fact. With them, this awareness often surfaces as a feeling of doubt whether one's own pronunciation of a certain word is "correct", as is to be expected in a speech community where the standard takes such a central and high prestige role.[1] This entails that the variation often acquires a strong, if puzzling, social semiotic. From my own point of view as a kind of bilingual participant observer, the following labels, some of them more evaluative than others, seem to me to be connected with different stress variants of individual words, cf. (1).

(1)
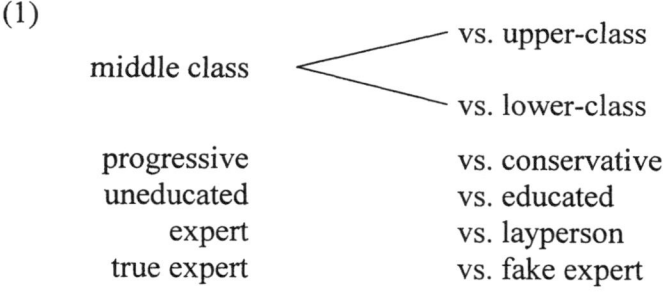

progressive	vs. conservative
uneducated	vs. educated
expert	vs. layperson
true expert	vs. fake expert

This list of value labels is, of course, rather *ad-hoc* and there is little doubt that it would merit the attention of in-depth socio-psychological informed linguistic study.

Historically, there is enough evidence to show that the variation of stress patterns is nothing new. Danielsson's (1948) mass of data with their numerous stress doublets give plenty of evidence of that. Equally, there are numerous indications that the concern with the social implications of stress-variation has been a persistent phenomenon among English speakers at least since the eighteenth century.

(2)   *For what can reflect more on a Man's Reputation for Learning, than to find him unable to pronounce or spell many words in common Use? Yet how often do we hear the grating sounds of Antipodes for anTIpodes, HORizon vs hoRIzon.*
(B. Martin 1749, *Lingua Britannica Reformata*)

The now fashionable pronunciation of several words is to me at least very offensive: CONtemplate is bad enough, but BALcony makes me sick.
(Samuel Rogers 1855, quoted in Crystal 1987: 64)

disPUTable and desPICable are intolerable "vulgarisms"
(J. Sargeaunt 1920 in a linguistic tract quoted in Danielsson 1948: 60)

only a berk stresses the second syllable [as in forMIDable]
(Amis 1996)

Today, in an age where statements such as those in (2) are unacceptable in the (public) discourse of language specialists, this concern often becomes objectified, as it were, by linking variation to dialect difference, mainly between the two main standard dialects

American and British English. A query on the Linguist List (volume 7-43) about stress differences between American and British English resulted in about 60 items reported back in the summary. On closer inspection these items fall into two categories. There are the stereotypical and apparently stable dialectal differences such as the famous *BAllet* vs. *baLLET, inQUIry* vs. *INquiry* etc. etc. (Examples always follow the order British – American). But there are more items on the list where I have the strong suspicion that an existing variation is ascribed to dialect difference without the variants actually being neatly split up between the dialects involved. Such cases would be *CONtribute* vs. *conTRIbute, LAmentable* vs. *laMENtable, teleVIsion* vs. *TElevision*. Both variants of all these examples can be found in British English, for instance. Should American English be consistent in having just one of them, then this might be a case of eastward transatlantic influence. On the other hand, the overwhelming majority of informants on the Linguist List query seem to have been Americans, who are apparently familiar with both variants. Given this, there are good reasons for thinking that they might well have translated their awareness of stress variation into a dialect difference which does not hold in any rigorous sense.[2] In the next section I will present a small-scale empirical study designed to shed some more light on this question.

3. A questionnaire survey

In order to gain some more information on the amount and distribution of word-stress variants I decided to carry out a small-scale empirical study among speakers of British and American English. As a working hypothesis I assumed that geographical distribution would not be the only variable which influences word-stress variation. A questionnaire of 54 items was drawn up.[3] Obvious British/American dialect markers such as *ballet* were excluded. However, the word-list contained some suffixed words where secondary stress on the suffix is deemed typical of American pronunciations (*defamatory, tergiversate*). Mainly the questionnaire consisted of technical ("hard") words from various disciplines (medicine, science) on the one hand, and general vocabulary items like *lamentable* on the other. Apart from this general distinction into "technical" and "general" words, the items were not controlled for frequency of occurrence, which is an undeniable methodological weakness. The words were presented in the form of a randomly ordered list and the respondents were asked to mark, underline or otherwise highlight that part of the word they would emphasise most on reading it out loud.

The questionnaire was completed by 14 speakers of American and 17 speakers of English English. Geographical attachment, however, was not the only variable along which the two populations differed. The British population had a somewhat wider age-range, and was slightly older on average.[4] Also, there was a marked difference in educational background. The U.S. informants were all university students (some of them postgraduates) while the UK informants had a more varied educational background with two university graduates, five with A-levels, and ten who left school at sixteen years of age. The US group was inhomogeneous in that it contained six speakers of English as a second language who were studying on an applied linguistics TESOL programme (i.e. they can be considered to be proficient users of English as a second language.)

Calibrating the size of the test population with its varied structure, it was thought pointless to analyse the data statistically. The interpretation of the results which follows is therefore qualitative rather than quantitative.

All in all the data show even more variation than anticipated: not a single one of the 54 test items was stressed in the same way by all the respondents. This remains true even if the results from the two dialects are considered separately and it shows that word-stress variation does not just exist across varieties but also within one and the same variety. With some items there is a clear majority for one variant on one side of the Atlantic and for another variant on the other, e.g. *INventory* vs. *inVENtory*. But in each group there are some speakers which use the respective "transatlantic" variant. That is to say, some British speakers use "American" stress patterns (which might be explained by the general influence American English has or is said to have on British English), but American speakers also use "British" forms.

Naturally, the number of attested variants for a particular word is also a function of the number of syllables in the word. The longer the word, the more variants it can theoretically have – in how far this correlates with actual variation cannot really be said without proper statistics. What can be said is that lower frequency of use in the language, that is, less familiarity with a word on the part of the respondents, goes hand in hand with a higher number of variants attested in the data.

This brings us directly to the question which strategies respondents seem to have applied in carrying out the task in the questionnaire. There presumably was a good deal of retrieval of known forms from memory, plus some morphological parsing with comparison of similarly structured words. An important case is raised by rare mono-morphemic words (such as *perone*) where stress assignment cannot use morphological analogy but has to rely on graphemic form. Generally, I think the role of graphemic form in on-line word-stress assignment should not be underestimated, but more will be said on this in section 3.

A question which has to remain open with the data at hand is whether the two groups of respondents differ in the amount of variability their responses show. It is certainly evident that being highly educated does not prevent one from using "variant" stress patterns, otherwise the American data should be much more uniform than they are. But the present data does not allow us to disentangle the factors "American" from "highly educated". My expectation is, however, that if there is significantly less variation in the American data it is due to the education factor rather than the geographical factor. In general, I think that the education factor is a very important one here. In reality of course, "education" is just a convenient shorthand for something like "amount of exposure to the standard in general and formal registers in particular", and I assume that the two stand in direct positive correlation. As to the effect of the second language speakers among the American respondents, it is difficult to say in which direction the influence went: first-language interference might have made for more variation, but the fact that they were all university educated teachers of English would suggest the exact opposite, namely stronger adherence to codified standards.

In sum, word-stress variation is a historical and contemporary fact in Standard English. Let me now turn to the question how this might translate into a theory of English word-stress.

4. Theoretical implications: parameters of a dynamic model of English word stress

4.1. Survey

The backdrop of the previous section has been an understanding of English word-stress which is more open to ambiguity and more dynamic than the current standard accounts. Some of the principles at work have already appeared in the shape of the factors discussed in connection with the data, notably "education" and "exposure to standard and formal registers", which is nothing else than saying that the way in which speakers use language has a strong impact on their grammar. In my view, then, word-stress assignment cannot be satisfactorily accounted for in terms of on-line application of one general rule but should be seen in terms of several, sometimes conflicting, principles which exist side by side. In addition to that, word-stress assignment is embedded in a network of other parameters such as memory and storage, social context, language use.[5] In the remainder of this paper I would like to draw a rough sketch of such an understanding of English word-stress.

The factors or principles which I am going to consider represent a "mixed bunch". They have various origins and are conceived of as either having entered the English language at different times during its history or as having arisen within English from a new constellation of facts caused by borrowings. This is the reason why some of them are linked more strongly to specific areas of the vocabulary, namely those through which they entered the English language in the first place. However, all are in principle applicable everywhere, and this is one way how synchrony and diachrony are inextricably intertwined.

Postulating an array of principles conditioning stress-placement in English words is not a new idea, at least not for diachronic treatments and I would like to mention in particular Danielsson's (1948) work because it has been so notably overlooked.[6] What is new about my proposal – it is far too loose to be called a model – is its claim to be valid for diachronic and synchronic concerns. Diachronically, my proposal amounts to an "additive-dynamic" or "incremental" understanding of the development of English word-stress: new principles are added to the language in accordance with the conditions of vocabulary development; they may fade or be reinforced according to the prevalent conditions of language use. Synchronically, my "proto-model" is also dynamic (or even "additive-dynamic" in language acquisition) as the principles may vary in weight according to the linguistic experience of individuals and groups of speakers. Let me now discuss the several principles in turn.

4.2. Initial root stress

"Always stress the first syllable of lexical roots. Or: Stress the first syllable of a word unless that first syllable is a prefix."

This principle is co-extensive with the Germanic Stress Rule. It amounts to morphological stress assignment because stress does not only have access to, but is crucially determined by, morpho-syntactic information. The rule works from left to right, and any material that is added to the lexical root through affixation does not change the position of stress. Consequently, affixes are never themselves stressed. Considering the time scale we are talking about (i.e. "English" and not Germanic) nothing can be said about its origins. It has been around ever since "English" began.

4.3. Parse morphologically

"See if you can identify a suffix, a prefix and a base or at least one of these items. Then proceed according to Initial Root Stress principle or (sometimes) not."

This is a weak version of the above principle, where morphological parsing is also required. Morphological parsing determines whether an item is compositional or not and tries to identify what the components are. The "sometimes not" option arises when, after stripping affixes, what is left does not look like a possible base for productive word-formation, i.e. a word. If I do not know the base I cannot preserve its stress pattern.

4.4. Donor principle

"With loan-words, look at how the word is stressed in the donor language and play around with primary and secondary stresses."

The donor languages most crucially involved here are Latin and French. The basic argument runs as follows: In the donor languages the main stress falls late in the word which is totally opposite to the Germanic Stress Rule. However, the secondary stress preceding Romance main stress provided a landing site for the main stress when such a loan was integrated into English. This has also been called stress retraction because to the measure that loans were integrated into English, main stress has tended to move further away from the end of the word. Pairs members like *GArage/garAGE*, or *BAllet/baLLET* can thus be seen as having or not having undergone stress retraction. The process may in fact lead to different results depending on whether French or Latin is the immediate source of the loan.

(3) Latin *acaDEmia*   > E *Academy*
     French *academMIE* > E *aCAdemy*

Both variants are recorded in historical dictionaries (Danielsson 1948). Depending on what is thought to be the "true" source of a particular word changes in codified stress patterns may and do occur. Therefore, donor stress may have recursive influence if the donor language has prestige and codifiers and dictionary makers refer back to it for disambiguation of variable practice.

4.5. Antepenult principle

Statistically, stress retraction tends to result in stress falling on the antepenult syllable. On this evidence the fully monolingual speaker who does not refer to outside linguistic "authorities" (French/Latin) is likely to conclude that certain kinds of words (foreign-looking, learned, academic, technical) are preferably stressed on the antepenult syllable. It is likely that this principle has been gaining in importance through the progressive loss of contact of educated speakers with Latinp. We could therefore say that the antepenult Principle is a historical consequence of the donor principle. It was first explicitly mentioned in 1582 by Mulcaster (cf. Danielsson 1948: 24).

4.6. Etymological prototypes

"This looks like a French word, so stress it on the last syllable. This looks like an Italian word, it ends in -o, therefore stress it on the penult."

This is another variation of the donor principle under different circumstances. It usually applies to a different section of the vocabulary consisting of later, non-scholarly or non-scientific loans which are typically from the modern Romance languages or "Mediterranean" in a wider sense (Greek, Arabic). These loans tend to pertain to non-formal, non-scientific styles.[7]

Thus, French loans which came into English after 1660 did not undergo stress retraction "treatment" straight away, but often kept their final stress (*cigarette, garage, ballet*) for some time with other principles taking hold later (stress fronting in *garage*). Also the derivational suffixes *-ee, -ette, -esque* (e.g. *interviewee, kitchenette,* *clownesque*), which attract stress onto themselves, were borrowed after the first great influx of complex loans in Middle English, which did not result in stressed affixes.

More recent sources of borrowing such as Italian and Spanish seem to have provided English with a kind of Mediterranean prototype or schema: such words are typically spelled with final *o/a/i* and receive stress on the penultimate syllable (*soPRAno, spaGHEtti, gonDOla, alFALfa, roDEo*) . Thus, Portuguese *VAranda* appears in English as *verANdah* (cf. Ronneberger-Siebold 1998). Loans from Modern Greek may be treated according to this schema (*mousSAka, retSIna*), but can also be found following the learned "Greek means antepenult"-schema, that is *MOUssaka, REtsina*. The original Modern Greek stress is *moussaKA* and *retSIna* respectively.

4.7. Graphemic likeness principle

"Search your mental lexicon for a word that looks like the word in question and assign word-stress according to this model."

In view of the quasi-axiomatic primacy of speech over writing, claiming that writing is relevant for stress assignment may seem a little risqué. I hope to show, though, that there are good reasons for this. What is opened up here, however, is the Pandora's Box-type question of the interaction of the two modalities of speech and writing and I will not be able to do justice to it in the space of this article.

Unless we take a radically processing-oriented approach under which word-stress is assigned on-line every time a word is uttered (as is done by the current standard accounts), the situation when a speaker has to assign word-stress does not really arise that often. If we assume that words tend to be stored and retrieved as wholes for an utterance, then the mental representation of a word would include, among other things, its (supra)segmental and graphemic form – all this being simply part of "knowing" the word (cf. Aitchinson 1994). If we subscribe to this view, a speaker actively assigns word-stress only when s/he needs to articulate or "create a phonological representation of" a word he or she has so far only encountered on the printed page.[8] Here, register and contexts of use enter the scene. It is commonly acknowledged that from Late Middle English onwards the written mode dominates both in learned borrowings and in "home-made" English formations on a Neo-Latin basis. It is no coincidence that this seems to be the area of the vocabulary where stress variability is highest. Many specialist terms originated from translations of written texts which were then read. Consequently the necessity for a loan (or a Neo-Latin formation) to also have a stress pattern arose (and arises) only when that word is used in oral communication, either within the specialist circle or when the word or a pattern associated with it gains wider currency in the language community at large. One consequence of knowing words in the written modality is that the influence of the graphemic image on an ensuing phonological representation should not be underestimated. While graphemic similarities usually do reflect morpho-lexical relatedness, this is not always the case so that graphemic "attraction" might work in totally idiosyncratic and thus unpredictable ways.

5. Integrating the principles: pattern recognition

So far, the principles which have been introduced are only loosely strung together and constitute a rather heterogeneous, disjunct, and sometimes conflicting array. As I have said above, the view of English word-stress introduced here is still a long way from being an integrated model. The principles are not hierarchically ordered and indeed a categorical ordering is explicitly undesirable for the present approach as it is intended to be able to account for variation. Different as the various principles are, we can, however, identify a common core that binds them together: they all embody the superordinate principle of pattern recognition. It is simply the case that in one and the same string several, sometimes clashing, patterns can be detected. A visual analogy can be found in the inversion pictures familiar from studies in Gestalt psychology.

Illustration 1. Two faces or a vase?

Some viewers will immediately see two faces in profile, some will see a vase and switching from one to the other will be the result of a conscious effort. It is our momentary disposition as well as our previous experience which seem to condition which picture emerges for us. In other words, it is our mind which prompts us which pattern to extract. I would claim that stress assignment in English answers to the same cognitive strategy. It is important for my argument about the social implications of English word-stress, that our mind is significantly shaped by experience which feeds back into underlying cognitive strategies. Whether these underlying strategies are universal or not, whether they are pre-linguistic, multi-modal or hard-wired is a fascinating question which shall, however, not concern us here.

In the realm of word-stress the "previous experience" mentioned above amounts to the structure of the vocabulary in terms of size but also in terms of frequency of use. Once again, this holds for the competence of a particular speaker as well as for "the language" over time. For instance, it seems that the presence of one or more morphologically related words in the vocabulary operates as an attractor for them to liken their stress patterns. Take as an example adjectives ending in *-ic*. There seems to be a competition between penultimate stress as in *democrátic, aromátic, irónic* and antepenult stress as in *chívalric*. While the former is clearly numerically dominant, the latter item seems to be stable because of *chívalry,* *chívalrous*. Diachronic switches in this respect are not only possible but frequent (see Danielsson 1948). What is interesting is that in individual cases they may go against general trends because of local solidarities or analogies. The pattern *luNAtic* which corresponded to that of *aromátic, irónic,* i.e. the dominant one, nevertheless changed to *LUnatic* presumably because of the pull of *lúnar, lúnacy*. Similarly, variants like *REputable* vs. *rePUtable* can be seen in terms of responding to the attraction of different principles. *rePUtable* groups with *repúted, repúte* while *REputable*, on the other hand, groups with other *-able* derivatives related to words like *reputation* or *separation* and, in fact, to any *-ation* word that has its secondary stress on the first syllable.

I can see no reason why pattern recognition should not operate across the boundaries of traditional linguistic components, i.e. involve phonology and morphology simultaneously in the sense that if a certain string is segmented as a suffix (such as *-ity, -ive,*) or a formative (such as *-pathy, -logy, -ferous*), the pattern involves putting the stress on the syllable to its left. The opposite sequence of events also holds: anything to the right of a non-initial, non-final stress stands a very good chance to be analysed as a suffix or formative. In the absence of any lexico-morphological clusterings, the alternative route is to go for more "shallow" patterns on the segmental-graphemic level. The lexico-morphological dimension may be absent because there simply isn't one and the word is simplex (or there isn't one within a reasonable etymological time-depth and it is a question in itself how far back one can reasonably go) or because the speaker does not recognise a morpheme when he sees one, which for all practical purposes amounts to the same thing (see below).

If there is a model to finally develop from these considerations, some thought will have to be spent on the relations holding among the different principles. I have already pointed out that the principles are certainly in no strict hierarchical order. Neither, however, are they chaotic. An idea germane to the approach embraced here is the suggestion that the English lexicon is somehow partitioned and different sets of principles have priority in each partition. Some principles, like Parse Morphologically would be pretty pervasive, others, like Initial Root Stress, would occupy the core, while yet others would be situated closer to the periphery and/or matched with specific sectors of the vocabulary. It is crucial that the spheres of operation have large overlaps in order to account for synchronic and diachronic variation.

6. Word-stress assignment as a problem-solving task

The understanding of English word-stress emerging here incorporates storage and processing and is thus akin to "dual path" models proposed in recent psycholinguistic work on lexical retrieval (Baayen, Dijkstra, and Schreuder 1997). For pattern recognition to operate the speaker obviously needs to have available a sufficient number of items which might pattern together. In any patterning which is not based on phonological-graphemic information alone, this is often directly related to how familiar a speaker is with a particular field of discourse. That is to say, which kind of pattern I am likely to recognise is dependent on the structure and frequency profile of my vocabulary. If I am a newcomer to the field of discourse and have fewer lexico-morphological fall-back strategies, I am more likely to have to look to the core vocabulary and to phonological criteria for data on which to build my pattern.[9]

Let me turn to the task which was put to respondents in the questionnaire described in section 3.: in effect, assigning word-stress to a new word is a classical problem-solving task. As with problem-solving in general, several strategies can be used. An example from the questionnaire is the noun *icosetetrahedron*. The codified stress pattern is on the antepenult: thus, *icosetetRAhedron*. To the respondents in my test, all syllables, even the last, seemed stressable. The antepenult principle supports the codified stress pattern, but obviously it is not powerful enough to overrule other principles in all instances. Those who felt they were familiar with geometry maybe connected the adjective *hedral*, and knew several other *"hedrons"* and stressed the word accordingly *icosetetraHEdron*.

A second example from the questionnaire is the medical term *peroneal*, for which the *OED* codifies the stress pattern: *peron*'[i:]*al*. The responses were divided between *peROneal* and *peroNEAL* but due to the written modality of the test the second version is ambiguous as to whether a respondent interpreted <neal> as one syllable or two. From the orthographic form we can only predict that the <o> must represent "some sort of *o*-vowel" while the <e> or the <ea> represents "some sort of *i*-vowel". But in order to apply the heavy syllable principle embraced by metrical accounts of English word-stress we would need to know exactly which *i*-vowel we have, because that makes all the difference to the heaviness or lightness of the syllable in which it is contained and therefore also to stress assignment. In terms of a metrical approach, stress assignment would roughly work as follows: a phonological representation with a long /i:/ is fed into the stress cycle, the /i:/ sits in the first heavy syllable from the right so there is no question that the main stress will fall on it. Only how do we know it is a long /i:/? In order for the heavy syllable principle to work we need to buy into a very specific understanding of how phonology is assembled "on-line", namely that all segments are fully in place before word-stress is assigned. I would, however, argue that we can see the whole thing in a different light: in solving the task we either recognise *perone* [pero'ni:] (part of the human skeleton) as the derivational base and go for *peroNEal*, or we don't. If we don't we might conclude that -*neal* must work like *deal* in which case the word has only three syllables, or we recognise a parallel with, say *baroneal*, in which case we are likely to opt for *peROneal*.

We have already said that the different principles apply with different degrees of probability in different parts of the vocabulary. Consequently, to the extent that the structure of different speakers' vocabularies differs, the weight of different principles will also differ. As the structure of one's vocabulary is largely defined by degree of literacy, degree of bilingualism vs. monolingualism, formal education and by the fields of discourse in which the speaker moves (typically these are occupationally defined in Western Industrialised

Societies), this is the place where the social dimension of English word-stress becomes visible.

Taking up the theme of social dimension of English word-stress in a more direct sense, the situation for an English speaker becomes socially critical (and presumably has been for a couple of centuries) when s/he needs to articulate or "create a phonological representation" of a word he or she has so far only seen on the printed page. Drawing the wrong conclusions, that is recognising a non-canonical pattern and thus producing the wrong stress, marks the speaker as a non-member of the particular discourse community who tend to use this particular lexical item and are thus familiar with it.[10]

> You might know exactly what porphyry means – might, indeed, be able to write a canonical essay about the use of the stone in Venetian monumental architecture – but if, when you come to say it aloud, you put the stress in the wrong place your knowledge will unfairly be turned to dust (Sutcliffe 1993).

7. Conclusion

The main argument of this paper has been that an account of English word-stress which does not exclusively revolve around syllable weight is in a better position to explain synchronic and diachronic linguistic reality. The reason why English word-stress is not amenable to monolithic rule-based accounts is due to the heterogeneous conditions under which the different principles now governing it came into operation; synchronically it may well be the case that there are pragmatic and stylistic pay-offs in non-unified stress-system (as Ronneberger-Siebold (1998) has shown for Modern German).

The approach presented does not assume on-line assignment of word-stress each time an utterance is made. Rather, on-line assignment is the exceptional case that springs into action when a speaker comes across an unfamiliar word. The default case is storage, and the stored stress-pattern is part of "knowing" a particular word. A similar case about the importance of prefabricated chunks has been made for syntax (Fillmore, Kay, and O'Connor 1988; Pawley and Syder 1983).

Moving storage back into the picture of linguistic modelling is tantamount to acknowledging that language use must have an influence on the language system – or, put differently, that language use is part of the language system. While frequency effects are the daily bread of psycholinguists, these facts have not really found their way into grammatical models. In its present state the approach presented here does not accomplish this integration either, but it is clear that, should it develop into a full-scale model, frequency effects of language use must be integrated. For the time being they are only being alluded to in the form of "familiarity with a field of discourse" and the like.

In invoking pattern recognition as the underlying strategy uniting the different principles suggested in the paper, I have placed myself in the vicinity of cognitive models of language, a fact about which I am not at all unhappy. More specifically, there is a good deal of affinity between the view of English word-stress sketched here and schema-based views of grammar (e.g. Barlow and Kemmer 1994; Fillmore, Kay, and O'Connor 1988). Advocating a schema-based view of syntax, Barlow and Kemmer (1994: 20) say: "The fact that some sentences appear to be clearly compositional does not mean that the central part of grammar is a generative rule-based system". The same can be said about English word-stress. Where phonology would seem to differ from syntax is that phonological schemas are not easily envisaged as being associated with a particular semantic configuration.

Another connection of my approach with functional-cognitive models is their common focus on the situatedness of language. In other words, the form language takes is not only determined by abstract rules but is closely related to contextual information such as previous discourse, people and objects within the discourse situation. In this sense grammar is a social construct like many other products of human culture. This situatedness with its integration of online information is the door by which the social enters grammar.

The currently standard treatments of English word-stress, and the historical accounts derived from them, assume that English word-stress can be successfully captured by high level generalisations i.e. rules, preferably one (e.g. Giegerich 1985, 1992; Katamba 1989; Burzio 1994; Lass 1992, 1994).[11] These approaches are firmly rooted in a general understanding that language exists and can be studied "by itself" (Saussure, Chomsky). Language is seen as essentially different from other cognitive-psychological capacities of humans and, although that is not a necessary consequence of this general position, linguistic practice has tended to produce descriptions and theories in which the "system" is totally independent of its users. That is to say, the possible psychological reality of descriptions has played a very minor role in most theories within this general paradigm. They aim to describe what we know, not how we know it.

The ideas presented in this contribution come from a radically different position which views language not as self-contained but as an open system connected with adjacent realities in multiple ways. This view has always existed but it has become more visible in recent years in the shape of "cognitive linguistics". This kind of outlook leads us head-on into problems which "language by itself" approaches have sought to avoid with good reason – but it is time to turn around and confront the rich reality of language in all its messiness.[12]

Calling language an "open system" has two important implications for this paper. Firstly, to the extent that language is part of the general cognitive faculties of humans, sharing certain strategies with other aspects of cognition (cf. Johnson 1987), we would expect linguistic description to develop an interest in psychological plausibility if not psychological reality of its products. This, however, happens relatively rarely, as a principled pursuit of this aim forces us to act in an interdisciplinary way rather than pay lip-service to it. So in practice, as I have done in this paper, the only accessible psychological reality is usually the one of the researcher herself by way of introspection. The second implication of adopting an "open system view" is that we cannot continue to regard language as persisting unaffected by the conscious communicative behaviour of its speakers. In other words, *"parole"* and "performance" in Saussurean and Chomskian terms can no longer be regarded to lie outside the concerns of linguistics proper. Separating them out can only be a thing of methodological convenience but not a matter of principle.

Notes

1. Readers will have noticed by now that I am making my points with specific reference to the situation of British English. I would claim though, and I think the data presented below indicate this, that much the same can be said of other varieties of English, notably American English. The role of the standard in highly developed modern societies tends to be very much the same, with differences among speech communities emerging more in the relative value of non-standard varieties.
2. Occasionally rather outlandish-sounding pronunciations have been ascribed to British English (*ferTILe, missILe*) where I suspect the motivation might have been something like "It sounds odd so it must be British".
3. The questionnaire contained the following words: *admirable, carbuncle, peroneal, lamentable, porphyry, tergiversate, epinephrine, incomparable, hegemony, annalistic, reputable, defamatory, aureole, norbornane, vitrificable, ancillary, actinophage, retsina, inexplicable, pademelon, diethylstilboestrol, revocable, siderosome, multiplicable, incognito, peromelous, norephedrine, disputable, mollusc, diatomaceous, inventory, illustratable, pacateness, moussaka, executable, icosetetrahedron, perone, minuscule, falsifiable, epigynous, elongate, refutable, contumacy, aureola, acidifiable, siderophage, particple, generalizeable, retina, pacificatoryness, locust, perosis, recognizable, phreatophyte.*
4. The average age of the British test-population was 34,3 years (age-range 15-55), that of the American population 28,4 (age-range 21-52).
5. The best-developed and most prominent standard accounts of English word-stress have arisen in the context of metrical phonology (cf. Giegerich 1985, 1992; Katamba 1989; Burzio 1994). Let me point out very briefly a couple of shortcomings or difficulties of this type of account: inasmuch a theory of word-stress assignment would be expected to cover the whole vocabulary of a language, the standard accounts show a notable preference for dealing with simplex lexical items. On the diachronic dimension it is notoriously difficult to settle on a time when the switch from left-handed to right-handed stress

assignment might have taken place (cf. Lass (1987, 1992, 1994) and the discussion in Minkova (1997)).
6. Speculating on the reasons for the lack of reception of Danielsson (1948), I am inclined to think that his rejection of the heavy syllable principle (which is at the heart of metrical treatments of stress) may well have played a part here.
7. This idea has been developed for German by Ronneberger-Siebold (1998), cf. also Berg (1997).
8. The development of text-to-speech systems as well as psychological modelling of reading aloud are based on similar premises. See Damper and Eastmond (1997).
9. Cf. Langacker's (1988: 131) usage-based model of language structure.
10. It is clearly necessary to do some empirical research in this area, but for the time being I would claim that the quotation which follows gives an accurate, if hyperbolic, reflection of linguistic reality.
11. Recently, Optimality Theory (cf. Minkova 1997; Pater 1995) has opened up new vistas in acknowledging that word-stress assignment operates via a number of ordered constraints rather than by rules, but it does not veer from the underlying assumption that language is a closed system.
12. De Beaugrande (1997) also regards the rise of "critical linguistics" as part of this general paradigm shift.

References

Aitchinson, Jean
1994   *Words in the mind.* (2nd edition.) Oxford: Blackwell.
Amis, Kingsley
1996   *The King's English: a guide to modern usage.* London: Harper Collins.
Baayen, Harald R., Ton Dijkstra, and Robert Schreuder
1997   Singulars and plurals in Dutch: evidence for a parallel dual-route model. *Journal of Memory and Language* 37: 94-117.
Barlow, Michael and Suzanne Kemmer
1994   A schema based approach to grammatical description. In: Susan Lima, Roberta Corrigan, and Gregory Iverson (eds.), 19-42.
Beaugrande, Robert de
1997   The "conscious and unconscious mind" in the theoretical discourse of modern linguistics. In: Maxim Stamenov (ed.), 9-47.
Berg, Thomas
1997   Lexical stress differences in English and German: the special status of proper nouns. *Linguistische Berichte* 167: 3-22.

Blake, Norman F. (ed.)
    1992   *The Cambridge history of the English language*, Volume 2. *1066-1476*. Cambridge: Cambridge University Press.

Burzio, Luigi
    1994   *Principles of English stress*. Cambridge: Cambridge University Press.

Damper, R. I. and J. F. G. Eastmond
    1997   Pronunciation by analogy: impact of implementational choices on performance. *Language and Speech* 40: 1-23.

Danielsson, Bror
    1948   *Studies on the accentuation of polysyllabic Latin, Greek and Romance loan-words in English: with special reference to those ending in -able, -ate, -ator, -ible, -ic, -ical and -ize*. Stockholm: Almqvist and Wiksell.

Eckhardt, E.
    1942   Der Übergang zur germanischen Betonung bei den Wörtern französischer Herkunft im Mittelenglischen. *Englische Studien* 75: 9-66.

Fillmore, Charles, P. Kay, and Mary Catherine O'Connor
    1988   Regularity and idiomaticity in grammatical constructions: the case of *let alone*. *Language* 64: 501-538.

Giegerich, Heinz
    1985   *Metrical phonology and phonological structure*. Cambridge: Cambridge University Press.
    1992   *English phonology*. (Cambridge Textbooks in Linguistics.) Cambridge University Press.

Hogg, Richard (ed.)
    1998   *Historical linguistics 1995: selected papers from the XIIth international Conference on Historical Linguistics, Manchester 1995*. (Current Issues in Linguistic Theory 162). Amsterdam/ Philadelphia: Benjamins.

Jones, Daniel
    1963   *English pronunciation dictionary*. London: Dent.

Katamba, Francis
    1989   *An introduction to phonology*. London/New York: Longman.

Langacker, Ronald
    1988   A usage based model. In: Brygida Rudza-Ostyn (ed.), 127-161.

Lass, Roger
    1987   *The shape of English: structure and history*. London: Dent.
    1992   Phonology and morphology. In: Norman Blake (ed.), 23-155.
    1994   *Old English*. Cambridge: Cambridge Univeristy Press.

Lima, Susan, Roberta Corrigan, and Gregory Iverson (eds.)
1994 *The reality of linguistic rules*. Amsterdam: Benjamins.

Mathesius, Walter
[1934] 1996 Zur synchronischen Analyse fremden Sprachguts. Reprinted in: Josef Vachek (ed.), 398-413.

Minkova, Donka
1997 Constraint ranking in Middle English stress-shifting. *English Language and Linguistics* 1: 135-175.

Pater, J.
1995 On the uniformity of weight-to-stress and stress preservation effects in English. MS, McGill University. Rutgers Optimality Archive: ROA-107.

Pawley, A. and F. H. Syder
1983 Two puzzles for linguistic theory: nativelike selection and nativelike fluency. In: J. C. Richards and R. W. Schmidt (eds.), 191-225.

Richards, J. C. and R. W. Schmidt (eds.)
1983 *Language and communication*. London: Longman.

Ronneberger-Siebold, Elke
1998 Phonological simplification vs. stylistic differentiation in the history of German word-stress. In: Richard Hogg (ed.).

Rudza-Ostyn, Brygida (ed.)
1988 *Topics in cognitive linguistics*. Amsterdam: Benjamins.

Stamenov, Maxim (ed.)
1997 *Language structure, discourse and the access to consciousness*. (Advances in consciousness research 12.) Amsterdam/ Philadelphia: Benjamins.

Sutcliffe, Thomas
1993 You open your mouth and a bomb goes off. *The Independent*. London, 19 July 1993.

Vachek, Josef (ed.)
1996 *A Prague School reader in linguistics*. Bloomington: Indiana University Press.

Wells, John C.
1990 *Pronunciation dictionary*. London: Longman.
1990 *Pronunciation theory*. London: Longman.

The modal verb *shall* between grammar and usage in the nineteenth century

Roberta Facchinetti

> The Verb by *shall*, States of fixed Order shows;
> Or States which Chance directs, as we suppose.
> And *shall* those verbal Future States declares
> Which *for itself*, an Object hopes or Fears,
> Thinks *of itself*, surmises, or foresees;
> But which for other Objects it decrees
> (Ward 1765).

1. Aim and scope of the study

The exact current semantic value of the modal verb *shall* is still unascertainable, due to its numerous shades of meaning, which have gradually been taking shape since the shadowy early history of modal auxiliaries and have come through the centuries up to the present time. Nonetheless, grammarians have always attempted to set some clear-cut distinctions between *shall* and its counterpart *will*, which originated from a different semantic context, but has met *shall* on the grounds of futurity. To prevent the fortresses of their categorisations from being attacked, grammarians have sometimes forced actual use into the boundaries of rational rules (see Tieken-Boon van Ostade (1985) for an interesting review of these rules) and at times they have even trespassed the limits of social discrimination so as to brand some *shall-* or *will*-clauses as typically Scottish, Irish, or American.

Starting from this premise, the present paper has a two-fold aim; first I will analyse the syntactic and semantic features of *shall* as it occurs in a nineteenth-century corpus, in an attempt to further dispel the mist still shrouding the history and development of this verb. Secondly, the analysis of real occurrences will allow me to discuss the socially biased remarks made by grammarians in the previous centuries and not yet totally abandoned.

The data sampled for this study are derived from a subset of the corpus *Changing Times* (1993) containing about 15,000 original articles selected from *The Times* and *The Sunday Times* over 200 years of history, from 1785 to 1992. The articles encompass accounts of events, letters, eye-witness reports and also personal reminiscences on a wide range of historical themes such as Trade and Industry, the Great War, the British Empire, the Second World War, the French Revolution, the Rise of Communism, the Rise of America, Moving European Boundaries, Women's Rights, World Conflicts, Special Events, and finally the Irish Question.

For the purpose of my study, I will analyse the 188 articles dealing with the Irish Question in the nineteenth century; undoubtedly, nineteenth-century Ireland was a source of social and political upheaval widely echoed in English newspapers. The declaration of the United Kingdom of Great Britain and Ireland in 1801, Daniel O'Connell's Association for promoting Roman Catholic emancipation in the 1820s, the "Young Ireland" movement in the 1840s, the disastrous famine of 1846-1851, the Home Rule League of Charles Stewart Parnell in the 1870s, William Gladstone's efforts to remedy the situation in the final quarter of the century, and finally the birth of the Irish Nationalist Movement Sinn Fein are only some of the many topics dealt with in the articles selected for the present analysis.

Since a large number of them are copies of reports and commentaries previously published in Irish newspapers, such as *The Cork Examiner*, *The Waterford Chronicle*, and *The Constitution*, the English language as it was used in nineteenth-century Ireland appears to be adequately represented alongside that of native English speakers.

2. Basic landmarks in the development of *shall*

The ancestor of *shall* was the Old English *sceal*, preterit of *sculan*, indicating, in Visser's words: "he has done something (probably committed an offence or a crime) in consequence of which he now 'is scyldig'" (Visser 1963-1973: 1581); the verb indicated that a person was "liable of a debt, had to pay, was in a person's debt for" (Visser 1963-1973: 549). The character or amount of the debt was originally conveyed by a direct object; gradually an infinitive verb replaced the complement, thus indicating that the person had to carry out an action.

Evolving from the narrow scope of pecuniary obligation or indebtedness to the wider moral obligation and command laid down by an external superior authority, including the operations of nature and gods and the allotments of fate, there was only a small step to reach the fully-fledged meaning of futurity, since commands necessarily have a future-time reference. Consequently, the idea of futurity also came about and was established as an integral part of the semantic value of this auxiliary with the two meanings of prediction and direction, "to which the lurking colour of necessity lodged in *shall* [gave] a certain added positiveness" (Bradley Beach 1911: 16). Indeed, the verb maintained its meaning of obligation and also conveyed the speaker's certainty about the necessity or the actualisation of the event. Moreover, when it simply indicated futurity, *shall* frequently occurred either with the infinitive form of the following verb or with some other words in the sentence like *weorþan*, clarifying the futurity of the event.

In Middle English *shall* was definitely more frequent than *will*, especially in predictive contexts, and its future value was further standardised also thanks to the examples provided by Wycliffe in his translation of the *Vulgate*, where *shall* was regularly used to translate the Latin future tense, while *will* was employed to gloss the Latin *volo*. In Late Middle English, the idea of futurity strongly increased at the expense of the force of obligation which was steadily weakened, up to Shakespeare's times, when the auxiliary gradually settled towards the present pattern, although Shakespeare himself, as testified by Kakietek's study, "did not subscribe to the rules generally associated with his English" (Kakietek 1972: 27).

From the seventeenth century onwards, grammarians were pressed by the increased use of *shall* and *will* in very similar contexts and wished to provide valuable reference books for foreign and native learners; hence they set out to make countless attempts to discriminate the semantics of the two modals and consequently to codify their uses.

3. *Shall* in grammar books up to 1900

Fries (1925) brings forth a detailed analysis, amended and integrated by Taubitz (1975), testifying to the fact that George Mason's *Grammaire Angloise* (1622) is the first one which posits a distinction between *shall* and *will*, although Mason does not provide a specific difference between the two modals. Only in 1653 does Wallis come to the conclusion that *shall* is employed with first person subjects to predict, and with second and third person subjects for promises or threats. Almost one hundred years later, in 1762 Robert Lowth remarks on the use of *shall* in interrogative clauses such as "*Shall I open the door?*", referring to another person's will, and in 1765 William Ward provides the first fully detailed account of *shall* as distinct from *will*, suggesting its specific uses in a variety of syntactic contexts.

A host of grammarians follow these linguistic milestones, and most of them acknowledge the rule of *shall* as indicating futurity with first person subjects and obligation with second and third. This norm is further standardised in the nineteenth century, when, as testified by Görlach's comprehensive list of English grammars by British and American authors (1998), hundreds of grammar books were published, only 894 of which, however, were totally new (Michael 1997: 25), the majority being either reprints or later editions of grammars from the previous century. Consequently they contributed to the preservation of the grammar conventions and the standards of correctness imposed in the previous centuries, which, indeed, result from perceptive, though incomplete descriptions of actual language use.

It is particularly during the nineteenth century that the use or misuse of *shall* and *will* gave reason to the English to accuse the Scots, the Irish and the Americans of incorrectly using the two verbs. For example, in 1864 Henry Alford, Archbishop of Canterbury, states: "Now here we are at once struck by a curious phenomenon. I never knew an English man who misplaced "shall" and "will"; I hardly ever have known an Irishman or a Scotchman who did not misplace that sometimes. And it is strange to observe how incurable the propensity is" (Alford 1864: 154).

Richard Grant White (1871) also points out that, while educated Americans make correct use of *shall* and *will*, equally educated Scottish and Irish people are totally unable to use the two modals correctly.

Similar remarks, particularly on the Irish, received wide echo in magazines, learned journals, and even transactions of philological societies, and have not even been totally abandoned in this century. Suffice Gowers' words:

> The idiom of the Celts is different. They have never recognized "I shall go". For them "I will go" is the plain future. The story is a very old one of the drowning Scot who was misunderstood by English onlookers and left to his fate because he cried, "I will drown and nobody shall save me". American practice follows the Celtic, and in this matter, as in so many others, the English have taken to imitating the American ... The Irish and the Scots are having their revenge for our bland assumption that English usage must be "right" and theirs "wrong" (Gowers 1954 [1987]: 141-142).

Undoubtedly, one cannot question the fact that the Irish, alongside the Scots and the Americans, did not (and do not) fully comply with British English grammar rules; on the other hand, right from the start grammarians have always attempted to pigeonhole usage into a set of rules bordering on arbitrariness and social discrimination, as suggested by the empirical evidence drawn from the corpus I have analysed.

4. *Shall* in the first half of the nineteenth century

4.1. The time under scrutiny has been divided into two periods coinciding with the two halves of the nineteenth century: 1800-1850 and 1851-1900. An overview of the behaviour of both modals in the whole *Changing Times* corpus is shown in figure 1:

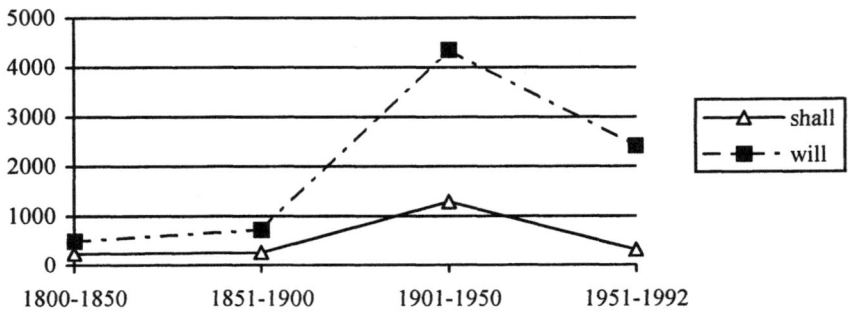

Figure 1. Occurrences of *shall* and *will* in *Changing Times*

Undoubtedly, no statistically valid conclusion can be drawn by separately charting the occurrences of the two modals in the period of time under scrutiny, on account of both the different number of articles encoded in the corpus for each period and their uneven length. Indeed, under the heading of one single article the compilers have frequently assembled many a text published by *The Times* and *The Sunday Times* on the same day and on the same topic. Consequently, the increased occurrence of both modals in the first half of the twentieth century might quite possibly be due to the much higher number of (longer) articles belonging to this period, 6691 compared to the 994 of the previous half of the century and to the 3936 of the second half of the twentieth century. Nonetheless, as figure 1 testifies, in the whole *Changing Times* corpus, *shall* has always been employed much less than *will* and its increase in use in the first half of the twentieth century was far less marked than that of *will*.

4.2. In the articles dealing with the Irish Question in the first part of the nineteenth century, *shall* totals 79 occurrences, none of which with second person subject. Interestingly, only 17 of them, all in declarative sentences, have been recorded with first person subjects, that is 21.51%, while the remaining occur with a third person subject. This may be justified by the fact that in journalistic writing first person subjects occur mainly in direct speech quotations or, though less frequently, in articles conveying the writer's personal involvement in the subject matter he/she is writing on.

In the corpus, the name of the person whose words are quoted is always clearly stated, and this leads to an interesting conclusion: although the grammarians claim that the Irish favour *will* and use *shall* improperly, or do not use it at all, at least with first person subjects, almost all the occurrences of *shall* with first person subjects in the corpus are not uttered by native English people, but by Irish politicians and religious leaders.

Moreover, a limited number of occurrences have been uttered by what I named pro-Irish writers, whose views on the Irish question are so Irish-orientated to betray a high probability of Irish nationality. On 17 January 1833, for example, a columnist of *The Times* comments on the rumour of Daniel O'Connell's arrest and, discussing the grievances of Ireland, writes:

(1) *There are three other grievances which we now have only space to glance at, but to the consideration of which we shall, without loss of time, return.*
    (17-01-1833 Irish Reforms)

With a pure futurity value of *shall*, the writer touches upon "the brutal persecution" of the "jealous" English government, rejoices that "Ireland has loosened the rivets of her chains", and deplores "the Grand Jury tyranny", "the Vestry Act tyranny". Nothing is known about the nationality of this writer, but his patriotic statements lead the reader to surmise his Irish nationality.

4.3. Indeed, as has already been mentioned, many of the articles dealing with the Irish Question are simple reprints of articles published in local Irish newspapers; example (2), for example, published on 30th July 1838 by the *Kilkenny Journal* and issued the following day by *The Times*, is the letter written by the former Mayor of the Irish city of Kilkenny, John Hume, to the newly appointed Mayor of the city. Hume, now representative of the Irish community, questions the proposal put forward by the House of Lords concerning the revision of the municipal reform bill for Ireland, and denounces "the repeated denial of justice to Ireland by the Imperial Legislature", "a reluctant and hostile party, for so many centuries against the people of Ireland"; then he remarks that:

(2) *There are such various other most unjust enactments, all against the people, that I would rather let matters remain as they are. I, however, shall be obliged to you to put me in possession of the opinion of my constituents on those particulars.*
(31-07-1838 The Irish Bills. Renewal of Agitation)

Pure futurity seems to be the main value conveyed in this example, as in example (3), that previously appeared in the *Constitution*, journal of the Irish city of Cork and then was republished by *The Times*; the writer is commenting on the distribution of corn during the potato famine:

(3) *We believe the fact to be, that in some places there is a sufficiency, – in others, the reverse; and we are not without hope that, with the precautions taken by Government, we shall be able to struggle on until the new crop comes in.*
(20-03-1846 The Apprehended Scarcity)

The clause "we are not without hope" clearly testifies to the feeling of expectancy and the consequent lack of deontic values in the modal verb. Again, Daniel O'Connell, the catholic lawyer who became commander-in-chief of the Catholic Association of Ireland, wonders:

(4)   *How I long to see the Ulster Association at work!
That is the point – will they work? We shall see.*
        (30-07-1840 The Repeal. Mr. O'Connell)

Interestingly enough, the Irish leader complies perfectly to the rule requiring *shall* with first person subject and *will* with second and third person subject to indicate futurity. Consequently, we may conclude that, in accordance with the rules of English grammar, dynamic futurity appears to be the core value conveyed by all the instances recorded in my corpus uttered by Irish speakers.

4.4. A legitimate objection is that the articles first published in Irish papers might have undergone a process of revision by the English editors, thus affecting their language and adapting it to the English standards. To dispel this doubt, a larger, purely Irish corpus should be employed, since the data drawn from the present corpus are not to be regarded conclusive. Moreover, these speakers were undoubtedly highly educated and their socio-political status might quite possibly have led them to comply with the English rules. Finally, one cannot rule out the possibility that, as far as politicians are concerned, they did not write their own speeches themselves; consequently their language might have been affected by the linguistic habits of the real authors of the speeches. However, nineteenth-century grammarians claimed that among non-English speakers, even the educated ones were frequently wrong in their use of *shall* and *will*. Henry Alford, for example, reports the following anecdote:

> It was but the other day that I asked a person sprung of Irish blood, whether he would be at a certain house to which I was going that evening. The answer was, "*I'm afraid I won't.*" Yet my friend is a sound and accurate English scholar, and I had never before, during all the years I had known him, discovered any trace of the sister island (Alford 1864: 154).

4.5. Nineteenth-century "sound and accurate English scholars", according to grammarians, employed *shall* with less frequency in subordinate temporal or conditional clauses. Kakietek (1972: 38) remarks that this pattern is a peculiarity of Shakespeare's English.

More precisely, the conditional construction was typical of Old English, Middle English, and Early Modern English, and became obsolete in 1700. In contrast, the temporal construction, denoting future contingency, began to be superseded by the present-tense form in the nineteenth century, and is now obsolete. Here again grammarians' texts do not reflect real use; suffice Murray's example, who specifies that when the verb is in the subjunctive mood, the meaning of *shall* and *will* undergoes some alteration (Murray 1824); he quotes examples like *if he shall proceed* and *if you shall consent*, yet he is unable to clarify the nature of the alteration; neither does he mention the occurrence of *shall* in temporal clauses, which, unlike *if*-clauses, was still frequent in nineteenth-century English.

This is further confirmed by the data yielded by my corpus, where a good number of *shall* occurrences are introduced by temporal subordinators, while only a limited number of them occur with the conditional *if*:

(5) *Look at Ireland the day after O'Connell shall have been imprisoned, – forget his history, his ambition, and his name.*
(17-01-1833 Irish Reforms)

(6) *It is intended to reserve issues from these depots for the more heavy pressure during the summer months, when farm labour shall have ceased.*
(15-04-1846 Government Relief)

(7) *That audience we take to comprise all Englishmen, of all ranks, and of all generations, from that day forth, so long as the monarchy shall stand.*
(23-03-1843 Poor Laws)

(8) *If again in the course of these proceedings any persons in this court shall conduct themselves in the manner we have just heard, I will beg leave to*

request that your Lordships will order the gallery to be cleared.
(17-01-1844 Repeal Association)

Interestingly enough, only a limited number of occurrences are uttered by Irish speakers (example (8)), who appear to favour the modern structure with the present tense, while most of them are uttered by native English speakers, mainly Government officials (example (6)) and English commentators (examples (5), (7)).

All the above instances occur with third person subject and convey a clear idea of futurity. In contrast, the remaining declaratives with third person subject do not merely convey futurity, as example (9) testifies:

(9) *Should any person be found so base as not legally to resist the rapacity of the plundering blood-sucking persons, their names shall be posted in the most public places! and their memory be execrated by posterity. Who will be found to cut their hay and corn in harvest? The vile mercenary attorney who degrades his legal profession by prostituting his services to enforce this unchristian tax, shall be branded with infamy, and the servile wretches who retain him at quarter sessions or assizes shall also be consigned to public scorn and contempt.*
(01-07-1832 Tithes)

Threat or menace of punishment appears to be the main value of *shall*, unlike *will*, which in the same context (*who will be found*) merely expresses futurity.

It appears, consequently, that in the first half of the nineteenth century *shall* was still linked to a strong idea of obligation. However, with a third person subject a few, though a much more limited, number of occurrences mainly uttered by native English speakers have been registered with a purely dynamic future predictive meaning:

(10) *That under-tenant is a middle-man; he offers to his landlord a rent proportionate to that which he conceives he shall be able to realize from the occupiers*

(23-03-1843 Poor Laws)

These are the words of an English commentator on the Irish agrarian system and, despite the rule viewing the use of *will* mainly in volitional contexts, particularly in the nineteenth century, it appears that the English, and not the Irish, do not totally comply with the rules.

The final interesting example of *shall* in this first half of the century is the following:

(11) *We see no escape for O'Brien from his ridiculous 'fix'. ... The modern Prometheus Vinctus is rather a perverse one. The original was persecuted for his unreserved benefits to all mankind; the Irish specimen for confining his interests to one little isle. The mythological philanthropist gladly accepted deliverance; his modern imitator refuses the most friendly aid. "I will be shut up," he cries, "and nobody shall help me."*

(01-05-1846 Arrest of O'Brien)

The example strongly echoes the one quoted by Gowers about the Scottish man who "wanted to drown"; however, in example (11) the Irish leader really wants to be put in jail and really wishes not to be helped. Hence, once more, it appears that the Irish do not disregard English rules, nor do they produce sentences which may be misunderstood.

5. *Shall* in the second half of the nineteenth century

5.1. In the second half of the nineteenth century, *shall* occurs 40 times in the articles dealing with the Irish Question. Only two instances of *shall* appearing in subordinate temporal context have been recorded, both in the same article written to the editor of *The Times* by some not better qualified Wm. Tighe Hamilton, commenting on the Irish land question:

(12) *The fact is that the plan is pregnant with litigation. Its very essence is that what is now a settled rule of property shall be unsettled, until lawyers shall have re-settled it again.*
(16-1-1869 The Irish land question)

(13) *In this conjuncture the people of England would do well to reserve their opinion until the real facts of the case shall have been found out for them.*
(16-1-1869 The Irish land question)

In examples (12) and (13) futurity appears to be the most feasible interpretation, as in the previous part of the century. It seems, however, that there is a growing tendency to follow the modern rule according to which *shall* – and *will* – occur only in apodosis.

Moreover, the data are consistent with regard to second person subjects, since, as recorded in the first half of the nineteenth century, no instance of *shall* with second person subject has been noticed. On the other hand, 67.5% of the occurrences of *shall* are with first person subjects (27 out of 40):

(14) *The practical breakdown of the round table negotiations is contemplated by Mr. Chamberlain with regret, but without alarm. "If we cannot agree quickly," he says, "we shall drift further apart."*
(14-03-1887 Parnellism and Crime)

Example (14) is the quotation of Lord Joseph Chamberlain's words, showing the use of *shall* in the apodosis of conditional clauses. A clear dynamic value of prediction is conveyed.

5.2. Unlike what was recorded for the previous half of the century, most of these utterances are not made by Irish speakers, but rather by English ones; indeed, the number of Irish speakers in this section is limited, since the majority of the articles are commentaries of the political turmoil determined by the Irish demands for land reform and an autonomous parliament. Consequently statements and speeches by such politicians as Joseph Chamberlain, as in example (14), and William Gladstone are very frequent, although other quotations from the Irish nationalist Charles Parnell and by Irish journalists are not totally absent, as example (15) testifies:

(15)   *We shall again enumerate some of those impediments of which we happen to be cognisant.*
                                        (24-10-1854 State of Trade)

This is an extract from an article dealing with the state of trade in Ireland, which appeared in the *Belfast Journal*; again, the writer, like the above-mentioned native English speakers, employs *shall* in this context to indicate futurity.

5.3. Consequently, judging from the data of this corpus, we may confirm that, all through the nineteenth century, *shall* with a first person subject mainly indicated future predictive meanings and only rarely exhibited some deontic overtones, when used both by the Irish and by the English:

(16)   *I think there are two duties incumbent upon us in regard to our friends of the Liberal party from whom we are momentarily divided, and the first is that we shall do nothing that can wound, that we shall say nothing that can wound and nothing that can embarrass them.*
                        (18-03-1887 Mr. Gladstone on the Irish Question)

These words, pronounced by William Gladstone, a native Englishman, at the time of the rift in the Liberal party due to Gladstone favouring Irish nationalism, betray some kind of determination further testified to by the word "duties".

Finally, in the few instances of *shall* employed with third person subject, the English once again appear not to comply with the rules. Undoubtedly, the majority of cases indicate rules and regulations or resolutions, be they uttered by the English or by the Irish as in example (17), however some of them also indicate pure futurity as in example (18):

(17) *The Irish race all over the world are hereby summoned to action! England is about to support those heartless land-robbers with her police, her army, her generals, and her treasure. Her greatest treasures – namely, her ships of commerce, are floating on the high seas. These shall be our prizes. These shall be our ransom until she hauls off from our kith and kin those infernal devils, the land robbers, the police, and her demoralising soldiery.*
(14-03-1887 Parnellism and Crime)

(18) *But what is a presumption of law? It is the inference which lawyers have from time immemorial been deciding – that certain acts or omissions, due to the weaknesses, or negligences, or failings, or perhaps kindnesses of men, shall be presumed to mean, whether they did mean so or not.*
(16-11-1869 The Irish Land Question)

In example (18) decision and resolution appear to be much less evident, while futurity seems to gain pace, despite the rules laid down with regard to second and third person subjects.

6. Conclusion

According to Fries and to the structuralist grammarians of the early twentieth century, *shall* and *will* have been codified in their present uses mainly due to the arbitrary speculations of the early grammarians. A different trend of discussion, first heralded by Hulbert (1947) and later endorsed by Taglicht (1970), Moody (1974), and Taubitz (1975), claims that such rules mirrored actual language use or at least possessed "an underlying rationale", specifically with regard to the pragmatic values of the two modals (Arnovick 1997).

Whatever their origin, these seventeenth- and eighteenth-century prescriptions were largely complied with in the nineteenth century, as the data from my corpus confirm. Indeed, the semantic discrimination between the two verbs suggested by grammarians in relation to their occurrence with first, second or third person subjects have been noticed: *shall* with first person subjects favours future values, while with second and third person subjects deontic contexts are more common.

One cannot totally confirm, however, the grammarians' sociolinguistic remarks on the Irish misuse or failed use of *shall* with first person subjects, since the data suggest that, at least in the first part of the nineteenth century, the Irish employed *shall* with first person subject even more frequently than the English.

Undoubtedly, the present results should be viewed merely as a starting point for further research to be carried out on a larger, exclusively Irish corpus; indeed, as previously mentioned, the Irish texts recorded in the corpus may have been revised according to the English norm when edited in England. Moreover, these writers were highly educated and they, or anyone on their behalf, might have chosen to meet with the English rules when writing political speeches and commentaries. Undoubtedly, working with historical data requires particular attention and no conclusive statement can be made. However I believe that the results of my analysis can find an authoritative and eloquent summa in Poutsma's (1924) words; while confirming the rules laid down by the English in regard to *shall*, and the failure of the attempts by non-British to conform to these rules, the grammarian also has doubts about the compliance to the same rules by the English themselves and remarks that:

> It may also be doubted that the "true-born Englishman", even when he constantly moves in educated circles, strictly observes the rules ... On the face of it, it seems incredible that he should be privileged, so to speak, with a sixth organ enabling him to tread unerringly in the maze of this bewildering problem (Poutsma 1924: 222).

The present study has indicated that grammar rules alone cannot lead us safely to the end of this "maze". On the contrary, it is only with the help of real language use, beyond social discrimination and imposed standards of correctness that we can attempt to scrutinise and analyse the nuanced English language.

References

Alford, Henry
    1864   *The Queen's English: stray notes on speaking and spelling.* London.

Arnovick, Leslie K.
    1997   Proscribed collocations with *shall* and *will*: the eighteenth-century (non-)standard reassessed. In: Jenny Cheshire and Dieter Stein (eds.), 135-151.

Bradley Beach, Cornelius
    1911   Shall and will – an historical study. *Transactions of the American Philological Association* 42: 5-31.

Changing Times
    1993   London: News Multimedia.

Cheshire, Jenny and Dieter Stein (eds.)
    1997   *Taming the vernacular.* London: Longman.

Fries, Charles C.
    1925   The periphrastic future with *shall* and *will* in Modern English. *Publications of the Modern Language Association of America* 40: 963-1024.

Görlach, Manfred
    1998   *An annotated bibliography of 19th-century grammars of English.* Amsterdam: Benjamins.

Gowers, Ernest
[1954] 1987 *The complete plain words.* (3rd edition.) Revised by Sidney Greenbaum and Janet Whitcut. Harmondsworth: Penguin Books.

Hulbert, James Root
1947 On the origin of the grammarians' rules for the use of *shall* and *will*. *Publications of the Modern Language Association of America* 62: 1178-1182.

Kakietek, Piotr
1972 *Modal verbs in Shakespeare's English.* (Uniwersytet im. Adama Mickiewicza Poznaniu, Wydział Filologiczny, Seria Filologia Angielska 3.) Poznań: Adam Mickiewicz University.

Lowth, Robert
1762 *A short introduction to English grammar: with critical notes.* London.

Mason, George
1622 *Grammaire angloise.* London.

Michael, Ian
1997 The hyperactive production of English grammars in the nineteenth century: a speculative bibliography. *Publishing History* 41: 23-61.

Moody, Patricia A.
1974 *Shall* and *will*: the grammatical tradition and dialectology. *American Speech* 49: 67-78.

Murray, Lindley
1824 *An English grammar: The principles and rules of the language, illustrated by appropriate exercises, and a key to the exercises.* Reprinted in *An English grammar*, volumes 1-2, 1996 [*Lindley Murray (1745-1826): The Educational Works*]. London: Routledge/Thoemmes Press.

Poutsma, Hendrik
1924 *A grammar of Late Modern English.* Groningen: Noordhoff.

Taglicht, Josef
1970 The genesis of the conventional rules for the use of *shall* and *will*. *English Studies* 51: 193-213.

Taubitz, Ronald
1975 *A study of* shall *and* will *by various grammarians.* Unpublished Ph.D. dissertation, Arizona State University.

Tieken-Boon van Ostade, Ingrid
1985 "I will be drowned and no man shall save me": the conventional rules for *shall* and *will* in eighteenth century English grammars. *English Studies* 66 (2): 123-142.

Visser, F. Th.
   1963/1973   *An historical syntax of the English language.* Leiden: Brill.

Wallis, John
   1653   *Grammatica linguae anglicanae.* Oxford.

Ward, William
   1765   *An essay on grammar.* London.

White, Richard Grant
   1871   *Words and their uses, past and present: A study of the English language.* New York.

Social relations and forms of address in the *Canterbury Tales*

Gabriella Mazzon

1. Introduction

Studies on Early Modern English uses revealed in full the potential of socio-pragmatic expression conveyed by terms and pronouns of address. It was found that some specific categories of participants in an exchange are always addressed with T (i.e. *thou* and related forms), others constantly with Y (i.e. *you* and related forms), not only according to immediate contextual factors such as emphasis and emotional value, but also in relation with their social status and/or their status as participants in the interaction. The analysis of some scenes from Shakespearian plays (Mazzon 1994, 1995) also revealed that the retractability of pronoun use (i.e. the possibility to switch from Y to T and back with the same interlocutor, even within the same exchange) is highly functional. It expresses the pragmatic-based dynamics of interaction between characters, including the expression of personal feelings and emotions and the "face-work" going on in several dialogues.

It is hoped, with this paper, to add some evidence for an earlier stage, i.e. the late fourteenth century, and for a different genre, although at times not very far from the liveliness and the mimetic quality of the theatre. Many of the examples that will be quoted have been already employed, and the uses they represent have been pointed at by others (see References); these phenomena have however rarely been interpreted, so far, in the light of modern pragmatic theories. It is now possible to venture some hypotheses about uses that our predecessors considered "erratic", "casual", or unexplainable.

2. The system and uses of pronouns and terms of address in the *Canterbury Tales*

At Chaucer's time, the use of Y as singular pronoun of address had already been introduced for some time and was gaining ground. The only significant changes in the system of second person pronouns before the fifteenth century are of a pragmatic, not of a morphological type, since the forms themselves evolved regularly from previous forms. A count of pronoun occurrences (and of their related forms) in the *Canterbury Tales* revealed that only very few cases of impersonal forms, or of forms inserted in otherwise peculiar constructions, seem to lead the way to further developments such as the extension of *you* to subject role: on the whole the system of forms as such is intact, but its uses clearly are not, as revealed by the figures in table 1:

Table 1. Occurrences of pronouns of address in the *Canterbury Tales*
Apart from the impersonal forms, there are 3 cases in which *ye* seems to be non-nominative, and 7 in which *you* seems to be nominative (significantly, out of these 6 are singular, only one plural)

T-forms	Y-forms singular	Y-forms plural	impersonal *you*
thou 743	*ye* 567	*ye* 290	singular 55
thee 308	*you* 377	*you* 251	plural 19
thy 683	*your* 492		

Table 1 shows that the use of Y as singular is already quite common indeed in Chaucer's work, and it could be interesting to investigate what triggers or constrains such uses. The origin of the "plural-as-singular" address is not very clear, as concerns both the time and the place of its introduction. Some influence from French has probably to be assumed, especially given the role of the high classes and of the bureaucrats in spreading this use. It must not be presumed, on the other hand, that the French model was followed blindly, since mismatches in translations show that this is not the case: in uses to strangers, for instance, i.e. in cases where a sort of "neutral politeness" is required, French documents use plural forms much more consistently than their English translations (Finkenstaedt

(1963: 67-73); for an account of the spread of "polite" singular Y cf. Strang (1970: 139, 262)).

The *Canterbury Tales* are interesting for this kind of analysis because they include several dialogues of various types, i.e. between various characters in various situations, and within tales representing, though with a certain background homogeneity, different sub-genres. The extent to which such evidence can be considered reliable to draw conclusions about the spoken language of the time is of course an open question. It must be recalled that most of the *Canterbury Tales* is in verse, which of course always influences the language forms chosen, and that the "language of Chaucer" cannot be uncritically assumed to be representative of any other language form. As was observed *à propos* other language phenomena (e.g. negation), some forms used by Chaucer seem rather atypical, and do not agree with other evidence about comparable forms of English attested in his time. This is of course aside from the very complex transmission issues, revealed, e.g., by interpolations which are involved in the tradition of this work (for some comments about the representativeness of Chaucer's uses and about the distance between literature and everyday language in this context cf. Finkenstaedt 1963: 69-73).

It is obvious that the further back in time we go, the less use of singular Y we should find, but in Chaucer's *Tales* the use of Y, if certainly not predominant, is already widespread, and it cuts across some straightforward social distinctions, suggesting that the "rules" for the choice of pronouns and for switching could be as refined as in Shakespeare's time, even though not identical. Similar considerations can be made about terms of address, whose progress or decline in time can be traced also in relation with developments in society and its structure; terms of address will be mostly mentioned in this paper for their correlations with pronoun uses, but they clearly represent a very interesting set of uses in their own right.

3. Some "special" types of addressing

The studies of Shakespeare's forms of address mentioned above revealed a use of T as a choice for addressing *"in absentia"* or when the addressed character is asleep, dead, mad, or otherwise not capable of taking on the "normal" status of participant. There are very few such cases in the *Canterbury Tales*; T is consistently used to address a corpse, but the other categories do not seem to determine the choice of T as strictly as in Shakespeare. There is a bias in favour of T for imaginary or reported dialogue (which is in some sense the analogue of the theatrical "aside"), but for instance there is also a tendency to adhere to "normal" usage for addressing a character absent from the "scene", and not to employ T in all such cases, as was found in Shakespeare's works.[1]

In the addressing of "external" entities, i.e. deities, natural forces, abstract entities, etc., T is more frequent[2], as well as when the narrator directly addresses a character, especially to pass judgement[3]. Conversely, the addressing of deities is not consistently with T; this is however not in contrast with the tendency to use "religious T" as a more and more marked form of address, since the uses of Y found in the *Canterbury Tales* are nearly always for pagan deities, not for the Christian only God, and the relationship is of course different because pagan gods (or rather the way pagan gods were seen in the Middle Ages) are closer to human beings than the transcendental God of Christianity; these uses of Y are all switches from introductory T, and are often accompanied by forms of address conveying respect, as they could be employed to humans in higher positions, such as *lord, lady*, etc. (e.g. see E.FR.1039-1042ff.)[4]; the latter phenomenon is extended to the Christian God as well. Cf. for example the following invocation in the *Franklin's Tale* (relevant forms are in italics, switching points also in bold type; for similar examples see B2.PR.453ff. vs. 486-487):

(1)   "Eterne God, *that thurgh* thy *purveiaunce*
*Led*est *the world by certein governaunce,*
In ydel, as men seyn, **ye** *no thyng make.*

> *But,* Lord, *thise grisly feendly rookes blake,*
> ...
> *Why han* ye *wroght this werk unresonable?*
> ...
> *Se* ye *nat,* Lord, *how mankynde it destroyeth?"*
> (F.FR. 865-876).

Of course things can be much more complicated than this, especially in invocations to pagan gods, e.g., Palamon to Venus in the *Knight's Tale* (the same alternation can be found in Emelye's invocation to Diana, at A.KN. 2297-2326):

(2)   *"... As wisly as I shal for everemoore,*
Emforth my myght, thy *trewe servant be,*
And holden werre alwey with chastitee.
That make I myn avow, so **ye** *me helpe!*
...
But I wolde have fully possessioun
Of Emelye, and dye in **thy** *servise.*
Fynd thow *the manere hou and in what wyse:*
...
For though so be that Mars is god of armes,
Youre *vertu is so greet in hevene above*
That if yow *list, I shal wel have my love.*
Thy *temple wol I worship everemo,*
And on thyn *auter, where I ride or go,*
I wol doon sacrifice and fires beete,
And if **ye** *wol nat so,* my lady sweete,
Thanne preye I **thee**, *tomorwe..."*
(A.KN. 2234-2255).

In this case, the switches to Y seem to coincide with places where the intentions and desires of the goddess are called into question, and thus indirectly her power; of course, it is difficult to justify all switches pragmatically in any precise way, especially given the distance in time and *Weltanschauung* that separates us from this work.[5] As we know, this oscillation will disappear, not in the more general direction of the spread of Y, but towards maintenance of exclusive T. Some examples of this exclusive T in addressing gods can be found at A.KN. 1543, 1559, 1623-1624, 2373.

Another kind of use that is connected to the Medieval code of behaviour is the use of Y in courting, as pronoun of respect towards the "lady" (Kerkhof 1966: 136-137; Finkenstaedt 1963: 84-87). This use, connected with the general tendency to use Y to women as a sign of respect, is not absolute, but predominant, in the *Canterbury Tales* (in some cases it is difficult to decide where courting is involved as opposed to "courtesy", but there seem to be three clear cases of "courting" T and ten of Y). Instances of courting language are the following:

(3) *"Naught may the woful spirit in myn herte*
Declare o point of alle my sorwes smerte
To yow, my lady, *that I love moost..."*
(A.KN. 2765-2767)

(4) *"Madame,"* quod he, *"by God that this world made,*
So that I wiste it myghte youre *herte glade,*
I wolde that day that youre *Arveragus*
Wente over the see, ..."
(F.FR. 967-970)

Note that this use is not always reciprocated, since the lady feels entitled to reply with T or Y according to whether she wants to grant some familiarity to her wooer or not; therefore, exchanges of this kind are often asymmetric in their use of pronouns (Finkenstaedt 1963: 84). The addressing of women by men (husband–wife and other family relationship excepted) is almost invariably with Y (20 cases vs. only one T), regardless of whether the woman has a status that is superior, inferior, or roughly equivalent to that of the male character addressing her; some examples follow:

(5) *"Suster", quod he, "this is my fulle assent,*

> *With al th'avys heere of my parlement,*
> *That gentil Palamon, youre owene knyght,*
> *That serveth yow with wille, herte and myght ...".*
>
> (A.KN. 3075-3078;
> Duke Theseus speaking to Emelye)[6]

(6)   *"Dame, I wolde praye yow, if youre wyl it were,"*
Seyde this Pardoner, "as ye bigan,
Telle forth youre tale, spareth for no man,
And teche us yonge men of youre praktike."

(D.WB. 184-187; Pardoner to Wife of Bath; notice that the imperative forms do not all agree with Y; this can be due to metrical or euphonic reasons)

(7)   *"A dagon of youre blanket, leeve dame,*
Oure suster deere – lo! Heere I write youre name –"

(D.SM. 1751-1752; Friar begging to woman)

4. Some comments on other pronoun uses

4.1. Family relationships

The *Canterbury Tales* do not yield many examples of direct parent–child address, but some tentative comments can nevertheless be offered. In these cases, there is often a term of address, i.e. a kinship term, and it is interesting to note that, when these terms are used non-literally, their correlation with specific pronoun forms may change, as in the case of *brother* and *sister*.

F(a)ader and *Mo(o)der*, for instance, tend to occur with Y; the few exceptions and, of course, the pronoun switches, concern non-literal uses or addresses in which the tone is emotional. This can be seen particularly in the last of the examples quoted below, where two different moments in the highly tragic story of Count Hugueline are juxtaposed; in the first, the son has not realised the atrocity of their destiny yet: the tone is still almost "normal", and so is the form of address. Not so in the second passage, whose dramaticity is much higher:

(8)   "Fader," *she seyde*, "thy *wrecched child Custance*,
              Thy *yonge doghter fostred up so softe,*
              And ye, my *mooder, my soverayn plesance*
              Over alle thyng, out-taken Crist on-lofte,
              Custance youre *child hire recomandeth ofte*
              Unto youre *grace, for I shal to Surrye,*
              Ne shal I nevere seen yow *moore with ye".*
                                      (B.ML. 274-280;
              notice the difference in pronoun of address between
              mother and father)

(9)   "Mooder", *quod she*, "and mayde bright, Marie,
              Sooth is that thurgh wommanes eggement
              Mankynde was lorn, and damned ay to dye,
              For which thy *child was on a croys yrent.*
              Thy *blisful eyen sawe al his torment;"*
                                      (B.ML. 841-845;
                            addressing of the Madonna)

(10)   *His yonge sone, that thre yeer was of age,*
              Unto him seyde, "Fader, *why do* ye *wepe?*
              Whanne wol the gayler bryngen oure potage?
              Is ther no morsel breed that ye *do kepe?"*
                                      (B2.MK. 2431-2434)

as against

(11)   "... Fader, *do not so, allas!*
              But rather ete the flessh upon us two.
              Oure flessh **thou** *yaf us, take oure flessh us fro ..."*
                                      (B2.MK. 2449-2451)

These exchanges are mostly asymmetric, in that addressing of offspring (with the terms *child, sone, doghter*) always correlates with T, both in literal and extended uses:

(12) "*Pees*, litel sone, *I wol do* thee *noon harm.*"
              (B.ML. 835; see also 855)

(13) "*Fareweel* my child*! I shal* thee *nevere see.*"
                  (E.CL. 555)

(14) "My sone, *thenk on the crowe, a Goddes name!*
    My sone, *keep wel* thy *tonge, and keep* thy *freend.*"
                 (H.MP. 318ff.)

The only two other examples of family relationship that are found in the *Canterbury Tales* are addresses to a niece (twice, with Y) and some which employ the term *cosyn* (whose application may well have been more extended than today, cf. the first two examples quoted below), where accompanying pronouns vary because politeness phenomena are involved in the specific interactions; uses of Y are however twice as many as uses of T (15 to 7 occurrences):

(15) "O deere cosyn myn, daun John" *she seyde,*
    What eyleth yow *so rathe for to ryse?*"
                 (B2.SH. 97-98)

(16) "*But* deere nece, *why be* ye *so pale?*
                 (B2.SH. 106;
  reciprocation of the previous example)

(17) *And with that cry Arcite anon up sterte*
    And seyde, "Cosyn myn, *what eyleth* thee,
    That art *so pale and deedly on to see?*"
                 (A.KN. 1080ff.)

4.2. Beyond the family: reflections of social relations in pronouns and terms of address

At Chaucer's time, Y-forms are well established as forms of deference and of respect, and are used rather regularly with one's superiors, and increasingly with strangers, since, in Strang's (1970: 139) words, "in all cases of doubt one would rather be polite than risk giving offence, and every precedent widens the range of cases of doubt". This decisive role of politeness rules is also determined by the fact that the use of singular Y spread among the high classes first; the *Canterbury Tales* contain several such examples, although they also show another phenomenon: when social distance is very high, there is again use of T, i.e. the king is treated like God. This of course depends also on the solemnity of some appeals to royals and other high authorities contained in the tales, as well as on the specific sub-genre that the individual tale draws upon, since whenever "courtly" genres inspire the tale, uses of Y prevail, also given the kind of social group most characters belong to, as in the *Squire's Tale* and in the *Franklin's Tale* (Blake 1992: 538-539; Finkenstaedt 1963: 72).

(18)   *"Who clappeth?" seyde this wyf, "benedicitee!*
       God save you, sire, *what is* youre *sweete wille?"*
                             (D.FR. 1584-1585;
                             in answer to a call at the door)

(19)   *Agayn the knyght this olde wyf gan ryse,*
       And seyde, "Sire knyght, *heer forth ne lith no wey.*
       Tel me what that ye *seken, by* youre *fey!"*
                             (D.WB. 1000-1002;
                             old woman to knight)

(20)   ... *"Lord," quod he "my willynge*
       Is as ye *wole, ne ayeynes* youre *lykynge"*
                             (E.CL. 319-320;
                             old man to nobleman)

(21) "O noble markys, youre *humanitee*
Asseureth us and yeveth us hardinesse,
As ofte as tyme is of necessitee,
That we to yow *mowe telle oure hevynesse"*
(E.CL. 92-95;
spokesman of subjects to lord, requesting)

(22) *But Daniel expowned it anoon,*
And seyde, "Kyng, *God to* thy *fader lente*
Glorie and honour, regne, tresour, rente ... "
(B2.MK. 2209-2211)

(23) ... "Sire, *what nedeth wordes mo?*
We have the deeth disserved bothe two.
Two woful wrecches been we, two caytyves,
That been encombred of oure owene lyves;
And as thou art *a rightful lord and juge,*
Ne yif *us neither mercy ne refuge,*
But sle *me first, for seinte charitee!"*
(A.KN. 1715-1721;
Palamon to Theseus; note the highly tragic tone and the strong difference on the pragmatic dimension of Power, also due to the situation).

(24) *The eldeste lady of hem alle spak,*
...
She seyde, "Lord, *to whom Fortune hath yiven*
Victorie, and as a conqueror to lyven,
Nat greveth us youre *glorie and* youre *honour,*
But we biseken mercy and socour.
Have mercy on oure wo and oure distresse!
Som drope of pitee, thurgh **thy** *gentillesse,*
Upon us wrecched wommen lat thou *falle, ... "*
(A.KN. 912-921;

women prisoners to Theseus, from paying respects to downright pleading)

Uses between friends also depend on the class of both speaker and hearer, and also on the situation; initially, the addressing of friends was with T, and then uses became more mixed. It has been noted that, when the exchange takes place in public, conforming to social conventions is felt as more important, and therefore it is common for a switch to Y to take place (Finkenstaedt (1963: 73, 77-79); cf. also Mazzon (1995: 24) for the persistence of this phenomenon as one of the few circumstances in which modern usage allows pronoun retractability).

(25) *Aleyn answerde,* "John, *and wi*ltow *swa?*
Thanne wil I be bynethe, by my croun,
And se how that the mele falles doun
Into the trough; that sal be my disport.
For John, *y-faith, I may been of* **youre** *sort*
I is as ille a millere as ar ye".
(A.RV. 4040-4045;
one of the students addressing the other)

(26) *Placebo seyde,* "O Januarie, brother,
Ful litel nede hadde ye, my lord so deere,
Conseil to axe of any that is heere ..."
(E.MC. 1478ff.;
face-work and polite public use among friends)

(27) *..., and seyde,* "Freend so deere,
That hoote kultour in the chymenee heere,
As lene it me; I have therwith to doone,
And I wol brynge it thee *agayn ful soone."*
(A.MI. 3775-3777;
Absolon to Gerveys)

In particular, there is variation in pronouns addressed by the Host to single pilgrims; this has to do not so much, or not always, with social class, but also with the circumstances in which the interaction takes place. The Host seems to take advantage of his position as "head" of the little company and organiser of the tale-telling (it is he, mostly, who decrees who should narrate next, etc.); he is often ironic and mocks several pilgrims, but is also ready to pacify and pursue his pragmatic aims by using deferential forms. In any case, he seems to decide on the status of the pilgrims, and thence on the way they should be addressed, on the basis of their more or less prosperous appearance and of their ability as narrators rather than of their social class. His interlocutors generally seem to accept this position of authority, since they address him generally with Y. Some examples will give an idea of the variety of his own uses:

(28)   "Sire Knyght," *quod he,* "my mayster and my lord,
         Now *draw*eth *cut, for that is myn accord.
         Com*eth *neer," quod he,* "my lady *Prioresse.
         And* ye, Sire Clerk, *lat be* youre *shamefastnesse,
         Ne studi*eth *noght; ley hond to, every man!"*
                                        (A.GP. 837-841;
                    addressing relatively high-status characters)

(29)   *Oure Hoost tho spak,* "A, sire, ye *sholde be hende
         And curteys, as a man of* youre *estaat;
         In compaignye we wol have no debaat
         Tell*eth youre *tale, and lat the Somonour be"*
                                        (D.FR. 1286-1289;
                                         pacifying the Friar)

(30)   "*Awake,* thou Cook," *quod he,* "God yeve thee sorwe!
         What eyleth* thee *to slepe by the morwe?
         Has*tow *had fleen al nyght, or ar*tow *dronke? ..."*
                                        (H.MC. 15-17;
                                 low-class addressee, reproach)

(31) *"But yet,* Manciple, *in feith* thou art *to nyce,*
Thus openly repreve hym of his vice.
Another day he wole, peraventure,
Reclayme thee *and brynge* thee *to lure; ..."*
(H.MC. 69-72;
rather low-class addressee, advice)

(32) *"What,* Frankeleyn*! Pardee,* sire, *wel* thou *woo*st
That ech of yow moot tellen atte leste
A tale or two, or breken his biheste".
"That knowe I wel, sire*", quod the Frankeleyn.*
I prey yow, *hav*eth *me nat in desdeyn,*
Though to this man I speke a word or two."
"Telle on thy *tale withouten wordes mo".*
"Gladly, sire Hoost*", quod he "I wole obeye*
Unto youre *wyl; now herkneth what I seye"*
(F.SQ. 696-704)

Notice the fact that address is asymmetric in the last example, with clear imposition of authority on the part of the Host, in spite of the fact that the Franklin, as an ancestor of the country squire, so to speak, is certainly not low class. By contrast, the Host addresses the Prioress (who is a woman, belongs to a religious order and is also very elegant and ostentatiously "polite" in manners) in a very deferential way, so unlike his usual behaviour that the author feels the need to highlight the Host's attitude with a descriptive phrase:

(33) *... and with that word he sayde,*
As curteisly as it had been a mayde,
"My lady Prioresse, *by* youre *leve,*
So that I wiste I sholde yow *nat greve,*
I wolde demen that ye *tellen sholde*
A tale next, if so were that ye *wolde.*
Now wol ye *vouche sauf,* my lady deere*?"*
(B2.SH. 445-451)

In this context, the use of terms of address can be mentioned in a somewhat more systematic way. It will be clear from the examples given so far that such terms are often used in the *Canterbury Tales*; the "rules" behind such uses, however, are not always easy to understand. Only two statements can be made at this point: first, that here, as in the use of pronouns, the pragmatic element of the situation seems as important as the social status of the addressee, and second, that correlations between pronoun use and terms of address can often be traced, but must not be taken as fixed and regular, because there are several counterexamples (Blake 1992: 537).

The main terms of address used from inferiors to superiors, for instance, are *sire, lord, lady, dame*, and *madame* (of the last two, the latter is more respectful and used particularly in courtly romance to address the "lady", cf. Blake (1992: 539); the fact that the former is in any case a term that indicates status and respect is suggested by the meta-comment at A.RV. 3956: "*Ther dorste no wight clepen hire but 'dame'.*").

The term *sire* is on the verge of being generalised to all strangers, for reasons of politeness, but in the *Canterbury Tales* it still retains some of its old meaning, in fact it is used as a term of respect, even for kings and other noblemen, and from wife to husband. It can be used, however, also in insults, probably to emphasise social distance, especially when used in combination with a "category name", indicating the occupation or status of the addressee, or in ironic utterances (see some examples above, among the Host's uses). The term occurs mainly with Y (95 cases against 23 T and 9 cases in which there is no pronoun), and this also indicates that it is mainly a term of respect as yet, a polite term (cf. for instance its use between Chanticleer and the Fox at B2.NP.3284ff., 3407). The highest term, however, is *lord*, used to address kings and gods (and thus with T), but also, especially in combination with a possessive, *my lord*, as a term of respect to address superiors (again including husbands), and thus with Y in 40 cases, against 8 with T and 4 with no pronoun.

As for women, who, as mentioned, generally receive more politeness, *lady* is a term of high respect (also used for the Madonna) and occurs with Y in 22 cases, with T in 7. The latter are all cases where divinity is involved, or the addressing of one's wife: in this sense, this term correlates differently from *lord*, because of the difference in status between husband and wife that will be mentioned later. *Dame* occurs with T in only one case out of 22, while *madame* appears in 15 cases, always with Y.

At this stage, *maister* is also partly a term of respect: it is used e.g. from boys and servants to adults at C.PD. 680, from the Host to the Physician at C.PD. 301, and from various characters to friars, e.g. at D.SM. 1781, 1800, 2184. It correlates mainly with Y (8 examples vs. 2; see fn. 9). *Fre(e)nd* is used rarely, and mostly with T, predictably correlating the more intimate relationship with the more intimate pronoun (e.g. see D.FR. 1363, C.PD. 832). Another term that is used in a similar way is *brother*, which also appears mainly in combination with T forms (see fn. 6; cf. D.FR.1395ff., 1474ff.; E.MC.1491, 1521; F.FR.1607ff.).

Addresses by first name fall into two categories: they can occur in intimate relationship between not very "high" characters, and in invocations to gods and external entities (often in the form "O + name". In both these cases, though for different reasons, there is strong predominance of uses of T (106 cases vs. 29 Y and 3 with no pronoun). For some comments on the strategic use of Christian names in specific exchanges see section 5.2.

T forms also prevail in the use of "category names" as terms of address, i.e. terms such as *Cook*, *Squier*, *Somonour*, *Messager*, *Juge*, *Preest*, etc. It must be noted that these uses are often connected to contexts of insult or of invocation, and these are both contexts in which we expect a predominance of T.

T is almost exclusively used, again predictably, with terms of address that are used as insults, such as *false traitour* (A.RV. 4268), *olde dotard* (D.WB. 331), *false theef* (D.WB. 800), *unsely wrecche* (G.SN. 468), *olde stot* (D.FR. 1630), etc. T prevails with terms of endearment, too, but not so overwhelmingly, because of the link between these uses and the courting/love relations. Thus, cf. with Y, *myn hertes queene* (A.KN. 2775), *sweete* (F.FR. 978), *O tendre creature* (E.MC. 1757) vs. *my sweete leef* (A.MI. 3729), *my dowve sweete* (E.MC. 2139) with T.

5. Some specific examples of strategic pronoun use and switching

5.1. The battle of the sexes

It should be recalled that the addressing of women, especially in the context of courting, emerges as a rather special case of addressing. Of course, pronoun use between husband and wife is even more complicated and richer in switches, which, however, appear nearly always clearly motivated by pragmatic reasons.

Notice that here the "conventional" use for spouses addressing each other mirrors that of the lovers. In agreement with the Medieval ideological outlook, it is now the woman who is in an inferior position, and thus uses Y in addressing her husband, who often replies with T, to emphasise the asymmetry of the relationship and to take on a patronising attitude. In this kind of convention we can see a reflex of the "double status" of women in the Middle Ages: revered as the "ladies" of courtly love, but considered inferior within marriage (Kerkhof 1966: 137; Finkenstaedt 1963: 86). In the *Canterbury Tales*, Y is predominant in wife-to-husband addressing, and the high amount of switching that the total figures reveal is mainly due to the particular dynamics of the dialogue between Melibee and his wife Prudence, more about which will be said later. In wife-to-husband, as well as in husband-to-wife exchanges, what triggers the use of T is mainly the expression of insult or of affection, and even husband-to-wife exchanges include a fair number of switches, mostly connected to the different "moods" expressed, or to a precise desire to overthrow this status scale (i.e. to "elevate" the wife or "debase" the husband), for specific pragmatic aims.

(34) "... *I am* thy *trewe, verray wedded wyf;*
 Go, deere spouse, *and help to save oure lyf."*
(A.MI. 3609-3610)

(35)   "Sire olde kaynard, *is this* thyn *array?* ..."
                              (D.WB. 235ff.)

(36)   *Thou sholdest seye:* "Wyf, *go wher* thee *liste;*
         Taak **youre** *disport; I wol nat leve not talys,*
         I knowe yow *for a trewe wyf,* dame Alys."
                              (D.WB. 318-320;
         imaginary dialogue; the switch expresses respect, cf.
         the address forms)

(37)   *Thanne wolde I seye,* "Goode lief, taak keep
         How mekely looketh Wilkyn, oure sheep!
         Com neer, my spouse, *lat me ba* thy *cheke!*
         Ye *sholde been al pacient and meke,*
         And han a sweete spiced conscience,
         Sith ye *so preche of Jobes pacience* ...".
                              (D.WB. 431-436;
                coaxing, humility, respect + intimacy)

(38)   "*Rys up,* my wyf, my love, my lady free!
         ...
         ...
         Com forth now, with **thyne** *eyen columbyn!*
         How fairer been thy *brestes than is wyn!*"
                              (E.MC. 2138-2142)

(39)   ... "*I* yow *forbede, up peyne of deeth,*
         That nevere, whil **thee** *lasteth lyf ne breeth,*
         To no wight telle thou *of this aventure* –
         As I may best, I wol my wo endure –
         Ne make no contenance of hevynesse,
         That folk of **yow** *may demen harm or gesse.*"
                              (F.FR. 1481-1486;
                switch to T = ordering, commanding?)

A partially different case is the dialogue in the following examples, where a social dimension is added: Grisilde addresses her husband invariably with Y, but he switches at points when he wants to stress the social inferiority and alleged "undesirability" of his wife: pronoun switches here seem part of a strategy of humiliating the interlocutor, which the husband pursues intentionally to test his wife's powers of endurance, and only the last switch corresponds to an expression of affection.[7]

(40)   "Grisilde", he seyde, "ye shal wel understonde
It liketh to youre fader and to me
That I yow wedde, and eek it may so stonde,
As I suppose, ye wol that it so be."
(E.CL. 344-347)

(41)   "Ye woot youreself wel how that ye cam heere
Into this hous, it is nat longe ago;
And though to me that ye be lief and deere,
Unto my gentils ye be no thyng so.
They seyn, to hem it is greet shame and wo
For to be subgetz and been in servage
To **thee**, that born art of a smal village.
And namely sith thy doghter was ybore ..."
(E.CL. 477-484)

(42)   "And yet, God woot, this is ful looth to me;
But nathelees withoute **youre** wityng
I wol nat doon; ..."
(E.CL. 491-493)

(43)   "The smok," quod he, "that **thou** hast on thy bak,
Lat it be stille, and bere it forth with thee"
(E.CL. 890-891)

(44)   "I have no wommen suffisaunt, certayn,
The chambres for t'arraye in ordinaunce

> *After my lust, and therfore wolde I fayn*
> *That* thyn *were al swich manere governaunce.*
> Thou knowest *eek of old al my plesaunce;* ...
>
> (E.CL. 960-964)

(45)   "*This is ynogh,* Grisilde myn, " *quod he;*
       "*Be now namoore agast ne yvele apayed.*
       I have thy *feith and* thy *benygnytee,* ...
                                    (E.CL. 1051-1053)

The specificity of the Melibee–Prudence dialogue lies in several circumstances: it is the only case in which the whole tale is based on dialogue, it is in prose and it is based more on the genre-based conventions of "philosophical" dialogues than on an attempt at the rendering of an actual conversation within a family. The pronoun uses by Melibee to his wife are quite readily explainable (and are not "incorrect uses" as in the hypothesis taken up by Finkenstaedt (1963: 75-76)), as they range from the indication of intimacy to the more respectful forms that seem triggered by a recognition of Prudence's "wisdom" and somehow of her authority, and also tend to signal submission to her better judgement.

(46)   *To thise forseide thynges answerde Melibeus unto his wyf Prudence: "alle* thy *wordes ... been sothe ...*
                                    (B2.ME. 1001ff.)

(47)   *This Melibee answerde unto his wyf Prudence: "I purpose nat ... to werke by* thy *conseil, ...*
                                    (B2.ME. 1055)

(48)   "*... And,* wyf*, by cause of* thy *sweete wordes, and eek for I have assayed and preved* thy *grete sapience and* thy *grete trouthe, I wol governe me by* thy *conseil in alle thyng."*
                                    (B2.ME. 1114)

(49)   "*I graunte wel that I have erred; / but there as* thou ha*st toold me heerbiforn that ...*"
(B2.ME. 1262)

as against

(50)   "**Dame**," *quod he*, "*as yet into this tyme* **ye** *han wel and covenably taught me .../ But now wolde I fayn that* ye *wolde condescende in especial / and telle me how liketh* yow, *or what semeth* yow, ...
(B2.ME. 1233-1235)

(51)   "*Certes," quod Melibee, "I se wel that* **ye** *enforce* yow *muchel by wordes to overcome me ...*
(B2.ME. 1427).

Prudence's own uses to her husband are considerably more complicated, since over 35 switches occur in her speech. Some of these can be explained as due to discourse "genre" rather than discourse strategies; assuming Y as the "unmarked" form,[8] there are several switches to T that can be explained by looking at the immediate co-text: the majority of them are in clauses where the verb *shal* is used (although the more tentative *shul* does not seem to have the same influence; it would be interesting to know whether a similar cline of "strength of obligation" could be established for the tale's language between *shal* : *shul* as in Modern English for *must* : *should*), or immediately following a maxim or other kind of "advising" discourse emanating from an external authority.

In this context, it must be mentioned that the "generic" address of maxims, proverbs, general statements and other similar speech formulae, nowadays expressed by *you* or by *one*, is operated invariably by T forms, unless the addressing is clearly in the plural (Kerkhof 1966: 139), and this holds both for maxims and proverbs quoted by characters and for the generic address forms used by narrators within their speech:

156   *Gabriella Mazzon*

(52)   *Touchynge swich thyng, lo, what the wise seith:*
"Withinne thyn *hous ne be thou no leon;*
To thy *subgitz do noon oppression, ... "*
(D.SM. 1988-1990)

(53)   *And therfore seith Seint Augustyn: "If* thou *hast desdayn of* thy *servant, if he agilte or synne, have* thou *thanne desdayn that* thou thyself *sholdest do no synne."*
(I.PS. 150)

(54)   *First in the temple of Venus may*stow *se Wroght on the wal, ful pitous to biholde, ...*
(A.KN. 1918-1919)

(55)   *To axen help* thee *shameth in* thyn *hert; If* thou *noon aske, with nede ar*tow *so woundid That verray nede unwrappeth al* thy *wounde hid!*
(B.ML. 101-103)

It is therefore not surprising to find switches to T in Prudence's speech triggered by such uses (not necessarily explicitly reported as quotations and not necessarily themselves containing pronoun forms, since, as mentioned, it is rather the attitude and general discourse mode of these quotations that trigger Prudence's uses), as in the following examples.

(56)   *"And therfore* yow *is bettre to hyde* youre *conseil in* youre *herte than to praye hym to whom* ye *han biwreyed* youre *conseil that he wole kepen it cloos and stille.*
For Seneca seith: 'If so be that thou *ne may*st *nat* thyn *owene conseil hyde, how dar*stou *prayen any oother wight* thy *conseil secrely to kepe?'*
But nathelees, if **thou** *wene sikerly that the biwreiyng of* thy *conseil to ... ".*

(B2.ME. 1146-1148ff.; in the first line, note *yow* in subject position, though still complement in function, with an impersonal expression)

(57) *"Wherfore Tullius seith, 'Amonges alle the pestilences that been in freendshipe the gretteste is flaterie'. And therfore it is moore nede that* **thou** *eschue and drede flatereres than any oother peple."*
(B2.ME. 1176ff.)

(58) *"... First shul* ye *clepen to* youre *conseil a fewe of* youre *freendes that been especiale; /*
for Salomon seith, 'Manye freendes have thou, *but among a thousand chese* thee *oon to be* thy *conseillour'. /*
For al it be so that **thou** *first ne telle* thy *conseil but to a fewe,* thou *may*st *afterward ..."*
(B2.ME. 1166-1168)

(59) *"...* **Ye** *shul also han in suspect the conseillying of swich folk as conseille* yow *o thyng prively and conseille* yow *the contrarie openly. /*
For Cassidorie seith that 'it is a manere sleighte to hyndre, whan he sheweth to doon o thyng openly and werketh prively the contrarie? /
Thou sha*lt also have in suspect the conseillying of ..."*
(B2.ME. 1195-1197)

(60) *"And Senec seith, 'If* thy *conseil is comen to the eeris of* thyn *enemy, chaunge* thy *conseil'. /*
Thou *mayst also chaunge* thy *conseil ..."*
(B2.ME. 1226-1227)

(61) *"Thanne shul* ye *eveeremoore contrewayte embusshementz* ... /
for Senek seith that 'the wise man that ...'/
.../
And al it be so that it seme that **thou** art in siker place, yet shaltow alwey do thy diligence ..."
(B2.ME. 1319-1322)

The co-occurrence of T forms with *shal* also fits with this explanation, since in these cases the speaker often takes on a similar role of "mentor" (the strong overtone of authority that seems involved in the use of *shal* is still present in its use in religious commandments).

(62) "... **Thou** <u>shalt</u> eek eschue the conseillyng of alle flatereres, swiche as enforcen hem rather to preise **youre** persone by flaterye than for to telle yow the soothfastnesse of thynges."
(B2.ME. 1175)

(63) "Now, sire, sith I have shewed **yow** of which folk ye <u>shul</u> take ... /
..., now wol I teche yow how ye <u>shal</u> examyne ... /
In the examynynge thanne of youre conseillour ye <u>shul</u> considere manye thynges. /
Alderfirst **thou** <u>shalt</u> considere that ..."
(B2.ME. 1200-1203)

(64) "And whan **ye** han examyned youre conseil, ... /
thanne <u>shal</u>**tou** considere if thou mayst ..."
(B2.ME. 1211-1212)

In other cases, especially when she wants to appear humble and not to seem to impose on her husband (to overcome his resistance at the notion of being advised by a woman), Prudence uses Y:

(65) "*Allas,* my lord," *quod she,* "*why make* ye youreself *for to be lyk a fool? ...*"
(B2.ME. 980ff.)

(66) "*My lord, ... I* **yow** *biseche, as hertely as I dar and kan, ne haste* yow *nat to faste ...*"
(B2.ME. 1052)

(67) "*My lord, ... as to* youre *firste resoun, certes ...*"
(B2.ME. 1065ff.)

(68) "*My lord,*" *quod she,* "*I biseke* **yow** *in al humblesse that* ye *wol nat wilfully replie agayn my resouns, ne distempre* youre *herte, thogh I ...*"
(B2.ME. 1236ff.)

Y forms often seem to re-appear also when there is a "recapitulative" function of the utterance, after e.g. a stretch of "didactic" discourse, as if to resume "normal" socio-pragmatic roles at turning-points in the dialogue, or to paraphrase maxims and "commandments" or strong advice, re-clothing them with more respectful forms in the process.

(69) "*Now, sith that I have toold* **yow** *of which folk* ye *sholde been counseilled, now wol I teche* yow *which conseil* ye *oghte to eschewe.*"
(B2.ME. 1172)

(70) "*And whan* **ye** *han examyned* youre *conseil, ... / thanne* <u>shal</u>**tou** *considere if* thou *mayst ...*"
(B2.ME.1211-1212)

(71) "*Now, as to the seconde point, where as* **youre** *wise conseillours conseilled* yow *to ...*"
(B2.ME. 1331ff.)

(72) "But now lat us speken of the conseil that was accorded by **youre** neighebores, ..."
(B2.ME. 1349ff.)

(73) "... and of hem <u>shal</u>t thou *aske* thy *conseil, as the case requireth.* /
I *seye that first* **ye** *shul clepe to* youre *conseil* youre *freendes that been trewe.*"
(B2.ME. 1156-1157)

(74) "... *but that* yow *oghte purveyen and apparaillen* yow *in this caas with greet diligence* ... /
.../
For Tullius seith, 'In every nede, er thou bigynne it, apparaille thee with greet diligence'. /
Thanne seye I that in vengeance-takyng, ... /
er **thou** *bigynne, I rede that* thou *appareille* thee *therto, and do it with greet deliberacion.*"
(B2.ME. 1342-1346)

(75) "... *the same Senek seith, 'the moore cleer and the moore shynyng that Fortune is, the moore brotil and the sonner broken she ir'.* /
Truste*th nat in hire, for she nys nat stidefast ne stable,* /
for whan **thow** *trow*est *to be moost seur or siker of hire help, she wol faille* thee *and deceyve* thee. /
And where as **ye** seyn that Fortune hath norissed yow fro youre childhede, ..."
(B2.ME. 1450-1453)

5.2. Strategic pronoun switching in face-work

We hope to have shown that pronoun use is manipulated in quite subtle ways according to precise discourse strategies, or responding to specific discourse modes.

One of the most important reasons for pronoun switching in Shakespeare was found to be connected with face-work, i.e. with the single speech-acts and their functions in specific stretches of dialogue where the status of some participants is unstable. Coaxing, promising, threatening, accusing are all possible loci for pronoun switching as additional marking of the attitude expressed.

Similar phenomena were found in the *Canterbury Tales*, several centuries earlier, suggesting that this strategic use of pronoun switching is not confined to the late stages of vitality of the T forms, when they represented more marked choices.

Our first set of examples of these uses is drawn from the *Summoner's Tale*. The dialogue between the friar and Thomas reported in this tale contains a number of pronoun switches, and it is particularly interesting because it represents an example of strategic behaviour, with coaxing, threatening, promising etc. The initial greetings employ formal pronouns on both sides, except for the phrase *thy savacion*, which may indicate a patronising attitude in the religious context:

(76)   "O Thomas, freend, *good day!"*
Seyde this free, curteisly and softe.
"Thomas, " *quod he,* "God yelde yow! Ful ofte
Have I upon this bench faren ful weel;*
...
"O deere maister, " *quod this sike man,*
"How han ye *fare sith that March bigan?*
...
"God woot," *quod he,* "laboured I have ful soore,
And specially for **thy** savacion
Have I seyd many a precious orison,*
...

I have to day been at youre *chirche at messe, ..."*
(D.SM. 1770-1788)

After this exchange, the friar enters into conversation with Thomas' wife, and here there is consistent use of Y, in agreement with what was said above about addressing women, and then launches into a stretch of preaching, whose persuasive and patronising tone comes out especially when he again addresses Thomas directly; the frequent use of the first name can be taken as a hint to this descending from the general to the particular, and is often found in correspondence with switches to T forms, as if to indicate a stressing of intimacy or, again, of patronising, at the expenses of his interlocutor who goes on addressing him with Y forms and *maister*.[9] Cf. the following:

(77)   "Thomas, Thomas! *So moote I ryde or go,*
         And by that lord that clepid is Seint Yve,
         Nere thou *oure brother, sholde*stou *nat thryve."*
(D.SM. 1942-1944)

This is followed by a protest by Thomas, claiming that he has been paying a lot of money to various religious orders but has not found that his lot has improved very much for it. Now the friar scolds him and also switches to Y as a form of distancing, to show how offended he is at Thomas's placing alms with other friars:

(78)   ... "O Thomas, *dos*tow *so?*
         What nedeth **yow** *diverse freres seche?*
         What nedeth hym that hath a parfit leche
         To sechen othere leches in the toun?
         Youre *inconstance is* youre *confusioun.*
         Holde ye *thanne me, or elles oure covent,*
         To praye for yow *been insufficient?"*
(D.SM. 1954-1960)

The switches between the "intimate-patronising" and the "distant-offended" modes continue in the friar's tirade aimed at obtaining the whole of Thomas's alms.

(79)   "Thomas, *of me* **thou** *shalt nat been yflatered;*
        Thou *wolde*st *han oure labour al for noght.*
        ...
        Thomas, *noght of* **youre** *tresor I desire*
        As for myself, but that al oure covent
        To preye for yow *is ay so diligent,*
        ...
        And therfore, Thomas, *trowe me if* **thee** *leste,*
        Ne stryve nat with thy *wyf, as for* thy *beste;*
        And ber this word awey now, by thy *feith;"*
                                    (D.SM. 1970-1987)

Another case of this kind of strategic switching can be found in the *Canon's Yeoman's Tale* (G.CY), where the exchanges between the canon and the priest, i.e. the swindler and his victim, lend themselves to a similar analysis in term of "face-work". The priest always uses Y, but the canon switches pronouns according to the kind of speech act he is performing or according to discoursal tone or intention. The first exchange is a request for a loan, performed with great protestations of honesty and using T forms to stress intimacy:

(80)   *"Leene me a marc,"* quod he, *"but dayes three,*
        And at my day I wol it quiten thee.
        And if so be that thow *me fynde fals,*
        Another day do hange me by the hals!"
                                    (G.CY. 1026-1029)

In the next exchange, the canon is still protesting his honesty and at the same time laying his trap, and he switches to more polite Y forms, and to the term *sire*, reciprocated by the priest:

(81)   *"Bileve*th *this as siker as* **youre** *Crede.*

...
And sire", *quod he,* "*now of my pryvetee,*
Syn ye *so goodlich han been unto me,*
And kithed to me so greet gentillesse,
Somwhat to quyte with youre *kyndenesse*
I wol yow *shewe, and if* yow *list to leere,*
I wol yow *teche pleynly the manere*
How I kan werken in philosophie."

(G.CY. 1047-1058)

The priest is easily trapped, and in the scene in which the two characters set about their alchemical activities there are also a number of switches; Y forms seem to be used for distancing, and in one case for reproach, T forms for intimacy, as if to stress the fact that the two are together in this secret and in the whole enterprise, which is of course the opposite of what is actually happening, but is perfectly plausible as a strategy to avoid attracting any suspicions. Some examples follow:

(82) *"This instrument," quod he, "which that* **thou** *seest,*
Taak in thyn *hand, and put* thyself *therinne*
Of this quycksilver an ounce, and heer bigynne,
In name of Crist, to wexe a philosofre.
...
For **ye** *shul seen heer, by experience,*
that this quyksilver I wol mortifye
Right in youre *sighte anon, withouten lye,*
And make it as good silver and as fyn
As ther is any in youre *purs or myn, ..."*

(G.CY. 1119-1129)

(83) ... *"for in tokenyng I* **thee** *love,"*
*Quod this chanoun, "*thyne *owene handes two*
Shul werche al thyng which that shal heer be do."

(G.CY. 1153-1155)

(84)   *This chanoun seyde, "*Freend, **ye** *doon amys.*
         That is nat couched as it oghte be;
         but soone I shal amended it ..."
                                            (G.CY. 1181-1183)

(85)   *And in the water-vessel he it caste,*
         Whan that hym luste, and bad the preest as faste,
         "Loke what ther is; put in **thyn** *hand and grope.*
         Thow fynde shalt ther silver, as I hope."
                                            (G.CY. 1234-1237)

(86)   ... *"Yet wol I make assay*
         The seconde tyme, that **ye** *may taken heede*
         And been expert of this, and in youre *neede*
         Another day assaye in myn absence ..."
                                            (G.CY.1249-1252)

There are of course other examples (see e.g. the progression that leads the accused to become the accuser in the dialogue between Cecily and the judge at G.SN. 428-463), but we hope to have shown that there is a clear correlation between discourse strategies and pronoun use and switching. Further studies of this kind are of course necessary, especially as regards medieval plays, but it seems clear that the choice between T and Y forms is certainly not connected only to the social relationship between the interlocutors, nor to the state of mind of a character or to the affective overtones of an utterance: it is also a perfectly viable additional politeness strategy, exactly as it was shown to be in Shakespeare's works, and it should be studied in further depth from this perspective.

Notes

1. Note that Finkenstaedt (1963: 81-82) reports exclusive use of T in addressing characters who are dead or asleep or absent, as well as in self-addressing, in

Troilus and Criseyde; he even feels the need to try and explain the only two exceptions to this in that work. Not so in the *Canterbury Tales*, where only one case out of five of addressing somebody absent involves use of T, while for imaginary or reported dialogue there are 28 T against 7 Y. Especially in imaginary husband-wife dialogues (e.g. at D.WB. 369, 433-434), there are frequent switches in pronoun uses, which suggests the primacy of the intention of discourse and of pragmatic orientation over the "non-reality" of the exchange. Conversely, results for the *Canterbury Tales* agree with Finkenstaedt's claim (1963: 83) that there is a generalised tendency to use Y when addressing a "lady". The rules of courtly behaviour, that is, seem stronger than the exceptionality of the situation, which is not a face-to-face encounter. Cf. A.MI. 3698-3701.

2. See for instance the invocations to "crueel firmament" (B.ML. 295); "O fieble moone" (B.ML. 305); "thou water" (D.WB. 974); "O sodeyn hap! O thou Fortune unstable!" (E.MC. 2057); "Fortune" (F.FR. 1355); "O glotonye" (C.PD. 512), which are all with T. On the other hand, "(Leeve) mooder", used to address the earth at C.PD. 731 and 734, is accompanied by use of Y.

3. E.g. at B.ML. 71, 72, 358-362, 445-446; E.MC. 1869; F.FR.1090; B2.NP. 3226-3229. The addressing of ancient heroes or other famous characters is invariably with T: cf. e.g. "O noble Sampsoun" (B2.MK. 2075); "O noble, O worthy Petro, glorrie of Spayne" (B2.MK. 2375); "O myghty Cesar" (B2.MK. 2679); "Lucan" (B2.MK. 2719); "O Golias" (B.ML. 934); "thou poete Marcian" (E.MC. 1732).

4. The edition of the text which was used is *The Riverside Chaucer* (Benson (ed.) 1988); abbreviated references to single tales follow those used in Oizumi (1991).

5. Kerkhof (1966: 138-139) reports this difference in address between Christian and pagan gods, as well as the alternations within such addresses, but offers no explanation for either phenomenon.

6. Note that the kin-term *suster*, used here in an extended, non-literal meaning, does not imply the choice of the intimate pronoun, as its correspondent masculine term *brother* does most of the time, both in the addressing of "real" brothers and in the more common use as term indicating intimacy, equal status etc. (overall about 20 T vs. 7 Y).

7. We cannot therefore agree with Kerkhof (1966: 137-138; my italics) that "in the beginning of the tale he [the husband] also uses *ye*, until he reveals his plan to kill her daughter, when *thou* and *ye* are found without any obvious difference in attitude".

8. Inverted commas are a must when mentioning such terms in the context of these analyses, it being far from clear what can really be considered unmarked even within the restricted scope of a single document. The term is used here only with reference to what seems to emerge from the text: wife-to-husband

uses of Y are more numerous and seem to apply to a wider range of contexts; for husband-to-wife addressing, T is more frequent, although the social discriminant seems to have a more important role here: noblemen and other "U"-characters are much more likely to use Y.
9. This term is most often found alone, though it can occur also with a first name or with an adjective like *deere* and/or a possessive. It is not used by "upper-class" characters but only by middle- to low-class to address a superior (not necessarily literally, e.g. by an apprentice) or as a polite form.

References

Benson, Larry D. (ed.)
    1988   *The Riverside Chaucer* (based on the edition of Chaucer's works by F. N. Robinson). Oxford: Oxford University Press.
Blake, Norman F.
    1992   The literary language. In: Norman F. Blake (ed.), 500-541.
Blake, Norman F. (ed.)
    1992   *The Cambridge history of the English language*, Volume 2. *1066-1476*. Cambridge: Cambridge University Press.
Finkenstaedt, Thomas
    1963   *You und Thou: Studien zur Anrede in Englischen (mit einem Exkurs über die Anrede im Deutschen)*. Berlin: de Gruyter.
Kerkhof, Jelle
    1966   *Studies in the language of Geoffrey Chaucer*. Leiden: Universitaire Pers Leiden.
Mazzon, Gabriella
    1994   Shakespearean *thou* and *you* revisited, or socio-affective networks on stage. In: Carmela Nocera Avila, Nicola Pantaleo, and Domenico Pezzini (eds.), 123-136.
    1995   Pronouns and terms of address in Shakespearean English: a socio-affective marking system in transition. *Views* 4: 20-42.
Nocera Avila, Carmela, Nicola Pantaleo, and Domenico Pezzini (eds.)
    1994   *Early Modern English: trends, forms and texts*. Bari: Schena.

Oizumi, Akio
    1991   *A complete concordance to the works of Geoffrey Chaucer*, Volume 2. Hildesheim: Olms-Weidmann.

Strang, Barbara M. H.
    1970   *A history of English*. London: Methuen.

Covert and overt language attitudes to the Scots tongue expressed in the *Statistical accounts of Scotland*

Robert McColl Millar (with the assistance of Dauvit Horsbroch)

1. Introduction

Attitudes to language condition what varieties of language we use and in what social contexts. In the case of lesser-used languages, these language attitudes often underlie language shift or even language death. Problems of this type are particularly acute when two closely related languages – such as English and Scots – are also in day-to-day, but socially unequal, contact and competition.

It is regrettable, therefore, that Scots is not better served when it comes to the discussion of the attitudes which must underlie its decline in status (Aitken 1979). Whilst there is some evidence, particularly from the eighteenth century, of negative language attitudes to Scots (Jones 1995), these derive largely from the major metropolitan centres. There is very little information about developments at "grass roots" level. There is one exception to this general tendency, one which has been generally disregarded by most commentators on these matters with the exception of a brief mention in an essay by Aitken (1990) – the returns to the *Statistical accounts of Scotland*. This essay will provide a more in-depth description and analysis of the language attitudes found in these three *Accounts*, published in the 1790s (SA1), the 1830s/1840s (SA2) and from the 1940s on (SA3).

The First *Statistical Account* (SA1) stems from the great interest from the mid-eighteenth century on in codification and enumeration which led to the development of the new sciences of statistics and economics: developments in which Scotland took a considerable part. The survey was instigated by Sir John Sinclair of Ulbster, Caithness (1754-1835), a man of affairs and MP as well as someone with a wide – if not necessarily deep – interest in a variety of issues (Mitchison 1962). The proceeds from these volumes (and indeed those of SA2 and SA3) were to go towards the upkeep of the widows and offspring of Church of Scotland ministers. Each parish was supposed to supply a report, based upon guidelines set down by Sir John, and indeed this was – with some arm-twisting – eventually achieved. Most of the reports were written by the parish minister or his assistant, although for a variety of reasons the task was occasionally written by the village schoolmaster or by "gentlemen" of some description or another.

Sir John had a largely statistical interest – thus reflecting his position as an "improver", someone who favoured the development of new industries and the redevelopment of old ones – an interest shared by many in "Enlightenment" Scotland. Nevertheless, as a man of his time, he was also interested in issues of culture and change which make the *Accounts* unique records of each of the Church of Scotland parishes in the kingdom at a time when the old peasant system of agriculture – the *runrig* – was being replaced by new, Capitalist, farming techniques. At the same time, the Industrial Revolution was in its initial phase, with its concomitant social problems, and urban (to a lesser extent rural) radicals in Scotland were learning lessons from political developments in America and particularly France – not something much to the taste of most ministers.

Unfortunately for our purposes, there was some confusion in Sinclair's instructions for the correspondents on the subject of language – despite the fact that he himself had published a book entitled *Observations on the Scottish dialect* (Mitchison 1962: 37) – so that many of them did not say anything on these matters. Sufficient did, however, to make a tradition of commenting on language relatively strong in both SA2 and SA3.

Both the *New statistical account* (SA2) and the *Third statistical account* (SA3) also stem from times of considerable interest to the social historian. At the time of SA2, revolutionary ideas – such as Chartism and early varieties of Socialism – were beginning to spread in the now heavily industrialised portions of Scotland, and at the same time the Church of Scotland was in ferment which ended in the "Great Disruption" of 1843, when more than half of the delegates walked out of the General Assembly to set up the Church of Scotland – Free. SA3 was largely written in the post-war period under a – relatively – radical Labour administration. Most of the correspondents to the *Accounts* look somewhat askance on many of these developments.

It will be the contention of this essay that many of these socio-historical developments and processes encouraged the language attitudes that will be analysed, and that discussion of the Scots tongue in the *Accounts* was by no means free of ideology.

2. Limitations of survey

There are a number of limitations to this survey. As has already been mentioned, the instructions originally given to the correspondents by Sinclair were a little ambiguous when it comes to language. Unfortunately, the earliest returns of reports – those written by those most keen to take part in the project – were also those which had not been asked about language use.

By the same token, the data is skewed considerably by the interests and obsessions of the ministers who replied. Whilst some might have had an interest in folk-life and culture, this need not always be the case. It is also true – particularly with SA1 – that the later a correspondent returned his report, the more perfunctory it was. Since *Language* was placed low down on Sinclair's list of topics for consideration, it could often be tacitly ignored. Further, in certain parts of Scotland, Church of Scotland ministers were not in regular contact with large portions of their ostensible parishioners because of the unusually high level of dissent, even before the Disruption. What comments they make may therefore not be representative.

Finally, all of the ministers and other correspondents might not be being entirely truthful in their reports. A certain degree of wishful thinking is encountered. For instance, in SA3, for my home parish, the minister, Mr Ramsay, writes:

(1) *The Unionist* [the name given in Scotland to the Conservative Party] *Association, a thriving local body, owes an allegiance beyond the bounds of the village ...*

(Renfrew SA3: Elderslie)

This comment is made despite (or perhaps because of) the fact that Elderslie has been either Labour or Nationalist in orientation since before the First World War.

3. Overt language attitudes

3.1. Language "mixing"

At first glance, the chief index of attitudes to language in the *Statistical accounts* is where direct reference to the language used in that locale is made – overt language attitudes. Sometimes this can be as simple as saying "x is spoken here". More interesting, however, is where correspondents elaborate on this type of bold statement in a variety of ways.

The first, and most perplexing, of these is the relatively common recording of a "mixture" of spoken language varieties. The most obvious of these is an implied mixture of Scots and Standard English. That this mixture might have something to do with the class-influenced choice of language developing at least since the Union of the Parliaments in 1707 (Aitken 1979) can be seen in the following:

(2) *Among the higher and better educated classes, the English language may be heard spoken in tolerable purity, both as to idiom and pronunciation. There are few who cannot express themselves in English, still fewer who do not familiarly understand it when distinctly spoken. Unmixed Scots is never to be heard. The most common dialect is a mixture of Scotch and English, the Scotch used being of the somewhat vicious kind, known, I believe, by the name of the Aberdeenshire. The Scotch, however, is gradually wearing out. Every person remembers the frequent use, in former years, of terms and phrases that are now seldom heard but among the older and more secluded. Even, however, in what is called, by courtesy, speaking English or using English words, there is often a sore lack of the genuine English pronunciation. ... Even in the matter of pronunciation, however, there is a great and progressive improvement.*

(Banff SA1: Banff)

Many of the opinions expressed here appear intrinsically connected to the "improvements" already discussed: the "mixture" reported is to be seen as part of an on-going process of "purification" in the direction of Standard English. Something similar can be seen in the following:

(3) *The language spoken here is neither English nor Scottish, but a mixture of both. With the exception of a few parochial words and phrases, the inhabitants speak with more propriety than those of the same station in most parts of Scotland.*

(Kirkcudbright SA1: Crossmichael)

Again "propriety" – a very eighteenth-century idea – is intrinsically connected to the move closer to Standard English. Other correspondents add comments on social developments within their parishes:

(4) *The language generally spoken is a mixture of Scotch and English. The use of the Scotch has decreased within the last forty years, in consequence, I apprehend, of the improvement in teaching at the schools. But when persons are under excitement, the language used is Scotch. Then, the writer has observed, here and in other parts of Scotland, that the lower orders of society, and many in the middling ranks, too, discover an acquaintance with that expressive dialect, which could not be inferred from their ordinary conversation.*

(Lanark SA2: Dalziel)

An ambivalence about the presumed change can be remarked here, perhaps because it derives from SA2, not SA1. There are a number of reports that are even less sanguine about the development in question:

(5) *The language generally spoken is a corrupt Scotch, with a barbarous admixture of English. A few only of the oldest of the people speak the Scottish dialect in its purity. These, however, are rapidly disappearing, and in a few years more in all probability there will not be one person alive who could have held converse with his grandfather without the aid of a dictionary.*

(Peebles SA2: Eddlestone)

What "mixing" in these reports means is not entirely obvious. It is very likely that, at least with reports from the *First* or *New statistical accounts*, a form of *diglossia* may be evident, a point made much clearer in a number of other entries, some from SA3:

(6) *Kilsyth children are bi-lingual. They speak English in school, in the playground and at play in the streets, they revert to broad Scots. The doric is not dead in Kilsyth; in the buses, the church meetings, churches, the tongue is the couthy Scots, though the speakers can switch automatically to English.*

(Stirling SA3: Kilsyth)

It is also rather dangerous to see the two tongues as being completely separate in the minds of speakers. As has been pointed out by McClure (1983), even by the end of the eighteenth century, Scots and English had been in intimate contact for a large number of years, at least since the early days of the Reformation. It is not unlikely, therefore, that a biblical style of English – albeit sometimes of a fragmentary type – should have developed among the people.

But if what we are seeing is actually the code-switching regularly found in diglossic situations, what is causing this? One answer might be that the reporters of the phenomenon are trapped within the *observer's paradox*. Since ministers are often perceived as figures of consequence in a community, and are regularly distanced by their office from their parishioners, the language used in their presence would be unlikely to be that normally used when they were not there. A more "standard" use of language might well have been aimed for by parishioners. Yet this assumption carries with it striking evidence that qualitative language attitudes were very much at large within the community as a whole.

In later reports we can be more sure that what is described is actually the process of Scots being "thinned" (to use McClure's (1979: 29-31) term), particularly in terms of vocabulary, and becoming little more than a Scottish accent used when speaking English. Evidence for the reasons behind this can, perhaps, be seen in the following:

(7) *The local dialect still persists in tone and vocabulary, though in a more limited and debased form. All classes and ages appear to have a wider*

> *power of expression in the use of English. ... but the considerable and continuous movement of population in and out of Galashiels, the long duration of school education, and familiarity with the spoken word on the radio are influences that tend inevitably towards greater standardization of speech.*
>
> (Selkirk SA3: Galashiels)

No doubt the correspondent is correct in many of these assumptions. This essay will suggest, however, that ideological concerns might also underlie his opinions, and similar opinions expressed by other correspondents.

3.2. The presence of other language varieties and cultural/ethnic groupings

A feature of a number of reports is that Scots – or the local dialect, no matter how defined – are mentioned largely in terms of the presence of another language variety and/or cultural/ethnic community. In a sense, in a situation where all – or nearly all – of the residents of a given area speak similar language varieties, there is little to say; it is when a notably divergent (and often antagonistically perceived) group or language variety is present that comment is encouraged.

3.2.1. Gaelic

Because of Gaelic's nature as a "retreating" language throughout most of the period under discussion (Durkacz 1983), it is not surprising that much comment – often in a similar vein to that describing the "mixing" cited before – should be elicited on language use in these "marginal" zones:

(8) *The language of the common people in this parish, like many of the parishes in the neighbourhood, is a*

mixture of Scotch and English. This jargon is very unpleasant to the ear, and a great impediment to fluent conversation. No language is more expressive than the Scotch, when spoken in perfection; and the accent be short and unmusical, yet it is by no means disagreeable to hear two plain country men conversing in the true Scotch tongues, but, in this parish, you seldom meet with such instances. – In the quarter towards Callander, the generality of the inhabitants speak Gaelic; and this is perhaps still more corrupt than even the Scotch, in the other quarters of the parish. It is impossible to conceive any thing so truly offensive to the ear, as the conversation of these people. The true Gaelic is a noble language, worthy of the fire of Ossian, and wonderfully adapted to the genius of a warlike nation; but the contemptible language of the people about Callander, and to the east, is quite incapable of communicating a noble idea.

It ought, therefore, to be earnestly recommended to the people of the parish, and, indeed, to other parishes in that quarter, to study a more perfect style; either to practice the true Gaelic, the true Scotch, or the true English tongue.

But all kinds of civilization in society go hand in hand; and when arts and sciences begin to flourish here, the language will gradually polish and refine.

(Perth SA1: Kilmadock or Doune)

Much of the same can be seen in the following:

(9) *The language generally spoken is the Gaelic, and it is evident from a little intercourse with the people, that it has lost ground very considerably within the last fifty years. The older people of the parish speak*

> *it with classical correctness, whereas the rising generation intermixes it with many Anglicisms.*
> (Perth SA2: Moulin)

What is meant by *Anglicisms*, whether these are lexical, phonological or grammatical, and whether Standard English or a contiguous dialect of Scots is being implied is not always certain, although elsewhere there is little doubt that the latter is the case, a point supported by evidence from other sources, as discussed in McColl Millar (1996) and Ó Baoill (1997).

3.2.2. Varieties of English

It is inevitable that the obvious linguistic differences between Standard English and Scots should be commented upon when they occur within the same area. That similar comments should be made on the English frontier is sociolinguistically and dialectologically interesting, however:

(10) *There may be a tendency to assimilate to the forms and sounds of the speech of Cumberland, but the local tongue is still characteristically Scottish, and shows little sign of becoming less so. When social custom does not call for "polite", or "school" English, the language the people use is still largely that of their fathers.*
(Dumfries SA3: Dornock)

There is a certain defensiveness in this report – most noticeably in the comment that the local dialect is "characteristically Scottish". What is interesting from a sociolinguistic point of view is that the writer appears – surprisingly – to associate Standard English with the local forms of speech across the border. There is a degree of truth in the fact that traditional dialect is in a somewhat healthier position in Dumfriesshire than in Cumbria (Glauser 1974: 4.2.4.1.), and that therefore to the ears of someone from Dumfriesshire those from Cumbria would sound rather more "standard" in speech. As likely an explanation would be the commonplace lack of knowledge of differences between English dialects and pronunciations encountered in Scotland, however (Macafee 1994). Most notable, perhaps, is the fact that those Cumbrians who now live in the parish, which is essentially one of the outer suburbs of Carlisle, would probably be of middle-class – and therefore rather more "polite", standard-speaking – backgrounds.

That this mixture of tongues need not always be the case on the border can be seen in the following, however:

(11) *In truth, in all that respects language, the natives of this district may be said to be* Scotorum Scotissimi. *Though at the distance of only five miles from England, they speak the Scottish tongue in the most Doric of its forms; nor does there appear any prospect of a steady improvement in this particular. It would indeed seem, that, in proportion as the two countries approach their respective confines, the Scotch and Anglian tongues, instead of gradually losing each its distinctive character so as, at the point of junction, to interblend and coalesce in a common dialect, assume each its harshest and most intractable form; as if for the purpose of keeping their respective* marches *clear and distinct. At least the fact is unquestionable that, all along the south side of the east marches, we have the Northumbrian* burr *bristling, like a fence of thorns, to prevent the Scotch accent from penetrating into England, whilst on the north side, the latter dialect assumes a breadth of guttural energy, which effectively protects "the ancient kingdom" against the inroads of the speech of the smoother-tongued* Sassenachs.

 (Roxburgh SA2: Kelso)

The "mixture" perceived on the Western border is categorically denied in the Centre/East. There is no reason to rehearse the many violent episodes along the marches which for a long time encouraged a mutual antipathy between Scots and English. This may explain the vociferous nature of these comments, but it has to be remembered that the "old quarrel" was as vicious to the West as it was to the East. Even if we discount the different dates and the probable differences in character of this and the preceding correspondent, something else must underlie such great divergences in viewpoint. Firstly, the topographical nature of the Roxburgh border – high hills, often with no obvious passes – is very different from the flat and relatively open nature of the Solway Moss. According to Glauser (1974: 4.2.4.1.), there are a bundle of isoglosses along the Middle Marches "opening up towards Northern England in the east, towards Scotland in the west". That the cultural distinction is favoured over the linguistic can be seen in the culturally and geographically inappropriate use of Gaelic, however.

3.2.3. The Irish

It could be argued that the single most significant change to have happened to the ethnic structure of the South of Scotland in the last few centuries has been the large-scale immigration of people of an Irish background. That this movement – particularly when at its height in the years following the Potato Famine – caused considerable tensions in both industrial and rural Scotland is a well-known fact, and one which is regularly commented upon by the correspondents to the *Statistical accounts of Scotland*. That this mass-movement had linguistic consequences is also recognised (Macafee 1983: 1.4.). Interestingly, however, it is not in these centres of mass migration, such as the Clydeside conurbation, that comment on language "mixing" is recorded. It is rather where there has been long-term "coming and going" between the two countries that much is made of linguistic influence:

(12)   *The language generally spoken is tolerably good. The lower orders (of whom a great many are natives of Ireland) have a good deal of the accent of that country. Indeed, strangers allege that all classes of the inhabitants have a good deal of the Irish accent. This, no doubt, arises from our proximity to Ireland, and our very frequent intercourse with the Irish.*
                                        (Wigtown SA2: Stranraer)

It might be argued that genuinely long-term language contact is the only kind which can produce true linguistic change for an entire speech community – save under very specific circumstances –, and that therefore it is inevitable that Western Galloway should have been singled out as a contact area. That attitudes to this contact should change can be seen in the following:

(13)   *[T]he spoken language for many centuries has been a rather distinctive form of Lowland Scots. It is true that the tongue, like the people themselves, is often referred to as Galloway Irish and many of our people, when they move into other parts of Scotland, are taken to be Irish. Yet an authentic Irish tongue is every bit as distinctive in Kirkmaiden as a true Highland tongue is in Glasgow.*
                                        (Wigtown SA3: Kirkmaiden)

It is interesting in fact that a number of contiguous regions, such as Southern Ayrshire, do not report an entirely positive response – to say the least – to the language of their more southerly neighbours and its influence upon them, thus, perhaps, explaining the rather careful use of phrasing in the excerpt.

3.3. Local "peculiarities"

Not all comments on local peculiarities or uniqueness in language in the *Statistical accounts* are due explicitly to contact across linguistic or political frontiers, or to migration. Often in the reports reference is made to specifics which mark off that region's speech from that of any other. Again, with a few exceptions, there appear to be patterns underlying the geographical placement of these comments.

Not surprisingly, one dialect region which stands out in terms of commentary is that of the North-East – perhaps the most distinctive – and, eventually, best preserved – of the Scots dialects. This difference is perceived in the *First Statistical account*, where the account for Auchindoir states that

(14) *The people in the south of Scotland say, that the tone is harsh, and to them has the appearance of passion and bad humour*
(Aberdeen SA1: Auchendoir),

a sentiment supported by the report from Duffus that

(15) [O]*ur accent is, in the ear of a stranger, snappish and provoking, assimilating to that of Aberdeen, but is said not to be quite as invincible as theirs.*
(Moray SA1: Duffus).

In entries to the later *Accounts*, the tone of disapproval expressed has disappeared, but not the sense of uniqueness:

(16) *Despite the educational advance and the inroads of the Southrons, the language heard on market day at Elgin or in the homes of farmers and field workers remains racy, of the soil, and of honourable ancestry.*
(Moray SA3: St. Andrews Lhanbryde),

a sentiment supported in the comment of the SA3 correspondent from Ellon who states that

(17) [T]*he Buchan accent ... is notably more distinct in the landward areas, where the speech is broader and rougher in tone, but by no means unattractive, and full of the sap of character*
(Aberdeen SA3: Ellon).

What is interesting is that very rarely do any of the correspondents say what marks off the North-East as a linguistic area: it is almost as if this is a given.

Other areas which stand out for specific treatment as "unusual" are Southern Berwickshire:

(18) *The local dialect is very broad, and the accent is soft and musical. Most people use the past tense "comed" for "came" regularly, and many soldiers serving in other than the local regiment had to change their speech to avoid ridicule by their comrades from other districts.*
(Berwick SA3: Cockburnspath),

the southern parts of Roxburghshire, as in:

(19) *The inhabitants of this parish and of the neighbouring parishes have several striking peculiarities of dialect. For instance, instead of me and he, they pronounce these words as if written* mei *and* hei; *instead of tree, they say* trei; *and three,* threi, *which is precisely the German* drei, *by the substitution of* th *instead of* d. *They pronounce the Scotch twa, with a peculiar drawl, making it a disyllable, as if written* tweah; *and brae they make* breah. *All these sounds are rather pleasant to the ear; but their pronunciation of the initial* h *in some*

> words is harsh, and cacophonous in no ordinary degree. Thus the proper name Hope, signifying a particular kind of glen, they pronounce as if written whupp; and hole, as if whull; horn as if whurn. These peculiarities, as far as the author has been able to ascertain, are confined to the higher district of Roxburghshire. ... These peculiarities of dialect are, of course, generally confined to the lower ranks of the people, – although, such is the effect of habit and imitation, you hear sometimes people, from whose education and rank you might augur differently, utter the same harsh and barbarous sounds.
>
> (Roxburgh SA2: Bedrule),

eastern Fife:

(20) *The language spoken is the dialect peculiar to Fifeshire, which contains a good many words not to be found in Johnson, though their number is gradually diminishing. The pronunciation is slow and rather drawling. The double oo, as in fool, is sounded as the French u in un, the l after p and b is often changed into a short i or y, plough and blue being pronounced piu and biu, a corruption similar to the change of the Latin planus into the Italian piano. The a in haste, hate, &c has a sound intermediate between the ay in may, and the e in me, which is in fact a distinct vowel, peculiar to the Kingdom of Fife. The short i, as in him, is pronounced nearly as the u in tub.*

(Fife SA2: Monimail),

and the boundaries of highland Perthshire:

(21) *The Stormont dialect, of course, prevails, in which the chief peculiarity that strikes a stranger is the pronunciation of the Scotch* oo *as* ee, *poor being pronounced* peer, *moon* meen, *aboon* abeen, *&c.*
(Perth SA2: Caputh).

What is significant about these apparently random examples is that they all lie on the periphery of the Scots-speaking area. With the possible exception of eastern Fife they exhibit evidence of the cultural and linguistic contacts already mentioned. Further, most of these areas are also outside the mainstream of present-day Scottish urban, industrialised life, associated more with traditional pursuits (McColl Millar 1999).

The chief exception to this general pattern is a number of parishes in the more upper reaches of the Clyde Valley in Lanarkshire, for example:

(22) *The language spoken is the broad Scotch dialect, with this peculiarity, very observable to strangers, that the voice is raised, and the sound lengthened upon the last syllable of the sentence.*
(Lanark SA1, Lesmahagow, 488)

Yet even this area might be considered peripheral by some lights, with the rapidly industrialising Central Belt to the North, and the Southern Uplands at its back. Indeed something of this feeling can also be found in more recent times in an equally traditional area close to Clydeside:

(23) *The speech is lowland Scots, the homely tongue of Renfrewshire and Ayrshire, pure, alas, only on older lips, and, for the rest, much vitiated by the unlovely "Glesca"* [Glasgow] *inflection.*
(Renfrew SA3: Lochwinnoch)

3.4. Summary

Overt language attitudes can therefore be seen to be of three types. The first is where perceived change is taking place within a speech community. In earlier *Accounts* the change was towards Standard English, and was seen as being a positive thing; in later *Accounts*, the move towards urban – often Clydeside – speech is described, and is seen in a negative light. The ideological assumption underlying this is that rural speech is safe because the countryside and its inhabitants are conservative. Urban speech is dangerous because the "mob" is dangerous. Anything dangerous is, by implication, also ugly.

The second overt spur to the recording of language attitudes – not truly distinct from the first, in fact – is where there is an outside – often subversive – force present within a community. This presence gives the correspondents an opportunity to say something about the "virtues" of the local community.

Again connected to this is the third distinction – the expression of local peculiarities in speech. Once more this emphasises a small-scale locale and the singularity of local experience.

That this rather patchy recording does not give the full story on attitudes to Scots can be seen if we turn to covert language attitudes, which pick up on, and amplify, much of what has already been said.

4. Covert language attitudes

4.1. In many of the articles in the *Statistical accounts*, Scots words and phrases appear to be being used to give some kind of "local colour" to the entry. This is natural enough, since perhaps the single most defining feature of a people as a culturally distinct body is their use of language. A "taste" of this for "outsiders" would therefore be expected in collections of this type. In a culturally and politically fraught nation such as Scotland, the reasons for the specific use is not always as straightforward as this, however.

The mid- to late-eighteenth century down to the present day is probably the first era in history that has perceived itself as passing through profound change. Strange as it might seem, the normal assumption today that our lives will be fundamentally different from our predecessors' in a number of ways previously unimaginable would have been considered somewhat abnormal until around the time of the invention of an economically viable steam engine (Morgan 1980). When this *Weltanschauung* altered, the "future shock" must have been particularly harsh in a country like Scotland which had begun the eighteenth century as an independent but backward kingdom on the brink of civil war but ended it as a part of the single most powerful country on earth at the time, at the centre of heavy industrialisation, and with social and ethnic problems which would have been unimaginable only fifty years earlier. That this speed of change has continued (if not accelerated) up to the present day is doubtless one of the reasons why many of the writers in the *Statistical accounts* make reference to the passage of time. What is significant, however, is that this passage is reflected in the use of Scots words and phrases, whether in a regretful sense:

(24) *And the many unclaimed* lairs *in the churchyard. tell of many families having passed away, who once lived here in simplicity and peace.*
(Stirling SA2: Drymen)

or as a means of showing how much more clear-sighted the present generation is when compared with the preceding:

(25) *They believed in benevolent spirits, which they called brownies*
(Kirkcudbright SA1: Tongland).

It is dubious whether either of the words cited are as unusual or outdated for the correspondents as they appear to suggest. What is important for our purposes is that they should feel it necessary to make such an assertion.

As these examples show, there is a dichotomy felt between those who believe in a Whig-historical model of Scottish life, that there is an ongoing improvement in manners, agriculture, culture, etc. which is reflected (as we have already seen) in the abandonment of Scots, and those writers who regret the past's passing and use Scots to evince sympathy with the "old ways".

The first of these viewpoints is, it is not too surprising to discover, particularly prevalent in the first two *Statistical accounts*, although it is not excluded from later writings:

(26) [T]*he poor child is placed upon the loom, there to "eik" out, by its 1s 6d or 2s. per week, the pittance of the half-starved parent.*
(Stirling SA2: Balfron),

(27) *Some of the farmhouses are exceedingly neat and cleanly about the doors. At Beatlaws, the front is graveled and tastefully laid out. Others of them, however, could "thole" amendment, – such, for instance, as protecting the front from all access by cows and pigs, &c. and removing dunghills.*
(Lanark SA2: Wandell and Lamington),

or:

(28) *Thirty-two years ago, there were only 7* hats *in the church, but at present there are not as many* bonnets.
(Roxburgh SA1: Lillies-leaf).

In each of these three examples, Scots words – or meanings of words exclusive to Scots – *eik, thole* and *bonnet* – are cited for what amounts to the same purpose: to highlight the fact that the "bad old days and ways" are passed, and that more "civilised" times have arrived. There is one striking difference between the first two excerpts and the third, however: in the first, genuine economic hardship is described; the second appears to highlight a rather less important matter, but actually describes something particularly germane to developments in the Scottish countryside at the time. On both of these occasions it can be argued that the correspondent's sympathies lie with the people whom he describes. The last example is of a rather less important nature; indeed, it might even be argued that it describes merely the loss of "local colour" in favour of a gradual cosmopolitanisation. It nonetheless demonstrates rather well the ideas about "improvement" held at this time.

Although, as has been seen, these viewpoints are largely confined to the first two *Statistical accounts*, this is not entirely the case, as the following shows:

(29) *People are well-dressed and no "orra" or ragged children are to be seen in the village.*
(Perthshire SA3: Meigle).

It might be argued, however, that the period immediately succeeding the Second World War (when this was written) was the last in which it was possible to take a "Whig" view of the economical and social development of Scotland.

On none of these occasions would it be accurate to say that the writers involved were by the nature of what they wrote reactionaries – indeed the opposite is the case at times. What is disappointing from the point of view of the long-term vitality of Scots, however, is their attitude to the language as a marker of older times.

That they are not alone in this is shown by similar tactics employed by their ideological opposites: those who regret the passing of the old ways, a viewpoint most prevalent in, although not by any means confined to, the *Third account*. Again they believe that one of the casualties of change is the Scots tongue itself, as examples such as the following demonstrate:

(30) *A farmer who walked "up the brae" from the carse to the village school at Kippen some thirty-five to forty years ago might have been one of sixteen cousins walking to school together, but to-day it would be difficult to find two.*
(Stirling SA3: Kippen).

A sub-set of this viewpoint is to place what amounts to the same dichotomy in the present:

(31) *He* [the local] *is keen on sport, loves a "flutter", enjoys the pub or club, the pictures and the crowded throng. On the other hand there are those, perhaps fewer in number, who prefer their own fireside, or book, the "bools", the silent loch or burn, and the hallowed hour of the Kirk.*
(Fife SA3: Ballingry).

This is a particularly interesting statement of this view. Especially revealing is the opposition set up between the "flutter" and the "bools" (note the symmetrical use of quotation marks): it is almost as if the correspondent has two separate templates for activity for the "lower orders": one essentially urban and ungodly, as emphasised by the use of a common "slang" term, the other essentially rural and god-fearing, as emphasised by the use of a number of specifically Scots words.

A number of correspondents take a "middle way", however. They see that much of value has passed away in the never-ending flux of modern society. They are not blind to the genuine nature of many of the improvements that modern society has brought:

(32) *The workers climbed the* Stey Brae *to the clearer air of the* Auld Toon *upon the hill when the day's darg was done. (Nowadays the bus company provides mill services morning, noon and night.)*
(Selkirk SA3: Selkirk),

(33) *Yet there was one predominant feature of the social life at that time that must not be forgotten. This was the spirit of comradeship, best described perhaps as "neeborliness", and not of course confined to Beath parish, but common to all miners' rows.*
(Fife SA3: Beath).

But again on these occasions the correspondents use Scots words to bring home the idea of the passage of time; inherent in this is the idea of the loss of much specifically Scots vocabulary – a fact of life for Scots for the last 100 years in particular. It may be that they are correct in this assumption. Yet, as will be seen, other, ideological explanations could be given for these assumptions.

4.2. Use of Scots as a marker of proverbial, local, wit and wisdom

Up until this point, it has generally been assumed that Scots was a marker of a passing age (whether this was seen as a good or a bad thing). Related, but separate from this is a category of uses of Scots which could be defined as an amalgam of proverbial wisdom, local knowledge, and general *couthiness*, the Scots word for the concept of native wit and wisdom, not necessarily the result of conventional education. This attribute was – and is – much prized in Scottish society. Like the above – but with a subtly different slant – examples of this type establish a strong sense of locality:

(34) *There [sic; i.e. the people of Muirkirk] turn of mind, so far as it is peculiar, is, in a great degree, formed by their situation and manner of life, and they discover a strong attachment to the place of their birth, and former residence, or, in their own words, "Weary sair for the Muirkirk", even when they remove to countries more fruitful and better cultivated.*
(Ayr SA1: Muirkirk)

Often the examples give strong evidence of the self-deprecating wit regularly associated with Scots speech:

(35)   *The climate is pithily summed up in the words of one farmer: "We may be flooded oot but never burned oot".*
(Ayr SA3: Old Cumnock),

or with a directness and power of expression not associated with standard speech:

(36)   *The folk of the parish have much weather lore and are very fond of proverbs – especially alliterative adages, such as "Burnt breid maks bonnie bairns" (said to induce a child to eat singed oatcakes).*
(Aberdeen SA3: Tough),

(37)   *Evening services are sparsely attended, particularly in summer; as the old beadle said, "When the weather's ower bad, they'll no come oot, and when it's ower guid, they'll no come in".*
(Stirling SA3: Grangemouth).

On these occasions the use of Scots is associated with traditional virtues such as fortitude, forbearance, and thrift. It is interesting that in the example from Grangemouth the "words of wisdom" are put into the mouth of an "old beadle" – the church warden in the Scottish Presbyterian tradition – a working-class figure who had a unique standing within the community as a whole. In this sense the minister distances himself both socially, and – by the use of the adjective *old* – in time, from the speaker, inevitably adding to the "proverbial" nature of the statement, and, indirectly, removing from himself the taint of being a Scots speaker. This same method is employed in the following:

(38)   *"A herd," said one, "would be a gey sillie body if he hadna a good dug. It doesn't matter how good a herd is, if you haven't a good dug you never got out of the bit."*
(Peebles SA3: County).

On all of these occasions the use of third person narrative could chime in well with the Scottish tradition of the *worthy*, the person of (actual or assumed) wisdom, strongly associated with a given area and not necessarily of an elevated social standing, although, because of his wit, given privileges that his position could not demand. Indeed the passing of such local characters, and their influence upon local speech, is explicitly mourned by a number of ministers. Yet by doing so, the writers are in danger of a ghettoisation of the use of Scots as a "twee" thing, rather than as a vital part of a people's everyday linguistic identity:

(39)   *Charlie Coulter, the old lamplighter, lit the lamps only on moonless nights, and worked strictly to the table in the Almanac, so that when it announced full moon the lamps were not lit. Taken to task by the villagers for not lighting the lamps when the moon was obscured by heavy cloud, Charlie would reply "if there'snae muin, there shoulda been ane".*
(Lanark SA3: Carmunnock).

On this occasion, whilst "old" Charlie's speech does represent a degree of *couthiness*, the story is being told essentially to mock him; his use of Scots is merely part of this. This exemplifies a danger inherent in the third-person use of Scots in these entries: the distancing effect may represent more an opportunity to demonstrate social distance rather than emotional attachment or engagement. In this sense their use bears a marked resemblance to the "mimicking" speech use by contemporary middle-class citizens of Ayr of working-class speech, as discussed recently by MacAulay (1991: 185-186).

The ideological assumptions already mentioned are at their most prevalent in these examples of "worthy's speech". This is particularly the case when working class speakers are quoted as putting forward ideas supporting the supposedly traditional Scottish virtue of independence from State help:

(40)   "Na, Sir, Guid be thankit I was never burden to kirk nor king".

(Aberdeen SA2: Fyvie),

or:

(41)   *Only last week the writer met a road worker, who had gone to live in a village council house, and asked him how he liked his new quarters. "Nae very weel", was the reply. "There's unco little freedom jammed in atween twa neebors, an' nae oot-rin at the back for hens or bees. I cud aye tak' abeen £20 a year oot o' th' gairden i' th' auld place; an' noo here A'm abeen £20 a year extra for rent an' taxes. That mak's mair than £40 a year doon on th'ower-turn. Practically aboot a poun' a week oot o' ma pey. Of course, th' wife his a'thing handy i' the hoose here, an' nae oot-gaun on an ill day t' th' wall for water – but it's some dear".*

(Aberdeen SA3: Lumphanan).

Both of these examples date from periods of major political and social upheaval. The first derives from the tail-end of the "hungry thirties", when the Scots poor law was under dreadful stress, and ministers in the second *Account* often make distinctions between the "independent" Scots and the peripatetic and sometimes destitute Irish. The second stems from the period immediately following the Second World War, when new social and health-care provisions were taking away a number of the functions of charity – a state of affairs unappreciated by certain elements within the Church. Since it is to be assumed that many ministers – even now, but particularly in the past – subscribed to a form of paternalistic conservatism, it is not surprising that such disconcerting – and often painful – changes should have distressed them.

As we have seen, putting "anti" messages into the mouths of worthies has both a distancing and enforcing effect upon their pronouncements. It also – perhaps sometimes unfairly – leaves correspondents open to charges of *kailyarding*, the Scots concept already hinted at of a rural, hierarchical Utopia. Interestingly, the chief proponents of the *Kailyard* literary school at the turn of the century – such as J. M. Barrie – were either ministers themselves or "sons of the Manse".

That such conservatism was not true of the whole Church can be seen in the following, where modern developments are seen as of benefit to the people – even when the people do not recognise the point themselves:

(42) *The nearest doctors – three of them – live in Gorebridge but visit regularly and frequently in the parish, as do also the district nurses. All are liked, trusted and appreciated; but, even since the institution of the National Health Service, they are often called in too reluctantly and too late, especially by older people who need them most. ("I wasna brocht up to lie in ma bed!")*

(Midlothian SA3: Temple).

Yet underlying the use of Scots here is exactly the same idea of its being part of a passing age.

4.3. Summary

It seems therefore that the covert language attitudes expressed in the *Statistical accounts* tell us much about the status of Scots among the Middle Classes – the natural source of candidates for the ministry – over the period. Scots words and phrases are often used to mark the passage of time; sadly, Scots is seen as an emblem of a passing – or passed – age and way of life. This has about it the makings of a self-fulfilling prophecy.

When Scots is put into the mouths of local speakers, it is often used to express the power and pithiness of local speech. It may also imply a hankering for simpler, less complex times. A subset of this is that it may be being used on these occasions to express reactionary views closer to those held by the ministry than the population as a whole.

Interestingly, the use of Scots in these contexts also implies – perhaps unconsciously – a considerable (albeit possibly passive) knowledge of the language.

5. Conclusion

From a positive point of view, therefore, the language attitudes – both covert and overt – expressed in the three *Statistical accounts of Scotland* often demonstrate that the Scots tongue – or its local varieties – are a vital part of the identity of localities across the whole of non-Gaelic Scotland. Other, less positive, attitudes can be extracted, however. In the hands of the correspondents to the *Accounts*, the assumed decline of the language – and even this very localised identity – are used for what can only be termed ideological goals. Such uses might not augur well for the long-term health of Scots as an essential of Scottish identity. A further point of interest is that it is in the covert – rather than the overt – attitudes expressed that the full range of these phenomena can best be described.

Primary Sources

The Statistical account of Scotland (SA1)
The New statistical account (SA2)
The Third statistical account of Scotland (SA3)
Note: In this essay, reference to the texts of the Accounts is given in the following way:
(Pre-1975 County [where appropriate, without -*shire* suffix], SA1/2/3, Parish [or, in the case of SA3, other section when appropriate])

Further, places are cited according to their present spelling, if that is different from that given in the *Account*.

References

Aitken, Adam J.
   1979   Scottish speech: a historical view, with special reference to the Standard English of Scotland. In: Adam J. Aitken and Tom McArthur (eds.), 85-118.
   1990   The good old Scots tongue: does Scots have an identity? In: Einar Haugen, J. Derrick McClure, and Derick S. Thomson (eds.), 72-90.

Aitken, Adam J. and Tom McArthur (eds.)
   1979   *Languages of Scotland.* (The Association of Scottish Literary Studies Occasional Paper Number 4.) Edinburgh: Chambers.

Durkacz, Victor Edward
   1983   *The decline of the Celtic languages.* Edinburgh: Donald.

Glauser, Beat
   1974   *The Scottish-English linguistic border: lexical aspects.* Bern: Francke.

Haugen, Einar, J. Derrick McClure, and Derick S. Thomson (eds.)
   1990   *Minority languages today.* (2nd edition.) Edinburgh: Edinburgh University Press.

Jones, Charles
   1995   *A language suppressed: the pronunciation of the Scots language in the 18th century.* Edinburgh: Donald.

Jones, Charles (ed.)
   1997   *The Edinburgh history of the Scots language.* Edinburgh: Edinburgh University Press.

Macafee, Caroline
   1983   *Glasgow.* (Varieties of English around the World 3.) Amsterdam/Philadelphia: Benjamins.
   1994   *Traditional dialect in the modern world: a Glasgow case study.* Frankfurt (Main): Lang.

MacAulay, Ronald K. S.
   1991   *Locating dialect in discourse: the language of honest men and bonnie lasses in Ayr.* (Oxford Studies in Sociolinguistics.) Oxford: Oxford University Press.

McClure, J. Derrick
   1979   Scots: its range of uses. In: Adam J. Aitken and Tom McArthur (eds.), 26-48.

    1983   Scots in dialogue: some uses and implications. In: J. Derrick McClure (ed.), 129-148.

McClure, J. Derrick (ed.)
    1983   *Scotland and the Lowland Tongue: studies in the language and literature of Scotland in honour of David D. Murison.* Aberdeen: Aberdeen University Press.

McColl Millar, Robert
    1996   Gaelic-influenced Scots in pre-revolutionary Maryland. In: P. Sture Ureland and Iain Clarkson (eds.), 387-410.
    1999   Some geographic and cultural patterns observable in the lexical/ semantic structure of Scots. *Northern Scotland* 18: 55-65.

Mitchison, Rosalind
    1962   *Agricultural Sir John: the life of Sir John Sinclair of Ulbster 1754-1835.* London: Bles.

Morgan, Chris
    1980   *The shape of futures past: the story of prediction.* Exeter: Webb and Bower.

Ó Baoill, Colm
    1997   The Scots-Gaelic interface. In: Charles Jones (ed.), 551-568.

Smout, Thomas Christopher
    [1969] 1985   *A history of the Scottish people 1560-1830.* London: Fontana Press.
    [1986] 1987   *A century of the Scottish people 1830-1950.* London: Fontana Press.

Tulloch, Graham
    1980   *The language of Walter Scott.* London: Routledge.

Ureland, P. Sture and Iain Clarkson (eds.)
    1996   *Language contact across the North Atlantic.* (Linguistische Arbeiten 359.) Tübingen: Niemeyer.

Fashionable idiolects?
The use of the negative prefix *dis-* 1520-1620

Roderick W. McConchie

1. Introduction[1]

It is sometimes asked, rather naively, whether Shakespeare was as creative a word-maker as the evidence in the *OED* suggests. Indeed, the question of whether the *OED* can tell us anything about the verbal creativity of a given author from the evidence of the first citations for its lemmas seems more often to be taken as already answered positively than inquired into. In this respect, Shakespeare's reputation precedes him, and makes it easy to find that whatever the *OED* offers confirms what was already felt to be true.

Previous work on the medical terminology of the sixteenth century and its treatment in the *OED* revealed the curious fact that a number of antedatings to the *OED* from the work of the physician William Clever, *The flower of physick* (1590), were words formed with the prefix *dis-* (McConchie 1983). An apparently significant number of the words with Shakespeare as their earliest citation also fall into this category. The present article draws attention to this fact, makes some comparison with other sixteenth-century works, and explores the possible ramifications for studies of the lexicon of Early Modern English as well as the possibility of identifying personal linguistic habits from such evidence.

The first problem is to clarify which prefix we are in fact discussing, *des-*, *dis-*, or *dys-*. The *OED* explanation indicates that *des-* formations had run their course by the end of the Middle English period. *Dys-* words, formed from the Greek prefix δυσ- are different again and, apart from one or two such as *dyscrasia*, for the most part postdate our period, according to the *OED*. In both cases then, there is relatively little likelihood of confusion.

The second problem is to distinguish the particular use of this prefix which is productive in English, particularly in the sixteenth century. The prefix *dis-* is discussed at length under its own headword in the *OED*. The category with which this paper is concerned is the last distinguished in the preamble to this lemma; namely, that which reanalyses the various uses of the prefix in both Classical and Late Latin, and in Old French. This is category 4, used "as a living prefix, arising from the analysis of categories 1-3, and extended to other words without respect to their origin."[2] In effect this means that words such as *dismiss, display, distinguish* and *disrupt* are effectively excluded from this discussion, though most of them would in any case fall beyond the chronological limitations specified in this study, mostly being earlier borrowings or formations. Exemplars of the kind of word included here are *disanagrammatize* [Donne 1610][3] or *disthrone* [Sylvester 1591]. The sense with which we are primarily concerned then is "II, as a living prefix, with privative force". It should also be noted that no words with further prefixation, such as *undiscernable* [Hooker 1586] or *all-disposing* [Hieron 1607] have been included in this study. In these particular cases, the root is certainly too early as well as not pertinent to this study, and the fact that many such formations are rather later than their bases would only confound the present study.

New data from thirteen medical texts dating from 1547 to 1613, the year of Shakespeare's last play, were examined for words which were absolute first citations for the *OED* formed with the prefix *dis-*. The *OED* itself has been searched for all *dis-* words whose absolute first citation[4] falls between 1520 and 1620. The *Helsinki Corpus* has also been searched for these words in the Early Modern period, the earliest date being 1500, which follows the *Helsinki Corpus* periodisation for convenience.

What is in the lists contained in this article therefore is words which are actual or potential absolute first citations for *OED*, at least in the present state of knowledge, and may thus represent idiolectal usages, although what exactly this might mean is rather obscure and a matter which the data offered here may go some way to clarifying. I deliberately eschew the word "coinage", since the *OED* first citations can prove nothing about them, apart perhaps from exceptional cases such as coinages explicitly stated to be such by their coiners, or such things as malapropisms. Even the latter will be familiar and conventional in many cases. To claim that a word must have been coined by a given author simply because it is the *OED*'s earliest citation is an absurdity which ignores the inescapable facts of making an historical dictionary.

The inherent interest of the words considered here thus arises not from the negligible possibility of their having been coined by an identifiable individual but, far more realistically, simply as perhaps representing a relatively early written occurrence of such terms and, if identifiable in sufficient numbers, as indicating a trend in their use. The other matter which will be inquired into is whether there are tendencies observable in individuals to use a particular word-formation, in this case the prefix *dis-*, in the sense already explained. The data from the medical sources is then put into the context of the *dis-* words from this period from the *OED* and those extracted from the *Helsinki Corpus*, and the practices of some lexicographers of the period are examined.

This article describes a process of interpreting information. The procedure involves deriving a table from a particular database, then modifying and adjusting it in the light of further evidence, so that instead of setting out the evidence in full from the beginning, I move by transitional stages to the point where some conclusions can be drawn.

2. The evidence of medical texts

All the medical texts listed here almost certainly contain such terms but, for the reasons outlined, only first citations are considered. The question asked is thus whether an author might have used such terms idiosyncratically, not whether he or she might have used them extensively. Not all the medical works yielded absolute first citations of *dis-* words. Those which did not were

Bailey, Walter
    1585   *A treatise of the medicine called mithridatium*
Baker, George
    1574   *The composition ... of the moste excellent and prestigious oil called oleum magistrale*
B(ostocke), R(obert)
    1585   *The difference betweene the auncient Phisicke ... and the latter Phisicke*
Cotta, John
    1612   *Ignorant practisers ... of physicke*
Langton, Christopher
    c.1550   *An introduction into physyke, with an vniuersal dyet*
Plutarch
    1549   *The gouernaunce of good helthe*

Turning to those which did, it should be noted that no words near in date to the *OED*'s first citation but not antedating it were included, since the question is whether some individual or social network might be the vector of introduction of such terms, rather than the extent of use of all terms of the type we are considering. No parallel first dates were recorded. The words are cited with the *OED* sense, word-type where necessary, date and author cited in square brackets, the signature or page number of the new instance, and the text in which it occurs. They are listed separately as antedatings and as unrecorded. New senses were not relevant unless they were also antedatings. Since postdatings, the other category usually cited in listing additions to the *OED*, do not bear on this study, they have been omitted. Those works which did yield *dis-* word first citations within the limitations of type and chronology already indicated were, with the instances produced:

John Banister
    1579   *The history of man*

Antedatings
1. *dislocate* (v, 2b, 1605, Shakespeare) Giir the small number of Bones, should offer ouer readyly occasion, vpon euery light motion to be dislocated, or rather *Luxated*
2. *dissimilar* (a, 1621, Burton) Cir *Dissimilar*, or *instrumentall*

Phillip Barrough
    1583   *The methode of physicke*

Antedatings
1. *discolorate* (1850 *Recent dicts.* and ns) 39 the second they terme *discolorata* (that is, hauing no colour)
2. *disobedient* (A, b, 1588, Read, J.) 276 for the most parte grosse and thicke and disobedient to resolution

Unrecorded
    distempure 1 a simple distempur without any humours

William Clever
    1590   *The flower of physicke*

Antedatings
1. *discoverture* (1818, Cruise *Digest*) 31 And yet in all sharpe sicknesses the same is no consequent discouerture.
2. *disequal* (a, 1622, Mabbe *Aleman's G.*) 45 then all passiue actions were dispropriated and vnperfectly disequalled.
3. *disflourish* (v, 1640, Sedgewicke, O *Chr. C.*) 20 or els disflorisheth the laudable generation of bloud in grosse bodies
4. *disframe* (1629, Layton) 49 their courses vtterly difframed [*sic*] one from an other
5. *disliking* (1, 1596, Norden) 123 all foode ministred vnto the bodie should be medicinable, sheweth some naturall effect eyther of liking or disliking propertie
6. *dismatch* (v, 1591, Sylvester *Du B.*) 100 For mordicat rewmes are hurtfull to all naturall operations ... astonieth hearing, dissmacheth tasting
7. *dispropriate* (v, 1613, Purchas *Pilg.*) 45 then all passiue actions were dispropriated and vnperfectly disequalled.

8. *disseason* (v, 3, 1628, Greville, F. *Poems M.*) 11 the elements thereby so offended in their naturall courses poure downe superaboundaunce of moisting showers, disseasoning the earthlie fruites of mans mortall estate
9. *dissociate* (v, 1a, 1623, Cockeram) 42 when they (the elements) were disframed and dissociated from their equall places

Unrecorded
1. *disapetite* 77 giddinesse distempereth the head, and disapetiteth the stomach
2. *disfashion* 65 what fashion or disfashion soeuer the body is
3. *disfashionment* 102 best outwardly regarded by the outward alteration, and disfashionment of hayres
4. *disframed* 43 disframed conditions and qualities
5. *disoner* 72 a dry body ... furnisheth the bodie with good blood, disonereth the body from raw excrementes
6. *disornate* 86 (in margin) nature wolde not disornate the beautie of the face with haire
7. *disseasonable* 22 by reason of a disseasonable winter or vnnaturall spring before
8. *disseparate* 54 they are so deseperate one from another
9. *disure* 44 their actiue qualitie must be disured and fall away therewith

John Hester
    1580   *A short discourse ... vppon chirurgerie*

Unrecorded
    distemperament Giv^v The other is caused of great heat, Feuer, and distemperament of Nature, and this is called *Disenteria*

Thomas Hill
    1579   *A ioyfull iewel*

Antedatings
    dishabit (1595, Shakespeare) Biii^v and for that cause many places are dishabited

Christopher Langton
   1547   *A very brefe treatise*

Antedatings
   distemperate (a. 2, 1548, Recorde) Ci^v And hereof it is euident, that sumtyme one temperament is equall and temperate in one opposicion, and distemperate, and not equall in an other.

Phillip More
   1564   *The hope of helth*

Antedatings
   discredit (v, 3 1579, Harvey) Aiiii^r as the vile Renobites and Papistes at this prese(n)t daie, do seke meanes to discredite preachers as muche as they can, by scrupulous serching and examininge of their liuing, which somtime they finde to disagree from their doctrine.

Unrecorded
   distempure[5] Avi^r And contrariwyse that disease chaunce to the body by distempure of the said foure qualities of the eleme(n)tes

The medical authors cited here have not been exhaustively reported, since neither concordances nor exhaustive corpora have been available, and more first citations of such words may be found. The Shakespearean corpus, however, has been very thoroughly excerpted for the *OED* (Schäfer 1980), so that it is highly probable that all instances of *dis-* words have been considered for inclusion in it. For all intents and purposes then, the following list of the *OED*'s Shakespearean first citations of *dis-* words is complete (cf. table 1). The character who uses the word is also listed where appropriate, and whether the context is prose.

Table 1. Absolute first citations of *dis-* words from Shakespeare (all works)

word	type	year	work	character
disbench	v	1607	*Cor.* 2, 2, 75	Julius Brutus
discandy	v	1606	*A&C* 3, 13, 165	Cleopatra
discarded	ppl a	1595	*KJ* 5, 4, 12	Melun

discase	v	1610	*Temp.* 5, 1, 85	Prospero
discontent	n	1588	*Tit.* A 1,1, 443	Tamora
disdained	ppl a	1596	*1H4*, 1, 3, 183	Hotspur
disedged	ppl a	1611	*Cymb.* 3, 4, 96	Imogen
disgraceful	a	1591	*1H6.* 1, 1, 86	D. of Bedford
disgracious	a	1594	*R3* 3, 7, 112	Gloucester
dishabit	v	1595	*KJ* 2, 1, 220	King John
dishearten	v	1599	*H5*, 4, 1, 117	King (prose)
dishonoured	ppl a	1603	*MM* 4, 4, 34	Angelo
dishorn	v	1598	*MWW*, 4, 4, 63	Mrs Page
disliken	v	1611	*WT* 4, 4, 666	Camillo
disliking	ppl a	1592	*V&A* 182	
dislimn	v	1606	*A&C* 4, 14, 10	Antony
dislocate	v	1605	*KL* 4, 2, 65	Albany
dismask	v	1588	*LLL* 5, 2, 296	Boyet
disorb	v	1608	*T&C* 2, 2, 45	Troilus
dispose	n	1590	*CE* 1, 1, 21	Solinus (the Duke)
disproperty	v	1607	*Cor.* 2, 1, 264	Junius Brutus
disproportion	v	1593	*3H6*, 3, 2, 160	Richard (D. of Gl.)
dispunge	v	1606	*A&C* 4, 9, 12	Enobarbus
dispurse	v	1593	*2H6*, 3, 1, 117	Gloucester
disquantity	v	1605	*KL* 1, 4, 270	Goneril
disquietly	adv	1605	*KL* 1, 2, 124	Gloucester (prose)
disseat	v	1605	*Mac.* 5, 3, 21	Macbeth
dissembly	n2	1599	*MA* 4, 2, 1	Dogberry (prose)
distrustful	a	1591	*1H6* 1, 2, 127	Joan le Pucelle
disturb[6]	n	1594	*R3* 4, 2, 73	King
disturbed	ppl a	1592	*V&A* 340	
disturbing	ppl a	1592	*V&A* 649	
disvalue	v	1603	*MM* 5, 1, 221	Angelo
disvouch	v	1603	*MM* 4, 4, 1	Escalus (prose)

It is interesting that among the extensive list of antedatings assembled by Bailey ((ed.) 1978), none for Shakespearean *dis-* words were discovered, so that *dislocate* and *dishabit* are the first of this group to have been antedated. A further point of interest is raised by the word *disgest* (*MW, LLL, JC*, etc.), listed by *OED* as a byform of *digest*, and omitted from this list both for that reason and because the first listed occurrence is 1494. The chronology also prevents this form from being seen as an instance of the development of *dis-*

words later in the sixteenth century influencing the form of earlier borrowings. Further research may, however, turn up instances of such a phenomenon.

Reduced to tabular form, the gross numbers of occurrences of all types of *dis-* words and senses is thus:

Table 2. Numbers of *dis-* words forming *OED* new data from medical texts; *dis-* word first citations from Shakespeare added for comparison

Author	antedatings	unrecorded	total
Banister	2	0	2
Barrough	2	1	3
Bostocke	1	0	1
Clever	9	9	18
Hester	0	1	1
Hill	1	0	1
Langton	1	0	1
More	1	1	2
Shakespeare	34	–	34

Shakespeare and William Clever obviously yield far more instances of these words than the other authors; indeed, far more than the rest put together. The figures for Banister and Barrough do not seem to be numerically significant, but it is hard to be sure on these figures.

It might also perhaps be helpful to see which characters in Shakespeare's plays use such terms; after all, it is just as accurate to say that Shakespeare ascribes these words to his characters as to say that he uses them himself. Table 1 shows that the great majority of characters using these words are at least of gentle birth, often aristocrats, and in some cases monarchs. Only two lowborn characters use them: Dogberry, who uses *dissembly* as a malapropism, and Joan of Arc in *Henry VI Part one*. For the most part they are used in verse, though there are some exceptions.

Do these figures then represent an instance of idiolectal or even eccentric use largely confined to the work(s) of Clever and Shakespeare, or is it likely that this is a more widespread phenomenon? The relatively large proportion of unrecorded forms in Clever does suggest the former, but it is known that there is much untapped material, even in sources already excerpted by the *OED* readers (McConchie 1997: ch. 7). Is it possible to call it a lexical fashion, and to ascribe it to a particular period, or perhaps generation?

The question of whether these words are *hapax legomena* or not provides an obvious opening. Clever's unrecorded words plainly are, while *discandy* (two Shakespearean citations only), *dishabit*, *disliken*, *disproperty*, and *disvouch* (an aphetic form of *(dis)avouch*) are listed as such in *OED*. *Disbench* and *disorb* have further citations, but only from the nineteenth century. *Hapax legomena* are not meaningful in themselves, since they may be interpreted as either barren, not having been productive introductions, and thus as of little consequence for the lexicon, or simply as words insufficiently recorded, which may not only have been more in use, but may also be antedated, as is precisely the case with *dishabit*.

It would seem on the face of the evidence thus far that Shakespeare and Clever share a predilection for such formations and that, pending further information, this might indicate some kind of fashionable, perhaps localised or socio-economically explicable usage, since their contemporaries seem not to share it. This figure is however a raw number, and must be reassessed relative to the number of words examined for each author, since the corpora in all cases are very significantly smaller than Shakespeare's. Looked at this way, Clever yields an absolute first citation *dis-* form once in every 1602 words, while Shakespeare yields one every 25,289 words. The real position is revealed still more clearly by calculating the number of *dis-* forms per 100,000 words for all these authors.

Table 3. Occurrence of *dis-* words per 100,000 words, from table 1, in descending frequency

Author	total	words (est.)	*dis-*/100,000 words
Clever	18	28,847	62.40
More	2	24,860	8.04
Hester	2	37,984	5.26
Shakespeare	37	859,857[7]	3.95 (3.72)
Langton	1	17864	3.94
Hill	1	34375	2.91

| Barrough | 3 | 265,065 | 1.13 |
| Banister | 2 | 199,888 | 1.00 |

Clever is far and away the most prolific user of such terms in this list, increasing the likelihood that this represents an idiolectal feature. In any case, Shakespeare's number must be reduced by the number of antedatings of him found here, so that presently his figure actually stands at 3.72/100,000 words. This figure is considerably more than that of Banister and Barrough, while the figures for Hester and More look rather more significant. However, the very small number of words militates against any confident assertions in these cases.

Further adjustments to these figures ought to be made, however. First, all terms not falling into the *OED*'s category 4 should be removed. This eliminates *discolorate* (Barrough) and *dissimilar* (Banister), both of which are direct Latinate borrowings, not creative uses of the prefix. Other words already omitted are *discoverture* (Clever) and *distinguished* (Bostocke), which are obvious derivatives of words which predate our period. Finally, other *dis-* absolute first citations in the *OED* for the authors listed in table 2 should be added (Baker 1, Banister 3, and Hester 1). All these adjustments to table 2 now give table 4:

Table 4. *OED* category 4 *dis-* word absolute first citations in medical texts and the *OED* (and Shakespeare)

Author	antedatings	*dis-*/100,000 words
Baker[8]	1	–
Banister	5	2.50
Barrough	2	1.89
Clever	8	65.86
Hester	1	2.63
Hill	1	2.91
Langton	1	3.94
More	1	4.02
Shakespeare	37	3.95 (3.72)

The figures for More and Hester now appear to be meaningful, but the number of occurrences is very low. In Hester's case there are works still to be excerpted.

3. The *Oxford English Dictionary* evidence

In order to provide the instances from medical texts and from Shakespeare with some kind of context, a list of all words beginning with *dis-* in the *OED* with a first date between 1520 and 1620 was prepared, comprising 870 items in all. The principles which were followed in preparing this list from the *OED* CD-ROM were that all fine-print lemmas have been included where the corresponding main entry falls between 1520 and 1620, but not main entries whose date falls before that range. Inflected forms (with *-ing*, *-ed*, etc.) with full lemma status have however been included. Fine-print lemmas with no quote at all, such as *discommodated,* have been omitted as undatable, though there were very few of these. Main lemmas such as *disdainish* or *disquare*, or *distackle*, taken by the *OED* editors to be established by a cited inflected or derived fine-print lemma, e.g. *disdainishly,* have not been included unless a first date in the period covered by this article was available. Where it was not, the fine-print form only has been retained, e.g. *distackled*. *OED* lemmas like *dismaiden*, illustrated by a citation containing *dismaidening* but no other, have been listed under the latter form. *Disconduce* and *disconducing* are doubtful in date.

Names which were doubtful attributions, such as H(arvey), J. have been treated as if resolved where the same name occurred as a certain attribution for another word. There was no need to resolve the cases of M(oufet) or W(oodcocke), since all attributions were doubtful. One doubtful attribution to Shakespeare was also included.

Any duplications created by the antedatings listed earlier should also be removed (Shakespeare 2, Southwell 1, Read, J. 2, Norden 1, Sylvester 1, Purchas 1, Recorde 1, and Harvey 1). Authors producing less than three first citations were omitted. The first citations of these words sorted by author or work cited then produces the following list:

Table 5. Numbers of absolute first citations of *dis-* words in the *OED* per author/ work (minimum 3; no subsequent antedatings removed; all types included)

Absolute first citations	Author/ work cited	Absolute first citations	Author/ work cited
50	Florio	4	Day, A.
46	Cotgrave	4	Dee
37	Shakespeare	4	Drayton
20	Spenser	4	Fenton
17	Sylvester	4	Fletcher. G.
15	Sidney	4	Folkingham
14	Holland	4	Foxe
14	Nashe	4	Gest
13	Daniel	4	Harvey, J.
13	Palsgrave	4	Jackson
11	Speed	4	Newton
10	Jonson	4	Phaer, T.
10	Pilgr. Perf. (W. de W. 1531)	4	Puttenham
		4	Raleigh
10	Udall	4	Stanyhurst
9	Chapman	4	Wilson, T.
9	Hall Chron	4	Wright, T.
9	Shelton	3	Banister
8	Golding	3	Bell
7	Barret	3	Breton
7	Berners, Ld.	3	Bright
7	More	3	Compl. Scotl.
7	Norton. T.	3	Davies, J.
6	Countess of Pembroke	3	Drant
		3	Greene
6	Heywood, J.	3	Guillim
6	Hooker	3	Hakluyt
6	Sandys	3	Hall, Bp.
6	Topsell	3	Harpsfield
6	Warner	3	Hieron
5	Act 35 Hen. VIII, c. 1	3	Hollyband
		3	Horsey
5	Coverdale	3	Huolet
5	Donne	3	Hyrde
5	Eden	3	Marston
5	Elyot	3	North
5	Latimer	3	St. Papers Hen. VIII, XI.

5	Mulcaster	3	Tomson
5	Stubbes	3	Tourneur
5	Tindale	3	tr. Pol. Verg. Eng. Hist. (Camden)
4	Bacon		
4	Bayne	3	Turberville
4	Collins	3	Whitehorne
4	Copland		

This list shows the absolute prominence of the lexicographers among the authors cited. John Florio and Randle Cotgrave, both compilers of English/vernacular dictionaries, dominate the latter part of the period considered, as does Palsgrave, who is comparably prominent in the earlier period. Together they account for 108 (12.4%) of these words. This relatively large contribution is probably explained by a large number of terms coined to account for the Italian prefix *dis-* in Florio, such as *discortegianato discourtiered*, and the French *des-* in Palsgrave and Cotgrave. Interestingly, by no means all of these are straightforward calques, however; witness Florio's *sfeminato diswoman'd*. Had they been, a simple explanation of their presence would have been to hand but, as it stands, it may be the case that Florio was responding to a current trend, and was perhaps inclined to use such terms himself. One must also keep in mind the efforts made in the later sixteenth century to incorporate material into dictionaries simply in the interests of copiousness.

Edmund Spenser (20), the translator Josuah Sylvester (17), Sir Philip Sidney (15), the translator of classical works Gabriel Holland (14), Thomas Nashe (14), Samuel Daniel (13), and the historian John Speed (11) are also prominent. Generally speaking these people were prominent in the literature of the time.

There are many interconnections between certain of these people. Sidney ought to be considered along with his sister, Mary Herbert, the Countess of Pembroke, who contributes six. Spenser was closely associated with Sidney, dedicating *The Shepheardes Calendar* to him, and "The Ruines of Time" to the Countess of Pembroke (Hannay 1990: 60, 78).[9] Samuel Daniel was among the circle of literary and learned friends Mary Herbert gathered about herself at Wilton.[10] The influence of French and particularly Italian literature among these writers was strong. The connections between the Florio family and the Herberts were of long standing (Hannay 1990: 74), and John Florio was involved in the revision of the *Old Arcadia* (Hannay 1990: 71). Others to come within their ambit include Nashe (14), Chapman (9), Golding (8), Raleigh (4), while Thomas Drant (3) was an early influence on the young Philip Sidney (Buxton 1954: 33-34). Unfortunately an accurate estimate of their contribution against the corpus they each provide is not possible. Fulke Greville and Sir Edward Dyer, both of whom were among the closest of the Sidneys' friends, are however conspicuous by their absence. In fact, not one such word is recorded for either of them. Michael Drayton (4), who emerged later, and who fell indirectly under the Sidneys' influence, does however appear on the list (Buxton 1954: 223-227).

The position of Thomas Nashe is curious. His colleagues Peele and Greene do not appear in the present list at all. He does seem, however, to have had indirect, if not always friendly, contact with the Sidney circle (Hannay 1990: 69, 140-142). Does his contribution to the list of *dis-* words represent conscious aping of the talk and writing of a learned circle he admired? He was after all involved in the publication of the unauthorised 1591 version of *Astrophil and Stella* (Hannay 1990: 69).

It is tempting to speculate that the Pembroke circle act as a kind of vector for the fashionable spread of this usage, taking it perhaps from the earlier humanists, so that by the 1590s it has been taken up by many others, including Nashe, Speed, Shakespeare, and Clever, but how much data would be required to demonstrate this adequately is not known.

The Sidney circle was not conspicuously aristocratic; indeed Fulke Greville (Lord Brooke), whose name does not appear in table 5, seems to have been the only one among them, although they were extremely well connected. Since there is not much evidence of the use of these words among aristocratic circles, apart from Lord Berners, who predates the Sidneys, it is interesting that Shakespeare frequently puts these words in the mouths of aristocrats, which might rather suggest the upward aspirations of his own class than being a real reflection of the register used by the aristocracy.

It is important at this stage to put this question in a still broader perspective, to see whether there is some degree of knowledge which will allow meaningful conclusions to be drawn from this welter of disparate information. Figure 1 shows the numerical spread of first citations of *dis-* words in the *OED* for the period under discussion. If the *OED* were entirely adequate in its coverage, one would expect a rising and relatively even trend to show up.

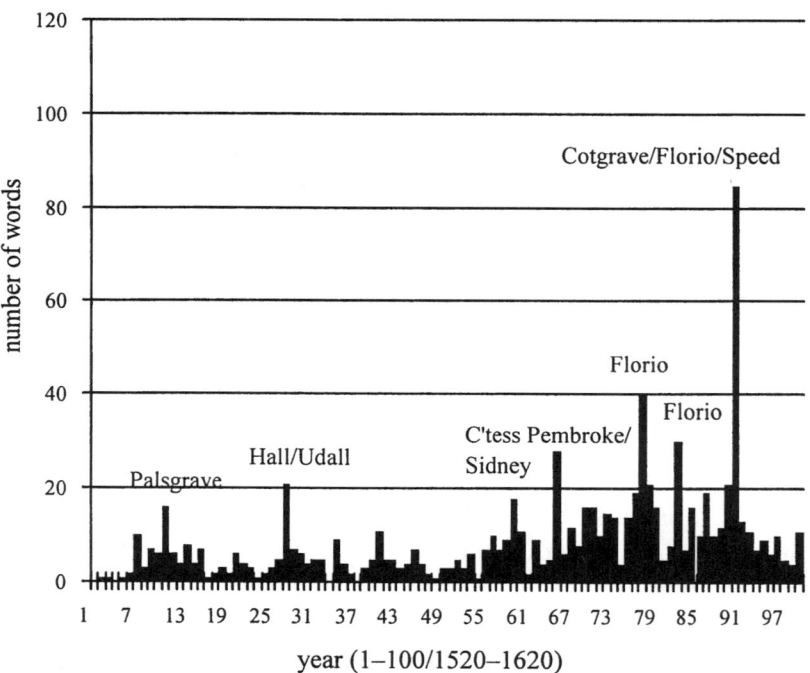

Figure 1. Numbers of first citations of *dis-* words in the *OED* 1520-1620

The difficulty in interpreting it is that it cannot be clearly shown that it represents a meaningful numerical spread of these occurrences rather than representing simply the state of the *OED*'s coverage of the period. In order to clarify this, the highest relative totals have had the names of the one or two most prominent contributors added, to indicate the relative reliance of the *OED*, despite the range of its sources, on particular authors and works. The numerical variation in the highest and lowest is between 0 (three instances) and 85. On the other hand, there is a steady overall rise, as is to be expected, until about 1600. Perhaps rather disturbingly, the coverage falls off from there to 1620. Other areas in which the coverage falls away somewhat are from 1533 to about 1577, conspicuously excluding 1549 (Hall/Udall). It cannot simply be assumed that the use of *dis-*compounds fell away in this period, since it is equally possible that the *OED* data represents it less well.

Consolidating the figures for individual years into larger blocks may overcome this difficulty, but the fact of the matter is that it is not known how many occurrences per unit of time (say, 1-10 years) would adequately represent the actual state of the lexicon. In this particular case, the bias towards lexicographers and literary authors, for whatever reason this might arise, is clear enough.

4. *Helsinki Corpus* evidence

The *Helsinki Corpus of English Texts* for the period 1500-1710 was examined to find out what contribution it could make to the present study. The spread of texts which comprises this period is more limited than that used by the *OED*, but is however less obviously literary, and included such things as legal transcripts and Statutes of the Realm (Kytö 1996). It is also possible of course to search this source exhaustively. The result was that eight antedatings and one unrecorded for the *OED* were found. These were, with their *Helsinki Corpus* codes:

Antedatings
1. *disbursyng* vbl. sb. (E1 XX CORO MOREWOL I, 205: Heading)
2. *discontent* sb (E1 XX CORO WOLSEY II, 17: Heading)
3. *discredit* sb (E1 NN BIO ROPER 92: Heading)
4. *disorder* (E1 XX CORO WOLSEY II, 20: Heading)

5. *dispeche* (E1 XX CORO BEDYLL I, 76: Heading)
6. *dissatisfied* (E1 XX TRI THROCKM I, 78.C2: Heading)
7. *dissembler* (E1 NI FICT MERRYTAL 134: Heading)
8. *disquiet* sb (E1 NN DIARY MACHYN 41: Heading)
Unrecorded
1. *diseased* sb (E1 STA LAW STAT3 III, 906: Heading)

While in absolute terms this does not look like much, it should be remembered that the 870 *dis-* words in the *OED* represent approximately 0.3625 of the total number of lemmas, and that if this number were extrapolated to a complete search of the *Helsinki Corpus* for all possible antedatings, it should yield 2206 such items of new data.

It is generally assumed that word-coinage is a good thing, an assumption pretty well unquestioned in respect of major literary figures. It is presumably felt to be both innovative and healthy for the language, expanding not only its lexical range but also its flexibility and subtlety, while assuring readers and critics of the originality of the writer concerned. All this has applied particularly to Shakespeare. There is, however, no necessity to make such an assumption. It is equally possible to explain the rash of *dis-* words as a rather pretentious, semilearned, and perhaps social affectation, perhaps the sixteenth century equivalent of yuppy slang, or a rough equivalent of the contemporary use of prefixes occurring in various registers, such as *macro-*, *mega-*, or *micro-* as in such forms as *megabucks*, *macrobiotic*, or *microminiaturisation*.

Another issue is whether the figures for the medical practitioners suggest some wider predilection for such forms among them especially, or whether this spread was typical of the population at large. Only a more extensive study will provide an answer to this question, the present data being too incomplete and open to misinterpretation.

5. The lexicographers

The question of whether the words which appear in the dictionaries of Palsgrave, Cotgrave, and Florio are examples of calques, invented to fill out their pages, which never had a genuine life in the language must also be considered. The *OED* provides the following information, including everything which falls after 1520, the *terminus post quem* obviously being the date of the relevant dictionary's publication. Words not in the *OED* category 4 are marked with an asterisk:[11]

Table 6. Palsgrave's *OED dis-* words' first citations

word	type	date	one or no citation[12]	calque
disappear	v	1530	no	no
disappointing	ppl a	1530	no	no
disburse	v	1530	no	no
disconsolate	v	1530	no	yes
**discreetness*	n	1530	no	no
disfaithful	a	1530	yes	no
disgree	v	1530	yes	no
disinhabit	ppl a	1530	yes	no
disinhabit	v	1530	no	no
disjunctive	a and n	1530	no	no
disorder	n	1530	no	yes
disquiet	v	1530	no	no
disused	ppl a	1530	no	no

Palsgrave's relatively small list provides only two clear examples of calques, both of which became firmly established. He also provides the useful remark about *disconsolate* that "This terme is nat yet comenly used."

Table 7. Florio's *OED dis-* words' first citations

word		date	one or no citation	calque
disaccompany	v	1598	no	no
disacknowledge	sb	1603	yes	no
disacknowledge	v	1598	no	no
disadorn	v	1598	no	no

disaggravate	v	1598	yes	no
disagreed	ppl a	1598	no	no
disassociate	v	1603	no	no
disbark	v 2	1578	no	no
disburdened	ppl a	1598	no	no
discomputation	n	1611	yes	yes?
disconclude	v	1611	yes	yes
discustom	n	1603	yes	no
disembowelling	v	1603	no	no
disembroil	v	1611	no	?
disenamour	v	1598	no	yes?
disenamoured	ppl a	1598	no	yes?
disengage	v	1603	no	?
disentangle	v	1598	no	no
disentomb	v	1611	no	?
disenwrap	v	1611	no	?
disestablish	v	1598	no	no
disesteem	n	1603	no	no
disgout	v	1611	yes	yes?
disgregation	n	1611	no	yes
disgust	n	1598	no	no
*dishevel	v	1598	no	no
disinfect	v	1598	no	no
disinteressed	ppl a	1603	no	no
disintricate	v	1598	no	yes
disinvolve	v	1598	no	yes
dismaidening	vbl n	1603	yes	no
disnun		1611	no	yes
disoblige	v	1603	no	no
disobstruct	v	1611	no	no
disopinion	n	1598	no	no
disorderer	n	1598	yes	no
disparting	vbl n	1611	no	yes
displayer	n	1611	no	no
disrepute	v	1611	no	yes
dissociable	a	1603	no	no
dissolubility	n	1611	no	yes
distaste	n	1598	no	no
*distracted	ppl a	1598	no	yes

Fashionable idiolects? 219

word	type	date	one or no citation	calque
disunite	v	1598	no	no
disuniting	vbl n	1611	no	yes
disveiled	ppl a	1611	no	no
disvirgin	v	1611	yes	yes
disvisage	v	1603	no	no
diswood	v	1611	no	no?

Table 8. Cotgrave's *OED* dis- words' first citations

word	type	date	one or no citation	calque
disabuse	v	1611	no	?
disabused	ppl a	1611	no	yes
disaccommodate	v	1611	no	yes
disadapt		1611	yes	yes
disadapted	ppl a	1611	yes	yes
disadapting	vbl sb	1611	yes	yes
disadjust		1611	yes	yes
disadjusting	vbl sb	1611	yes	yes
disadmonish	v	1611	yes	yes
disadvantageously	adv	1611	no	yes
disadvest	v	1611	yes	yes
disadvesture		1611	yes	yes
disappearing	vbl n	1611	no	yes
disappointable	a	1611	yes	yes?
disapt	v	1611	no	yes?
disassemble	v	1611	yes	yes
disassure	v	1611	yes	yes
disaugment	v	1611	no	yes
discontinuation		1611	no	yes
discontinuing	vbl n	1611	no	yes
discontinuingly	adv	1611	yes	yes
discredited	ppl a	1611	no	no
*disdainable	a	1611	no	yes
disembarking	vbl n	1611	no	yes
disembellish	v	1611	no	yes
disenchanted	ppl a	1611	no	yes
disenclose	v	1611	no	yes
disencumbered	ppl a	1611	no	yes
disentreat	v	1611	yes	no
disesteemer	n	1611	no	no

disimmure	v	1611	no	yes
disimpeach	v	1611	no	yes
disimprison	v	1611	no	yes
disinhabitate	v	1611	yes	yes
disinter	v	1611	no	no
disjust	v	1611	yes	no
dismantling	vbl n	1611	no	yes
disorderable	a	1611	yes	no
*disparager	n	1611	no	no
dispraiseress	n	1611	yes	yes
*disputed	ppl a	1611	no	yes
dissociated	ppl a	1611	no	yes
dissociation	n	1611	no	yes
*distillable	a	1611	no	yes
distrustfully	adv	1611	no	no
disunition	n	1611	no	yes

In these tables columns 4 and 5 show the extent to which these lexicographers have tended to produce calques which have not entered the language. "Yes" and "yes" obviously suggests a stillborn calque. "Yes" and "no" suggests a still-birth, although not a calque, while "no" and "yes" suggests a calque which has found its way into use, although these tables make no attempt to show how well-established the word may have become. Two quotes in the *OED* are sufficient here to put it in this category, which may still mean very restricted use. "No" and "no" suggests either a word already established in the language or, less probably, a successful introduction.

There is a clear difference in the distribution of these classes among these three lexicographers.

Table 9. Distribution of one or no citation instances among lexicographers

lexicographer	yes and yes (%)	yes and no (%)	no and yes (%)	no and no (%)	total
Palsgrave	0 (0%)	3 (23%)	2 (15%)	8 (62%)	13
Florio	4 (8%)	6 (12%)	11 (22%)	25 (51%)	49
Cotgrave	14 (30%)	3 (7%)	23 (50%)	5 (11%)	46

The percentage figures, which are far more revealing than the raw numbers, have been rounded out to the nearest whole number. Although Palsgrave's figures are relatively small, they suggest that he was recording words already in the language, 77% falling into the last two classes. These figures are comparable to those for Florio. At the other end of the scale Cotgrave has 17% in the classes with only one citation, and as little as 11% in the "no and no" category, strongly suggesting that he was interested in fleshing out his work with what we might call dictionary words, and paid rather less attention to current usage in English.

It is of even more interest, to return to the matter of the Sidney circle, that Florio was closely associated with them, whereas Cotgrave was not. The connections between the Florio family and the Herberts is outlined in Hannay (1990: 74). The interest of the Sidneys in Italy is of course also well attested. We may I think speculate that Florio was recording words in use among people that he knew quite well. This provides another hint that the Sidneys and their influential circle may have been the catalyst for the accelerating spread of *dis-* words from the 1580s on. Figure 1 shows that 1577 might indeed be a turning point but, given the remaining doubts about the adequacy of the *OED*'s coverage, the fact that the evidence adduced here adds to it only marginally, and the rate at which antedatings have been and presumably will continue to be found, it seems possible that the trail will lead to earlier groups of humanists, including Thomas Drant, Nicholas Udall, the chronicler Edward Hall, and perhaps even Thomas Phaer (to hazard a guess), and that the configuration of figure 1 will shift appreciably to the left as more data becomes available. The role of familiarity with French and Italian remains unexplored; tantalisingly so, since both Cotgrave's and Florio's works date from 1598-1611.

6. Conclusion

In a sense, this investigation has come full circle, and we are still left with William Clever's unexplained contribution. Studies of the

Sidneys do not throw up his name, the only doctors regularly mentioned being Matthew Gwinne, none of whose writing was excerpted for the *OED*, and Thomas Moffet.[13] It seems rather unsatisfying simply to suggest that what the Sidneys said one year was all the rage the next, in spite of its perhaps containing a grain of truth. Neither is there a satisfactory reason for the failure of Dyer and Fulke Greville to appear, though perhaps this means that a reassessment of their terminology is called for, along with that of Gabriel Harvey.

The fundamental problem raised here is the nature of the evidence. The *OED* seems to show a usage centring on the Sidney circle as might be expected from its coverage of the literature of the time, but the nine unrecorded words from Clever raise the question of how complete the *OED* record of these forms is in the first place. It also seems that the *OED* may be overreliant on data from those associated with the Sidney circle in any case. The Shakespearean evidence has been shown to be less significant than it might have seemed. The *Helsinki Corpus* has a little to offer over and above the *OED* from the Early Modern English period, but a great deal of information must remain untapped, as the Clever evidence suggests. Surely the whole story of the *dis-* prefix, and presumably other features of the sixteenth century lexicon, is yet to be told.

Notes

1. My grateful thanks to Terttu Nevalainen, whose painstaking and helpful suggestions on the text have been greatly appreciated.
2. There is a full discussion of the principles of negative prefixation and its typology in Colen (1980-1981), in which distinctions are made between its reversative, privative, and ablative functions. These matters have also been discussed in Funk (1986); however, for the present purposes I confine myself to the broader sense of "privative" which the *OED* adopts, since much of the primary data here comes from that source. On prefixal negation more generally see Baldi, Broderick, and Palermo (1985: 33-35).

3. The references in square brackets are to the author or work and date listed in the *OED*.
4. This term is used to distinguish these from first citations of particular senses of a word which are not the earliest under that lemma. They are not absolute in any stricter sense, and of course may be themselves antedated at any time. The accuracy of the *OED*'s summary is another matter worth attention, but is beyond the scope of this paper.
5. Although this may in fact be a form of *distemper*, the *OED* lists no variant form which suggests that it is not a separate formation analogous to *closure, investiture, disposure, ructure*, etc. from the Latin *-ura*. It is less likely to have derived from the *-erare* verb ending in Latin as with *distemper*.
6. A disputed quarto reading; elsewhere *disturbers*, but the *OED* has been followed.
7. This figure is taken from Schäfer (1980: 61).
8. A figure for Baker cannot be produced, since this antedating is from a work not examined here. The one which was used here contains about 16,380 words, which would produce a result of 6.11, but this is clearly too high.
9. Spenser also had a long-standing friendship with the humanist don and pamphleteer Gabriel Harvey, who contributes only two *dis-* words, but whose works have in all likelihood been only perfunctorily read for the *OED*. His brother, John Harvey, contributes four.
10. Monsarrat (1982) shows Daniel's dependence on French sources for Seneca, but also shows, on the subject of this paper, that on one occasion he renders *d'incommoditez* by *incommodities* whereas other translations use *discommodities*.
11. Leaving other categories of *dis-* words in these lists gives some sense of the relativities involved.
12. The *OED* is a little inconsistent in recording the status of these words (xi, "General Explanation"). The term "rare" with the superscripts $^{-1}$ or $^{-0}$ is given as the code for words with no or one citation only respectively. However, "obs^{-1}" and "obs^{-0}" both occur. It is also clear that "no citation" in practice means "no citation other than one given in a dictionary" so that *disinhabitate* is listed as "rare^{-0}", but has a citation from Cotgrave. There are also words such as *disinhabit* [ppl a Palsgrave] where neither status marker is given, but there is only one dictionary citation. I take this to mean that this was indeed the only citation available, despite the lack of the marker. In view of all this, I list these instances with "yes" under the heading "One or no citation" in the tables, column 3. Under *disadmonish*, there is the additional entry "In Halliwell", which I take to mean that the word is listed in Halliwell's *A*

Dictionary of Archaic and Provincial Words (1847), since no actual quote accompanies it. Instances like this are listed as "yes" in column 3.
13. Matthew Lister became physician to the Countess of Pembroke after Moffet's death in 1603. See Hannay (1990: 201).

References

Bailey, Richard W. (ed.)
    1978   *Early Modern English: additions and antedatings to the record of English vocabulary, 1475-1700.* Hildesheim: Olms.
Baldi, Philip, Victor Broderick, and Davis S. Palermo
    1985   Prefixal negation of English adjectives: psycholinguistic dimensions of productivity. In: Jacek Fisiak (ed.), 33-57.
Buxton, John
    1954   *Sir Philip Sidney and the English renaissance.* London: Macmillan.
Colen, Alexandra
    1980-1981   On the distribution of *un-*, *de-* and *dis-* in English verbs expressing reversativity and related concepts. *Studia Germanica Gandensia* 21: 127-152.
Fisiak, Jacek (ed.)
    1985   *Historical semantics. Historical word-formation.* (Trends in Linguistics. Studies and Monographs 29.) Berlin/New York: Mouton de Gruyter.
Funk, Peter
    1986   Towards a definition of semantic constraints on negative prefixation in English and German. In: Dieter Kastovsky and Aleksander Szwedek (eds.), 877-889.
Hannay, Margaret P.
    1990   *Philip's Phoenix.* Oxford: Oxford University Press.
Kastovsky, Dieter and Aleksander Szwedek (eds.)
    1986   *Linguistics across historical and geographical boundaries.* (Trends in Linguistics. Studies and Monographs 32.) Berlin/New York: Mouton de Gruyter.
Kytö, Merja
    1996   *Manual to the diachronic part of the Helsinki Corpus of English Texts: coding conventions and lists of source texts.* (3rd edition.) Helsinki: Department of English, University of Helsinki.

McConchie, Roderick W.
1983   Additions to *OED* from William Clever's *The flower of physicke, 1590*. *Notes and Queries* 30: 396-401.
1997   *Lexicography and Physicke: the record of sixteenth century English medical terminology.* Oxford: Oxford University Press.

Monsarrat, G. D.
1982   Samuel Daniel, Seneca and Mornay. *Notes and Queries* (New series.) 29: 420-422.

OED
1979   *The compact edition of the Oxford English dictionary.* London: Book Club Associates.

Schäfer, Jürgen
1980   *Documentation in the* OED: *Shakespeare and Nashe as test Cases.* Oxford: Oxford University Press.

Wood, Anthony
1691   *Athenae Oxoniensis.* London.

On the conditioning of geographical and social distance in language variation and change in Renaissance Scots

Anneli Meurman-Solin

1. Space, time, and genre

Problems of historical dialectology in the field of Scottish studies have been highlighted in recent research by pointing out that until recently the evidence scholars had to rely on was mostly "documents written by a small, unrepresentative section of Older Scots society, often a specialised, 'set-piece' type of text such as a will, a deed, a public record or a literary work" (Johnston 1997: 48). To take a somewhat different perspective, data extracted from Scottish texts representing this rather limited selection of genres has not been thoroughly studied, because the texts have not been readily available to scholars. The *Edinburgh Corpus of Older Scots* (*ECOS*), which is being compiled by Keith Williamson at the Institute for Historical Dialectology, University of Edinburgh, will allow us to draw on a rich source of legal and other documents originating from the different areas of Scotland, all of them checked against the manuscript.

In addition, partly because of the diversification of the social functions of written texts and partly for other reasons such as the general increase in literacy, a much wider range of prose genres is extant, starting from the mid-sixteenth century, as is amply demonstrated for example by the bibliography of the *Dictionary of the Older Scottish Tongue*. A relatively representative variety of chiefly non-literary texts is also available in computer-readable form in the *Helsinki Corpus of Older Scots* (*HCOS*) (Meurman-Solin 1995b), 1450-1700, which comprises texts extracted from fifteen different genres: acts of Parliament, burgh records, trial proceedings, histories, biographies, travelogues, diaries, pamphlets, educational treatises, scientific treatises, handbooks, private letters, official letters, sermons, and the Bible (Meurman-Solin 1993, 1995a, 1995b). A new corpus of Scottish correspondence, including some private records such as diaries and autobiographies by women writers, will provide evidence of language use in more private, often informal settings. In the reconstruction of regional variation, non-professional or untrained writers, who can be assumed to be linguistically and stylistically less competent and less experienced, can be indispensable as informants as regards both phonological and morphosyntactic variation.

In legal texts, especially in the public documents, the dimension of "space" is usually unproblematic, as the majority of these texts are relatively easily localisable. However, despite the precise date of production, the variable of "time" must be redefined to allow for the important role of conventions and formulae, which increases the general degree of conservatism in legalese. While the date of a letter allows us to specify a particular point of time in a person's idiolect in a particular communicative situation, the variable of "space" calls for a scalar system of parameter values when applied to texts by geographically and socially mobile writers.

If the degree of systematicity in the choice of variants is sufficiently high, idiolects reflecting a high degree of "mixed speech" can provide important evidence of the relative importance of norms in contact.[1] In other cases, informants who have left their place of origin, and have perhaps continued moving from one place to another, add to the extent of variation and variety in a given area. Members of the clergy and professional soldiers have been put in separate groups of their own because of the more or less regular pattern of mobility in their lifestyle.

Localisation may also be difficult as regards women who, as a result of marriage (or marriages), moved from one place to another. Moreover, as we do not usually know where and when a female informant became literate, it may be impossible to tell which area the spelling practices she learned belong to and how they relate to her pronunciation. Systematic use of phonetic spellings of a particular kind has been shown to provide relevant diachronic evidence (Meurman-Solin forthcoming a). However, in historical dialectology, as suggested by Keith Williamson (personal communication), letter-writers used as informants could be graded according to how detailed information about language-external factors related to mobility and degree of literacy is available. In contrast with England (for information about the *Corpus of Early English Correspondence*, see Nevalainen and Raumolin-Brunberg 1996), the scarcity of fifteenth- and sixteenth-century autograph letters in Scotland means that also informants that cannot be prosopographically described in sufficient detail have to be included in the text corpora.

Johnston (1997: 51) discusses the influence of stylistic competence, claiming that the more mobile people would use a "watered-down" style to communicate with people from other regions; beside this enhanced ability to differentiate between speech styles, the upper classes and professionals, in general more mobile, would act as the main guardians of a "Standard Scots style". He also introduces the concepts of town vernaculars as opposed to countryside vernaculars. However, polarisations of this kind are too simplistic to provide a relevant set of criteria for categorisation. For example, the network of family castles scattered around on the map of Scotland may give the impression of places on the periphery or in isolation, but their distance from administrative centres varies, depending for instance on a particular family's or family member's role in national politics, the economy or culture. Therefore, in addition to the geographical distance between the various places of origin of the texts and their writers, the concepts of economic and social distance must be applied in order to explain differences, for instance between members of self-contained tightly-knit speech communities and those regularly in contact with people originating from various other areas within the rather diffusely-patterned framework of national administration and the economy.

In the present study,[2] the focus is on tracing developments in the mid-sixteenth century, when a number of major changes in the differentiation process from Northern English to Scots have taken place in a considerable number of texts (Meurman-Solin 1993, 1997a, 1997b; Devitt 1989); this has been considered a time-period which is sufficiently free of standardising (i.e. anglicising) tendencies (cf. McIntosh 1978: 42-43 as quoted in Romaine 1982: 2). With reference to the replacement of Scots by English starting from the late sixteenth century, Johnston (1997: 50) suggests that "there seems to be a sort of hiatus in the provinces, where the pull of the Edinburgh Standard is declining and that of London not quite dominant". In the present study, my question is the extent to which the so-called Edinburgh Standard spread to the other regions of Scotland in the sixteenth century. The general assumption is that major changes in progress in certain areas, for instance in the Central Scots area, may never have reached certain other areas such as the south-western counties, or were interrupted under the pressure of new, more forceful trends.

2. Informants

In a diachronic study of regional variation, letter-writers are especially important informants for the following reasons.
1. Rather than being exclusively produced by trained and competent writers, as is the case with for example statutory texts or "high styles" of literature, letters have also been written by less trained and less experienced writers, for instance by women.
2. Letters provide direct evidence of more varying degrees of linguistic and stylistic competence, and also of how the varying addressees affect linguistic and stylistic choices. In contrast with texts representing some other genres, where the audience of a text can sometimes be defined only with reference to the abstract concept "the implied reader", in letters the addressee is almost always specified as a particular person or a body of persons. I am interested in the multidimensionality of pressures a writer experiences in choosing between different levels of usage; the degree of pressure and the writer's linguistic and stylistic performance will depend first and foremost on his or her competence as well as the topic and

purpose of the text and its addressee. Important conditioning factors are related to the circumstances of production, whether the text is a product of careful planning or a hurriedly written note; whether it is a polite gesture with the necessary clichés or an appeal written in sophisticated argumentative prose, etc. At one end of the continuum depicting variation in the written idiom in epistolary style there are thus letters that are syntactically complex and stylistically highly elaborated texts epitomising characteristics of some of the most sophisticated written texts, and at the other prose styles where shorter sentences and paratactic structures prevail (Meurman-Solin 2000b).

In earlier research the focus has often been restricted to the writers themselves. The Helsinki corpora have specified the participant relationship between the writer and the addressee in terms of degree of intimacy and distance, labelling the presumed differences in social status by the parameter values "up", "equal" and "down". I would like to claim that, at least in the reconstruction of regional variation, a much more detailed set of criteria must be used. A well-trained writer may be conscious of the linguistic and stylistic expectations of his or her addressee; he or she may resort to the linguistic and stylistic resources of his or her own variety but is perhaps also influenced by the recipient's language variety, especially if that variety enjoys prestige.

Can letters provide useful information about practices of spoken language, even colloquialisms (cf. the discussion in Romaine (1982: 154))? In my earlier research I have been able to show that phonetic spellings frequently used in letters by less trained writers do indeed allow us to study the spoken form of words spelt in this way. For example it has been possible to antedate the shortening of long vowels in the first half of the sixteenth century by analysing the texts of writers who tend to resort to phonetic spellings as a result of their ignorance of established spellings. As regards other features I would be very reluctant to consider letters a source of evidence for the reconstruction of the spoken idiom. In the genre of letters we can identify a wide range of levels of written usage, styles or registers. The more rarely a writer takes a pen in hand, the more unpredictable – ranging from imitative to idiosyncratic – his or her use of linguistic resources may be as a result of inexperience and lack of confidence. Like Romaine (1982: 16), I would wish to stress McIntosh's view (1978: 4) that "We must educate ourselves to recognise that the written word as such will often display its own regional habits and characteristics; a realisation of this will help to jolt us out of habitual obsession with spoken dialect characteristics and enable us to understand and interpret specifically written-dialect characteristics".

In the present study the evidence has been extracted from the *Correspondence of Mary of Lorraine* (1542-1560) (Cameron (1927), from here on quoted as *Corr. M. L.*). The edited letters have been checked against manuscript (Scottish National Archive SP2: 1-4). The thirty-eight informants represent thirteen different counties besides the city of Edinburgh; only localisable authors writing autograph letters have been included. There are four women writers.

Table 1. Localisation of writers of autograph letters in the *Correspondence of Mary of Lorraine*

ABERDEENSHIRE	ANGUS
Sir George Meldrum of Fyvie	Patrick, Master of Ruthven, later the third Lord Ruthven
George, fourth Earl of Huntly	
Elizabeth Keith, Countess of Huntly (spouse of the fourth Earl of Huntly)	FIFE
	William Bruce of Earlshall
Alexander Gordon, younger brother of George, fourth Earl of Huntly	Andrew Fernie of Fernie
	Mr. Henry Balnaves of Halhill
	William Mudy of Breckness and Downreay
PERTHSHIRE	William, fourth Lord Sinclair
Henry, first Lord Methven	Sir James Stewart of Beath; third son of second Lord Avondale
Margaret Robertson of Strowan, Countess of Erroll	
EDINBURGH	EAST LOTHIAN
James Henrison	William, fourth Earl Marischal
Sir Adam Otterburn of Auldhame and Reidhall	Sir George Douglas of Pittendreich[3]
James Stewart, Earl of Moray	ROXBURGHSHIRE
Catherine Bellenden	John, sixth Lord Erskine, Commendator of Dryburgh
SELKIRK	Thomas, Master of Erskine, Commendator of Dryburgh
Sir Walter Scott of Buccleuch and Branxholm	Marion Haliburton, Lady Home (spouse of George, fourth Lord Home)

LANARKSHIRE Sir Alexander Shaw (Schaw) of Sauchie James, fifth Lord Somerville John, second son of Hugh, fourth Lord Somerville	AYRSHIRE Ninian, third Lord Ross Mr. John Hepburn, parson of Dalry William Cunningham of Glengarnock Gilbert, third Earl of Cassillis Sir Hew (Hugh) Campbell of Loudoun William Cunningham, third Earl of Glencairn
KIRKCUDBRIGHT James Gordon of Lochinvar	
WIGTOWN Malcolm Fleming, prior of Whithorn; second son of John, second Lord Fleming Fynlay Campbell of Croswell	DUMFRIES Malcolm, third Lord Fleming Sir James Douglas of Drumlanrig Robert, fifth Lord Maxwell

Data of this kind is assumed to show how internally homogeneous the various idiolects are and what sort of variability is reflected when idiolects are grouped together on the basis of the geographical area informants originate from. Romaine (1982: 11) reminds us of Bailey's (1973) assumption "that the individual is homogeneous and that variability results from the aggregation of internally consistent lects which are different from each other with respect to one or more linguistic features". The data is analysed taking into consideration possible intracounty differences. Besides time and space, other conditioning factors such as social status, contacts with the court, education, and mobility may influence the choice of variants; these will be discussed in paragraphs summing up the findings at the end of each section, and in section 4. The general assumption is that the frequent contacts of many of these informants with members of other speech communities and their more or less regular participation in various activities in the political, judicial, and ecclesiastical institutions of the nation must have influenced their idiolectal preferences. Information about the families and the lands they possessed and about places where the letters were written thus offers primary evidence for the localisation of the various writers; further evidence is provided by the description of the education and the social status and network of each informant. A sophisticated method for including information of this kind in electronic corpora of letters has been applied in the *Corpus of Early English Correspondence* (Nevalainen and Raumolin-Brunberg 1996).

3. Diffusion of *i*-digraphs

Long vowels have undergone major changes in the late fifteenth-century and sixteenth-century Scots (Aitken 1977); the use of *i*-digraphs to mark vowel length has been considered one of the features diagnostic of the rise of the so-called Scottish English Standard (Meurman-Solin 1993: 126-135). The following data will illustrate the diffusion of these spellings in the various counties listed in table 2.

Table 2. Vowel and diphthong systems of Early, Middle and Modern Scots: a rough outline

Early Scots	Middle Scots	Modern Scots	Modern Scots examples	Older Scots spellings
1a	iː → ei	aɪ	*rise, byre, dry, ay* 'yes'	iCe, yCe, y; yi, ay: y#
1b		ʌi	*bite, bide, wyce* 'wise'	
2	eː → iː	→ i	*meet, see*	e, eCe, eC-; ei, ey; eaː
3	ɛː		*deaf, dead, deave* 'deafen'	e(e#
4	aː → eː	→ e	*gate, baith* 'both', *hale* 'whole', *gae* 'go'	a, aCe, aC-; ai, ay, e, ea: a#, ay#
5	oː → oː	→ oː	*coat, before, close* [klos] n., [kloːz] v.	oCe, oC-, o; oi, oy: o#, oo#
6	uː → uː	→ u	*crouse* 'jaunty', *loud* [lud], *dou* 'dove'	ou, ow: ow#
6a	ul		*multure, pull, full*	ul(l), (w)ol: ull#
6b	ul- → ul	→ ʌl	*bullet, pulley*	ull-
7	øː → øː	→ ø	*use* [øs] n., [øːz] v., *fruit, mune, do*	oCe, oi, oy, o(me), o(ne), (w)o, uCe, wCe, ui, uy, wi, wy, ou, ow, oo: o#, oe#, oo#, ou#, ow#, u(e#, w#
		i		
		e		
		eː + ɪ		

A larger corpus of letters will be needed to present statistically significant findings about the frequencies and distributions of *i*-digraphs.[4]

3.1. The digraph yi

Instead of the *i/y(-e)* predominant in pre-1450 texts (Aitken 1977: 3-4), the spelling *yi* was later used for /iː/, possibly reflecting the transition from /iː/ to /ei/ which has been attested from the last quarter of the fifteenth century (Aitken 1977: 7). Thus, beside the prevalent spellings of the period such as *tyme, devyse* for *time, device*, George Gordon, fourth Earl of Huntly (Aberdeenshire), for instance, differentiates between graphs for /iː/, so that pronunciations perhaps gradually approaching /ei/ are spelt *yi*, as in *desyir, lyik, thyink, quhyit, prowyid, devyis, wyiffe* (PrE *desire, like, think, quit, provide, devise, wife*), while the pronunciation /i/ is perhaps reflected in spelling variants with double consonants, for instance *lyff(e), gyff* (PrE *life, give*). The later change from /ei/ to /aɪ/ or /ʌi/ has been dated to around 1600 (Aitken 1977: 7). Beside its use as part of an inflectional ending (for instance *quenyis*, usually *quenis*, for *queen's*), the spelling *yi* also occurs in word-final position (*redyie* for *ready*). When we try to find evidence for the direction of the change, it may be significant that the Countess of Huntly, unlike her husband, does not use such variants.[5] The third informant representing Aberdeenshire, Sir George Meldrum of Fyvie, writes *myin* for *mine*, but otherwise there are no variants of this kind in his idiolect. In his numerous letters, Alexander Gordon, a younger brother of the Earl of Huntly, usually an early adopter of new variants (see below), has only *lyik* for *like*, and *hapax* occurrences of *-yin* in the past participle forms *wreittyin* and *fwnddyin*.

This spelling has not been attested in letters by writers representing the counties of Angus, Selkirk, Roxburgh, Dumfries, Kirkcudbright and Wigtown, and only occurs sporadically in Fife (*Fyiff* for *Fife*, *syid* for *side*, attested at Cupar and Leuchars). The shortened quality (as above) may be reflected in spellings such as *tymmis* and *crymmis* (PrE *times, crimes*) and the variants *wyff, lyff* (PrE *wife, life*) used by Perthshire writers. These could be compared with one of the three informants representing Lanarkshire. John Somerville alternates between *dissyir* and *dissir*; as he also has *plissir* (suggesting /i(:)/ in the second syllable), instead of variants such as *plesuyr* (/ø:/), he seems to make a distinction between /dissi:r/ or /disseir/ and /dissir/.

Two of the Edinburgh informants choose the digraph exclusively in words of native origin such as *vyis, utherwyis, alwyis, twyis, lyik, wyif, almychtyie* (PrE *(other)wise, always, twice, like, wife, almighty*), while French borrowings are spelt *avis/avys/awys* and *devis* (PrE *advice/advyse, device/devise*). In East Lothian, the graph *yi* has not been attested in the Earl Marischal's letters but, in his letter written at Tantallon Castle, Sir George Douglas of Pittendreich has *wyisle* for *wisely* in addition to the prevalent *syd, lyk(maner)* for *side, like*.

In Ayrshire, one writer has *liif* for *life*, and sporadic instances of *yi* (*syid, Tyisday, wyit, wyislie, wyin* for *side, Tuesday, wit, wisely, wine*) have been attested in letters by three of the six Ayrshire informants; these variants are particularly frequent in Gilbert, Earl of Cassillis' letters (*tyim, adwyis, dessyir(r)it, lyik, syin (syne, adv.)*). William Cunningham of Glengarnock differs from other informants in choosing spellings such as *taym, maynd, Tayesday, Klayd, layk, desayres* (PrE *time, mind, Tuesday, Clyde, like, desires*), evidently suggesting diphthongisation (/teim/, /meind/, etc.).[6] Similarly the female informant of Roxburghshire, Marion Haliburton, Lady Home, never uses *yi*, but there is evidence of a lower quality of /i:/, approaching /e:/ (*henes* for *highness*); her variant *weyn* for *wine* may also suggest pronunciation as a diphthong.

To sum up, the shortened quality of /i:/ is reflected in variants attested in Perthshire and Lanarkshire, whereas various degrees of diphthongisation are reflected in the spelling *yi*, which is especially frequent in the Earl of Huntly's (Aberdeenshire) and the Earl of Cassillis' (Ayrshire) letters, in the spelling *ay* in William Cunningham of Glengarnock's letters, and in the spelling *ey* in Lady Home's (Roxburghshire) letters.

We will find the Earls of Huntly and Cassillis repeatedly mentioned as writers who have adopted the full range of new spelling practices earlier than many others. This can perhaps be explained with reference to extralinguistic variables other than time and space. The Earl of Cassillis was educated at St. Andrews, and was also a pupil of George Buchanan, both a well-known writer and tutor of James VI. He travelled abroad for some years, was later also commissioned for various official tasks, and regularly attended the Parliaments of Scotland from 1535 until his death. In 1554 he became Lord High Treasurer of Scotland. The Earl of Huntly spent his youth chiefly at Court, as he was of approximately the same age as his uncle King James V. He retained his direct contacts with the court, was one of the Regents of the kingdom during the King's absence in France in 1536, and in 1542 one of the Council for the government of the realm during the minority of the young Queen. Like Cassillis, Huntly was a wealthy landowner; in 1548-1549 he was given the lands and earldom of Moray as a gift from the Queen. Further research will be necessary to find out whether the use of variants with *yi* originated in coalitions close to the court and among high government officials. That this question is worth closer study is suggested by the fact that the informants using diphthongs of a clearly more open quality, Glengarnock and Lady Home, had lower social status, their role in national politics subsisting only through intermediaries such as their relatives.

3.2. The digraph ei/ey

As in the case of *yi*, a strong tendency to prefer the *i*-digraph has been attested particularly in the Earl of Huntly's letters in Aberdeenshire, as well as in some lexical items where the vowel is generally short (*keyng, leyf* for *king, live*). The past participle *been* is spelt *bein* or *beyn*, sometimes also with the word-final *-e* retained (*beyne*). Variation in the genitive forms of *queen* also provides evidence of the markedly long vowel: besides *queynis, quheyingis, queyneis* and *qwieyneis* have been attested. There are four instances of *quenis* as compared to five variants with *ei/ey*, a pattern of co-variation in the use of the earlier and later spellings which is also in general terms one of the striking features of mid-sixteenth-century letters examined in this study (for the generally high degree of variation in Middle Scots, see Aitken (1971)). The trend towards marking vowel length by *i*-digraphs can be contrasted by variants reflecting a shortening of the vowel: *belyffe* and perhaps also *quyneis*. Some of the examples quoted above provide evidence of some degree of overlapping in the variational space of /iː/ and /eː/ as regards both quality and length. The proportion of *i*-digraphs is lower in the Countess of Huntly's letter as compared with her husband's letters; in Meldrum of Fyvie there is co-variation between *gret, well* and *pleis, deidis*. In the Angus informant's letters, despite the use of the *i*-digraph, the word-final *-e* has been retained in *seine* (*seen*), but also *bene* (*been*) occurs.

The number of items where *ei* is chosen is considerably high in Perthshire, so that 85% of the variants of *please* and *great* have an *i*-digraph. *Herof, -for, -upon, -to* (40%) co-vary with *heir/heyr* (60%). The digraph also occurs in final syllables: *fineill, eterneill, Octobeir, casteill*, and in word-final position in *supley*. The more frequent pattern *remeid, remedit* occurs in Lord Methven's letters in the form *remeid, remeiddit*. Henry, first Lord Methven, who married the Queen-Dowager, Margaret Tudor, widow of James IV, is one of the informants whose full range of *i*-digraphs may suggest that this spelling practice was favoured by members of discourse communities that had close contacts with the court and the government.

All the Fife informants have variants with *ei/ey*, mostly in monosyllabic words or bases: *keipe, seik, beseik, conwein, weill, heir, neirhand, beir, yeirlie, cleirlie* (PrE *keep, seek, beseech, convene, well, here, nearhand, bear, yearly, clearly*), but *kepyng, chetis, quenis, yeris* (PrE *keeping, cheats, queen's, years*). Andrew Fernie of Fernie, writing at Cupar, supplies an instance of *beleyiff*, where the additional *i* after *ey* can be assumed to stress vowel length and perhaps to suggest a higher quality of /eː/. Mr. Henry Balnaves of Halhill is the only Fife informant who has introduced the incoming spelling of /eː/: *greater, bearis, feare, earnestlye, knawleage*, even *preas* for *pres* (PrE *press*). Unfortunately, the only thing we know of his English contacts is that he was appointed one of the commissioners for Scotland to meet the English commissioner for the settlement of some disputes on the Border.

Sir Adam Otterburn was Provost of Edinburgh for a certain time, and was one of the original senators of the College of Justice (*Corr. M. L.*: 36). His preferred practice is to use variants with *i*-digraphs when the long vowel is immediately followed by *r* (*heir, weir, yeir, geir, feir* 92%), *d* (*dreid, deid* 'deed', *deid* 'dead', *speid, neid, remeid, proceid, steid* 84%), *k* (*speik, seik* 'sick', *seik* 'seek', *beseik* 100%), and *s* (*pleis, eis, eiselie* 91%). However, there are practically even proportions of *weil(l)* and *wele*, *keip(e)* and *kepe*. Moreover, the occurrences of the variant *grete* represent 75%, *gret* 13%, and *greit* 12%; similarly *bene* is chosen in 89% of the cases, but *bein* only in 11%. The Earl of Moray's (Edinburgh) practice shows a somewhat higher proportion of spellings such as *ples* (6; *pleis* 3), but there are fewer letters, so that there is not enough quantitative evidence of most variants. Henrison has *mene* and *quene*, but otherwise the monosyllabic words have *ei*, while Catherine Bellenden's letters illustrate an almost regular practice: *bein, weil(l), keip, geir, greit, seiknes* but *belevis, quenis, yeris, berar*. In addition she writes *arreistit* and *arreistment*.

Sir George Douglas of Pittendreich, brother of the sixth Earl of Angus, indicates a shortened and higher quality of /eː/ by spellings such as *kyp, kyppyng, kype* for *keep(ing)*. On the other hand, there are variants of an infrequent type such as *nobeill* and the genitive form *Grayeis* (cf. Lord Methven above). The early shortening of /eː/ to /i/ is abundantly evidenced by Alexander Gordon's idiolect. There are variants such as *hyr* for both *here* and *hear*, *wylfair* for *welfare*, *swstyne, obtyn* for *sustain, obtain*; *byne, quyn, belyff, beliwis, besyk, myn* and *ryff* for *been, queen, belief, believes, beseech, mean* and *reave* 'to tear'. These variants allow us to antedate the shortening of /eː/ to /i/, so that the change seems to have taken place as early as the 1540s and the 1550s (see also Meurman-Solin 1999, forthcoming a, b) instead of approximately 1600 (Aitken 1977: 7). This shortening has also been attested in the Borders in Lady Home's letters, where *plis, plissis* for *please, pleases* have been attested.

In Roxburghshire there are no *i*-digraphs of this kind among Lord Erskine's spellings, but *pleis, greit, beseikand, weile*, which belong to the high-frequency items in epistolary style, have been attested in the Master of Erskine's language. Lady Home uses the two main groups of variants interchangeably: *beseik, speik, keip, weill, beyn, pleis, heir/heyr, beir*, but also *gret, nedfull, sped, belef, well*. Her spelling *geit* (*get*) suggests the pronunciation /ge:t/. The Selkirk informant chooses an *i*-digraph in words and base elements presumably pronounced as monosyllabic (*beyne, beseyk, heir(for), heir(in), weill*), but otherwise *e* is used.

Beside a couple of examples such as *weil/veill, heir*, the informant of Sauchie, Lanarkshire, writes *belew, ben, her*, and also suggests a long vowel in *geit* and *leis* (PrE *get, less*). There are very few examples in the letters of the other two Lanarkshire informants, but their practices reflect a pattern of co-variation between the two systems (*beseik, pleis* but *beleve; greit* and *gret*).

In Ayrshire, all informants show variation between the English and the distinctively Scottish spellings, except William Cunningham of Glengarnock, who does not use the graphs *ei/ey*. The Earl of Cassillis clearly prefers variants with *i*-digraphs, as compared to the other Ayrshire writers, in whose idiolects the two competing practices are relatively evenly applied. James Gordon of Lochinvar (Kirkcudbright) uses only *i*-digraphs (*bein, seik, yeit, seiknes, seyne, geif (if), keiping*), whereas the Dumfries writers use a mixed system. A change in the stress pattern is perhaps reflected in Wigtown variants such as *kepeyne* and *eweyne* (*keeping, even* 'evening').

Evidence from Aberdeen, Angus and Fife also reflects overlapping between phonemes 3 (Early Scots /ɛː/ > /iː/ > /i/, as in *meet*, or /ɛː/ > /eː/ > /e/, as in PrE *deaf*) and 4 (Early Scots /aː/ > /eː/ > e) in table 2. In the Earl of Huntly's and the Countess of Erroll's letters the occurrence of the variant *plais*, instead of the more frequent *pleis* for *please*, perhaps makes explicit the difference between /eː/ and /ɛː/, the spelling variants for both being primarily the same before the introduction of the differentiating graphs *ee* or *ie* and *ea*. The phoneme /ɛː/ is spelt *a* in *hartlie/hartly, hard and tratyt* (*heartily, heard, treated*) by Lord Ruthven (Angus). Lord Methven (Perthshire) uses the variants *arly/ayrly/ayrle* for *early*. An adventitious *dail* (for *deal*) occurs in a letter by the Earl of Cassillis.

We can thus conclude that the digraph *ei/ey* has spread to all the counties, and almost all informants use it. However, no writer uses this graph exclusively, although writers such as Catherine Bellenden carefully contrast between *yeir* and *yeris*. She was the daughter of Patrick Bellentyne, parish clerk of Holyrood and steward of Queen Margaret, wife of King James IV, and Marion Douglas. To understand her good linguistic and stylistic competence, it is perhaps significant that John Bellenden, the translator of Livy and Hector Boece may be her brother. In a wider corpus, it may be possible to find evidence of the influence of the following consonant on the choice of a digraph (see Otterburn above). Phonetic spellings reflecting the shortening of /eː/ to /i/ have been attested in Aberdeenshire, Roxburghshire and East Lothian. The graph *ai* is used for /ɛː/ in Perthshire (Countess of Erroll, Lord Methven), Aberdeenshire (Earl of Huntly), Ayrshire (Earl of Cassillis) and Angus (Lord Ruthven), the graph *ea* only in Fife (Balnaves). The digraph *ei/ey* occurs in word-final syllables in Aberdeenshire, Perthshire, East Lothian and Wigtownshire.

3.3. The digraph oi/oy

The variant spelling *oi/oy* for /oː/ is much more unevenly spread in the different regions than *ei/ey*. There are sixteen informants (42%) with no *oi/oy*-variants. A further fourteen use this digraph only when /oː/ is followed by *r*, a length-maintaining consonant in Middle Scots; in addition a number of these informants write *purpois* and *suppois*. The frequency of *oi* in *purpois* and *suppois* seems to indicate that the stress pattern attracts the *oi*-spelling in loanwords of this kind.

Thus only 21% of the informants use this digraph in a way which is more varied than that described above. While in Lord Methven's letters variants such as *hope* and *hoip* covary, Sir Adam Otterburn, the Edinburgh informant, uses *oi* more frequently than the alternative spellings, for instance, *befoir* 86%, *befor* 14%. Beside the typical contexts (*quhairfoir, thairfoir, foirsaid, purpois, suppois*), only the variant with *oi* occurs in the spellings of the following lexical items: *hoip(e), lois, Boithuile* (*hope, lose, Bothwell*). Another Edinburgh informant, James Henrison, has *moir* and *moist*. In this collection of letters, only Henrison and Alexander Gordon show a rounding of /aː/ in these frequently occurring lexical items; in fact the only other pre-1550 instances have so far been attested in Sir Patrick Waus' letters from school at Musselburgh, East Lothian, in 1540. Of the Roxburghshire writers, Lady Home has *loifis* (*loves*) and *toik* (*took*), which shows her awareness of the distinctively Scottish spelling practice. It is noteworthy that, as a daughter of Patrick, last Lord Haliburton of Dirleton, her language is presumably a mixture of the East Lothian and Roxburghshire varieties.

The use of *oi/oy* is particularly widespread in Alexander Gordon's letters; unlike other mid-sixteenth-century letter-writers in this collection, he has variants such as *doid, shoyt, woittit, thoycht, wroycht, broycht* and *Scoitland* (*did, shoot, voted, thought, wrought, brought, Scotland*). There is variation in the quality of the vowel when followed by *n*, as reflected in *done, doune* (for *done*), *sone* and *sonair* (*soon, sooner*). The spellings reflecting /uː/ (*doun(e)/downe, noun/nowne, stoun*), rather than the prevalent /oː/, have also been attested in Angus, Selkirk and Roxburghshire. Further study will be necessary to establish the geographical and social distribution of *done, doin, doun(e)* and *dwin*; in the present material, the last-mentioned variant only occurs in Meldrum of Fyvie's (Aberdeenshire) and the Earl of Cassillis' (Ayrshire) letters. Meldrum also spells *dweng* and *dwis* for *doing* and *does*.

In addition to the five informants mentioned above, there are two Ayrshire letter-writers in whose letters the digraph has been attested in words such as *thoill* (Lord Ross), and *doyn* and *soyn* (*done, soon*) (Hew Campbell). The Earl of Cassillis again differs from all the other informants by choosing spellings reflecting a higher quality of the long vowel: *dwin, nuin, twik*, instead of the more frequent *done/doin, none/noin, toke/toik*.

Thus the eight writers using the digraph represent Aberdeenshire, Perthshire, Edinburgh, Roxburghshire and Ayrshire. Among these there are two of the early adopters of the whole system of digraphs: Sir Adam Otterburn and Alexander Gordon.

3.4. The digraph ui/uy

The Earl of Huntly's spelling practices indicate that the variational space of /uː/ and /øː/ overlap to some extent, as he has both *souerly* and *suyrly* for *surely*. The variants *concluid, persuit/perswyt, behuif, puir, displesuyr* also suggest the pronunciation /øː/. There are however spelling variants such as *gud, reffus, excus* and *us* (*use*), which in other idiolects frequently have variant forms *guid/gwid, re(f)fuis, excuis* and *(h)uis*. The Countess chooses *uy* in *assuyr, aventuyr, plesuyr*; it is perhaps significant that in her variants the following consonant is *r*. Meldrum has *gud/gwd* but *exswis, rwid, swir* (*excuse, rude, sure*). Lord Ruthven (Angus) has only one *ui*-spelling rendering phoneme 7 in table 2, namely *cuist* (*cast*). Otherwise, only variants with /uː/ occur: *gud, doun* (*done*), *noun* (*noon*). Also in Perthshire we find a mixed set of variants: *pwyr, suir, Tuisday,* but *gud, assur(e), indure, aventur, plesour, surty*; as regards the verb *use*, the vowel is shortened in *ussit* for *used*. The Countess of Erroll does not use the *ui/uy*-graph. Only one of the Fife informants, William Mudy, spells *suirle*, and there is variation in a place-name: *Muiraldhouse/Murhaldhous*. William Bruce of Earlshall has *lowk* for *look*, instead of *luik/luyk*. He has no *ui*-graphs.

The markedly Scottish *i*-digraph co-varies in three of the four Edinburgh idiolects. Otterburn belongs to those writers who now and then choose *ui* when followed by *r* or *s*: *puir, suirly, uis, Tuisday,* but these co-vary with *pur, sur(elie), assur(e), use*. Only *gude, tuke, luke* have been attested in his idiolect. The Earl of Moray has *guid* and *Tuisday,* but otherwise *brut, gud, indure, surlie*. Henrison does not use *ui*-graphs. Bellenden has *puir* but *gude, surname*.

South of Edinburgh, either intra- or interidiolectal variation prevails. In East Lothian, for instance, Sir George Douglas does not use the graph *ui*, preferring *plessur, sur, gud*. In contrast, the Earl Marischal consistently uses *guyd, gwidnes, plesuyr*. In Roxburghshire only *tuik* occurs in Lord Erskine, but he uses *serwiture* instead of the more frequent *servitour*. The Master of Erskine suggests a higher quality by the variant *behuif*, but spells *gud(e), servitour*. Lady Home uses *suir*, but *pur, gud, adventour* (cf. her *doun*, for *done*). She also has the graph *i* for phoneme 7 in table 2 in *assirans*, possibly suggesting /i(:)/. In Lanarkshire, John Somerville may suggest the same quality by *plessir* for *pleasure* as Lady Home by *assirans* for *assurance*, although his variant may also reflect the French etymology (French *plaisir*). There is also another etymologising variant *serviture* in his idiolect. The other two Lanarkshire informants do not use the graph *ui/uy*.

With the exception of the Earl of Glengarnock, who writes *sower* and *sowerle* (*sure, surely*), the digraph *ui/uy* occurs in all Ayrshire idiolects. John Hepburn, the parson of Dalry, has a whole set of these variants: *huis, duisun, puit, luif, suir, suirnam, huisand, tuichand*, while variants with an additional *i* such as *houis, touin, douit* may also suggest a similar pronunciation, rather than merely marking vowel length. That the dominant pattern in Ayrshire is that of co-variation is highlighted by the fact that the Earl of Glencairn has *guid* but also *gud, sur, us*; Lord Ross chooses *suyrlye* but *souerte*, Hew Campbell *servituir/servetuir, guid, fuit* but *gud, excus*, Cassillis *excwis, retwirning*, but *gwd* (cf. his *wi/ui*, instead of *oi*, above).

Dumfries and Kirkcudbright informants do not use *ui/uy*. Lord Maxwell has *towin* for *town*, Malcolm Fleming, prior of Whithorn, *youir* for *your*. The variational space in the area ranges from the Lochinvar (Kirkcudbright) variant *tryblit* to James Douglas of Drumlanrig's *sowr* varying with *surlie*. There is also *twyk* (*took*) in Campbell of Croswell, and *guid* by the prior of Whithorn (Wigtownshire).

In Alexander Gordon's letters, the digraph is infrequent: *suir* varies with *surly*, and *towyn* with *toune/towne*, but the graph *ow* is otherwise prevalent, so that for instance only *powre* occurs for *pure* or *puir* (*poor*), and also *fowrtht, lowsit, rowine, cowm, cowmin*, etc.

(*forth, losed* [lost], *ruin, come, coming*), where the dominant graph in the period is *o* or *u*.

To sum up, fifteen writers (39%) do not use the graphs *ui/uy/wi/wy* for /ø:/ (the Countess of Erroll, 5 Fife informants, Henrison, Douglas of Pittendreich, 2 Lanarkshire informants, the Earl of Glengarnock, 4 Dumfries and Kirkcudbright informants). The graph *oui/owi* has been attested in the south-west, *i* in Roxburghshire and Kirkcudbright. The majority of writers vary between the earlier graphs and the later *i*-digraphs.

3.5. The digraph ai/ay

3.5.1. The type *make/maik*

As with other *i*-digraphs, George, fourth Earl of Huntly (Aberdeenshire) uses a rich variety of variants with *ai/ay* in both open and closed syllables, and in some suffixal elements (*haiste, haistlie, plais, plaice, graice, daytit, dyssait, glaid, maid, remaid, declair, declairyng, quhair, sayme(n), nayme, waikis, rayther, ansair, devisair*). However, the repeatedly attested interchangeability of the two main types of variants can be illustrated by his use of sets such as *grace* 78%, *graice* 15%, *gracis* 2%, *graceis* 2%, *graicis* 3%; *sayme(n)* 69%, *sam* 31%. In the Countess's letter, *ai* only occurs in the variant *maid*. Variation also characterises Sir George Meldrum of Fyvie's spelling practices (*grais, maid, wair*, but *grace/gras, part(t)*).

Lord Ruthven (Angus) has adopted the practice (*quhairfor, haist, skayth, persaife, resaife*), as has Lord Methven (Perthshire), the latter's usage being abundantly illustrated by *ai/ay*-spellings in open and closed syllables and in suffixal elements (*lait, laytlie, estait, maid, staid, laif, gaif, rasaif, persaif, bagsaif, remayn, tayn, graic(e), haist, maik, eschaip, bairnis, spairis, skaythis, contrair, contenwaill*). In the rather scanty evidence of the Countess of Erroll's practices in a single letter, earlier spellings such as *charge, grace, persave* are perhaps somewhat more prominent than those with an *i*-digraph (*maid, pairt, skayth*, also *traittit*). Her phoneme /ɛː/ is sporadically spelt *plais*, instead of *pleis*, while spellings such as *chengit* and *bernis* instead of *changit/chaingit*, *barnis/bairnis* perhaps suggest a changed quality in the prevalent /ɛː/ to /e(ː)/.

All informants from Fife use a mixed system (for instance *graice/grayce* co-varying with *grace*); even variants such as *madaym*, which are otherwise rare in this period, have been attested in Bruce of Earlshall's letters. In addition, the graph *e* occurs in *hesty* for *haisty* and *forenemit* for *forenamit*. Fernie uses the graph *a* in *rade* and *hartle* (*ready, heartly*), as does Lord Sinclair in *hartlie*.

As regards Edinburgh informants, there is a richer variety of lexical items with the *i*-digraph in Otterburn, but the proportion of *i*-less variants is considerable: *skaith, graitht, persaif(f), saif, saifty, gaif, haist(e)(ly), laitlie, debait, aige, maid, perswaid, invaid, glaidlie, declair, quhair, cais, saik(leslie)*. For example, the type *quhair* has been chosen in 71% of occurrences, *quhar* in 29%. The Earl of Moray uses *maid, laitlie, payrtit, haiste(ly), quhairof, Clydisdaill*, but *part, quharfor* and *quhartrow*. Henrison has the digraph *ai* only before *r*: *quhairfor, laird*, the latter varying with *lord*. Bellenden's variants with *ai* are *weilfair, quhairthrow, maid, skaith* and *traist*.

In East Lothian only *rasaifit* and *fair* (*far*) have been attested, and *maitter* varies with *matter*. Otherwise, *hast, part, spar, gar* are used. Marischal has *lait/layt(lye), mayd, quhayr(for), mariaig*, but *charg, discharge*. The Selkirk informant spells *invaid, mayk, taykis, nayme, wair* (v.), *quhair, hayst, waygis, sayff*, but *change* and *depart*. The mixed system is also prevalent in Roxburghshire, so that for instance Lady Home uses both types of spellings: *mad, part, quhar, skath* and *maik, maid, pairt, spair*. In Lanarkshire John Somerville's variants are *rasaif, astait, dait, persuaid, quhairthrow*, the last-mentioned varying with *quharfor*, but in Lord Somerville's letter there are no instances of the digraph except in *maist* (see section 3.5.2.).

In Ayrshire, the idiolectal profiles differ considerably. Hepburn of Dalry, the Earl of Glencairn, Campbell of Loudoun, and the Earl of Cassillis apply mixed systems of orthography, with *ai/ay* varying with *a-e*, whereas Lord Ross has no *ai/ay* in the type *make/maik* (cf. /aː/ > /oː/ in section 3.5.2.); besides *grays, plays, saym, qwayr* (*where*), Glengarnock uses *sornem* (*surname*). Hepburn of Dalry's *dale* for *daily* probably reflects uncertainty in his use of graphs for /ɛː/ and /ai/, rather than an early example of the monophthongisation of the diphthong in *day*. It is noteworthy that the digraph *ai/ay* has also spread to the south-western counties, although informants such as Gordon of Lochinvar use them only in *hais* and *haif*.

There is thus evidence that the spelling *ai/ay* leads the spread of the incoming digraphs with *i*, since there is a wider variety of lexical items, and the practice has been adopted by all writers. However, it is noteworthy that the variants with an *i*-digraph regularly occur with the earlier alternative spellings.

3.5.2. The type *mast/maist*

The digraph *ai/ay* also occurs in spellings where variation has mostly been attested between /aː/ spelt either *a-e* or *ai/ay*, as in *mare* and *mair*, rather than between these and variants reflecting the rounding of /aː/ to /oː/ such as *more* (also *moir*, as shown in section 3.3.).

In Aberdeenshire the Earl and the Countess of Huntly differ from one another in the use of *ay* in word-final position. While the former uses variants such as *nayne, haym, hayff, baytht* alongside *nay, say/suay/sway, fray*, the latter has *ay* in *wrayt* 'wrote', but *a* in *fra* and *quha*. In the Earl's idiolect, *maist* is still a minority variant (8%) as compared with *mast* (85%) and *uttermest* (7%). Meldrum of Fyvie uses *saye* (*so*) and *mast* (*most*) but, interestingly, some of his variants reflect an early rounding of /aː/: *sowbeit, no, onely*.

While Lord Ruthven (Angus) restricts his use of the digraph to closed syllables *mair, maist* as opposed to *a* in word-final position (*na, fra, sa*), Lord Methven (Perthshire) shares the Earl of Huntly's practice, as illustrated by such variation as *haill, maist, mayr/mair/evyrmair, nayn, bayth(e), gayn, stayn, wrait* and also *quhai/quhay*. Like Meldrum of Fyvie, the Countess of Erroll also has variants reflecting the rounding of /aː/. Apart from *nane, maist, quhay*, she uses *quhome*, which is the prevalent oblique form of *who*, co-varying with the prevalent nominative form *quha* (Meurman-

Solin 2000a). She also has *frome*, which is infrequent in Scots at this early stage.

The Fife pattern of variation is that of the Countess of Huntly and Lord Ruthven, so that the digraph does not occur in word-final position. The only idiolect with a rounded variant (again *quhom(e)*) is that of Henry Balnaves. Andrew Fernie of Fernie's spelling *mayist* (*most*) can perhaps be interpreted as emphatically indicating vowel length. William Mudy has *spak, halele* (*wholly*), *fra, twa, na, quha*, but no corresponding *i*-digraphs.

Like the Earl of Huntly and Lord Methven, Otterburn (Edinburgh) spells not only *mair, maist* and *baith(t)/bayth, haill, wrait*, etc., but also uses *mast*. He has no variants with rounding, in contrast to the Earl of Moray, in whose letters there is variation between the two types of main variants such as *fra, na, nane, spak, quham* and *bayth, maist, mayr(e)*, and sporadic uses of *quhom(e)* and *boyth*. Henrison also has on the one hand *sa, bygane, baith* and on the other *moir, moist*. Similarly, Catherine Bellenden uses *quhom*, but otherwise *sa, bygane, wrait, haill*.

It is significant that the pattern of co-variation also prevails in East Lothian, Selkirk, Roxburghshire, and Lanarkshire. In East Lothian, besides the relatively widespread *quhom*, the nominative form *quho* also occurs, otherwise *bath, ga, haill* illustrate the pattern of presumably free variation. Although preferred in *haym(e), nayme, bayth, maist, haill* (Earl Marischal), the digraph *ai/ay* does not seem to occur word-finally; for instance only *quha* has been attested. Besides *quhome, wtermest/wtermost*, the Selkirk informant spells *maist, baytht, nayne, haill*, and *fra, quha, swa/sa*. In Roxburghshire, the only *ai/ay*-spelling in Lady Home's letters is the word-final *suay* (*so*); otherwise, she has *sa, forga, na, quha, hale, hamly, mar*. All the Roxburghshire informants show rounding in the co-variation of *nane* and *none, maist* and *most, quhay* and *quhome, bath(t)* and *both*. A similar co-variation of the graph *a* (*nan, rad* (*rode*)*, ham, quha, fra*), the digraph *ai/ay* (*bayth, maist, mair*) and *non* (John Somerville), *quhom* (Lord Somerville) has been attested in Lanarkshire. A pattern of this kind also characterises the Ayrshire writers; however, two (Hepburn of Dalry and Campbell of Loudoun) also use the graph *e* as in *nen*, which co-varies with *nane* and *nain* in the former's idiolect; the latter also chooses *wttermest*, *hyndmest*. Unlike Dumfries, where all the main variants (*maist*, *mair*, *wrait*, *baith*; *hale*, *fra*, *na*, *twa*; *quhom*) occur, there are no variants with rounding in Kirkcudbright and Wigtown (*mair/mayr*, *mayst*, *fra*, *twa*).

Thus only one informant, William Mudy (Fife), does not use *ai/ay* in words representing the type *mast/maist*. Five letter-writers (the Earl of Huntly, Meldrum of Fyvie, Lord Methven, the Countess of Erroll and Lady Home) also use the digraph in word-final position. Variants reflecting the rounding of /aː/ to /oː/ have been chosen by Meldrum, the Earl of Moray, Henrison, the East Lothian and Roxburghshire informants and John Somerville; in addition the variant *quhom* occurs in the letters of the Countess of Erroll, Henry Balnaves, Catherine Bellenden, Scott of Buccleuch, the Dumfriesshire informants, and Lord Somerville. The phonetic spelling *nen* co-varies with *nane/nain* in an Ayrshire idiolect (Hepburn of Dalry). An especially high degree of intracounty variation has been attested in Fife.

4. Concluding remarks

In these mid-sixteenth-century autograph letters, the variable of space is reflected in the varying pace and patterns of diffusion of the different *i*-digraphs. While the digraphs *ai/ay* and *ei/ey* generally co-vary with the earlier graphs *a-(e)* and *e-(e)* in almost all the writers' letters, the other digraphs have been adopted only by some informants, or are used very sporadically by a somewhat more numerous group of them. The use of the spelling *oi/oy* seems to be particularly conditioned by locality, so that it is rare or absent in the western counties of Scotland, and in certain regions in the east, for instance in most idiolects in Fife. Only two writers use this digraph for the phoneme /oː/ in more varied contexts: Alexander Gordon, who, as a younger brother of the Earl of Huntly, had an ecclesiastical career, and Adam Otterburn. Similarly, the digraph *ui* is used only by 61% of the informants, *yi* only by 29%.

Although in Edinburgh the two writers higher on the social ladder, the Earl of Moray and Adam Otterburn, use *yi* in contrast with Catherine Bellenden and James Henrison, in whose letters the graph is absent, further evidence will be necessary to draw conclusions about the possible conditioning factors related to social status. As regards variation between the established /eː/, frequently spelt *ei* in words such as *keip, pleis,* and *beleif,* and the incoming shortened /i/, spelt *i/y,* as in *kyp, belyff(e),* and *plis,* shared language-external characteristics are difficult to identify between the four informants who use the latter types of variant: the Earl of Huntly, Alexander Gordon, George Douglas of Pittendreich, and Lady Home.

Indications of the widened variational space of a phoneme or phonemes, which leads to some degree of overlapping in the choice of graphs, have been attested in a number of idiolects. The Early Scots phoneme /iː/ either seems to have a lower quality, approaching /eː/, or has developed into a diphthong /ei/ in variants such as Lady Home's *weyn (wine)* and Cunningham of Glengarnock's *taym (time)*. Rather than claim that only these two writers represent early adopters of the diphthongised pronunciation, it is possible to conclude that phonetic spellings of this kind offer relevant evidence of a change in vowel quality. While the same change may also have taken place in some other informants' idiolects, it remains covert because of conservative spelling practices or because of a writer's insensitivity to a faithful graphic representation of phonetic variants. There seems to be a direct correlation between the generally high degree of variation in an idiolect and a higher percentage of incoming variant spellings. For instance, the Earl of Huntly varies between a short and a long vowel in items such as *belyffe, lyff(e), beleif(f), wyiff(e),* and *keyng* for *king*; he also uses both *suyrly* and *souerly* for *surely, concluid* and *gud, affor* and *af(f)oir, therfor* and *therfoir.*

Data illustrating the use of *i*-digraphs highlights the role of factors other than space and time in the spread of variants. This can be further illustrated by converging evidence offered by the analysis of the relative pronoun *who* after animate/personal antecedents in the same autograph letters (Meurman-Solin 2000a). According to evidence provided by these letters and texts in the *HCOS,* this pronoun occurs for the first time in this function and position in Scots as late as the mid-sixteenth century. It is noteworthy that, in contrast with other Ayrshire informants, the Earl of Cassillis, who has been shown to have adopted the whole range of *i*-digraphs, is also one of the five informants (others represent Perthshire, Fife and East Lothian) who have been identified as early adopters of the relative pronoun *who* after immediately adjacent antecedents other than personal names.

The present study has tried to show that both geographical and social distance may be relevant as factors conditioning the diffusion of spelling variants. The question of whether the so-called Edinburgh Standard spread to the other regions has been shown to be irrelevant for two reasons. There are no clear indications of an internally uniform norm in the Edinburgh region, and the direction of change is not definable simply in terms of a spread of variants from the Central Scots area to peripheral or isolated areas. It is evident that the relatively low degree of uniformity in idiolects representing the same geographical area can be explained with reference to type and intensity of contact with other speech communities in the case of letters to Mary of Lorraine, particularly the court and other wielders of political power. A wider range of texts, including family letters, will be necessary to see whether the practice of using *i*-digraphs to mark vowel length originated in formal styles of writing.

As part of the next stage in this large-scale project, it will be necessary to examine the system of local and regional varieties in detail, keeping in mind that some or all of them may have remained internally heterogeneous, and that it may not be possible to provide evidence of one of these varieties having developed into a relatively uniform national standard, the so-called Scottish English Standard. In addition, the later developments will have to be discussed in terms of when and where the influence of the Southern Standard becomes evident.

Notes

1. The concept "norm" here refers to shared linguistic practices attested in a number of texts that form a relatively coherent group of core texts, along with a varying number of other texts scattered around them at varying distances from the core depending on their degree of divergence, rather than to internally more or less uniform varieties used in a particular area, conventionally labelled the Scottish English Standard, and a number of regional and local norms.
2. I am very grateful to Robert McColl Millar, University of Aberdeen, for his valuable comments on the present study.
3. Both of the East Lothian informants have a North-Eastern background, as the Earl Marischal originated from North-East Scotland, and, although the Douglas family had its power base around Tantallon Castle, there is an Angus connection (McColl Millar, personal communication).
4. For information on the spread of *i*-digraphs in the first version of the *Helsinki Corpus of Older Scots* (1993), see Meurman-Solin (1993: 196-200).
5. The Countess also wrote at least one of her husband's letters (*Corr. M. L.*: 20, footnote); it is interesting that in this letter spellings with *yi* are also consistently avoided.
6. Cunningham of Glengarnock does not use *ei/ey* (cf. for instance *men* for *mean* in *the men taym*); the digraph *ay* renders the pronunciation /ɛː/ in *plays* 'place', *rayd* 'rode' and *nayn* 'none'.

References

Primary source

Cameron, Annie I.
    1927   *The Scottish correspondence of Mary of Lorraine, 1542-1560 (Corr. M. L.)*. Scottish History Society, Third Series, 10. Edinburgh.

Secondary sources

Aitken, Adam J.
    1971   Variation and variety in written Middle Scots. In: Adam J. Aitken, Angus McIntosh, and Hermann Pálsson (eds.), 177-209.
    1977   How to pronounce Older Scots. In: Adam J. Aitken, Matthew P. McDiarmid, and Derick S. Thomson (eds.), 1-21.

Aitken, Adam J., Matthew P. McDiarmid, and Derick S. Thomson (eds.)
    1977   *Bards and Makars: Scottish language and literature, mediaeval and renaissance.* Glasgow: University of Glasgow Press.

Aitken, Adam J., Angus McIntosh, and Hermann Pálsson (eds.)
    1971   *Edinburgh studies in English and Scots.* London: Longman.

Barisone, Ermanno (ed.)
    forthc.   *The history of English and the dynamics of power.* Alessandria: Dell'Orso.

Bermúdez-Otero, Ricardo, David Denison, Richard M. Hogg, and Charles B. McCully (eds.)
    2000   *Generative theory and corpus studies: a dialogue from 10ICEHL.* (Topics in English Linguistics 31.) Berlin/New York: Mouton de Gruyter.

Devitt, Amy J.
    1989   *Standardizing written English: diffusion in the case of Scotland 1520-1659.* Cambridge: Cambridge University Press.

Hickey, Raymond, Merja Kytö, Ian Lancashire, and Matti Rissanen (eds.)
    1997   *Tracing the trail of time.* Proceedings from the Diachronic Corpora Workshop, Toronto, May 1995.

Johnston, Paul
    1997   Older Scots phonology and its regional variation. In: Charles Jones (ed.), 47-111.

Jones, Charles (ed.)
    1997   *The Edinburgh history of the Scots language.* Edinburgh: Edinburgh University Press.

McIntosh, Angus
    1978   The dialectology of Mediaeval Scots: some possible approaches to its study. *Scottish Literary Journal*, Supplement No. 6: 38-44.

Meurman-Solin, Anneli
    1993   *Variation and change in early Scottish prose: studies based on the Helsinki Corpus of Older Scots.* (Annales Academiae Scientiarum Fennicae, Dissertationes Humanarum Litterarum 65.) Helsinki: Suomalainen Tiedeakatemia.
    1995a   A new tool: The Helsinki Corpus of Older Scots (1450-1700). *ICAME Journal* 19: 49-62.

1995b	*The Helsinki Corpus of Older Scots*: a WordCruncher version. 850 000 words of running text. Oxford Text Archive, Norwegian Computing Centre for the Humanities.
1997a	Text profiles in the study of language variation and change. In: Raymond Hickey et al. (eds.), 199-214.
1997b	On differentiation and standardization in Early Scots. In: Charles Jones (ed.), 3-23.
1997c	A corpus-based study on *t/d* deletion and insertion in Late Medieval and Renaissance Scottish English. In: Terttu Nevalainen and Leena Kahlas-Tarkka (eds.), 111-124.
1999	Letters as a source of data for reconstructing Early Spoken Scots. In: Irma Taavitsainen, Gunnel Melchers, and Päivi Pahta (eds.), 305-322.
2000a	Geographical, socio-spatial and systemic distance in the spread of the relative *who* in Scots. In: Ricardo Bermúdez-Otero et al. (eds.), 417-438.
2000b	Genre as a variable in sociohistorical linguistics. *European Journal of English Studies* 1.
forthc. a	The centre and the periphery: competing norms on the dialect map of Renaissance Scotland. In: Ermanno Barisone (ed.).
forthc. b	Women's Scots: gender-based variation in Renaissance letters. In: Proceedings of the International Conference on Medieval and Renaissance Scottish Literature and Language, Oxford, August 1996.
forthc. c	Change from above or from below? Mapping the *loci* of linguistic change in the history of Scottish English. In: Laura Wright (ed.).

Nevalainen, Terttu and Leena Kahlas-Tarkka (eds.)
1997	*To explain the present: studies in the changing English language in honour of Matti Rissanen.* (Mémoires de la Société Néophilologique de Helsinki 52.) Helsinki: Société Néophilologique.

Nevalainen, Terttu and Helena Raumolin-Brunberg (eds.)
1996	*Sociolinguistics and language history: studies based on the Corpus of Early English Correspondence.* (Language and Computers: Studies in Practical Linguistics 15.) Amsterdam/ Atlanta, GA: Rodopi.

Romaine, Suzanne
1982	*Socio-historical linguistics: its status and methodology.* (Cambridge Studies in Linguistics 34.) Cambridge: Cambridge University Press.

Taavitsainen, Irma, Gunnel Melchers, and Päivi Pahta (eds.)
    1999   *Writing in non-standard English.* (Pragmatics and Beyond. New Series 67.) Amsterdam: Benjamins.

Williamson, Keith
    forthc.   Edinburgh Corpus of Older Scots. Institute for Historical Dialectology, University of Edinburgh.

Wright, Laura (ed.)
    forthc.   *The development of Standard English: theories, descriptions, conflicts.* Cambridge: Cambridge University Press.

The influence of political correctness on lexical and grammatical change in late-twentieth-century English

Stephen J. Nagle, Margaret A. Fain, and Sara L. Sanders

1. Introduction

At various periods in the history of the English language, prescriptive attitudes toward language and conscious manipulation of linguistic forms have come to effect lasting changes in the language. As the twentieth century has drawn to a close, a new wave of prescriptivism has emerged as part of a social movement sometimes called "political correctness". "*Political correctness*" has become over the past two decades a cover term for a range of prescribed and proscribed verbal behaviours both written and spoken. Growing out of the movements for ethnic and gender equality, the drive to encourage or mandate linguistic sensitivity toward diversity has come to influence not only what may be considered a proper topic of comment or discussion, but also the type of terminology and, as we shall show, phrasal structure used to describe occupations, ethnic groups, sexual orientation, physical features, religion and various perceived physical and mental "challenges". The often virulent indignation and certainty of proponents of political correctness has led Rees (1991: xii) to dub the bulk of the recent neologisms as "euphemisms with attitude".

The linguistic effects are especially pronounced in the United States, which for forty years has legislatively defined and guaranteed the rights of members of minority groups in an increasingly broad fashion. The concept of what constitutes a "minority group" has redefined itself as well, with women – who represent over 50 percent of the population of the United States – now being recognised as a minority group of sorts. Adherents of the underlying socio-political movement which has championed the rights of minorities have sometimes been intolerant of critical discussion of issues and concern over individual pieces of legislation or judicial rulings. Thus, the term *political correctness* reflects critics' frustration with the apparent self-righteousness of the minority-rights movement, in which the particulars of various legislative and legal proposals are not to be called into question because the cause is right. The animosity is so widespread that we, in our research on the linguistic influences of political correctness, risk pre-judgment and criticism from both sides. Further, simply by using the term *political correctness*, which has no transparent neutral synonym, we raise eyebrows in both the liberal and conservative camps of our university colleagues, since it is in the intellectual community where the rancour is most bitter.

Political correctness originally had a very different meaning from its current one. The origins are in some dispute. Most observers agree that the term came from the political left and may be several decades old. However, Bush (1995: 42) claims that it was a "term of disparagement towards radicals and extremists"; Losey and Kurthen (1995: 228) state that leftists in the 1960s used *not politically correct* to criticise other leftists who "did something that was not consistent with their professed political belief"; and Miles (1995: 16) says that it came from the Communist Party "where it referred to the party's practice of deciding matters of policy and even of fact not on the merits but in its own interest". Allen (1995: 112) argues that starting in the 1930s it was "used by liberals to criticize Marxist orthodoxy", then used later by the New Left to affirmatively refer to the thoughts in Chairman Mao's *Little Red Book*, and now has regained its critical sense, this time toward the left in general.

As a rightist twist on a leftist term, *political correctness* was not used in its current sense until the 1980s, although the first prescriptive surge of the incipient movement now dubbed "political correctness" came in the 1970s against gender-biased language. Targets included the generic use of masculine *he/his* as in *Everyone must bring his book*, the use of *man* in terms for professions (e.g., *businessman*) and the use of masculine anaphoric pronouns that presumably indicate bias in certain professions toward or by males (e.g., *A manager should set his priorities*). Certainly, the social climate of and since the 1970s has accelerated interest in a substitute for generic *he*. Interestingly, while proponents of these types of proposals often, and erroneously, indict eighteenth-century prescriptivists for creating generic *he* and hence, the problem, they implicitly appear to agree with early prescriptivists by preferring neologisms to singular *they*, which has been in the language since Late Middle English (cf. Wales' (1996: 126) references to discussions in the *OED* and Jespersen (1914)).

Many of the attempts in the 1970s to draw attention to and eliminate gender bias in language were polemical writings which had such an effect in educational, professional and media circles that by 1980 one could seek guidance in Miller and Swift's *The handbook of nonsexist writing*, which appeared in a second edition in 1988 followed by the arrival of Maggio's *The nonsexist word finder: a dictionary of gender-free usage* (1989), each with extensive bibliographies. By the 1990s, public reaction to the pervasiveness of political correctness motivated a popular book-length spoof (Beard 1993) and Rees' more empirical if still humorous *The politically correct phrasebook: what they say you can and cannot say in the 1990s* (1991). The popular columnist and author William Safire, ever a satirical observer of language, has written several columns and articles in the past two decades on the linguistic offerings of what he has dubbed the "vocabulary vigilantes" (1991). Deborah Cameron devotes a quarter of *Verbal hygiene* (1995) to examining the social history and context of political correctness, the grounding of assent and dissent to it, and the questionable validity of individual politically correct neologisms as euphemisms. As she points out, the cause for the gains of gender-neutral usage is itself in dispute: Crystal (1984) has credited prescriptivism, while Cheshire (1984) calls it a case of natural change due to societal developments. Beyond purely linguistic concerns, Bush's brief history (1995) of political correctness and selected annotated bibliography cites one hundred and sixty-three articles and books, some of the latter anthologies of essays, and mentions that his surveys of indexes have found hundreds of references.

Part of the reasoning underlying the linguistic prescriptivism associated with political correctness is that if people are taught to avoid what some perceive as disparaging, insensitive, or biased language, societal attitudes will in turn become less disparaging, insensitive, and biased. This prescriptive twist on Whorf's view (e.g., Whorf 1956) that language shapes cultural perceptions may or may not be validated in the behaviour of future generations. What is certain now is that in public and professional life and the scholarly community, there is considerable pressure to use politically correct language. In these sectors of society, political correctness has to a significant degree accomplished much of its linguistic mission. It remains to be seen whether over the course of time the linguistic influence of political correctness will affect society as a whole, entering the vernacular mainstream. Certainly, some of its output has made the transition from self-conscious editing to everyday professional usage.

In the sections that follow we examine specific changes in progress in neologisms, derivation and phrase structure, as well as general prescriptive recommendations for less biased usage. Our sources include journalistic writing, introductory social science texts, a database of scholarly abstracts (Wilson 1997), and communications manuals and texts for aspiring professionals. Our intent is to assess the extent to which prescription is becoming practice in an increasingly wider swath of American society and the English-language community in general.

2. Language revision in the academic trenches: undergraduate training

Political correctness has been most influential in the intellectual community; and scholarly texts and instructional materials illustrate the increasing effects of the movement. Sometimes, efforts to avoid generic *he* result in considerable differences in sequential editions of the same book. For example, in the first four editions of *Child development and personality* (Mussen, Conger and Kagan) generic *he* is common. As shown in (1) below, generic *he* in (1a) from the 1974 fourth edition is avoided in the fifth edition (1979) by various strategies (1b-c) such as pluralising the nominal or pronominal subject agent (*infants*) or avoiding referring to an agent (*One of the earliest smiles*). The stiff, clinical tone of *One of the earliest smiles* in (1b) or *The social smile* in (1d) almost seems to announce the absence of a pronoun. In the seventh edition (1990), impersonal *it* appears in the section on smiling and the more clinical *the social smile* is gone:

(1) a. *When the young infant has acquired a schema for a face, he is likely to smile*
(Mussen, Conger and Kagan 1974: 195)
b. *One of the earliest smiles appears around 3-4 months of age*
(Mussen, Conger and Kagan 1979: 158)
c. *Four-month-old infants from varied cultural environments are likely to show a smile*
(Mussen, Conger and Kagan 1979: 158)
d. *The social smile appears at 7 or 8 weeks of age*
(Mussen, Conger and Kagan 1984: 126)
e. *The 3-month-old may smile in response to most human faces because it recognizes*
(Mussen, Conger and Kagan 1990: 145)

In the first and second editions of *Conditions of learning* (Gagné 1965, 1970), generic *he* is prevalent. In the third edition (Gagné 1977), *he* and *she* sometimes alternate by paragraph. Yet if there is an extended case isolated from other generic examples and generic *he* is employed, the passage such as (2a) viewed in isolation makes the text look like it might use generic *he* throughout (2a). This may be why in the next edition (Gagné 1985) the pronoun is sometimes replaced by repetition of the formerly antecedent noun and deletion of the possessive where possible as in (2b):

(2) a. *For example, the speaker might begin with the high cost of oil, imagining that this idea located at the left of the doorway to the room. Then, proceeding clockwise, he might locate his next point (say, the scarcity of food supplies) at the closet door along the lefthand wall. If his next point concerns the incidence of starvation, this might be located in the left corner of the room. He would then continue this process until he had completed the main parts of his speech.* (Gagné 1977: 36)
b. *Then, proceeding clockwise, the speaker* [he] *might locate the* [his] *next point ...* (Gagné 1985: 56)

One of the most recent fields for linguistic revision has been in the description of people who have disabilities. Certain students described as *handicapped* in early editions of Good and Brophy's *Educational psychology* are called in the fifth edition (1995: 585, 700) *students with disabilities* and *students with special needs*. A similar development is found in the labelling of Down's Syndrome. Replacement of the terms *mongolism* and, especially, *mongoloid* began somewhat before broad attention was directed to the language of disabilities in general, possibly because describing people with this condition as having oriental features raises ethnic sensitivities, an area of social concern which preceded concern with rights of the disabled. The 1963 second edition of *Child development and personality* (Mussen, Conger and Kagan 1963) discusses "Mongolism, a condition of severe mental retardation" and "the mongoloid". In the third edition (Mussen, Conger and Kagan 1969) the only term used is *Down's Syndrome*, but the condition is only briefly mentioned. Interestingly, however, in 1974 we find in the fourth edition "mongolism, which is also called Down's Syndrome" but not the term *mongoloid*. This description is repeated in the fifth (1979) edition. In the sixth edition (Mussen et al. 1984) one finds "Down's Syndrome (mongolism)".

While language use in textbook discourse reflects concerns about bias and may in turn influence the usage of students, prescriptions of unbiased usage found in communications texts may be even more influential. In the U.S.A., much of the college population will take a course in communications, especially students in various subject areas under the rubric of business administration. This potentially provides an avenue for diffusion into the larger working population. Once again, there has been a gradual shift in communications manuals toward recommending unbiased language and a similar progression from gender issues to the other principal areas of concern.

In the first of three editions of *Business communications* (Harcourt, Krizan and Merrier 1987), over six pages are devoted to "assuring unbiased language" with only gender bias considered. The second edition (1991) also deals only with gender issues. The third edition (1996) devotes only three pages to the topic but briefly discusses race, religion and physical/mental condition. The fourth edition (Krizan, Merrier, Jones and Harcourt 1999) contains similar concerns but for the first time provides as part of its teaching aids a transparency on "Using unbiased language". Ober's *Contemporary business communication* (1992) offers over four pages (95-99) of specific recommendations for "nondiscriminatory language" ranging from now common gender-neutral replacements such as *chair* for *chairman* to suggestions for representing disabilities such as *Mary, who has epilepsy,* instead of *Mary, an epileptic,* In ten volumes of communications texts dating from 1961 written by William C. Himstreet with a variety of co-authors, publishers and title changes, the first prominent discussion of gender issues and recommendations to avoid "sex-biased language" appears in *Business communications: a guide to effective writing, speaking, and listening* (Himstreet, Maxwell and Onorato 1982). The focus on gender continues in subsequent works until in Himstreet, Baty and Lehman (1993) there are between four and five pages on "bias-free language" touching on various categories, including a recommendation that *typical* should be used in place of *normal*, since the latter may imply that others are abnormal.

Whether such substitutions are much of a solution to the issue is certainly questionable and points to the particular difficulty of finding neutral terms for physical and mental conditions. This has become of considerable importance within the disability rights movement. *Crippled* decades ago gave way to *handicapped* and *disabled*; *physically challenged* has gained currency in the last decade and now *differently abled* has been suggested. The integral concern with language within the movement is further indicated in the discussion at the 1997 conference of the Society for Disability Studies on the lack of a single cover term for a person's physical and mental status similar to those for other personal aspects such as race, gender, ethnicity, religion, and nationality. *Physicality* was proposed but not favoured by some discussants, and *embodiment* was subsequently proposed.[1]

The recency of the linguistic prescriptivism now associated with political correctness is evident in the variety of terms for the type of usage that is being recommended: *nondiscriminatory*, *bias-free* and *unbiased* are all in use. It is curious that so influential a trend has no cover term other than *political correctness*, which pejoratively denotes the movement. As recent and diverse as the movement is, however, its effect on the lexicon has been accompanied by some morphological and syntactic ramifications as well.

3. Change in progress: from the lexicon to derivation and phrase formation

3.1. An expanding lexicon of political correctness

As our preceding discussion might suggest, the lexicon is the area that has been most extensively affected by attempts to mandate sensitivity to diversity in society and culture. Even before the political correctness movement had its, for better or worse, current name and before the rise of the term *multiculturalism* in the 1980s, *undeveloped* referring to the economic condition of a country gave way to *underdeveloped* by 1949 (first *OED* citation) and it in turn to euphemistic *developing* by 1964 (first *OED* citation). We noted above a similar shift from *crippled* to *handicapped* and *disabled*, and the recent rise of *physically challenged*. The latter is the prescribed term of choice in the intellectual community, and *challenged* with a preceding adverbial has become the canonical adjectival descriptor for physical, mental or social differences. Variously, one may be *physically challenged, visually challenged, financially challenged,* and so on. The intent is to avoid words such as *disabled, blind* or *bankrupt*.[2] In the case of physical condition, it has been argued that using *handicapped* or *disabled* suggests a permanent lessening of ability whereas using *challenged* puts the given ailment in the context of the myriad possibilities of things, "challenges", that people have to deal with in their daily lives. Terms with *challenged* have become for many people, whether friend or foe of the broader political correctness movement, symbolic of the associated linguistic editing and prescription to the extent that constructing such terms has become something of a joke as in (3):

(3) Examples of facetious *challenged*:
metabolically challenged = *dead* (Davies 1993)
generationally challenged = *old, young* [depending on the age of the user]
conversationally challenged = *boring*

It is sometimes a stylistic "challenge" to tell whether a writer or speaker is being serious or attempting humour when using a term such as *vertically challenged* instead of *short* or *folically challenged* for *bald* or *balding*. Similarly, while *intellectually challenged* or *cognitively challenged* might be used in place of, say, *mentally retarded* or *brain damaged*, similar to Singapore Airlines' use of *intellectually disabled* in a 1997 advertisement mentioning its charitable contributions, they could also be used informally for comic effect in place of *stupid*. However, just as extensive use of a certain metaphor may ultimately render it a cliché, the use of a euphemism whether for intentional evasion or for transparent levity may ultimately lead it into common usage, without a euphemistic or satirical sense. Two syndicated articles on professional football appearing in the Somerville, New Jersey *Courier-News* on October 19, 1997 respectively referred to a certain stadium as *acoustically challenged* (Palladino 1997) and to a team as *pass-rush challenged* (Corbett 1997). The articles were not editorials, in which journalists often try to impress each other as well as their broader readership. Nor, should we point out, were they strictly local journalism, since they were distributed by the national Gannett News Service. Yet, if the primarily middle-class readership of such newspapers continues to see neologisms with *challenged* in the daily press, the still self-conscious *challenged* pattern may become an everyday, non-self-conscious derivational form.

3.2. Derivational -centric *and* -ism/-ist

With the rise of multiculturalism as a social and educational movement in the United States, it has been fashionable to criticise fields such as history for having focused primarily on Europe and the West and, therefore, to have contributed inadvertently or intentionally to historical inaccuracy, incompleteness and societal bias in favour of the West. Thus, *ethnocentric* is now more often used pejoratively than not, as are derivatives such as *Eurocentric*, *Anglocentric* and numerous others. The suffix itself has not clearly become pejorative, however. *Afrocentric* studies and accounts of history abound and are promoted as alternatives to purely Western-based histories of civilisation. In science, technology and business, *-centric* is generally neutral and assumes any favourable or unfavourable connotation in context.[3] For example, in the 62 tokens of *-centric* which we gathered from *General science abstracts* (cf. Wilson 1997), *client-centric, document-centric, network-centric* (in computing), *info-centric, Web-centric,* and *user-centric* were used affirmatively, while *PC-centric* and *hospital-centric* were used negatively, and still others such as *host-centric* (in computing) and *process-centric* (in database research) were apparently neutral. In social and political discussion, however, we find that *-centric* derivatives quite often appear in a negative context: *adult-centric biases and ideologies, hetero-centric bias, a less media-centric way, WASP-centric views*. Yet in contrast with the latter examples from the abstracting data, *Afro-centric (curriculum), Hindu-centric,* and *China-centric* ranged from neutral to affirmative sense, again in context. What we may conclude is that *-centric*, though still denotatively neutral, has become in many fields at least semantically heavy and polemic, and in today's intellectual climate, pejorative (e.g., *phallocentric* in Rees (1991: 41)).

If the core sense of *-centric* has increasingly polemic undertones, derivative *-ist* and *-ism* are even more polemic, semantically heavy, and potentially negative in sense. According to the *OED* (XIII: 74-76) *racism* first meant "the theory that distinctive human characteristics and abilities are determined by race", but the sense of *racism* and *racist* evolved by the 1940s, a decade after the *OED*'s first citations, to encompass the sense of earlier *racialism* (first cited for 1907), "belief in the superiority of a particular race leading to prejudice and antagonism toward people of other races...". The earlier, less pejorative sense of *racism* has disappeared, and *racism/racist* has undoubtedly been responsible for analogous *-ist* coinages such as *sexist/sexism*, first cited by the *OED* for 1965 and *ageist/ageism*, first cited for 1970 (as *agist*).

Earlier in the century, especially in the United States, Cold War hysteria enhanced the newer, negative sense for *socialist* and *communist*, while from the political left *militarist* and *militaristic* became primarily negative. With the notable exception of *rapist*, first cited by the *OED* for 1883, *-ist* and *-ism* once denoted primarily a professional or personal interest without an implied negative sense. However, it is difficult to imagine a neutral professional term such as *economist* or *dentist* gaining currency in today's usage, where neologisms with *-ist* or *-ism* denote bias toward or against the referent of the stem. These now prevalent senses are not new, however. *Feminist* is first cited by the *OED* for the 1890s, and *racism* acquired the bias sense of *racialism* by the 1940s. More recent examples of *-ist* in its 'bias against' sense include the four citations from the late 1980s provided by Rees (1991) for *fattist* and *fattism* (bias against those traditionally called *fat*), and one from 1989 for *heterosexist/heterosexism* (bias against homosexuals). On the model of *feminist* and, in its contemporary sense, *environmentalist* (which until fifty years ago meant one who believes in the preeminence of environment over heredity or other factors in shaping individuals and cultures), Rees cites two 1980s examples of *animalist*, and Siegenthaler (1993) pokes fun at Smith College's disdain of and possible coinage of *lookism*, 'belief that appearance is an indicator of a person's value'.

3.3. The demise of generic he*?*

Although the assault on impersonal generic *he* has gathered new strength in the last three decades, proposals for eliminating it are by no means new. Baron (1986) states that more than eighty bisexual pronouns have been promoted since the eighteenth century. Among these, nominative/objective *thon* (with genitive *thons*) was widely discussed and has appeared at times in dictionaries since it was first proposed by Converse (1884). In the last thirty years, competitors have proliferated. In her proposal of *heesh, hiser(s)*, and *herm* as (respectively) nominative, possessive, and objective third-person-singular personal pronouns, Timm (1978) cites no fewer than six other paradigmatic proposals in the 1970s (Orovan 1972, Densmore 1970, Miller and Swift 1972, Darnell and Brockride 1976, Mackay 1978, Longwell 1978[4]).

In contrast with these largely failed offerings, many writers now use one or more of a variety of alternatives such as *he or she, one* and *s/he*. As we saw in section 2., a stilted or detached tone is often a product of using these forms, especially in extended discourse, which may be amplified when paradigmatically extended to possessive *his or her* and objective *him or her*. Plural *they* is often prescribed in manuals as one strategy for avoiding biased language, as is eliminating personal pronouns where possible. In some academic discourse, writers alternate between the *he* paradigm in one sentence, paragraph, or chapter and the *she* paradigm in another, but this has little currency outside of academia.

The attempts of the early prescriptivists to eradicate singular *they* have proven futile, despite two centuries of presence in virtually every handbook of English. The argument against singular *they* continues to be that a pronoun cannot or should not have two grammatical senses, here, singular and plural. Despite the new presciptivists' tacit conformity with this long-standing proscription if perhaps not the reasoning behind it, singular *they* persists and may survive its proscription. Singular/plural *they* is certainly no more or less logical or illogical than, for example, standard singular/plural second-person *you* or the use of third-person-singular verb forms as second-person-singular forms in formal registers in Spanish as in example (4):

(4)   *Habl-a*   *espanol?*
        speak   Spanish
        third person singular/
        second person singular (formal)
        'Does he/she speak Spanish?'
        and 'Do you speak Spanish?'

In a study concluding that generic *he* has been a successful target of efforts for nonsexist language, Prögler-Rössler (1997) finds that in the responses of the 121 teenage British participants in her elicitation experiment *they* was used 59.7% of the time and generic *he* only 11.7%. Although measures were taken to obscure the purpose of the survey and to minimise attention to form, perhaps this figure would have been even higher if the students had completed their survey outside of their English class. For whatever reason, users of English apparently want a third-person-singular generic pronoun without the attendant awkwardness of *he or she* and *his or her*. Generic singular *they* may prove to be the successful candidate. Stringer and Hopper found in a (1998) study of a conversational corpus no examples of generic *he* but many instances of generic *they*. They did, however, find occasional usage of what they call "pseudo-generic *he*", the use of *he* to refer to "sex-unspecified incumbents of traditionally male social categories" (Stringer and Hopper 1998: 213).

3.4. The internal structure of noun phrases

The collocation of adverbials with *challenged* and to a lesser degree with other past participles is an attempt at euphemism through lexical choice and complex adjective phrase formation. Similar attempts at semantic lenition have led to revision of noun modification from preposed to postposed modifiers. Since English does not allow adjectives normally to occur after the nouns that they modify, the switch to postposed modifiers entails the use of prepositional phrases and relative clauses as in example (5):

(5) a. *disabled people* > *people with disabilities/ people who have disabilities*
   b. *poor people* > *people in the lower income bracket*
   c. *coloured people* > *people of colour*

Example (5c) is particularly interesting in that *coloured* was once discouraged as a racist term, superseded by *Negro*; then *Negro* in turn was superseded by *black*; and, most recently in the United States, *African-American* has gained ground against *black*. *People of colour* is sometimes used as an inclusive, dignified cover term for all non-whites by both members and non-members of various ethnic communities and has a long history (cf. Safire's (1988) discussion and references). Even though the term may have been in use since the late eighteenth century, it would be purely speculative to propose that *people of colour* was a model for the new trend toward postmodification. Whatever the origin of this trend, so-called "people-first language" is often prescribed to focus on people and not their physical or mental features (cf. Himstreet, Baty and Lehman (1993: 210) and Krizan et al. (1999: 107), following Tyler 1990). The trend is further illustrated in the title *Americans with Disabilities*

Act (1990), by which the United States Congress legislated equality for disabled people in areas ranging from employment to physical access to and within hotel facilities.

4. Conclusions

Unless there is some radical social shift away from promoting the acceptance of diversity, the linguistic influence of so-called "political correctness" will continue, especially in the United States, where litigation and legislation continue to prescribe methods of equitable treatment of various segments of the population designated as minorities. However, the trends toward linguistic innovation based on sensitivity toward diversity are apparently limited largely to the intellectual community. Therefore, at this point we are hesitant to conjecture that a wide swath of changes in the English language such as those we have discussed will ever reach the non-self-conscious vernacular of the broad English-speaking population. Singular *they* is well established in vernacular English, but generic *he* also is still sometimes found in non-self-conscious colloquial usage. Yet the results of studies such as Prögler-Rössler (1997) and Stringer and Hopper (1998) suggest that the days of generic *he* may be numbered. Indeed, even Kilpatrick (2000), among the more conservative and prescriptivist commentators on the English language, has all but given up the battle against generic singular *they*, noting in his column on language which is nationally syndicated in the United States that "The masculine referent pronoun is in feeble shape; two generations down the road, everybody will be driving their car and reading their paper, and I will be revolving in my grave".

The *challenged* pattern is spreading but still retains its satirical effect in many cases.[5] As for the distribution of new and old terms for disabilities and the disabled, our survey of the 1997 hotel guide to facilities at over 2000 Holiday Inn hotels in the United States turned up over 100 instances of *handicap* or *handicapped* (e.g., *handicap rooms*) but only three instances of *physically challenged*, although we found 22 instances of collocations with *wheelchair* (e.g., *wheelchair accessible*) and eight instances of *ADA* or *Americans with Disabilities Act*. Clearly, diffusion of the new terms and structures has a long way to go to reach common usage; yet in the 1999 guide to Bass Hotels (the parent group of the Holiday Inn chains) most of the specific references to these special rooms have disappeared, replaced by a section in the introduction which discusses the company-wide commitment to facilities for "travellers with special needs".

The phenomenon that we have explored in this study is wide open to further and more extensive research. Written and spoken texts and larger corpora should be quantitatively examined in a broad spectrum of disciplines, occupations and registers. The snapshots that we have presented of textual revisions would appear to offer enticing prospects for future investigation. The specific changes that we have examined could in the future turn out to have been tenuous, and could later seem to be curious artefacts of a passing linguistic trend. Even if they persist, diffuse somewhat, and are accompanied by continued innovations, they may remain limited primarily to the intellectual realm. We feel that they will persist because of the prevailing legal and legislative climates in many English-speaking countries. We look forward to future studies of this new prescriptivism in English and its parallels in other languages as well.

Notes

1. We would like to thank Anne Swanson of Sonoma State University for this information.
2. A guest commentator on the Cable News Network recently described a young woman who abandoned her newborn baby in a bathroom trash can at a school dance (after just giving birth) as "morally challenged", an unintentionally humorous if legally useful strategy in the litigious United States, especially since she had not yet come to trial.
3. Hyphens are sometimes used with *-centric* but often are not.
4. For Mackay's proposal, Timm (1978) refers the reader to the article "Alternative pronoun proposed by professor", *University* [of California] *Bulletin* 26 (30 January): 70. She further refers the reader to Wicker (1978) for Longwell's proposal.

5. Even as or perhaps especially as detached investigators, we appreciated the wit (while not concurring with the judgment) of sports columnist Jay Mariotti's (*Chicago Sun Times*, 6 December 1998) reference to our home state of South Carolina as *glitter challenged*.

References

Primary sources

[Bass Hotels]
    1999   *Bass hotels & resorts worldwide directory*. Bass Hotels & Resorts.
Corbett, Jim
    1997   Rattling Bledsoe goal for trash-talking Jets. *The Courier-News* (17 October): F-3.
Gagné, Robert A.
    1965   *The conditions of learning*. New York: Holt, Rinehart and Winston.
    1970   *The conditions of learning*. (2nd edition.) New York: Holt, Rinehart and Winston.
    1977   *The conditions of learning*. (3rd edition.) New York: Holt, Rinehart and Winston.
    1985   *The conditions of learning and theory of instruction*. New York: Holt, Rinehart and Winston.
Good, Thomas L. and Jere E. Brophy
    1995   *Contemporary educational psychology*. New York: Longman.
Harcourt, Jules, A. C. Buddy Krizan, and Patricia Merrier
    1987   *Business communication*. Cincinnati, OH: South-Western.
    1991   *Business communication*. (2nd edition.) Cincinnati, OH: South-Western.
    1996   *Business communication*. (3rd edition.) Cincinnati, OH: South-Western.
Himstreet, William C., Gerald W. Maxwell, and Mary Jean Onorato
    1982   *Business communications: an effective guide to writing, speaking, and listening*. Missions Hills, CA: Glencoe.
Himstreet, William C., Wayne M. Baty, and Carol M. Lehman
    1993   *Business communications*. (10th edition.) Belmont, CA: Wadsworth.

[Holiday Inn]
    1997   *Holiday Inn worldwide directory*. Holiday Inns.

Krizan, A. C. Buddy, Patricia Merrier, Carol Larson Jones, and Jules Harcourt
    1999   *Business communications*. (4th edition of Harcourt, Krizan, and Merrier 1987.) Cinncinnati, OH: South-Western.

Mussen, Paul H., John J. Conger, and Jerome Kagan
    1963   *Child development and personality*. (2nd edition.) New York: Harper and Row.
    1969   *Child development and personality*. (3rd edition.) New York: Harper and Row.
    1974   *Child development and personality*. (4th edition.) New York: Harper and Row.
    1979   *Child development and personality*. (5th edition.) New York: Harper and Row.
    1984   *Child development and personality*. (6th edition.) New York: Harper and Row.
    1990   *Child development and personality*. (7th edition.) New York: Harper and Row.

Ober, Scott
    1992   *Contemporary business communication*. Boston, MA: Houghton Miflin.

Palladino, Ernie
    1997   Giants want Lion crowd to be a silent partner. *The Courier-News* (19 October): F1.

Wilson, H. W.
    1997   *Wilson select database*. On line: http://wilsonweb3.hwwilson.com/ cgi-bin/webspirs.cgi.

Secondary sources

Allen, Irving L.
    1995   Earlier uses of *politically (in)correct*. *American Speech* 70: 110-112.

Bailey, C.-J. N.
    1973   *Variation and linguistic theory*. Arlington, VA: Center for Applied Linguistics.

Baron, Dennis
    1986   *Grammar and gender*. New Haven, CT: Yale University Press.

Beard, Henry
    1993   *The officially politically correct dictionary and handbook*. New York: Random House.

Bush, Harold K.
1995 A brief history of PC, with annotated bibliography. *American Studies International* 33 (1): 42-64.
Cameron, Deborah
1995 *Verbal hygiene.* New York: Routledge.
Cheshire, Jenny
1984 The relationship of language and sex in English. In: Peter Trudgill (ed.), 33-44.
Converse, Charles C.
1884 A new pronoun. *The Critic* 55 (2 August): 55, 79.
Crystal, David
1984 *Who cares about English usage?* Harmondsworth, UK: Penguin.
Darnell, Donald and Wayne Brockride
1976 *Persons communicating.* Englewood Cliffs, NJ: Prentice-Hall.
Davies, Andrew
1993 Dead or metabolically challenged? *Times Educational Supplement* (28 May): Extra 1.
Densmore, Dana
1970 *Speech is the form of thought.* Pittsburgh, PA: Know.
Jespersen, Otto
1914 *A Modern English grammar*, Part II, Volume 1. Heidelberg: Carl Winter's Universitätsbuchhandlung.
Kilpatrick, James
2000 Dialects are no exception. *The Sun News* (2 February): 13A.
Losey, Kay M. and Hermann Kurthen
1995 The rhetoric of "political correctness" in the U.S. media. *Amerikastudien* 40 (2): 227-245.
[Mackay]
1978 Alternative pronoun proposed by professor. *University* [of California] *Bulletin* 26 (30 January): 70.
Maggio, Rosalie
1989 *The nonsexist word finder: a dictionary of gender-free usage.* Boston, MA: Beacon.
Miles, Jack
1995 Political correctness and the American newspaper: the case of the *Los Angeles Times* Stylebook. *English Today* 41 (5 January): 14-18.
Miller, Casey and Kate Swift
1972 What about new human pronouns. *Current* 138: 44.
1980 *The handbook of nonsexist writing.* New York: Harper and Row.

OED = Murray, James A.H., Henry Bradley, William A. Craigie, and Charles T. Onions
    1989   *The Oxford English Dictionary.* (2nd edition.) Oxford: Clarendon Press.

Orovan, Mary
    1972   *Humanizing English.* (3rd edition.) Hackensack, NJ: Art and Copy.

Prögler-Rössler, Karin
    1997   Sexism in language – a study on pronoun usage in generic context. *Views* 6: 34-48.

Rees, Nigel
    1991   *The politically correct phrasebook.* London: Bloomsbury.

Safire, William
    1988   People of color. *New York Times Magazine* (20 November): 18-19.
    1991   Linguistically correct. *New York Times Magazine* (5 May): 18-19.

Siegenthaler, John
    1993   Politically correct speech: an oxymoron. *Editor/Publisher* (6 March): 48, 38.

Stringer, Jeffrey L. and Robert Hopper
    1998   Generic "he" in conversation? *Quarterly Journal of Speech* 84: 209-221.

Timm, Lenora A.
    1978   Not mere tongue-in-cheek: the case for a common gender pronoun in English. *International Journal of Women's Studies* 1: 555-565.

Trudgill, Peter (ed.)
    1984   *Applied sociolinguistics.* London: Academic Press.

Tyler, Lisa
    1990   Communicating about people with disabilities: does the language we use make a difference? *Bulletin of the Association for Business Communication* 53: 65-67.

Wales, Kathleen
    1996   *Personal pronouns in present-day English.* Cambridge: Cambridge University Press.

Whorf, Benjamin L.
   1956   *Language, thought and reality: selected writings of Benjamin Whorf.* Edited by J. B. Carrol. Cambridge, MA: MIT Press.

Wicker, Tom
   1978   He or she or what. *The New York Times* (18 April): 39.

The changing role of London on the linguistic map of Tudor and Stuart England

Terttu Nevalainen and Helena Raumolin-Brunberg

1. Introduction[1]

Our study relates language change to linguistic differences between centre and periphery in late medieval and early modern England. London had become the political and economic capital of the realm in the late medieval period. In the sixteenth century, it was by far the largest city in the country and its rate of growth was extraordinary. Assuming that this key position of London also had its linguistic consequences, as is often claimed to be the case, we shall compare the spread of a number of language changes in London with their diffusion in East Anglia and in the northern counties of England. Several interrelated factors will be discussed: internal migration, dialect contacts in the capital, and the time courses of linguistic processes. Of particular interest is the variable input to these processes, resulting in the generalisation of one variant or set of variants as part of the supraregional standard. All the processes we have investigated are morphological.

As will be shown in section 3., London's phenomenal growth in this period depended on immigration, because epidemic and endemic diseases kept its mortality rate at a very high level. The language spoken in London must therefore have represented a mixture of regional dialects, which were partly levelled down in everyday communication. There is also evidence of social stratification in London English as far back as the fourteenth century (Kristensson 1994). London must therefore have continued as a less than homogeneous speech community in the following centuries. Various levels of speech in sixteenth-century London are referred to by Dobson ([1955] 1969), Blake (1981: 47-49) and Leith (1984).

At the same time, it is commonly argued that the variety which later came to be codified as Standard English had its origins in London. The capital and its vicinity were singled out by such well-known contemporary commentators as John Hart and George Puttenham as the area where the "best English" was spoken in the latter half of the sixteenth century (see Danielsson 1955; Dobson [1955] 1969). London English of a certain kind must therefore by this time have acquired a prestige status. Part of it may be related to the fact that London was the seat of the national government, including the Court, and that the bulk of its paperwork was produced in London. This is nothing new. The language of the Chancery had served as a model, albeit a variable one, for a written standard back in the fifteenth century before the era of the printing press (John Fisher, Richardson, and Jane Fisher 1984).

The question we address in this paper is whether it was indeed the case that the linguistic features that eventually made their way into Standard English were typically first promoted in London before spreading to the rest of the country. This hypothesis agrees with the findings of modern sociolinguists, who attach particular importance to the role of large cities in language change (Trudgill 1986; Labov 1994). However, in many cases it conflicts with the traditional view of dialects being diffused according to a regular wave-like pattern. As sociolinguistic generalisations cannot be taken for granted historically, the issue becomes an empirical one.

In order to test the hypothesis, quantitative corpus-based studies were carried out on the following structural features in Late Middle and Early Modern English: 1) present-tense indicative inflections, especially the third person singular *-(e)s* and *-(e)th* (in what follows, *-s* and *-th* will be used to refer to both their syllabic and non-syllabic realisations); 2) the relative pronouns *the which* and *which;* 3) the subject pronouns *ye* and *you;* 4) the third person singular possessive form *its;* 5) the prop-word *one;* and 6) indefinite pronouns with singular human reference. The material used in this study comes from the electronic *Corpus of Early English Correspondence, CEEC,* which covers the period 1417-1681 (Nevalainen and Raumolin-Brunberg 1996).

We shall introduce these features and their alternative expressions from a typological perspective in section 2., and then move on to discuss the position of London in early modern England in socio-historical terms in section 3. How dialect contact is understood by historical dialectologists and present-day sociolinguists is discussed in section 4. In the rest of the paper, we shall provide the systematic linguistic evidence that we have so far accumulated for and against the metropolitanist hypothesis. While the hypothesis is clearly supported by the data in the sixteenth and seventeenth centuries, our results indicate that it cannot be upheld without further qualifications in the fifteenth century.

2. The changes studied in a typological perspective

Earlier research has shown that our six morphological variables underwent significant transformations in Late Middle English and/or Early Modern English. Their rates of change vary from slow and gradual to extremely rapid. Table 1 lists these changes and the temporal ranges analysed.

A general characterisation of these developments could be morphological simplification, although this term is applicable to some of the changes only in an indirect manner. Most changes can be associated with the general shift from synthetic to analytic, in other words, from a complex inflectional morphology towards a simpler one, so that the role of free morphemes and features of word order come to play a more significant role in grammatical coding. This "drift", a term introduced by Sapir (1921), has been going on in Germanic languages at different rates for a long time, but, as Ferguson (1996) points out, unexpected innovations at times interrupt long-term general trends (see also Danchev 1992).

The discussion of present indicative subject-verb concord has very much concentrated on the third person singular.

Table 1. The changes studied

Change	Temporal range
1. Subject-verb agreement in present indicative	1460-1680
2. Relative pronoun *the which* versus *which*	1460-1680
3. Subject pronoun *ye* versus *you*	1460-1600
4. Possessive determiner *its*	1600-1680
5. Prop-word *one*	1600-1680
6. Indefinite compound pronouns with singular human reference	1600-1680

Nevertheless, during the time of our study, after the demise of the Old English regular inflection system, suffixes could be used in both the third person singular and the plural, and occasionally also in the first person singular. Examples (1) and (2) illustrate the use of the third person singular endings *-th*, *-s* and zero. Example (3) shows how the suffix *-th* was also employed in the third person plural, and (4) has both zero and *-s* in the plural. Example (5) illustrates the use of *-s* in the first-person singular.

(1) **The Kyng** *purposeth* as to morow to be at Wendesor, and from thens to Notyngham. **My Lord Chamberleyn** *rides* to morue hame to Leycestre.
(STONOR, Richard Page, II: 59, 1478?)[2]

(2) *Also,* **my godfather** *onderstond that Ze haue sent to Thomas Kesten ...*
(CELY, Richard Cely junior, 8, 1476)

(3) *for* **Saint Gregorie** *sayeth that we ar more bounde to* **them that** *bringeth us up wel than to our parents, for* **our parents** *do that which is natural for them, that is* **bringeth** *us into this Worlde ...*
(ORIGINAL 2, Princess Elizabeth, 154, 1548)

(4) **The judges** *gifues* her no favour, for **they** *say* **they understand** by credible informations that ...
(PLUMPTON, Godfrey Greene, 35, 1476?)

(5)   *as yet* **I** *am on my journey, but* **hopes** *in due time to reach home.*
         (FLEMING, Daniel Fleming, 38, 1654)

The inflectional pattern described above can be seen as one stage of a development the ultimate aim of which would be a present tense without subject markers and a simple contrast between the present and the past (Lass 1992: 135). The loss of endings happened gradually, spreading from one person to another. This development did not proceed in a straightforward manner but was affected by other processes, such as the spreading of one suffix to other persons and/or numbers. As examples we can mention the past indicative and subjunctive plural *-en* finding its way into the indicative present in Middle English, as well as the adoption of *-s* into the first person singular, as example (5) illustrates. The spreading of one suffix to other persons and numbers could have led to a system in which one ending marks the present indicative. This is what has happened in some non-standard varieties of English (e.g. the Reading dialect described in Cheshire (1982: 31-43)) and in another Germanic language, Swedish. It is important not to forget that in Early Modern English the indicative marking was functional, expressing contrast with the subjunctive, which was still in current use.

According to Ferguson (1996: 179), both of the above tendencies are apparent from Middle English onwards. Section 5. will further explore how these divergent patterns of verbal agreement developed in Late Middle and Early Modern English. We shall conclude this discussion with Ferguson's pertinent comment on the path that led to Present-day English:

> The limitation of agreement to the 3sg is an important feature of the standardization of English. It is an instance of an unnatural, marked construction becoming accepted as a sign of the standard language as opposed to various nonstandard dialectal variants. By Middle English times, the spread of various changes had resulted in divergent patterns of present tense inflection in the Northern, Midland, and Southern dialect areas. Every one of these changes represented a morphological simplification, but the final outcome – limitation to 3sg singular subject marker on the verb –

represented a kind of compromise among the changes that is not so obviously simplifying (Ferguson 1996: 179).

Another long-term typological trend may, however, account for some of the internal changes in the third person singular. It is noteworthy that third person singular present-tense forms underwent a gradual implementation of vowel deletion in inflectional endings similar to those undergone by the preterite and past participle forms in *-ed,* and the nominal plural and genitive forms in *-es.* As pointed out by Kastovsky (1992, 1998), some of these developments began in pre-Old English while others were later and were only generalised in Early Modern English. In the course of time, morphophonemic alternations like this became an integral part of the typological shift away from stem-variability and towards consistent word-based morphology in English (Kastovsky 1992: 415).

The case of third person singular endings is interesting in that, according to Luick ([1921] 1964: 546-548), the deletion of the vowel in the suffix took place earlier in the North than in the South. The process also advanced more rapidly in colloquial speech than in other registers. Luick ventures a guess that around 1500 the suffix *-es* might already have reached a stage where the uncontracted form was confined to verbs ending in a sibilant sound but the vowelless form occurred elsewhere in colloquial registers. His dating will probably have to be modified in the light of more empirical research (cf. e.g. Stein 1987: 427-428). Given, however, that the pace of vowel deletion was slower in the South than in the North, we may argue that the generalisation of *-s* in London in the late sixteenth century may have been boosted by the growing demand for and acceptance of a vowelless suffix in colloquial speech. Evidence like this suggests that a step backwards in the overall scheme of morphological simplification of the English language may represent a regular development at the level of its morphophonemic restructuring (see further note 9).

The obvious way of explaining what happened to the synonymous pair of relative pronouns *the which* and *which* (example (6)) in terms of morphological simplification, is to say that the simple form *which* overcame its complex rival, as we shall see in section 6 (see also Raumolin-Brunberg 2000). It would have been uneconomical to have one compound member among the relative pronouns, which in general are simple. The demise of *the which* in broad terms coincides with other changes among the relative pronouns, such as the semantic differentiation between *who* and *(the) which*, the former becoming limited to personal reference and the latter to non-personal reference. This specialisation, which took place at an early stage of linguistic standardisation on the national level, may have contributed to the loss of one of the two variants.

(6)   *There was a countrey in **the which** there were almoste none but foolys, sauynge a fewe **which** were wise.*

(MORE, Alice Alington, 512, 1534)

On the other hand, a question can be posed as to why the complex form *the which*, popular in Middle English, came about at all. The argument presented above may not be so strong as it looks at first sight. When we examine the whole relative marker system, we find a number of complex forms, i.e. the relative adverbs, e.g. *whereat, wherefrom*. The forms *that that* and *that which* may also be understood as complex, although their first elements represent the matrix-clause antecedent, while in *the which* both parts belong to the relative clause. Nevertheless, what happened was that the complex variant disappeared, and in the long run *the which* could be characterised as one of the unexpected innovations that Ferguson speaks about.

The third change to be discussed, the replacement of the nominative *ye* by the oblique form *you* (examples (7)-(8)), may be examined in the light of two long-range tendencies suggested by Sapir (1921: 180). The distinction between the subjective and objective case is against the drifts "toward the abolition of most case distinctions" and "toward position as an all-important grammatical method".

(7)   *Yf ye knowe they complayn with cawse, I praie you se it amendyd:*
          (JOHNSON, John Johnson, 250, 1545)

(8)   *but that I wolde yow were in myne armes or I in yours, for I thynk it long, syns I kyst yow.*
          (HENRY8, King Henry VIII, 144, 1528)

The case distinction between the nominative and the oblique disappeared from nouns in Early Middle English. The genitive prevailed in most varieties,[3] but the periphrastic *of*-phrase increased its domain at the cost of the genitive case. In fact, there was also a tendency to limit the use of the genitive, expressed by Sapir (1921: 176-177) as a drift "towards the restriction of the inflected possessive forms to animate nouns and pronouns". The personal pronoun system and the relative pronoun *who* retained case distinctions, though, before the change in the second person subject pronoun in the sixteenth century there was in fact already one member without this distinction: the third person singular *it*.

The personal-pronoun paradigm has retained its mixed character up until our own times, obviously supported by linguistic standardisation. Although no items have been ousted from the system, the usage has changed towards a positional distinction of subject and object "territories", and the objective has become the unmarked case form in informal or non-standard English, as shown by examples like *It's only me* and *Him and Mary are going abroad for a holiday* (Quirk et al. 1985: 337-338).

The possessive determiner *its* was introduced into English around 1600 (example (9)). In structural terms, it filled a hole in the possessive pattern (Nevalainen and Raumolin-Brunberg 1994). After the demise of grammatical gender, the original neuter possessive *his* gradually became associated with masculinity and was increasingly avoided in the neuter. Post-nominal paraphrases like *of it* and *thereof* were often used instead (examples (10)-(11)).

(9) ... *the returneing you my most faithfull thankes for your extraordinary Friendship exprest upon the occasion of **it's** contents.*
(PEPYS, Samuel Pepys, 162, 1680)

(10) *He had a letter to thee from me. I pray be mindfull of the contents **of it** assoone as you can ...*
(KNYVETT, Sir Thomas Knyvett, 144, 1644)

(11) *it would be necessary for the government of the City that the chiefe Governor **thereof** should at all times have libertie*
(COSIN, Miles Stapylton, II: 386, 1660s?)

The introduction of the possessive *its* is not in harmony with the typological drift from synthetic to analytic. The innovation *its* with a suffix and the older form *thereof* are both more synthetic than their alternative *of it*. It seems that the need for a prenominal element was so strong that it was possible to create an analogical extension of the genitive which was in opposition to an all-pervading tendency. The position of *its* still appears unshaken, although Sapir argued (1921: 176-177) that the possessive *its* was weakening in English, since its use contradicted the drift "towards the restriction of the inflected possessive forms to animate nouns and pronouns". Sapir's claim predicts that the postnominal variants, in particular *of it*, will in the end carry the day.

Nevertheless, there is a general trend that can further explain the rapid adoption of this innovation. The introduction of *its* may be associated with a gender shift that raised the feature [+*human*] to a prominent position in the pronominal system. As mentioned above, a parallel Early Modern development took place among the relative markers, where *(the) which* came to be used in non-personal reference and *who* became the only pronoun of the *wh*-series with solely personal reference.

The last two changes are indirect consequences of the loss of the nominal inflectional system in English. Analyticity increased when it gradually became necessary to have an explicit headword in the noun phrase. If the phrase had none, a dummy element, i.e. the so-called prop-word *one* could be added (example (12); Rissanen 1997; Raumolin-Brunberg and Nurmi 1997).

(12) *... has already had the villainy to write one untruth (and **soe bold a one**) concerning you ...*
          (PEPYS, Samuel Pepys, 147, 1680)

(13) *Deare Semandra, **none** deserves more love from **everybody** then you ...*
          (ROYAL3, Princess Anne, 108, 1679)

(14) *Sir, I beseeche yow, if I may serve yow in anything, command mee for thear is **noe man** liveinge that enjoyes so litle of himselfe;*
          (LOWTHER, Roger Kirkby, 225, 1641)

(15) *soe greateness or virtue the sparke of primitive grace is in **every one** alive ...*
          (WILMOT, John Wilmot, Earl of Rochester, 270, 1670s?)

(16) *he may goe in a Reasonable Creditable way and without chardge too **any** butt his master.*
          (PEYTON, Thomas Barrow, 214, 1641)

The increase in the use of the compound variants of the indefinite pronouns with singular human reference apparently also reflects the new noun phrase structure. Examples (13)-(16) illustrate this paradigm and the full inventory of the elements is found in note 17, below. This group of pronouns consists of compounds in *-body* (example (13)), those in *-one* (example (15)) and *-man* (example (14), as well as simple pronouns like *any* (example (16) and *none* (example (13). The oldest alternatives, the simple forms and compounds with *-man* gradually gave way to the pronouns in *-body* and -*one*, which both go back to Middle English (Raumolin-Brunberg and Kahlas-Tarkka 1997).

The development of compound pronouns is an illustration of a further phenomenon that plays a significant role in language change, namely grammaticalisation. Among the pronouns discussed here we can observe two kinds of grammaticalisation: a lexical word becomes a grammatical word (*body*) and a grammatical word becomes more grammatical (*one*; Hopper and Traugott (1993: xv)). Compounds in -*man* must have undergone a process of grammaticalisation very early, since their pronominal uses go back to the earliest periods of Old English.

It is worth pointing out here that, contrary to what was said about relative pronouns, complex forms are quite natural among peripheral pronouns like the indefinites. This is connected with the position of the indefinite pronouns close to the noun phrase end of the continuum from full noun phrases to central pronouns. Although the changes among the indefinite pronouns increase compounding and hence complexity, they were still a consequence of morphological simplification, as apparently the old simple forms without inflectional endings could no longer convey all the grammatical information that was felt necessary. On the other hand, this change was also connected with the gender shift raising the feature [+*human*] into a prominent position. The compound pronouns refer to human beings only, while the simple ones, such as *any* and *none*, have a broader range of reference.[4]

The development of the six changes at issue corroborate Ferguson's argument (1996: 188) that "a drift does not proceed in a straight line but zigs and zags, regresses here and advances there, while the overall trend continues". Drifts are composed of apparently separate changes, which at times may even counteract the main current. Different types of innovation, including grammaticalisations, find their places among the paradigmatic variants from which the speakers make their unconscious selections that often prove to be cumulative in some special direction (Sapir 1921: 166). In addition to linguistic factors, the choices are also constrained by various non-linguistic phenomena, such as standardisation, language contact, social structure, and the speaker's gender. External embedding is the focus of our present research project, and this paper concentrates on regional variation, migration and dialect contact.

3. Early Modern London

It goes without saying that neither England nor London remained the same during the two hundred and twenty years this study covers (1460-1680), and indeed there were changes in most fields of life. The phenomenal growth of London that will be discussed below has given rise to various analyses on London's role in early modern society. An extreme view is to see London as a parasite that devoured a large part of the country's resources, but since the publication in 1967 of Wrigley's article on the importance of London in changing English society and the English economy 1650-1750 the evaluations have mostly been positive. Wrigley presented an interlocking network of demographic, economic, and sociological factors which together paved the way to the Industrial Revolution in the eighteenth century. London played an important part in this network acting as a potent force for change in English society.

Although it is perhaps unusual to turn to economic and social historians for information relevant for linguistic research, we have found Wrigley's model stimulating in our work in historical corpus studies (e.g. Nevalainen and Raumolin-Brunberg 1989: 88-89). Demographic and sociological developments in particular can help us to understand how linguistic changes possibly proceeded in London and throughout the country.

3.1. "Soon London will be all England" (James I)[5]

Table 2 compares the size of London's population with that of the whole of England. The statistics only begin from 1550, and the two different sets of figures for London indicate how difficult it is for historians to estimate the size of past populations.[6] As regards the number of inhabitants in medieval London, Dyer's (1991: 33) estimate for 1377 is about 40,000, which grew to c. 50,000 in 1500 (Rappaport 1989: 61).

Both columns in table 2 describing the increase in London's population testify to a phenomenal growth which continued even in the second half of the seventeenth century, when the total population of England began to decrease. This means that, in 1700, 10-11% of the English people lived in London, while the corresponding proportion in 1550 had only been 2-4%. The earlier figures mainly refer to the population that lived in the City within and without the walls. With time suburbs emerged round the City, and urban settlement came to connect London with Westminster.

Table 2. The population of England and London 1550-1700

	England	London	
		Boulton (1987: 3)	Finlay and Shearer (1986: 39)
1550	3,010,000	70,000	120,000
1600	4,110,000	200,000	200,000
1650	5,230,000	400,000	375,000
1700	5,060,000	575,000	490,000

London's growth was much faster than that of the provincial towns, among which Norwich was the largest, although its population was less than 30,000 during our period (Patten 1976: 112; for different figures, see Coleman and Salt 1992: 27). From an international perspective, too, London's growth was quite extraordinary, and by 1700, London surpassed all West European cities in size (Wrigley 1967: 44; Beier and Finlay 1986: 3). This phenomenal growth clearly depended on a steady flow of migrants, since recurrent endemic and epidemic diseases meant that London's mortality rate exceeded its birth rate. At times the mortality was so high in London that the total population surplus of England was absorbed by London (Wrigley and Schofield 1981: 168-169). Sixteenth- and seventeenth-century court records suggest that only 15% of Londoners were born there (Coleman and Salt 1992: 27). Immigrants often settled down in the new suburbs that developed outside the City proper (Finlay and Shearer 1986).

Beier and Finlay (1986: 11-14) attribute London's massive growth to two basic developments that encouraged migration: centralisation of the nation's political and economic life, and upheavals in the provincial economies, including the agrarian changes and urban crises. It is the centralisation of both political and economic life in one city which also happened to be the country's main port that made London's development unique in comparison with other European capitals.

Most of the migrants to London were young adults. Some scholars make a distinction between "betterment" migrants, who came to find advancement, for instance, through apprenticeship, and "subsistence" migrants, who had to leave their home towns and villages when unable to find a living there (Wareing 1980: 249). Kitch (1986: 239), for his part, speaks about a rural "supply push" and an urban "demand pull" aspect of migration. The wage level in London was higher than elsewhere in the country, and employment was easily available.

Another division can be made on the basis of the length of stay. Although many immigrants stayed in the capital, a number left London after spending some time there. This type of mobility was not uncommon, since it has been estimated that one English adult in eight in 1550-1650 and one in six in 1650-1750 had some experience of life in London (Wrigley 1967: 49). Visits to London were also part of country gentlemen's life. Earlier during our period, they only came to London to see to various legal or administrative matters or to attend the Parliamentary sessions. Later they also brought their families with them to participate in the capital's social events (e.g. Finlay and Shearer 1986: 46).

Unfortunately, extant documents hardly allow systematic investigations into the immigrants' places of origin. However, some groups have left sufficient material for research. The prominent role of the northern counties as suppliers of immigrants to London may be surprising. According to John Fisher (1977: 885), the majority of Chancery clerks came from the northern counties during the Lancastrian era. Another group of people whose origin has been relatively well documented is London apprentices. Wareing (1980:

243) shows that the share of those who came from the north was very high in the late Middle Ages (61% 1485-1500), gradually decreasing towards the end of the early modern era (11% 1654-1674) at the same time as the proportion of the Midlands increased from 10% to 45%. Wareing's figures are based on studies of apprentices to different companies at different times, which, of course, diminishes comparability, but, no doubt, his general trend holds. Kitch (1986: 228-229) corroborates the argument by showing that the proportion of London apprentices travelling long distances decreased considerably after the Restoration, but London's migration field nevertheless remained nationwide.

Figure 1 from Rappaport (1989: 79) describes the origin of 876 immigrants who acquired London citizenship in the early 1550s. Even here the proportion of the northern counties is the highest (about 30%), the south-east also playing an important part (24%). Although the number of people studied may appear small, Rappaport (1989: 28-29) claims that they are representative of male London citizens, since "by the middle of the sixteenth century approximately three-quarters of the city's adult males were freemen and thus entrants' careers are indeed representative of the experiences of the majority of the men who lived and worked in Tudor London".

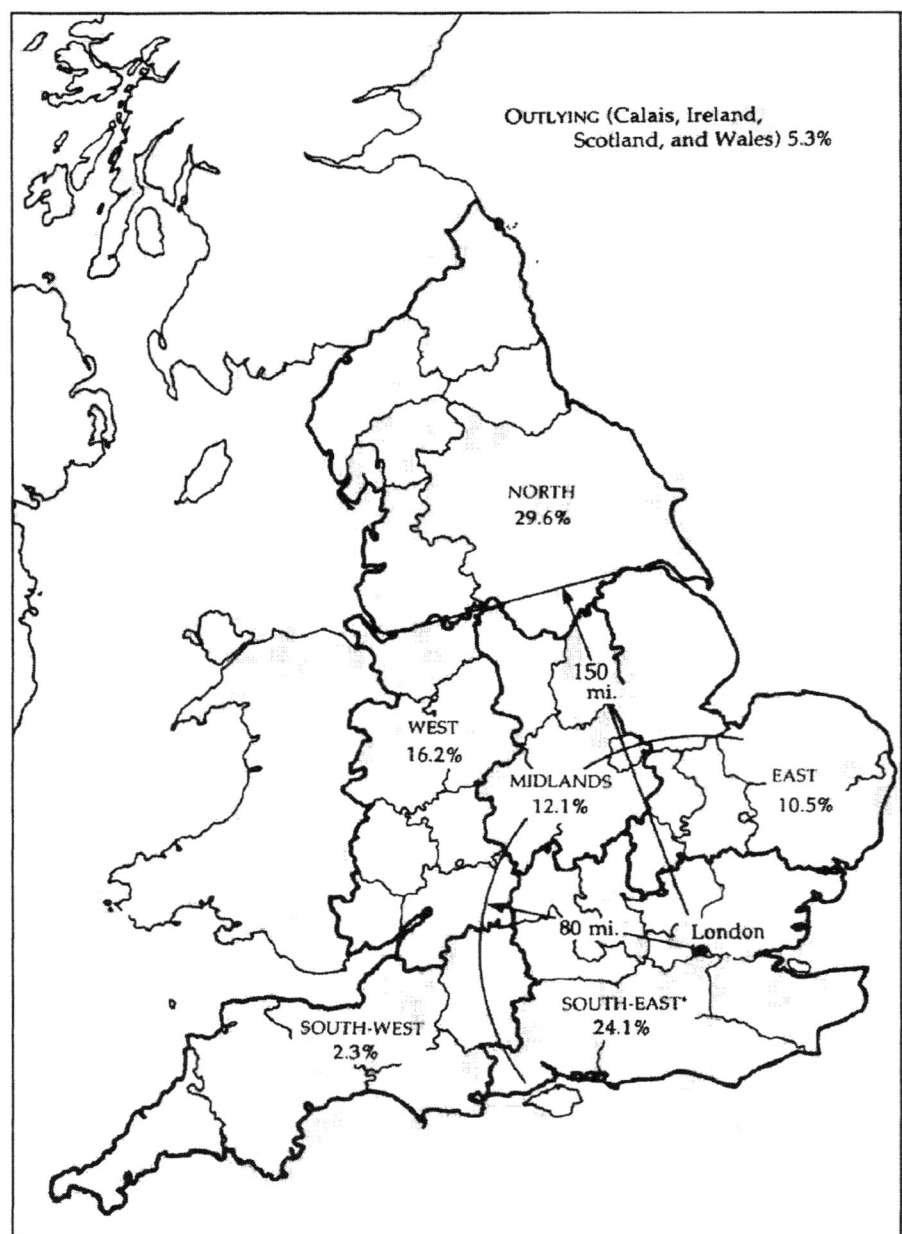

Figure 1. Regions of origin of 876 immigrants who became citizens of London during 1551-1553 (from Rappaport 1989: 79)

Since this study compares the language of northerners (people living north of Lincolnshire) and inhabitants of East Anglia (Norfolk and Suffolk) with that of Londoners, a few words on these areas are in order. The close relationship that prevailed between the North and London has already been demonstrated, at least as regards the number of apprentices sent to London. East Anglia, on the other hand, was a rather self-sufficient area in which it was more natural to move to Norwich for apprenticeship than to London (see Patten 1976). According to figure 1, the eastern counties accounted for about 10% of apprentices to London from 1551 to 1553, but in fact the share of Norfolk and Suffolk was very low, only 2%, since it was Lincolnshire that sent more than half of the young men included in this group (Rappaport 1989: 78). Wareing's statistics (1980: 243) also show low figures for the East with a declining trend, from 8% in 1486-1500 to 3% in 1654-1674. Kitch (1986: 229, 235), too, comments on the relative paucity of migrants from East Anglia and stresses the character of East Anglia as a coherent area, undisturbed by the direct influence of London.

The massive influx of migrants naturally affected London English. Nor is it unexpected to discover differences in linguistic behaviour between northerners and East Anglians. Sections 5. and 6. below will provide in-depth analyses of our six linguistic changes in relation to the three dialect areas.[7]

3.2. Social structure and social relations

Table 3 gives a schematic description of rank and status in early modern England (mainly based on Laslett 1983: 38), depicting the social structure of the sixteenth and seventeenth centuries. The fifteenth century was not quite the same, as English society was still undergoing transformation from the medieval division into three estates, clergy, warriors and labourers, into a more complicated social hierarchy.

Table 3. Rank and status in Tudor and Stuart England

Estate	Grade	
GENTRY	Royalty	
	Nobility	Duke, Marquess, Earl, Viscount, Baron
		Archbishop, Bishop
	Gentry proper	Baronet (1611-), Knight, Esquire, Gentleman
	Professions	Army Officer (Captain, etc.), Government Official (Secretary of State, etc.), Lawyer, Medical Doctor, Teacher, Clergyman, (wealthy) Merchant
NON-GENTRY		Yeoman, Merchant, Husbandman, Craftsman, Tradesman, Artificer, Journeyman, Labourer, Cottager, Pauper

The main dividing line in early modern social:~ structure was between the gentry and non-gentry, and it was primarily based on land-ownership. Another important factor was manual labour: those who did not need to work with their hands called themselves gentlemen. This criterion raised the in-between professional group to gentility, and on the whole, the professions provided an important route for social mobility especially during the Tudor and early Stuart times (e.g. Stone 1966; for further discussion on the social structure, see Raumolin-Brunberg 1996b; Nevalainen 1996).

London's urban social structure differed from the countryside because of the significant role of merchants and craftsmen. The centralisation of government meant that London's population came to include a considerable number of civil servants, representing both the upper ranks and professions. Alongside the royal government came the Court with a large number of full-time officials (Beier and Finlay 1986: 11-12).[8] Gradually London also housed families whose wealth and way of life did not differ from that of the gentry, although these families did not own land. This new social group was called the "pseudo-gentry" by Everitt (1966). On the whole, London had a varied population consisting of all social orders except for those that were directly connected with agrarian manual work.

Life in a densely populated city meant frequent day-to-day contacts with people in their different social roles. Social networks were more often loose-knit and uniplex, i.e. single-function, than in the countryside (for social networks, see J. Milroy and L. Milroy (1985); L. Milroy (1987)). Social mobility was easier in London, and innovations of all kinds were accepted and new consumption patterns established here before other parts of the country (Wrigley 1967: 50-51; see also Nevalainen and Raumolin-Brunberg 1989: 88-89).

Studies of Early Modern London's social topography (Power 1985, 1986) show that people of different social status did not necessarily live isolated from each other. John Stow's *Survey of London* (Power 1985) indicates that there was a concentration of substantial building and economic enterprise in the central City. The West End and Westminster were settled by a landowning and governing elite and the East End and Southwark by a lower working population. The pattern that emerges represents occupational clustering rather than wealth clustering, which developed later (Power 1986: 216-219). How far one's regional origins affected residential patterns is not clear, but people from the same shires at least formed clubs and gathered together for feasts (Beier and Finlay 1986: 21). Despite some segregating tendencies there was, according to Power (1985: 11), "a considerable intermingling of rich and poor, commerce and craft, skilled and unskilled in the same parishes and even in the same streets".

In general, the relatively fluid social structure and numerous opportunities for social contacts made London a place which is likely to have promoted rapid diffusion of linguistic change. This assumption will be pursued in the ensuing discussion of the six morphological changes that are under examination in this study.

4. Dialects in contact

4.1. An answer to Wyld's dilemma

The traditional view of dialect contact is based on the wave model. It is reasonable to expect that people who live in adjacent areas will have more contacts with each other than people who are geographically separated by longer distances. Neighbouring areas are therefore expected to converge linguistically, forming a dialect continuum. In England, northern regional dialects share more features with each other than with southern regional dialects. However, as Samuels (1972: 90) points out, gradual changes best apply to areas where the population is distributed evenly. It is especially the case with changes that lead to a regional or national standard that these natural expectations based on regional proximity may not be fulfilled.

We shall illustrate these exceptions to the wave model in the history of English by what might be called Wyld's dilemma. It concerns the spread of the originally northern third person indicative present tense ending in -*s* (i.e. a sibilant form) to the south of the country, where -*(e)th* (a form with a dental fricative) continued to be used well into the seventeenth century and even later. Both Wyld ([1920] 1936) and Holmqvist (1922) were puzzled by the fact that they did not find many instances of the third person singular indicative suffix -*s* in the intervening East Midland texts in the late fifteenth and early sixteenth centuries. Wyld (1936: 336) summarises the point at issue as follows:

> We are placed in this dilemma, that the only apparent possible intermediary between the North and London and the South, by which a dialectal peculiarity could pass, is the E. Midland area, whereas this peculiar characteristic does not appear to be especially widespread in the E. Midland dialects, or among such writers as might be expected to show direct influence from these dialects in the fifteenth and sixteenth centuries.

He solves the problem by suggesting that the spread of -*s* may perhaps have nothing to do with dialect contact. Instead, he resorts to a "multiple births" hypothesis:

> It is possible, however, that the starting point of the -*s* forms has nothing to do with Regional influence, but that the extremely common Auxiliary *is* may have provided the model. I am inclined to think that this is the true explanation of the 3rd Pers. Pres. in -*s* in the Spoken dialect of London and the South, and in the English of Literature (Wyld 1936: 336).

In his monograph on -*s* and -*th* variation, Holmqvist (1922: 138) shares Wyld's dilemma, but offers a different solution. Without the backing of actual textual evidence, he tries to salvage the dialect-diffusion model by suggesting that

> -*s* attained general currency in the spoken language ... probably as early as about 1500. And it is probable that from the early 16th cent. it was universally used in ordinary conversation, not only in vulgar speech or by middle-class people (such as the Celys or Machyn) (Holmqvist 1922: 185).

Holmqvist's idea of a uniform pronunciation of -*s* in the early sixteenth century is clearly untenable. He ignores, among other things, the fact that -*s* and -*th* were not the only variants that appeared in the third person singular. As we shall show below, zero forms were also common in the third person singular, and -*th* in the plural. Moreover, the wealth of empirical evidence accumulated on both genre variation and lexical diffusion in the course of the change points to a register-governed process "from below" proceeding from colloquial spoken and informal written language to more solemn speech and formal writing (see e.g. Barber [1976] 1997: 166-168; Stein 1987; Kytö 1993; Ogura and Wang 1996).[9] Nor does Holmqvist's view fit the facts in more recent times which show that the third person ending with the dental fricative persisted well into the late nineteenth century in some regional dialects, including Somerset and Devon (Wright 1905: 296-297). We therefore argue that the case calls for careful reconsideration on the basis of systematic regional evidence.

The main thesis advanced in our study is that cities are instrumental a) in promoting dialect mixtures and b) in spreading linguistic innovations. The first part of our argument is the uncontroversial traditional one: in frequent contact situations, people from different regional backgrounds will accommodate to each other linguistically. Individual accommodation in face-to-face interaction is the mechanism leading to diffusion of linguistic changes in a speech community (Trudgill 1986: 1-38). In the case of -*s* and -*th*, the two classic studies referred to failed to consider dialect contacts outside the dialect regions proper, and therefore ignored the phenomenal rate of immigration into London as a factor promoting dialect contacts and diffusion.

Our study highlights the importance of social networks in language change. According to this sociolinguistic model, particularly promoted by J. Milroy and L. Milroy (e.g. 1985), loose-knit social networks provide channels for the diffusion of language change, whereas close-knit networks promote language maintenance and consequently hinder change. As already pointed out, we shall assume that in London, social networks were looser and more uniplex than in country villages, and the diffusion of language changes was therefore faster in the capital.

The second part of our argument focuses on innovations spreading from cities and urban centres to the surrounding rural areas. Trudgill (1986) has shown in detail how language changes first hop from one urban centre to another, bypassing the countryside in between. Trudgill's model is based on the population sizes of the communities in interaction and the distances between the different centers. His studies trace the diffusion to Norwich and elsewhere in East Anglia of a number of London features, including the merger of the fricatives /θ/ and /f/ in words like *thin* and *fin*. The geographical diffusion of this feature was extremely rapid: in Trudgill's sample, speakers born in 1957 did not have it at all, while those born in 1967 used it extensively (Trudgill 1986: 53-54). Other processes may be slower. The loss of /h/, for instance, has been diffused outward from London into East Anglia within the past 150 years and is now well established (Trudgill 1986: 44).

A mathematical model has been presented by Ogura and Wang (1996) to account for the rate of diffusion of changes taking place in the lexicon, in individual speakers, and different locations. The model predicts a similar series of consecutive S-curves of diffusion for all three aspects of change and suggests that their progress from inception to completion is a gradual process. As far as changes from site to site are concerned, the model clearly caters for the wave-model kind of diffusion.[10] To what extent it can accommodate the chronologies of changes hopping from one area or city to another is an empirical question. What particularly interests us is the "snowball effect" detected in the process: the curves for chronologically more recent words, speakers, and sites participating in the change appear to rise more sharply than the earlier ones.

In what follows, we shall test these aspects of dialect diffusion, the role of loose-knit social networks and increased contacts in one location, i.e. London, on the one hand, and the diffusion of changes from site to site, on the other. We shall begin by discussing the variation between *-s* and *-th* in the third person singular in Late Middle and Early Modern English in section 5.1., and then expand on the topic of subject-verb agreement with a more detailed discussion of both the singular and the plural inflections in a large number of individuals in our corpus in section 5.2. The evidence provided by pronominal changes is introduced in section 6.

4.2. Delimiting the material

The empirical part of our research is based on the *Corpus of Early English Correspondence (CEEC)*, (Nevalainen and Raumolin-Brunberg 1996) produced by the Sociolinguistics and Language History project at the University of Helsinki. This electronic corpus covers the period from 1417 to 1681 and consists of a total of 2.7 million words of personal correspondence collected from 777 writers. The 1998 version of the corpus has served as the basis of this study, supplemented by some data from the 1996 full version of the *CEEC*. Both versions of the corpus provide personal files for each writer with more than 2,000 running words (see Nevalainen and Raumolin-Brunberg ((eds.) 1996)). To facilitate real-time studies, the corpus has been divided into 20-year periods. The part of the corpus covered by this study consists of two hundred and twenty years from 1460 to 1681.[11]

The *CEEC* has been developed to enable the use of sociolinguistic methods in historical linguistics. To that end every writer has been entered into an electronic "sender database", which records his or her date and place of birth, occupation, social rank, domicile and migration history, father's occupation and social status, and so on

(Nevalainen and Raumolin-Brunberg 1996). The writers for this study have been drawn from three categories: those whose domicile was
1) London, including the City, Westminster and the Court, and Southwark (= Londoners),
2) Norfolk or Suffolk (= East Anglians), and
3) the counties north of Lincolnshire (= Northerners).

This classification does not make a basic distinction between those inhabitants of a locality who had migrated from elsewhere and those who were born there. Nor does it include those who had emigrated from their native area and permanently settled somewhere else. The number of informants included in the study is shown in table 4.

Table 4. Number of writers from the three dialect areas

Period	London *CEEC* 1996	East Anglia *CEEC* 1998	North *CEEC* 1998
1460-1499	42	47	8
1500-1539	22	3	34
1540-1579	36	34	9
1580-1619	35	44	13
1620-1659	21	26	31
1660-1681	13	4	20
Total	169	158	115

It is telling of the migration history of the period that, in the case of East Anglia, nearly all our writers were in fact native East Anglians. Also, as far as we can ascertain, the vast majority of the Northerners in the data were born in the North. The picture of London is rather different: out of the total of all the writers included in the *CEEC* who permanently lived in London less than one fifth are recorded as having been born there. This comes very close to the estimates of the proportion of native Londoners based on the sixteenth- and seventeenth-century court records discussed in section 3.1. For our purposes, therefore, London English is the language used by the people who lived and worked in the metropolis on a permanent basis, regardless of whether they were born there or not.

In view of the variability of London demographics, on what grounds are we entitled to treat the metropolis as one speech community? London did not constitute a typical Labovian speech community, because not all Londoners were native to the community. Neither do we know whether all linguistic variation presented uniform patterns in London, that is, whether the frequency of a given linguistic feature always increased and decreased with both social status and formality of speech style. Most likely it did not.

One way of looking at the situation is to distinguish between two different levels of abstraction in the notion of speech community, just as Kerswill (1993) has done in his research on the city of Bergen in Norway. We may assume that there were some small-scale communities in London, such as those associated with the negatively valued Kentish dialect from the mid-fifteenth to the sixteenth century (see Blake (1981: 47-49)). We may further assume that there was an overarching, larger-scale community, containing the mainstream native community and various "minorities", in so far as the two could be distinguished (see Boulton (1987)). The fact that Londoners' evaluations converged on varieties like "Kentish", on the one hand, and on the best spoken Englis, on the other, suggests some shared attitudes in London to language variation as a whole. We shall therefore treat London as a two-tiered speech community. In practice, that is what dialectologists have always done when they have studied regional dialects consisting of a number of localities.

A further consideration is the possible diffuseness of norms in a dynamic community like London which has considerable social mobility and intermingling of social groups. Kerswill (1993: 52) points out that speakers in communities like this may be more influenced by publicly legitimised norms such as standard languages. In our period, the standard was not yet codified and cannot therefore have provided any ready-made model. But what we can see happening is the consolidation of a nationwide speech community gradually agreeing on forms to be admitted into the evolving supra-regional standard. We can now sharpen this aspect of our research question: by studying these would-be standard language features in

Early Modern English we hope to learn to what extent and for how long it is indeed possible to distinguish three separate dialect areas, London, East Anglia and the North, as opposed to only one, i.e. supraregional agreement, on the use of a given linguistic feature.

5. Subject-verb agreement

5.1. -th versus -s in the third person singular

Table 5 presents the diffusion of the incoming form -*s* numerically in the three areas in the period 1460-1681, divided up into six subperiods. The same information is shown in figure 2, which indicates the averages of the individual writers' -*s* scores for each subperiod (also included in table 5). The relative frequency of -*s* was calculated for each writer with more than ten instances of the -*s*/-*th* variable. The rest were treated in the aggregate. This calculation was performed in order to avoid any skewing of the total means by individuals who provide large samples of data in the corpus. None of the figures include *have* and *do,* which were the last verbs to acquire the suffix -*s* (see e.g. Holmqvist (1922), Kytö (1993)).

The fact that -*s* was of northern origin is obvious from our results. The form was first attested in the Northumbrian dialect in the tenth century both in the plural and in the singular (Berndt 1956) and continues to predominate in the North in the fifteenth century. These findings are supported by the data in the last Middle English subperiod in the *Helsinki Corpus*, which extends from 1420 to 1500. As opposed to 1% in the East Midland texts and 17% in the southern, the relative frequency of -*s* in the northern texts of the period is over 80% of all the cases of the third person singular present indicative which end in a suffix other than zero.

Table 5. The frequency of -*s* versus -*th* in the third person singular indicative in three dialect areas: variable totals (N), total means of -*s* per period (%) and averages of individual scores per period (A) (1460-1681; excluding *have* and *do*)

	London			East Anglia			North		
	N	Freq. of -*s*		N	Freq. of -*s*		N	Freq. of -*s*	
Period		%	A		%	A		%	A
1460-1499	503	29%	31.8	690	1%	0.9	35	60%	59.6
1500-1539	675	1%	0.1	11	0%	0.0	139	22%	21.4
1540-1579	813	9%	6.3	428	4%	4.8	22	32%	32.0
1580-1619	1059	63%	60.7	202	10%	5.2	84	45%	41.2
1620-1659	268	87%	83.2	390	75%	59.8	452	59%	75.0
1660-1681	270	99%	99.2	126	71%	84.1	227	90%	91.0
Total N	3588			1847			959		

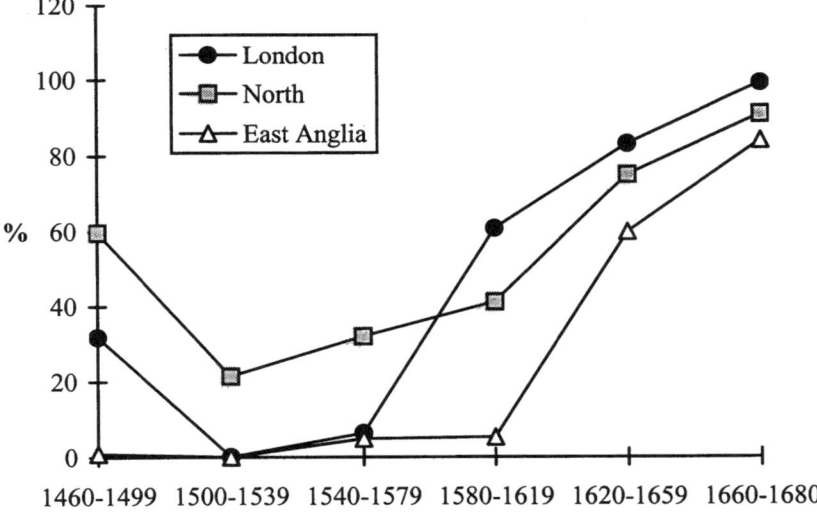

Figure 2. -*s* (%) versus -*th* in the third person singular indicative in three dialect areas; averages of individual scores (1460-1681; excluding *have* and *do*)

Our figures also very clearly show that -*s* appeared early in London. The high figure in the first subperiod is largely due to the Cely family and their circle of London merchants. It is equally apparent from these figures that -*s* was not used in East Anglia. Thanks to the Paston letters, the area is particularly well covered in this period. Our parallel data clearly speak against the traditional wave model of dialect diffusion in the case of -*s*. The suffix could not have reached London via East Anglia, as Wyld (1936) and Holmqvist (1922) expected. A more likely explanation is migration into the capital from the North.

Now, something unexpected happens in the middle of the diagram: -*s* rapidly recedes in London during the first half of the sixteenth century, only to make a comeback in the second half of the century. The change cannot be attributed to lack of data. The decades from 1540 to 1560 and from 1580 to 1600 are particularly well represented in our corpus. There is however a discrepancy in the social continuity between the late fifteenth and early sixteenth century that may overemphasise the decline of -*s* in London. Our late medieval Londoners largely consist of wool merchants, while our corpus does not contain writers below the gentry–professionals line in the first few decades of the sixteenth century. But as the decades around 1550 are socially well represented we must conclude that, instead of following a regular S-shaped curve as modern sociolinguists would anticipate, the diffusion of the incoming form in the South makes a U-turn. A clue to understanding this process is suggested by the fact that a similar dip is also evidenced in our northern data.

What we are witnessing in our sixteenth-century northern letters is best explained as an effect of the evolution of a supraregional standard. This explanation is offered by Holmqvist (1922), who finds that from the fifteenth century onwards, -*th* gradually becomes more and more common in the present indicative with northern writers. Holmqvist (1922: 50) accounts for this new trend by stating that: "Evidently this change is exclusively due to influence from the 'Standard' language". By "Standard", he refers to the language of London documents. Holmqvist may have a case here, at least in so far as the Chancery Standard is concerned. John Fisher, Richardson and Jane Fisher (1984: 45) note that the third person with -*s* does not occur in the Signet letters of Henry V and is only found in eight of the other 136 documents. In our fifteenth-century material, the use of -*s* in London was largely but not entirely confined to the merchant community, which evidently did not have much influence on the language of the Chancery at the time.

A hundred years later, even the merchant community (or the section of it that is now accessible to us) appears to be returning to the traditional southern form. This is suggested by the apparent-time material drawn from the Johnson family and their peers. There is a marked contrast between successive generations, a master and his former apprentices. While the older man, Anthony Cave, still uses a fair number of -*s* forms, some 20% of the cases, the younger merchants are unanimous in preferring -*th* (see Raumolin-Brunberg (1996b)). Although it is suggested (Winchester 1955: 23-26) that Anthony Cave also taught his apprentices the skills of writing, his influence is clearly not extended to the details of their morphology.

We are inclined to interpret this situation as a change in the social evaluation of the two forms. It is worth noting that, to varying degrees, -*th* had been a minority variant even with those Londoners who favoured -*s* in the fifteenth century. This dual morphology must have coexisted for a long time, and may even have been evaluated in dialectal rather than in social terms by contemporaries. However, the changes in the apparent time pattern in the Johnson letters may reflect a change in attitude. It is in the mid-sixteenth century that we also find the first signs of the two variants being sharply stratified socially. Our evidence comes from analysing the social embedding of -*s* in the entire 1996 version of the *Correspondence Corpus* in subperiod 1540-1559. This information is given in figure 3. It shows the relative frequency of -*s* out of the total incidence of -*s* and -*th* in the data for male writers. (The number of cases is 1,204; excluding *have* and *do*; see the appendix for numerical information).

Figure 3 suggests that the incoming form was strongly preferred by the nonprofessional non-gentry: their relative frequency of -*s* exceeds 70% of the cases. By contrast, professional people, consisting of lawyers and representatives of the lower clergy, appear to have disfavoured it, as did the successful social aspirers Thomas Cromwell, the first Earl of Essex, Stephen Gardiner, Bishop of Winchester, and William Paget, Lord Paget of Beaudesert. All these men had risen from humble origin to the top of the early modern English society. We may therefore assume that *-th* was not only the traditional southern regional form but it had probably become a literate and prestigious variant by the mid-sixteenth century throughout the country. It was, after all, the traditional Chancery form, which had also been propagated by Caxton and other early printers. *-s*, by contrast, may have been interpreted as a colloquial or even stigmatised form, and would therefore have been largely avoided by members of the middling and upper ranks. None of our sixteenth-century northern writers, showing a decline in the use of the original northern form, represented the non-professional, non-gentry category.

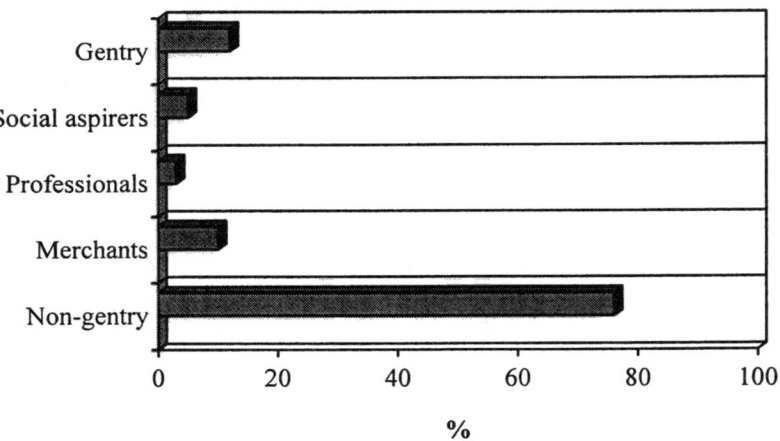

Figure 3. The use of *-s* (%) as opposed to *-th* in the third person singular in the whole corpus 1540-59; excluding *have* and *do* (*CEEC* 1998, male informants only)

At the same time, it is noteworthy that *-s* still continued in steady use in the North. Although our material is not ideally representative of the northern usage in this period, even at its lowest the average frequency of -*s* remains at the 20% level in the northern data. The dwindling use of -*s* in London could have been replenished from this stock, had it been merely a matter of continuing immigration (see section 3.1.). Or perhaps we need not go so far as the North. Although East Anglia remained the stronghold of the southern -*th*, the spread of -*s* southwards would presumably have continued. It would have been further advanced in the Midlands area in the mid-sixteenth century than it had been a hundred years earlier (Holmqvist 1922: 140-145). We therefore suggest that the mid-sixteenth-century situation in London arose from the social markedness of the two variant forms.

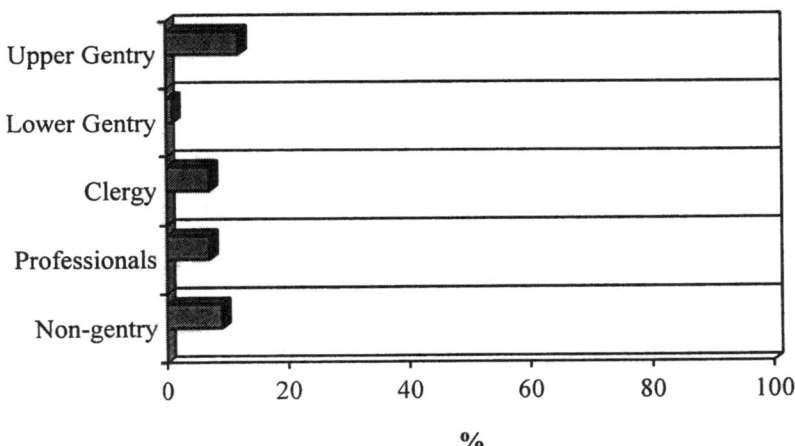

Figure 4. The use of -*s* (%) as opposed to -*th* in the third person singular in East Anglia in 1560-79, excluding *have* and *do* (*CEEC* 1998, male informants only)

No such markedness evidently existed in East Anglia at the time. As is shown in figure 2, -*th* was in general use in East Anglia throughout the sixteenth century. The region is well represented in the corpus in the latter half of the century, especially for the period 1560-1579. Figure 4 indicates that the mean frequency of -*s* in East Anglian male writers in this period is no more than 5% of the cases

(N = 414), and that there is remarkably little social variation in the data. The figures suggest no dramatic concentration of the incoming form in the lowest ranks below the gentry (see the appendix, and Nevalainen, Raumolin-Brunberg, and Trudgill forthcoming).

Returning to figure 2, it is obvious that -*s* made a successful breakthrough in London in the latter half of the sixteenth century and was also soon diffused supraregionally. Towards the end of the century, it rapidly gained momentum first in our London-based writers and then in the North. Although -*s* does appear to be spreading from below in terms of social status, the differences among social ranks even out towards the end of the century. In the period from 1580 to 1599, the average frequency of -*s* in our London data is as high as 45%, calculated from individual scores. It is interesting to find that such an influential individual as Queen Elizabeth I is among those reaching the 50% mark (N = 82). Clearly there could no longer be any social stigma attached to -*s* in London at the time.

East Anglians, too, begin to accept -*s* in the first quarter of the seventeenth century. The process accelerates in the 20-year period from 1620 to 1639, and the mean frequency of -*s* reaches 50%. As in the North, the form is finally generalised during and after the Civil War period, 1640-1659, forty years later than in London. Comparing the S-curves in figure 2 with Ogura and Wang's (1996) model for site-to-site diffusion, we can see that the predicted "snowball effect" also applies in this case, not just in the traditional wave model of dialect diffusion. The last area to adopt -*s*, East Anglia, shows the steepest S-curve and hence the fastest rate of diffusion of the change in the seventeenth century, while the curve for the North has the slowest rate of the three.

Briefly summarising our argument so far, it appears that in real time the diffusion of the emerging supraregional forms need not be linear. In the second half of the fifteenth century, we have three regional alternatives for the third person singular suffix: -*s* in the North, -*th* in the South and East Anglia, and the two forms in competition in London. At the beginning of the sixteenth century, the southern form strengthens its position supraregionally, to the extent that it effectively spreads to the North, and largely replaces the traditional northern form in the writing of the upper ranks. We may argue that *-th* was promoted from above at least in terms of social awareness: it was the form used in the official documents issued by the Chancery, and was favoured by early printers and other professionals at the time. In so far as agencies like these can be localised, most of them were associated with London. If Standard English had been codified in the first half of the sixteenth century, it would have included *-th* in the third person singular present indicative.

However, a new phase in the process begins in the latter half of the sixteenth century. Far from extinct in the various local speech communities in London and elsewhere, *-s* is now diffused from below, in the sense that it spreads from colloquial language and from the lower social ranks. It is first admitted into wider use in correspondence in London. The process gathers momentum and leads to a unified supraregional usage at the end of our period: unmixed *-s* throughout the country, with the exception of the two verbs *have* and *do*, which take longer to acquire the ending. In two centuries, and after a remarkable U-turn in mid-course, the three regional patterns were consolidated into one. This sorting-out was largely channelled through the power base of London.

5.2. The present indicative paradigm

Illuminating though it is, the above examination of *-th* and *-s* in the third person singular is not the whole story. A full picture can only be achieved by looking at the whole paradigm of indicative subject-verb agreement. The following study is based on random samples of 2,000 to 4,000 words by 65 individuals, who were chosen according to different external criteria, such as domicile, rank, migration history, and authenticity of writing.[12]

The late medieval inflection system forms the background for our analysis. Schendl's (1996) article on the origins of the third person plural suffixes argues that the "Northern Present-Tense Rule", presented in table 6, proved to be an amazingly vital syntactic rule, finding its way into the emerging Early Modern English standard (see example (4) in section 2.).

Table 6. Middle English northern paradigm of the present indicative (Schendl 1996: 148)

(i) subject not a personal pronoun in contact with verb	
third person singular	-es
first, second and third person plural	-es
(ii) personal pronoun in contact with verb	
third person singular	-es
first, second and third person plural	-e, -0; in the south of N area also -en

In Late Middle English this rule roughly operated north of the Chester-Wash line, in other words an area slightly larger than the one we define as the North in this study. Between the Chester-Wash line and a line running from Shrewsbury to the Thames estuary, the Midland paradigm was used, i.e. *-(e)th* in the third person singular and *-e* or zero in the plural. South of this line the *-(e)th* ending was in use in the third person singular and the whole plural.

According to McIntosh (1983) there was also a mixed paradigm which had developed through dialect contact between the North and the Midlands. In this system *-(e)th* was used when the subject was not a personal pronoun in contact with a verb, and in the third person singular with personal pronouns in contact with the verb, in other words the rule was similar to the Northern Present-Tense Rule, but the suffix was different. The plural with personal pronoun subjects had the suffix *-en* or *-e* or zero.

Our aim was to analyse the whole of the indicative paradigm, but it soon became evident that some material could be left out. The second person plural had to be excluded, since there was not enough material in the letters, which were mostly written by one individual to another. We also left out the second person singular with the subject pronoun *ye/you* and the first-person plural, which both had practically always a zero ending.[13] The occasional instances of *thou* were invariably followed by the verb in *-(e)st*, and no further attention was paid to them. Only one case of the first person plural with an *-s* ending was found in our early northern material, which shows that the Northern Rule only seldom applied in the first person plural during the period at issue.

On the basis of the above, it turned out that the suffixes in only three persons merited detailed scrutiny, the first and third singular plus the third plural. Tables 7-9 contain the results of our analysis. An overall look at them reveals that the first person singular was expressed by a zero in London and East Anglia, but an occasional ending could occur in the North.[14] Much more variation can be observed in the third person, both singular and plural, neither of which became fully regularised during the time our study covers. In fact, what looks like a unified supraregional usage in the aggregates discussed in section 5.1., still contains a great deal of variation in many individuals' language.

The inventory of the third person endings included, apart from -*th*, -*s* and zero, -*t* and -*z* as their variant forms (examples (17)-(18)). As tables 7-9 show, zero was a real (though rare) alternative in the singular throughout our period. It was not always easy to distinguish between the indicative and the subjunctive in the analysis, but we made every effort not to overinterpret the indicative. In the plural the inventory also includes the medieval Midland suffix -*(e)n* in East Anglia (example (19)).

(17) **my master youre fader and my maysterys yowre moder** *faryt* well ...
        (CELY, William Maryon, 36, 1478)

(18) *And Syr, as touchynge the ffelles of Robert Turbotes of Lamberton,* **it** ***makez*** *no matter as yit ...*
        (STONOR, Thomas Betson, II,3, 1476)

(19) *for there be* **tenauntes þat varyen** *fro his billes and he can best answere there-to.*
        (PASTON, James Gloys, II: 377, 1466?)

As table 7 shows, medieval Londoners had a great deal of variation in the third person singular. Most informants had at least three alternatives, and both -*th* and -*s* appear as main variants. In the plural, on the other hand, variation is not very extensive. It is known that many of the informants were immigrants to London – hardly surprising in the light of the facts discussed in section 3. The abundance of variation suggests that a great deal of diversity was tolerated in medieval London. Migration to London did not mean loss of dialectal features, and standardisation was yet to come.

The early part of the sixteenth century shows remarkable uniformity. Among the King's administrative servants, both native Londoners like Sir Thomas More and immigrants like Cardinal Wolsey only used -*th* in the singular. An occasional -*th* suffix also occurs in the plural. This seems to be in harmony with Holmqvist's (1922: 153) observation that -*th* in the plural was on the increase in what he calls the written standard after about 1500. As shown earlier, -*s* began to gain ground again from the 1540s onwards. At the end of the century, the domination of -*th* in London and the Court begins to erode. The standard of the earlier administrators is still observed in the letters of Queen Elizabeth's principal Secretary of State William Cecil, Lord Burghley, and in those of the Recorder of London, William Fleetwood. But the Earl of Leicester, Robert Dudley, uses -*s* even in the plural and Philip Henslowe, theatrical manager and proprietor, has a variety of forms in both the plural and the singular. Philip Gawdy, in turn, is an immigrant from Norfolk, and hence his preference for -*th* is not surprising. After moving to London his use of -*s* increased gradually (Raumolin-Brunberg 1996b: 34).

Table 7. Present indicative inflection in London (Calais) and the Court (*have* and *do* excluded)

	First person singular	Third person singular	Third person plural
Before 1500			
Thomas Betson	0 [ff]	th [*s z 0*]	[0]
George Cely	0	th *s* [*0*]	0
Richard Cely sr	0	t [th 0]	0
Richard Cely jr	0	s 0 [*th*]	0 s
Richard Page	0	s [*th*]	0
John Dalton	0	s [*th t 0*]	0
William Maryon	0	t [*th 0*]	t 0

Edmond Paston 2	0	th s *0* [*t*]	[0 s]
John Paston 2	0	**th** [*t s*]	0
1500-1540			
Henry VIII	0	th	[0]
Thomas Cromwell	0	th	0 [*th*]
Thomas More	0	th	0 [*th*]
Stephen Gardiner	0	**th** [*0*]	0
Thomas Wolsey	0	th	[0]
Thomas Wyatt	0	th	0
1540-1560			
Princess Elizabeth	0	th s	th [*0*]
Anthony Cave	0	th s	[0]
John Johnson	0	**th** [*s*]	0
Otwell Johnson	0	**th** [*s*]	[0]
Richard Johnson	0	th	0
1560-1600			
Elizabeth I	0	th s [*0*]	0 s
William Cecil	0	th	0
Robert Dudley	0	[s th]	0 [*s*]
William Fleetwood	0	th	0
Philip Henslowe	0	s th	[s th 0]
Philip Gawdy	0	**th** [*s*]	0
1600-1640			
Anthony Antony	0	**th** [*s*]	0 [*s*]
John Chamberlain	0	**s** [*0*]	0
Robert Daborne	0	s	0
Thomas Meautys 2	0	s	0
1640-1681			
Samuel Pepys	0	**s** [*th*]	0
John Wilmot	0	s	0
Thomas Oxinden	0	s	0
Joseph Williamson	0	s	0

Note to table 7. The suffixes in bold type represent the main variants, i.e. those used in 80% of the cases or more. The endings in italics are rare variants, only up to 20% of the occurrences. The remaining endings represent the frequencies between 21% and 79%. The forms in square brackets are rare in absolute terms, viz. only one or two occurrences.

Figure 2 already testified to a rapid increase in the employment of -*s* in London in the seventeenth century. Table 7 suggests that the plural was also almost fully regularised by this time. The inflectional norms similar to Present-day Standard English had been adopted by native Londoners, such as the dramatist Robert Daborne and John Wilmot, the Earl of Rochester, as well as immigrants to London, like Thomas Oxinden from Kent and Joseph Williamson from Cumberland.

The pattern that emerges for East Anglian English in table 8 markedly differs from that of London. The earliest informants preferred the Midland -*th* in the third person singular. It was also quite frequent in the plural, in which the old nasal suffix was also possible at this time. If we believe that -*th* gained prestige at the expense of -*s* in the early sixteenth century, it was natural for people in Norfolk and Suffolk to go on using their prestigious native alternative. Until the first decades of the seventeenth century, -*th* holds its position as the main variant in East Anglia, but -*s* slowly gains ground in the seventeenth century. On the basis of what we know of Present-day East Anglian dialects, it is rather surprising that zero, which is now common, does not play a more important role there than the table indicates (Trudgill 1996; see Nevalainen, Raumolin-Brunberg, and Trudgill forthcoming). It is, however, interesting to see that those who have zero as a real alternative in table 8 are either women, such as Katherine Paston or Dorothy Browne, or represent lower social orders, like John Mounford. We may assume that these people were more likely to use their local dialect than their better-educated contemporaries.

Table 8. Present indicative inflection in East Anglia (*have* and *do* excluded)

	First person singular	Third person singular	Third person plural
Before 1500			
Richard Calle	0	**th** *0* [*s*]	**0** [*th*]
James Gloys	0	th 0 [*s*]	n 0 [*th*]
John Paston 1	0	**th**	0 [th]
John Paston 3	0	th t [*s*]	**0** *th*
Thomas Playter	0	**th** [*s*]	**0** [*th*]
William Worcester	0	**th** [*s*]	th [n 0]
1500-1540			
Thomas Howard	0	th	0
1560-1600			
Edward Bacon	0	th	0 [th]

Nathaniel Bacon 1	0	th [s]	0 [th]
John Mounford	0	th 0 [s]	0
Francis Wyndham	0	th [t s]	0 [th]
1600-1640			
Nathaniel Bacon 2	0	th [s]	[0 th]
John Heveningham	0	th [s]	[0]
Thomas Knyvett	0	s [th]	0 s
Katherine Paston	0	s 0 [th]	0
1640-1681			
Dorothy Browne	0	s 0	0
Thomas Browne	0	s th	0
Thomas Corie	0	s *th*	0

Note to table 8. For conventions, see table 7.

Let us then look at the northern informants in table 9. It is not surprising that the two medieval gentlemen Greene and Plumpton used -*s*, but we can see that it was not Robenet Plumpton's main variant. Among the northerners of the early sixteenth century, the nobleman Thomas Dacre is the only one to show traits of the northern paradigm, while two others, John Wilson, prior of a monastery called Mountgrace, and Sir Thomas Wharton rely on -*th* in both the singular and the plural. Their non-use of -*s* could be explained by the high prestige of -*th* even in the North. On the other hand, these people did not fully adopt the London zero plural but used a suffix according to the analogical mixed Midland paradigm. The fact that Wilson uses -*th* even in the first-person singular may be a sign of hypercorrection.

Table 9. Present indicative inflection in the northern counties (*have* and *do* excluded)

	First person singular	Third person singular	Third person plural
Before 1500			
Godfrey Greene	0	s [0]	0 s
Robenet Plumpton	0	th [s 0]	[0 s th]
1500-1540			
Thomas Dacre	0	th [s]	[0 s]
Thomas Wharton	0	th	[0 th]
John Wilson	0 [s th]	th [0]	th 0
1560-1600			
Matthew Hutton	0	th	0

1600-1640			
Arthur Ingram	0	th [s 0]	0
Christopher Lowther	0	**th** [*s*]	0
Chr Wandesford	0 [*s*]	s [*th 0*]	0
Thomas Wentworth	0 [*s*]	s [*th*]	[0 *s*]
William Wentworth	0	th s	[0]
1640-1681			
Frances Basire	0	s [*th 0*]	0 [*s*]
Daniel Fleming	0 [*s*]	[s]	0
Andrew Marvell	0	s th [*0*]	0

Note to table 9. For conventions, see table 7.

While the late-sixteenth-century Bishop of York, Matthew Hutton, favoured the standard paradigm of his time, during the first part of the seventeenth century -*s* became the main variant in the language of northern gentlemen such as Sir Thomas Wentworth and Christopher Wandesford. It is worth noticing that they also employed the Northern Present-Tense Rule in the plural and the first person singular. Among our latest informants it is interesting to compare the language of the northern gentleman Daniel Fleming with that of his friend Joseph Williamson in table 7, who had moved to London. Fleming kept some northern patterns, while Williamson did not.

This section can be summed up by stressing the extent of individual variation both in the third person singular and plural. Our material does not include any one who would have consistently applied either the Northern Rule, the mixed paradigm, or the southern inflection system. On the other hand, the Midland paradigm was thriving, but by no means exclusively. While late medieval Londoners displayed extensive variation, the Midland pattern appeared as a fairly regular court and administrative standard in the early part of the sixteenth century; relatively few people however had it as their only choice. -*th* spread to the North, but traits of the northern plural can be found throughout our period.

In the third person plural, an interesting implicational relationship emerges: if a person has -*s* in the plural, -*s* also appears as one of the variants in the singular. The same is true of -*th*. In other words, there are no examples of an exclusive -*s* in the singular and -*th* in the plural or *vice versa*. How this should be interpreted is not quite clear.

Analogical extension may be suggested, but the usage may also be a sign of the application of either the Northern Rule or the mixed Midland paradigm. The latter argument is supported by the fact that both the proximity principle and the character-of-subject condition are met in practically all cases. A notable exception is the Londoner Sir Thomas More, who in his younger years wrote *they wisheth*. This expression was apparently a reflection of the medieval southern plural form. Our observations are well in line with Schendl's argument that the -*s* and -*th* suffixes in the third person plural were a consequence of dialect contact, i.e. an intersystemic development, rather than an intrasystemic analogical extension.[15]

Nevertheless, analogical extension also seems to be working in the paradigm, as the first person singular was not originally affected by the Northern Present-Tense Rule at all. The proximity and character-of-subject conditions are fulfilled in cases with a suffix in the first-person singular (see example (5) in section 2.). The use of the zero suffix in the third person singular was not predicted by the Northern Present-Tense Rule either, nor by any other paradigm introduced at the beginning of this section. The scarcity of occurrences prevents any quantitative analysis of the linguistic environment of the verbs with the zero suffix, but we have observed that zero occurred with both noun and pronoun subjects which could be adjacent or non-adjacent to the verb.[16] There are no signs of a development towards one suffix becoming the present tense marker with all kinds of subject, like -*s* in some present-day non-standard varieties.

Our material suggests that immigrants' linguistic behaviour changed with time. Medieval migrants to London seem to have kept at least some of their dialectal features in full use. Later on, there appears to have been more accommodation to the usage of other Londoners, as we can see from the linguistic behaviour of Philip Gawdy and Joseph Williamson. On the other hand, people like Sir Thomas Wentworth who had an important role in national politics could retain regionally conditioned choices, such as the first person singular -*s*.

Overall, our analysis of the whole indicative present paradigm, more varied though it is, suggests a process similar to that of the third person singular. London leads the development towards the norms of verbal inflection of Present-day Standard English.

6. Pronominal changes

Let us now turn our attention to five pronominal changes which may shed more light on the question of London's role in linguistic change. Figure 5 and the corresponding table 10 show how the relative pronoun *which* quickly proved to be the winner over its rival *the which*. In Late Middle English both alternatives were in frequent use with similar grammatical profiles, i.e. both were employed with personal and non-personal reference in non-restrictive and restrictive clauses in different syntactic functions and with different antecedents (Raumolin-Brunberg 2000).

Table 10. The frequency of *which* versus *the which* as relative pronouns in three dialect areas: variable totals (N), total means of *which* per period (%) and averages of individual scores per period (A) (*CEEC* 1996; 1460-1681)

Period	London N	Freq. of *which* %	A	East Anglia N	Freq. of *which* %	A	North N	Fr. of *which* %	A
1460-1499	479	39%	23.0	384	85%	84.3	32	69%	58.2
1500-1539	685	90%	89.6	2	100%	100.0	177	87%	90.4
1540-1579	1075	91%	88.8	582	94%	89.1	16	94%	93.7
1580-1619	1093	98%	97.7	401	95%	97.0	144	97%	94.1
1620-1659	287	94%	95.8	466	98%	97.7	747	98%	95.4
1660-1681	131	99%	99.0	115	100%	100.0	256	100%	100.0
Total N	3588			1950			1372		

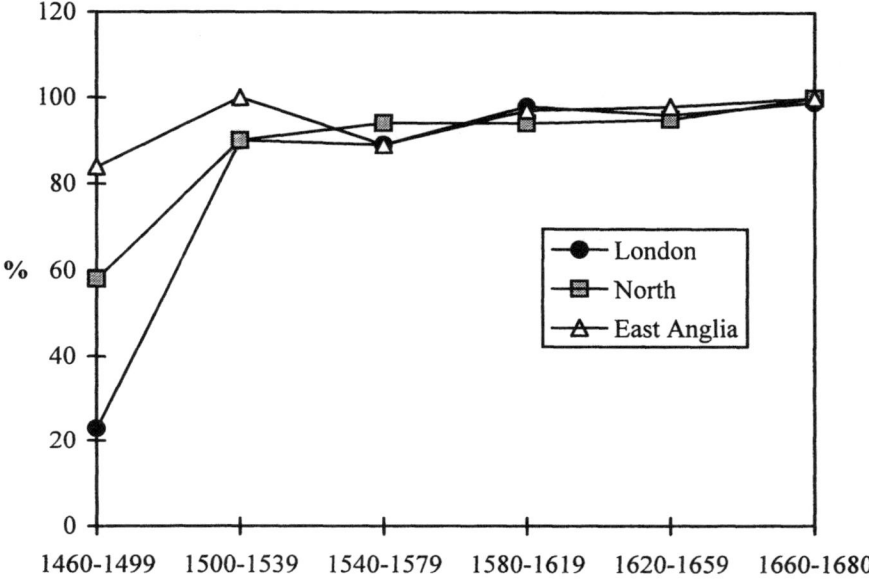

Figure 5. Which (%) versus *the which* in three dialect areas; averages of individual scores (1460-1681)

The which, a form of northern origin, was very frequent in Middle English. It was commonly used in Chancery English, and in the *Helsinki Corpus* last subsection of Middle English (1420-1500) its proportion was 44%, while during the hundred years from 1417 to 1519 in the *CEEC* it covered 35 % of the occurrences. There was remarkable individual and textual variation in its use, and it is not easy to establish clear patterns of external conditioning. In general, women tended to use this form more than men, and there is one distinct group of people who preferred it in the latter half of the fifteenth century, namely London wool merchants (Raumolin-Brunberg 2000).

There are in fact quite a number of similarities between *the which* and the third person singular suffix *-s*. Both were originally northern forms that had found their way to London, apparently in immigrants' language, and gained ground there, *the which* even more widely than *-s*. Neither form was used in East Anglia to any significant degree, and neither was adopted in the evolving standard during the first decades of the sixteenth century. But here the similarities end. As we have seen, the third person *-s* entered Standard English later on, while *the which* disappeared. In this case, a form that had been popular in medieval London gained no supraregional position. Perhaps its complex form in the end was the factor that worked against its entrance into the standard language.

The next set of curves (figure 6) illustrates a remarkably rapid change. Although some occasional instances of the oblique pronoun *you* can be found in the subject position from the fourteenth century onwards (Mustanoja 1960: 125), figure 6 and table 11 show that its real breakthrough took place between 1520 and 1600. Here London clearly leads the change. Londoners chose *you* instead of the nominative *ye* in half of the instances of second person subject pronouns in 1520-1559 (measured in terms of score averages), while the subject function was assigned to *you* only in about one tenth of the cases both in the North and in East Anglia. This change nicely agrees with the "snowball pattern" identified by Ogura and Wang (1996): those dialect areas, or sites in their terminology, that participate in a change temporally later tend to exhibit sharper S-curves than areas where the change takes place earlier. The model works despite the non-adjacency of the areas.

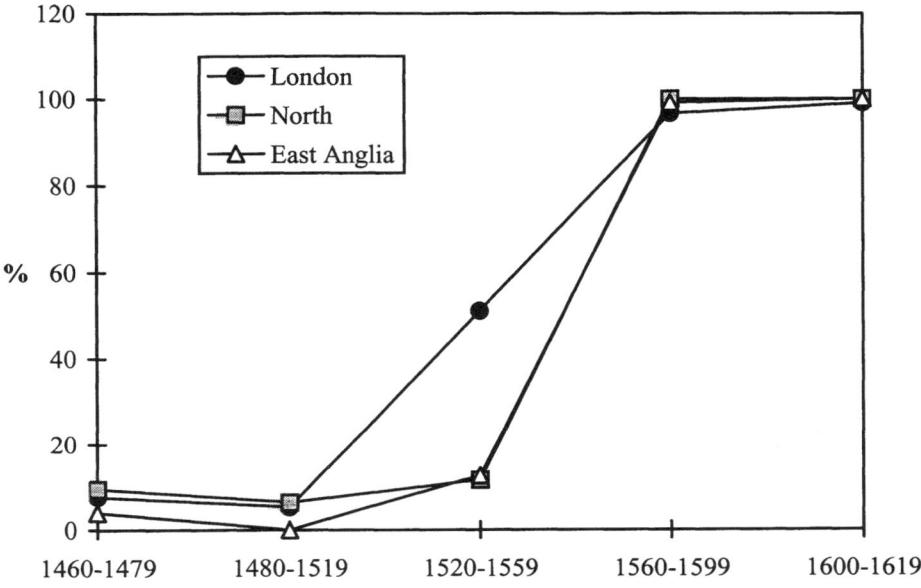

Figure 6. You (%) versus *ye* in three dialect areas; averages of individual scores. (1460-1681)

Table 11. The frequency of *you* versus *ye* in the subject function in three dialect areas: variable totals (N), total means of *you* per period (%) and averages of individual scores per period (A) (*CEEC* 1998; 1460-1619)

	London			East Anglia			North		
	Freq. of *you*			Freq. of *you*			Freq. of *you*		
Period	N	%	A	N	%	A	N	%	A
1460-1479	718	4%	7.5	1283	1%	3.9	57	9%	9.4
1480-1519	514	3%	5.2	75	0%	0.0	170	6%	6.3
1520-1559	1950	39%	51.1	16	13%	12.5	124	13%	11.5
1560-1599	721	91%	96.6	944	99%	99.1	27	100%	100.0
1600-1619	638	100%	99.0	99	100%	100.0	72	100%	100.0
Total N	4541			2417			450		

The variation between *ye* and *you* does not seem to have had any dialectal basis. The leading role of London may be understood against this background (see also Nevalainen 2000). It is interesting, though, that the North follows the distant capital as closely as East

Anglia when the process is gaining momentum. The linguistic behaviour of East Anglia therefore at least to some extent reflects the self-sufficiency that social historians have attributed to this area (see section 3.).

The following three changes take place in the seventeenth century. It is more than likely that the mid-century turmoils of the Civil War had an accelerating effect on all three (Raumolin-Brunberg and Nurmi 1997; Raumolin-Brunberg 1998). The literature contains no suggestions of a regional background for any of these developments. Since we know from earlier research that gender is an important external constraint on at least two of the changes, the prop-word *one* and the indefinite pronouns with singular human reference, the material was solely limited to men's letters. This choice was due to the uneven representation of women in the three dialect areas at different times.

As mentioned in section 2., the possessive determiner *its* was introduced into the language at the turn of the seventeenth century (Nevalainen and Raumolin-Brunberg 1994). Its paradigmatic alternatives consisted of *of it* and *thereof*. The oldest variant *his* was not included in this study, as it disappeared from the language quite early. Our results in table 12 do not contradict the suggestion made in the *Oxford English Dictionary* (s.v. *its*, poss. pron.) that the origin of *its* was colloquial southern English (London and Oxford). Table 12 indicates that Londoners adopted the innovation before East Anglia and the North. East Anglia however no longer appears to be a conservative area which lagged behind, as it did in the fifteenth and sixteenth centuries, but follows London before the North. The table further shows that the increase in the use of *its* is compensated by the decrease in the frequency of the old synthetic variant *thereof*.

Table 12. The use of *its* and its alternatives in 1600-1681 (*CEEC* 1998; male informants); absolute figures

	its		of it		thereof		Total
	N	%	N	%	N	%	N
London and Court	21	34	30	49	10	16	61
East Anglia	4	17	13	54	7	29	24
North	7	11	33	54	21	34	61

Let us next turn our attention to the increasing use of the prop-word *one*. This pronoun had existed in the language from the Middle English period onwards, but it was only in the seventeenth century that it began to gain broader currency (see Rissanen 1997; Raumolin-Brunberg and Nurmi 1997). The present analysis only includes premodified noun phrases (as in example (12)). Although the number of instances is low, table 13 suggests that by 1680 East Anglia had reached the same frequency of use as London, but the North lagged behind.

Table 13. The use of the prop-word *one* in 1600-1681 (*CEEC* 1998; male informants); occurrences per 10,000 running words

	N	Running words	N/10,000 words
London and Court	45	246,366	1.8
East Anglia	14	76,797	1.8
North	14	148,032	0.9

Our last pronominal change deals with the paradigm of compound indefinite pronouns with singular human reference such as *anybody* and *everyone* (see Raumolin-Brunberg 1994; Raumolin-Brunberg and Kahlas-Tarkka 1997).[17] The seventeenth century was a time when the proportion of the *-body* pronouns grew at the cost of the other members of the paradigm, i.e. compounds in *-man* and in *-one*, and the simple pronouns like *none* and *any*. Table 14 presents a familiar picture: the increase again follows the order London, East-Anglia, and the North.

Table 14. Indefinite pronouns with singular human reference in 1600-1681 (male informants); absolute figures

	-body		-one		-man		other		Total
	N	%	N	%	N	%	N	%	N
London and Court	46	34	15	11	34	25	41	30	136
East Anglia	6	23	3	12	7	27	10	38	26
North	5	4	23	21	25	23	58	52	111

Table 14 especially shows that the *-body* pronouns were rare in the North, where people to a large extent still relied on the simple forms of the group *"other"* (e.g. *none, any*). The large proportion of compounds with *one* in the North may be a coincidence, since the form is strongly favoured by one of our northern informants, Sir Christopher Lowther, with a contribution of over 30,000 words in the corpus.

These three seventeenth-century changes provide a different picture from what we saw a century before. Geographical distance has apparently begun to play a more important role, so that linguistic changes no longer reach the North before East Anglia. The leading role of London, however, remains undisputed.

7. Conclusion

Our findings corroborate the general idea of the significance of London that students of Early Modern English have probably always had. It shows, however, that London's role did not remain unchanged in the Tudor and Stuart periods. General demographic developments and patterns of migration inevitably affected the linguistic features that were encountered in London and diffused from London to different parts of the country.

The fifteenth century witnessed considerable linguistic variation. It is obvious that immigrants, among whom the number of northerners was not insignificant, introduced new elements into the language of London. The originally northern third person singular *-s* and the relative pronoun *the which* gained currency in London, but were not accepted as part of the rising standard in the sixteenth century. Occasional examples of the Northern Present-Tense Rule in the third person plural and the mixed Midland paradigm with *-th* also testify to a northern influence which did not last in the standard. The third person singular *-s*, which persisted in the language of lower-rank Londoners throughout the sixteenth century, however later superseded *-th* (perhaps in the wake of another ongoing change, vowel-deletion in inflectional endings), and developed into a supra-regional suffix. London also led the generalisation of the second person subject form *you* in the sixteenth century. The fact that the change took place in the North as rapidly as in East Anglia may be taken as a further indication of relatively close contacts between the capital and the North at the time.

The three seventeenth-century pronominal changes discussed in this study undoubtedly emphasise the role of London as the centre from which innovations emanated to the rest of the country. If Wyld had focused his attention on that century, he might not have been faced with a dilemma, since the diffusion of linguistic changes tended to proceed in a wave-like manner. This can only, of course, be said on the basis of the three dialect areas we investigated. Research into other regions is necessary to establish general validity for this suggestion.

Appendix

The use of -s (%) versus -th in the third person singular in the whole corpus in 1540-1559, excluding *have* and *do* (*CEEC* 1998, male informants only). Totals of the variable shown in brackets. See figure 3 in the text.

social rank	-s	%	(-s + -th)
nobility	0	0%	(4)
gentry	20	12%	(165)
professionals	2	3%	(65)
social aspirers	14	5%	(256)
merchants	63	10%	(659)
other non-gentry	44	76%	(58)
women	19	33%	(58)
total	162	13%	(1265)

The use of -s (%) versus -th in the third person singular in East Anglia in 1560-1579, excluding *have* and *do* (*CEEC* 1998, male informants only). Totals of the variable shown in brackets. See figure 4 in the text.

social rank	-s	%	(-s + -th)
upper gentry	1	12%	(8)
lower gentry	3	2%	(196)
clergy	10	7%	(145)
professionals	3	7%	(43)
merchants		(no data available)	
other non-gentry	2	9%	(22)
total	19	5%	(414)

Notes

1. We should like to thank Dieter Kastovsky and David Denison for their most useful comments on earlier versions of this paper.
2. The references in the examples give the abbreviated name of the letter collection used, name of informant, page number and year of writing. For further information on the data used, see section 4.2. in this study and the appendix in Nevalainen and Raumolin-Brunberg ((eds.) 1996).
3. There was a loss of the genitive inflection in the northern dialect area (Klemola 1997).
4. Some compounds in *-one* can also have non-personal reference in partitive constructions, such as *every one of the books*. These forms are usually emphatic and the pronoun is written as two words even in Present-day English. These items do not affect this study, since partitive constructions are excluded anyway, because two of the variants, i.e. pronouns with *man* and *body* never appear in them.
5. This pertinent quotation is from Wrigley (1967: 44).
6. Although the two sets of figures, which both frequently appear in the literature, seem to be in contradiction, this is not necessarily the case. Especially the differences prior to 1600 may be explained by the use of different criteria in defining the area of London. Rappaport (1989), who uses Boulton's (1987) figures, concentrates on the City proper, while Finlay and Shearer (1986) include the fast-growing suburbs in their estimates.
7. For a similar approach, i.e. analysis of demographic factors in connection with the use of periphrastic *do*, see Klemola (1996: 185-194).
8. We have employed the category Court as one of the alternatives in assigning domicile to the informants. This term refers to people who were courtiers or otherwise belonged to the royal household and also to those who worked as high-ranking government officials directly reporting to the Queen, King, or the Lord Chancellor. This division of Londoners into two groups is significant when we try to understand which linguistic changes are natural, i.e. coming "from below", and which represent the more prestigious type of language use, leading to changes "from above" (Nevalainen 2000; for the concepts, see Labov (1994: 78)).
9. This conclusion is also supported by contemporary phoneticians and orthoepists. In view of our argument it is interesting to find that those who commented on the pronunciation of third person present indicative endings were either native Londoners (Hart, Hodges) or long-term residents in the capital (Bullokar, Gill; see e.g. Danielsson (1955: 174-176) and Dobson 1957: II, 883-885)). It appears that these early commentators regarded *-s* (both its

voiceless and voiced realisations) as a contracted form of the syllabic *-eth*. This suggests that, unlike *-eth*, *-es* should have undergone vowel deletion in non-sibilant contexts by the late sixteenth century. The dental fricative still represented the regular third person ending for John Hart, whose works appeared between 1551 and 1570, although he also includes a few instances of *-s* in his transcriptions (e.g. in *methinks*).

Writing in 1586, William Bullokar allowed the use of *-s* as a poetic contraction of *-eth*. In the 1620s, Alexander Gill labels *has* as a northern variant of *hath*, regarding the forms with the dental fricative, *hath* and *doth*, as normal, but adds that in other verbs *-eth* can shorten to *-s* or *-z*, or become *ez* after a sibilant. Finally, in 1643 Richard Hodges notes that, although *-(e)th* may appear in writing, it is commonly pronounced *-s* or *-z* in ordinary speech. His general usage is characterised by Dobson (1957: I, 186) as "real and unaffected" and "in many ways somewhat advanced". It is however often forgotten, but mentioned by Danielsson (1955: 176), that Hodges, too, uses the "uncontracted" suffix with the dental fricative in his transcriptions of liturgical speech in *The English primrose* (1644). Register variation is therefore clearly in evidence in the speech of Londoners even in the middle of the seventeenth century.

10. Ogura and Wang (1996: 130) base their account of the site-to-site diffusion of *-s* solely on Holmqvist (1922).
11. The Sociolinguistics and Language History project has been funded by the Academy of Finland and the University of Helsinki. The team consists of four junior members, Jukka Keränen, Minna Nevala, Arja Nurmi, and Minna Palander-Collin, and of two senior ones, Terttu Nevalainen and Helena Raumolin-Brunberg.
12. One of the main criteria for the choice of the informants was authenticity: only material edited from autograph letters was included. Exception had to be made in the case of two informants. The northerners Robenet Plumpton and Godfrey Greene were selected, although their letters had been edited from copies, because there is no autograph material from the North before 1500.

    The random sampling was made as follows: all the material in the corpus was analysed for writers with less than 4,000 running words. For people with more data, the material included in the analysis was limited to twenty WordCruncher screens, which roughly amounts to 4,000 words. The search of the suffixes was made manually.
13. The zero suffix also includes *-e*, which in this study has been interpreted as a spelling variant of zero rather than a suffix in its own right.
14. The Londoner Thomas Betson's unexpected suffix *-ff* has been analysed by Nevanlinna (1996).
15. Occasional evidence for analogy can be found in the literature. Gómez-Soliño (1982), for instance, points out that Thomas Deloney's choice of the third

person plural suffix follows that of the singular. In his early work -*th* is frequent, but in the later writings -*s* becomes the predominant ending. On the other hand, Gómez-Soliño also shows that the character-of-subject condition is met in Deloney's writings in that zero always follows the personal pronoun *they*. Interestingly, the article also claims that zero was the third person plural suffix that was preferred by Deloney's fictional nobility. This alleged prestige of zero does not contradict what we have seen in table 7, but the fact that Queen Elizabeth also used -*s* and -*th* in the plural suggests that the prestige could hardly have been very high.

16. Bailey, Maynor, and Cukor-Avila (1989) present a study of the third person suffixes in the Cely collection. Their observation is that, even in the singular, zero more often followed a pronoun than a noun-headed noun phrase.

17. Table 15 presents all the linguistic items included in this study.

Table 15. Indefinite pronouns with singular human reference

	-body	-one	-man	other
assertive	some body	some one	some man	some (other)
non-assertive	any body	any one	any man	any (other)
negative	no body	no one	no man	none (other)
universal	every body	every one	every man	each
				each man

Note: Classification from Quirk et al. (1985: 377). The compounds are usually spelled as two words in the letters.

There were considerable problems in the interpretation of some of the items on both the type and token levels. On the type level, it was difficult to decide which lexemes to include. *A man*, for instance, in some contexts had the meaning 'someone' and *another* 'someone else'. Our decision was to discuss the central variants only. On the token level, it was especially difficult to find out whether instances of *any* and *some* represented the singular or the plural. Some of our decisions inevitably remained subjective, but we nevertheless believe that the general quantification is adequate (for further discussion, see Raumolin-Brunberg and Kahlas-Tarkka 1997).

References

Bailey, Guy, Natalie Maynor, and Patricia Cukor-Avila
    1989   Variation in subject-verb concord in Early Modern English. *Language Variation and Change* 1: 285-300.

Barber, Charles L.
    1997   *Early Modern English*. London: Deutsch. [First edition 1976.]

Beier, A. L. and Roger Finlay
1986 The significance of the metropolis. In: A. L. Beier and Roger Finlay (eds.), 1-33.
Beier, A. L. and Roger Finlay (eds.)
1986 *London 1500-1700: the making of the metropolis.* London/New York: Longman.
Bermúdez-Otero, Ricardo, David Denison, Richard M. Hogg, and Charles B. McCully (eds.)
2000 *Generative theory and corpus studies: a dialogue from 10ICEHL.* (Topics in English Linguistics 31.) Berlin/New York: Mouton de Gruyter.
Berndt, Rolf
1956 *Form und Funktion des Verbums im nördlichen Spätaltenglischen.* Halle (Saale): VEB Niemeyer.
Blake, Norman F.
1981 *Non-standard language in English literature.* London: Deutsch.
Blake, Norman F. (ed.)
1992 *The Cambridge history of the English language*, Volume 2. *1066-1476.* Cambridge: Cambridge University Press.
Boulton, Jeremy
1987 *Neighbourhood and society: a London suburb in the seventeenth century.* Cambridge: Cambridge University Press.
Britton, Derek (ed.)
1996 *English historical linguistics 1994.* (Current Issues in Linguistic Theory 135.) Amsterdam/Philadelphia: Benjamins.
Cheshire, Jenny
1982 *Variation in an English dialect: a sociolinguistic study.* Cambridge: Cambridge University Press.
Coleman, David and John Salt
1992 *The British population: patterns, trends, processes.* Oxford: Oxford University Press.
Danchev, Andrei
1992 The evidence for analytic and synthetic developments in English. In: Matti Rissanen et al. (eds.), 25-41.
Danielsson, Bror
1955 *John Hart's works on English orthography and pronunciation,* Part II, *Phonology.* Stockholm: Almqvist and Wiksell.
Dobson, Eric J.
[1955] 1969 Early Modern Standard English. *Transactions of the Philological Society,* 25-54. Reprinted in: Roger Lass (ed.), 419-439.
1957 *English pronunciation 1500-1700,* Volume 2. *Pronunciation.* Oxford: Clarendon Press.

Dyer, Alan
1991　　　*Decline and growth in English towns, 1400-1640.* Houndmills/London: Macmillan.

Everitt, Alan
1966　　　Social mobility in Early Modern England. *Past and Present* 33: 56-73.

Ferguson, Charles A.
1996　　　Variation and drift: loss of agreement in Germanic. In: Gregory R. Guy et al. (eds.), 173-198.

Finlay, Roger and Beatrice Shearer
1986　　　Population growth and suburban expansion. In: A. L. Beier and Roger Finlay (eds.), 37-59.

Fisher, John H.
1977　　　Chancery and the emergence of standard written English in the fifteenth century. *Speculum* 52: 870-899.

Fisher, John H., Malcolm Richardson, and Jane L. Fisher
1984　　　*An anthology of Chancery English.* Knoxville: University of Tennessee Press.

Fisiak, Jacek and Marcin Krygier (eds.)
1998　　　*Advances in English historical linguistics.* (Trends in Linguistics 112.) Berlin: Mouton de Gruyter.

Fisiak, Jacek and Peter Trudgill (eds.)
forthc.　　*History of East Anglian English.* Cambridge: Boydell and Brewer.

Gómez-Soliño, José S.
1982　　　Formas verbales de plural en 0, *eth* y *(e)s* en la prosa de Deloney. *Revista de la Filologia de la Universidad de La Laguna* 1: 113-121.

Gray, Douglas and Eric G. Stanley (eds.)
1983　　　*Middle English studies presented to Norman Davis in honour of his seventieth birthday.* Oxford: Clarendon Press.

Guy, Gregory R., Crawford Feagin, Deborah Schiffrin, and John Baugh (eds.)
1996　　　*Towards a social science of language: papers in honor of William Labov,* Volume 1. *Variation and change in language and society.* (Current Issues in Linguistic Theory 127). Amsterdam/Philadelphia: Benjamins.

Hogg, Richard and Linda van Bergen (eds.)
1998　　　*Historical linguistics 1995: selected papers from the XIIth international Conference on Historical Linguistics, Manchester 1995.* Volume 2: *Germanic linguistics.* (Current Issues in Linguistic Theory 162). Amsterdam/Philadelphia: Benjamins.

Holmqvist, Erik
1922 *On the history of the English present inflections, particularly* -th *and* -s. Heidelberg: Carl Winter's Universitätsbuchhandlung.
Hopper, Paul and Elizabeth Traugott
1993 *Grammaticalization.* Cambridge: Cambridge University Press.
Kastovsky, Dieter
1992 Typological reorientation as a result of level interaction: the case of English morphology. In: Günter Kellermann and Michael D. Morrissey (eds.), 411-428.
1998 Morphological restructuring: the case of Old English and Middle English verbs. In: Richard Hogg and Linda van Bergen (eds.), 131-147.
Kastovsky, Dieter (ed.)
1994 *Studies in Early Modern English.* (Topics in English Linguistics 13.) Berlin/New York: Mouton de Gruyter.
Kellermann, Günter and Michael D. Morrissey (eds.)
1992 *Diachrony within synchrony: language history and cognition* (Duisburger Arbeiten zur Sprach- und Kulturwissenschaft 14.) Frankfurt (Main): Lang.
Kerswill, Paul
1993 Rural dialect speakers in an urban speech community: the role of dialect contact in defining a sociolinguistic concept. *International Journal of Applied Linguistics* 3: 33-55.
Kitch, M. J.
1986 Capital and kingdom: migration to later Stuart London. In: A. L. Beier and Roger Finlay (eds.), 224-251.
Klemola, Juhani
1996 *Non-standard periphrastic* do: *a study in variation and change.* Unpublished Ph.D. thesis, University of Essex.
1997 Dialect evidence for the loss of genitive inflection in English. *English Language and Linguistics* 1: 349-353.
Klemola, Juhani, Merja Kytö, and Matti Rissanen (eds.)
1996 *Speech past and present: studies in English dialectology in memory of Ossi Ihalainen.* Frankfurt (Main): Lang.
Kristensson, Gillis
1994 Sociolects in 14th-century London. In: Gunnel Melchers and Nils-Lennart Johannesson (eds.), 103-110.
Kytö, Merja
1993 Third-person present singular verb inflection in early British and American English. *Language Variation and Change* 5: 113-139.

Labov, William
1994 *Principles of linguistic change: internal factors.* Oxford: Blackwell.
Laslett, Peter
1983 *The world we have lost – further explored.* London: Routledge.
Lass, Roger
1992 Phonology and morphology. In: Norman Blake (ed.), 23-155.
Lass, Roger (ed.)
1969 *Approaches to English historical linguistics.* New York: Holt, Rinehart and Winston.
Leith, Dick
1984 Tudor London: sociolinguistic stratification and linguistic change. *Anglo-American Studies* 4 (1): 59-72.
Luick, Karl
[1921] 1964 *Historische Grammatik der englischen Sprache.* Volume 1, Part 1. Stuttgart: Tauchnitz.
McIntosh, Angus
1983 Present indicative plural forms in the Later Middle English of the North Midlands. In: Douglas Gray and Eric G. Stanley (eds.), 235-244.
Melchers, Gunnel and Nils-Lennart Johannesson (eds.)
1992 *Non-standard varieties of language.* (Stockholm Studies in English 84.) Stockholm: Almqvist and Wiksell.
Milroy, James and Lesley Milroy
1985 Linguistic change, social network and speaker innovation. *Journal of Linguistics* 21: 339-384.
Milroy, Lesley
1987 *Language and social networks.* (2nd edition.) (Language in Society 2.) London/New York: Blackwell.
Mustanoja, Tauno F.
1960 *A Middle English syntax.* Part I. *Parts of speech.* (Mémoires de la Société Néophilologique de Helsinki 23.) Helsinki: Société Néophilologique.
Nevalainen, Terttu
1996 Social stratification. In: Terttu Nevalainen and Helena Raumolin-Brunberg (eds), 57-76.
2000 Processes of supralocalization and the rise of Standard English in the early modern period. In: Ricardo Bermúdez-Otero et al. (eds.), 329-371.
Nevalainen, Terttu and Helena Raumolin-Brunberg
1989 A corpus of Early Modern Standard English in a socio-historical perspective. *Neuphilologische Mitteilungen* 90 (1): 67-111.

1994   *Its* beauty and the beauty *of it*: the standardization of the third person neuter possessive in Early Modern English. In: Dieter Stein and Ingrid Tieken-Boon van Ostade (eds.), 171-216.
1996   The Corpus of Early English Correspondence. In: Terttu Nevalainen and Helena Raumolin-Brunberg (eds), 39-54.

Nevalainen, Terttu and Helena Raumolin-Brunberg (eds.)
1996   *Sociolinguistics and language history: studies based on the Corpus of Early English Correspondence.* (Language and Computers: Studies in Practical Linguistics 15.) Amsterdam/ Atlanta, GA: Rodopi.

Nevalainen, Terttu and Leena Kahlas-Tarkka (eds.)
1997   *To explain the present: studies in the changing English language in honour of Matti Rissanen.* (Mémoires de la Société Néophilologique de Helsinki 52.) Helsinki: Société Néophilologique.

Nevalainen, Terttu, Helena Raumolin-Brunberg, and Peter Trudgill
forthc.   Chapters in the history of East Anglian English: the case of the third person singular. In: Jacek Fisiak and Peter Trudgill (eds.).

Nevanlinna, Saara
1996   Interpreting the orthographic token *-vef(f)* for *ve* in the epistolary style of some [late] fifteenth century Londoners. In: Juhani Klemola, Merja Kytö, and Matti Rissanen (eds.), 265-283.

Ogura, Mieko and William S.-Y. Wang
1996   Snowball effect in lexical diffusion: the development of *-s* in the third person singular present indicative in English. In: Derek Britton (ed.), 119-141.

Patten, John
1976   Patterns of migration and movement of labour to three preindustrial East Anglian towns. *Journal of Historical Geography* 2 (2): 111-129.

Power, M. J.
1985   John Stow and his London. *Journal of Historical Geography* 11 (1): 1-20.
1986   The social topography of Restoration London. In: A. L. Beier and Roger Finlay (eds.), 199-223.

Quirk, Randolph, Sidney Greenbaum, Geoffrey Leech, and Jan Svartvik
1985   *A comprehensive grammar of the English language.* London/ New York: Longman.

Rappaport, Steve
1989   *Worlds within worlds: structures of life in sixteenth-century London.* (Cambridge Studies in Population: Economy and Society in Past Time 7.) Cambridge: Cambridge University Press.

Raumolin-Brunberg, Helena
1994   The development of the compound pronouns in -*body* and -*one* in Early Modern English. In: Dieter Kastovsky (ed.), 301-324.
1996a   Apparent time. In: Terttu Nevalainen and Helena Raumolin-Brunberg (eds.), 93-109.
1996b   Historical sociolinguistics. In: Terttu Nevalainen and Helena Raumolin-Brunberg (eds.), 11-37.
1998   Social factors and pronominal change in the seventeenth century: the Civil War effect? In: Jacek Fisiak and Marcin Krygier (eds.), 361-388.
2000   *Which* and *the which* in Late Middle English: free variants? In: Irma Taavitsainen et al. (eds.), 209-228.

Raumolin-Brunberg, Helena and Leena Kahlas-Tarkka
1997   Indefinite pronouns with singular human reference. In: Matti Rissanen, Merja Kytö, and Kirsi Heikkonen (eds.), 17-85.

Raumolin-Brunberg, Helena and Arja Nurmi
1997   Dummies on the move: prop-*one* and affirmative *do* in the 17th century. In: Terttu Nevalainen and Leena Kahlas-Tarkka (eds.), 395-417.

Rissanen, Matti
1997   The pronominalization of *one*. In: Matti Rissanen, Merja Kytö, and Kirsi Heikkonen (eds.), 87-143.

Rissanen, Matti, Ossi Ihalainen, Terttu Nevalainen, and Irma Taavitsainen (eds.)
1992   *History of Englishes: new methods and interpretations in historical linguistics.* (Topics in English Linguistics 10.) Berlin/ New York:: Mouton de Gruyter.

Rissanen, Matti, Merja Kytö, and Kirsi Heikkonen (eds.)
1997   *Grammaticalization at work: studies of long-term developments in English.* (Topics in English Linguistics 24.) Berlin/New York: Mouton de Gruyter.

Samuels, Michael L.
1972   *Linguistic evolution, with special reference to English.* Cambridge: Cambridge University Press.

Sapir, Edward
1921   *Language: an introduction to the study of speech.* New York: Harcourt, Brace and Company.

Schendl, Herbert
1996   The 3rd plural present indicative in Early Modern English – variation and linguistic contact. In: Derek Britton (ed.), 143-160.

Stein, Dieter
1987   At the crossroads of philology, linguistics and semiotics: notes on the replacement of *th* by *s* in the third person singular in English. *English Studies* 68: 406-431.
Stein, Dieter and Ingrid Tieken-Boon van Ostade (eds.)
1994   *Towards a Standard English 1600-1800*. (Topics in English Linguistics 12.) Berlin: Mouton de Gruyter.
Stone, Lawrence
1966   Social mobility in England 1500-1700. *Past and Present* 33: 16-55.
Taavitsainen, Irma, Terru Nevalainen, Päivi Pahta, and Matti Rissanen (eds.)
2000   *Placing Middle English in context*. Berlin/New York: Mouton de Gruyter.
Trudgill, Peter
1986   *Dialects in contact*. Oxford: Blackwell.
1996   Language contact and inherent variability: the absence of hypercorrection in East Anglian present-tense verb forms. In: Juhani Klemola, Merja Kytö, and Matti Rissanen (eds.), 412-425.
Wareing, John
1980   Changes in the geographical distribution of the recruitment of apprentices to the London companies 1486-1750. *Journal of Historical Geography* 6: 241-249.
Winchester, Barbara
1955   *Tudor family portrait*. London: Cape.
Wright, Joseph
1905   *The English dialect grammar*. Oxford/London/Glasgow: Henry Frowde.
Wrigley, E. A.
1967   A simple model of London's importance in changing English society and economy 1650-1750. *Past and Present* 37: 44-70.
Wrigley, E. A. and Roger C. Schofield
1981   *The population history of England 1541-1871: a reconstruction*. London: Arnold.
Wyld, Henry Cecil
[1920] 1936   *A history of modern colloquial English*. (3rd edition.) Oxford: Blackwell.

The rise and regulation of periphrastic *do* in negative declarative sentences: a sociolinguistic study

Arja Nurmi

1. Introduction

This paper looks at the development of the periphrastic auxiliary *do* in negative declarative sentences in the course of the sixteenth and seventeenth centuries. There are two main areas of interest: the overall development of the construction and the sociolinguistic variables connected with it. The material used comes from the *Corpus of Early English Correspondence*, which offers a single genre and a wide range of sociolinguistic variation.

2. The material used

This study uses the 1998 version of the *Corpus of Early English Correspondence (CEEC)*, which consists of 2.7 million words of personal correspondence written between 1417 and 1681. It is compiled by the Sociolinguistics and Language History project team at the University of Helsinki, and is intended to enable the application of the methodology developed by modern sociolinguistics to the historical study of language. The corpus is supported by a sender database, containing information on all our informants, including their dates of birth and death, domicile, migration history, education, as well as their social rank and details of social mobility. (For more information on the corpus, see Nevalainen and Raumolin-Brunberg ((eds.) 1996) and Nurmi (1999a).)

For this study nearly the whole corpus, almost 2,300,000 words, was used. The fifteenth century was left out because of the scarcity of the periphrastic construction in the early letters (Nurmi 1999b). The corpus material used is divided fairly evenly throughout the two centuries, though the first two decades of the sixteenth century offer too little data for any definite conclusions (see table 1 for word counts).

Comparative material is provided by the Early Modern English part of the *Helsinki Corpus* (for details see Kytö ((ed.) 1996) and Rissanen, Kytö and Palander-Collin ((eds.) 1993)).

3. The construction studied

In Present-day English, according to Quirk et al. (1985: 133-134), *do* is compulsory in the absence of another operator "in indicative clauses negated by *not*, where the verb is simple present or simple past"; this category also covers negative imperative clauses (with some reservation). In subjunctive clauses there is normally no *do*-support, and negative words other than *not* do not require *do*-support.

In this study I shall look at clauses negated by *not*, indicative as well as subjunctive. Examples (1)-(2) illustrate the instances chosen. The imperatives, being too rare, have been left out. Making the difference between subjunctive and indicative sentences is not easy, and I have not attempted it for the whole material. However, when looking at the third person singular instances, it becomes clear that in both the sixteenth and the seventeenth centuries the use of *do* varied in subjunctives as it did in indicative sentences, see examples (3) and (4). Thus there is no urgent need to separate indicatives and subjunctives.

(1) *Item I* doe not meane *to pase the lease of Redbourne unles I maie have eyther present money or ells present assuraunce*
          (Bacon: 1579 Nicholas Bacon, II, 101)[1]

(2)   Item I meane not *to pase eny assuraunce of landes or leases in generall wordes*
        (Bacon: 1579 Nicholas Bacon, II, 101)

(3)   [A]*nd therfor if it* take not *effect according to your mynd, blame not me, and so I sayed to my said syster your wiff.*
        (Johnson: 1546 Otwell Johnson, 795)

(4)   [M]*y maister sayed unto me: if Mr. Cave* do not like *his prices, lett him sett either sorte at xij d more in a dossen*
        (Johnson: 1547 Otwell Johnson, 867)

I have included the instances where *do* is used in negative declarative sentences, illustrated by example (1) as well as those where it might have been used – what Ellegård (1953) calls simple forms, as in example (2). This means that clauses with another auxiliary (examples (5) and (8)) have been excluded as well as main verb *be* (example (6)), since they are never used with periphrastic *do* in declarative sentences. I have also omitted verbs which show a variant use of *do* in Present-day English, but are never used with *do* in my data: main verb *have*, (example 7) and the marginal modals *dare*, *need* and *ought to* (examples (8)-(9)). The only instance of *need* where *do* is used (example (10)) is a full verb use of *need*, and appears in the 1650s in the language of one highly individual writer, whose use of *do* was altogether more modern than that of her contemporaries: Dorothy Osborne. Her language will be discussed further below.

Used to behaves in some ways differently from the other marginal modals – as it still does in Present-day English. It is only beginning to take its place in the language in the Early Modern English period and could be used with the periphrasis or without it (example (11)).

(5)   *which was the cause I* cold not have *so soone an oportunitii to talke with hiim at leisure.*
            (Bacon: 1587 John Stubbe, III, 38)

(6)   *for they trow that* ys not *the Kings mynd*
            (Plumpton: 1503 William Plumpton, 176)

(7)   *his conscience will lett me have that which is myne althoughe he* hathe not *the commoditie of the bargayne.*
            (Bacon: 1580 Edmund Banyard, II, 119)

(8)   *What it is I* can not tell, *and therfor I* dar not *write depely in it, but yit rogatus rogo.*
            (Fox: 1513 Richard Fox, 69)

(9)   *Suerly I* nede not *instructe your Lordship, of whome I wold learne willinglye, that such is the subtill sleight and old pollicie of Sathan*
            (Bacon: 1573 William Heydon, 191)

(10)   *and for example though I know you* doe not need *my Councell, yet I cannot but tell you that I think 'twere very well that you took some care to make my Lady R. your friend*
            (Osborne: 1653 Dorothy Osborne, 29)

(11)   *But this I know, that it* did not use to *bee soe, nor I trust in god will bee here after*
            (Pepys: 1663 Samuel Pepys, 2)

4. Development in the sixteenth and seventeenth centuries

In the course of the sixteenth century, negative declarative sentences increasingly began to demand the presence of the periphrastic auxiliary *do*. The standard study referred to in most research is Ellegård (1953); he has mapped the rise of periphrastic *do* from 1400 to 1700. Figure 1 reproduces Ellegård's results for the negative declaratives: the sixteenth century shows a rapid rise until the 1570s, after which there is a notable drop in the percentage of *do*, and again a rise in the early seventeenth century. It should be noted that the division into subperiods is not even, but ranges from 25 to 50 years. (I have collapsed two of his shorter subperiods in the first half of the sixteenth century).

Ellegård's famous graph (1953: 162) shows that by the end of the seventeenth century approximately 80% of negative declaratives seem to have *do*, but when calculating the frequencies from his tables this frequency is not even approximately reached (the result for 1650-1700 in his table 7 on p. 161 gives only 46%). This is explained by the early eighteenth century sample of Swift, with a frequency of well over 80%. According to Ellegård (1953: 162-163) "the humps on the curve for negative declarative sentences should ... be regarded as significant" – these "humps" are also reflected in figure 1, drawn according to Ellegård's results.

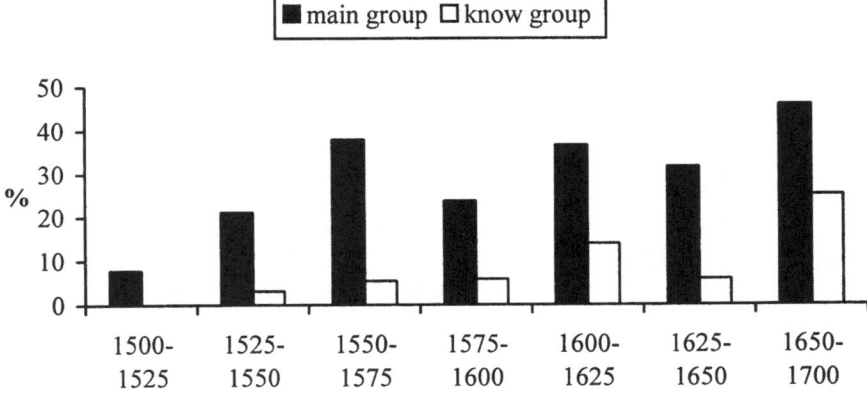

Figure 1. The development of periphrastic *do* in negative declarative sentences in 1500-1700 (after Ellegård 1953: 161, 199)

It should be noted, however, that the oft-quoted line of development only includes what Ellegård calls the main group of negative declarative sentences; there is also the so-called *know* group which consists of some 10 verbs which only rarely appear with the periphrastic auxiliary. The results for Ellegård's *know* group are included in figure 1, and, as can be seen, they mirror the general development of *do*, although with a considerably lower level of frequency. The *know* group, and the questionable need to separate it from the main group of verbs, is discussed in more detail below in connection with the results obtained by studying the *CEEC*.

Another problem with Ellegård's results is his use of mixed genres, which may well explain at least part of the fluctuation. The development of periphrastic *do* in affirmative declarative sentences happens at a different rate in various genres (Rissanen 1991), and there is little reason to doubt that similar trends can be attested in negative declarative sentences as well. In the eighteenth century text types seem to play some part in the choice of the periphrastic or simple form in negative declaratives, although more important is individual variation, which is mostly connected to the level of education (Tieken-Boon van Ostade 1987: 188-191).

The diachronic part of the *Helsinki Corpus* offers a balanced collection of genres and is therefore an interesting comparison to Ellegård's results. Table 1 and figure 2 present the development of *do* in the *Helsinki Corpus*. Unlike figure 1 with Ellegård's results, figure 2 shows a fairly even development of the construction. This is no doubt mostly due to the long subperiods of the *Helsinki Corpus*. It is interesting to note that the *know* group here too follows the main group of verbs faithfully, although with lower frequencies.

Table 1. The development of periphrastic *do* in negative declarative sentences in the *Helsinki Corpus*

	main group				*know* group			
	do	simple	total	% *do*	*do*	simple	total	% *do*
1500-1570	46	200	246	18.7	1	59	60	1.7
1570-1640	58	176	234	24.8	8	84	92	8.7
1640-1710	116	68	184	63.0	28	45	73	38.4

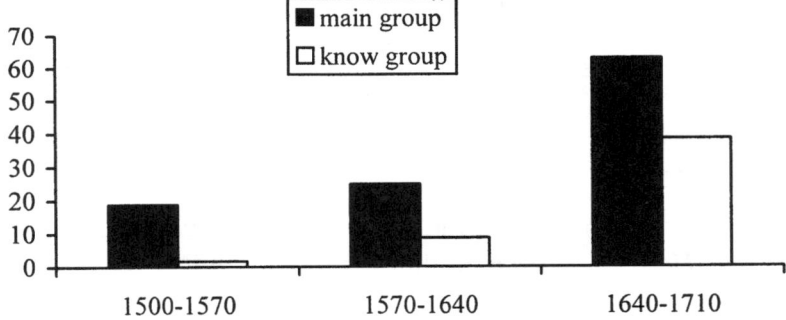

Figure 2. The development of periphrastic *do* in negative declarative sentences in the *Helsinki Corpus*

The low overall frequency of the construction studied makes it impossible to make a detailed analysis of the various genres, but separating oral genres from non-oral ones provides interesting results, which are shown in table 2. I have followed Raumolin-Brunberg and Kahlas-Tarkka (1997: 65) in classifying autobiography, comedy, diary, fiction, private letters, and trial proceedings as oral and all other genres as non-oral. Here I have not separated the two groups of verbs, but have included all instances of the variable in these results, as table 1 and figure 2 seem to show that there is no great difference in the overall trends of development between the main group and the *know* group but merely a difference of frequency.

The *Helsinki Corpus* material seems to show a non-oral origin for the periphrastic construction in negative declaratives, with a sudden change in the last subperiod, where oral genres introduce the use of *do*. The application of the chi-square test makes the results slightly less puzzling: the differences in the first and last subperiods are statistically significant ($p<0.05$), but in the middle period (1570-1640) the apparent gap between the oral and non-oral genres is not statistically significant. Obviously, something happens in the development of the periphrastic construction exactly where Ellegård's figures show a decline.

Table 2. Periphrastic *do* in oral and non-oral genres in the *Helsinki Corpus*

	oral				non-oral			
	do	simple	total	% *do*	*do*	simple	total	% *do*
1500-1570	7	76	83	8.4	40	183	223	17.9
1570-1640	24	107	131	18.3	42	153	195	27.1
1640-1710	77	43	120	64.2	67	70	137	48.1

One of the advantages of the *CEEC* over Ellegård's material as well as the *Helsinki Corpus* is that it presents only one, reasonably well defined genre, although it does not separate private and official correspondence, as the *Helsinki Corpus* does. The *CEEC* sample is also four times the size of the relevant *Helsinki Corpus* subperiod and spreads more evenly over the two centuries I am concerned with. So the *CEEC* allows a more accurate comparison with Ellegård's data in that respect. Unlike Ellegård's unstructured corpus, here there is less danger of the different pace of change in genres influencing the results. Table 3 and figure 3 present the development of periphrastic *do* in negative declarative sentences during the course of the sixteenth and seventeenth centuries. I have divided both centuries into five smaller subperiods, each consisting of 20 years. Apart from the first subperiod the division provides well over 150,000 words of text for each period of twenty years.

There is a rather steady rise in the frequency of *do* in the sixteenth century; the development is, according to the chi-square test, statistically highly significant ($p<0.001$). The percentage of *do*-periphrasis goes up all through the century, just as it does in affirmative declarative sentences (Nurmi 1998). As the development of the periphrastic construction in affirmative statements was calculated in relative frequencies I have given the normalised frequencies of *do*-forms/10,000 words in each subperiod (the last column in table 3) to help the comparison with affirmative statements. This shows that the shape of the graph would be the same even if the whole linguistic variable was not taken into account.

At the turn of the sixteenth and seventeenth centuries, there is a drop in the use of *do* from 26% to 15%. There is no corresponding drop in Ellegård's data: he has two drops, the first in the late sixteenth century and the second twenty years later than the one in my material. The latter drop Ellegård attributes to the noncolloquial nature of some of the texts in his sample, which is supported by the *Helsinki Corpus* finding that oral genres lead in the use of the periphrastic construction in the 1640-1710 subperiod. It is therefore plausible that different genres show the development in different order, and this explains at least some of the differences in the two graphs.

Table 3. The development of auxiliary *do* in negative declarative sentences 1500-1681

years	do	simple	total	% do	words	/10,000
1500-1519	1	53	54	1.9	45,882	0.2
1520-1539	24	224	248	9.7	199,514	1.2
1540-1559	99	382	481	20.6	276,794	3.6
1560-1579	61	217	278	21.9	165,022	3.7
1580-1599	115	333	448	25.7	255,291	4.5
1600-1619	71	397	468	15.2	259,450	2.7
1620-1639	154	531	685	22.5	374,227	4.1
1640-1659	385	426	811	47.5	356,980	10.8
1660-1681	354	354	708	50.0	365,902	9.6
without Dorothy Osborne						
1640-1659	203	370	573	35.4	285,681	7.1

As for the drop in the *CEEC* at the turn of the century, it does correspond to a drop in the use of affirmative *do* (Nurmi 1998 and Raumolin-Brunberg and Nurmi 1997). It may be that although the two constructions, affirmative and negative, were already leading somewhat separate lives in the sixteenth century, there was still enough connection to occasion a drop in the use of both at the same time. This is also the time which the *Helsinki Corpus* showed to be the changing period between oral and non-oral genres.

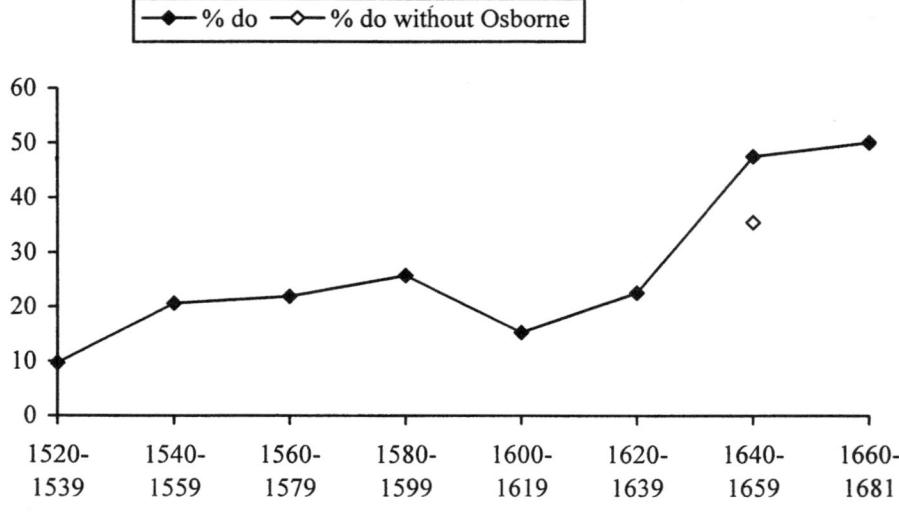

Figure 3. The development of auxiliary *do* in negative declarative sentences 1520-1681 in the *CEEC* (percentage of *do*)

For the rest of the seventeenth century the use of the periphrastic construction rises steadily again. The only anomaly is in the penultimate subperiod. This is due to Dorothy Osborne, who was referred to earlier. In table 3 as well as in figure 3 I also calculated the development without Dorothy Osborne's fairly large contribution (ca. 71,000 words), and once she is left out the development in the seventeenth century looks very even. Both lines of development are highly significant according to the chi-square test, but as Osborne differs from other writers in almost every change we have studied, I would like to suggest that the more even rise shown when she is excluded perhaps more accurately describes the real state of affairs.

Why is Dorothy Osborne so different? There are two plausible explanations for this. She herself writes in one of her letters that "all letters mee thinks should bee free and Easy as ones discourse, not studdyed, as an oration, nor made up of hard words like a charme" (Osborne: 1653 Dorothy Osborne, 90). This style, combined with an unusual linguistic sensitivity and the very private nature of her letters (they were all love letters to her future husband) may partly explain the way she seems to lead in almost every change. For a discussion of Osborne's writing, see also Raumolin-Brunberg and Nurmi (1997: 404-405).

Table 4 and figure 4 show what happens, if we take into account Ellegård's division into two kinds of verbs. The low point still comes in the early seventeenth rather than the late sixteenth century, although here (unlike table and figure 3) the main group of verbs is separated from the *know* group (*know, boot, trow, care, doubt, mistake, fear, skill* and *list*). I have followed Ellegård's division in order to provide fair grounds for comparison (except that I have also included one instance of both *misdoubt* and *misknow* in the *know* group), but the only verbs in Ellegård's list worth looking at separately in my material are *know* and *doubt*, the others either do not appear at all (*boot, trow, list*), or only rarely (*care, mistake, fear, skill*). Examples (12)-(15) give instances of *know* and *doubt* in both periphrastic and simple constructions.

(12) *considryng the comaundement gyven in Spaine that no man myght go afore th'emperor, And that he knew not of my being here for your maiestie*
(Wyatt: 1539 Thomas Wyatt, 107)

(13) *I answared that I dyd not knowe of no end that was maed*
(Johnson: 1545 Sabine Johnson, 515)

(14) *Whereunto his Highnes answerd that your Grace, as he doubted not ye wolde, removing for the tyme with your company to Saint Albons, it shulde serve of the while he wolde tarye there.*
(Gardiner: 1529 Stephen Gardiner, 27)

(15) *and than I do not doubt but your good fatherhode will thinke my motion reasonable*
(Parkhurst: 1574 John Becon, 248)

Tieken-Boon van Ostade (1987: 190-191) also points out the important role of *know* and *doubt*; in her eighteenth-century material there also seems to be a correlation between a more frequent appearance of *do*-less sentences and the use of other verbs besides *know* and *doubt* without the periphrastic auxiliary. Another verb that never appears with the periphrastic construction is *wot*, but this was not included in Ellegård's list, although he comments on its aversion to *do*. *Wot* appears in my data during the sixteenth century, always in the simple form, and has been included in the main group of verbs in order to make the figures comparable to Ellegård's.

Table 4. The development of auxiliary *do* in negative declarative sentences 1500-1681: main group versus *know* group of verbs

years	main group			*know* group		
	do	simple	% do	do	simple	% do
1500-1519	1	38	2.6	0	15	0.0
1520-1539	24	121	16.6	0	103	0.0
1540-1559	84	262	24.3	15	120	11.1
1560-1579	50	132	27.5	11	85	11.5
1580-1599	104	191	35.3	11	142	7.2
1600-1619	61	220	21.7	10	177	5.3
1620-1639	133	292	31.3	21	239	8.1
1640-1659	342	162	67.9	43	264	14.0
1660-1681	297	163	64.6	57	191	23.0
without Dorothy Osborne						
1640-1659	181	151	54.5	22	219	9.1

The main group of verbs shows here too the steady rise during the sixteenth century that could be seen in figure 3, which included all instances, and here again the development is highly significant in both centuries ($p<0.001$). There is the familiar drop at the turn of the centuries, from 35% to 22%, but after that, the rise continues steadily. The development of the *know* group shows a clear fall in the frequency of *do* in the last subperiod of the sixteenth century, falling further in the early seventeenth century, and as the changes in the graph are statistically significant ($p<0.01$) there seems to be a correspondence to Ellegård's drop, albeit in the wrong group of verbs.

In the main group of verbs, the influence of Dorothy Osborne again makes a clear impact on the shape of the graph: the frequency of *do* seems to drop in the last subperiod, but only if we include Osborne, otherwise there is a reasonably steady rise. In the *know* group her influence can also be seen, but here the difference is not as great as in the case of the other group.

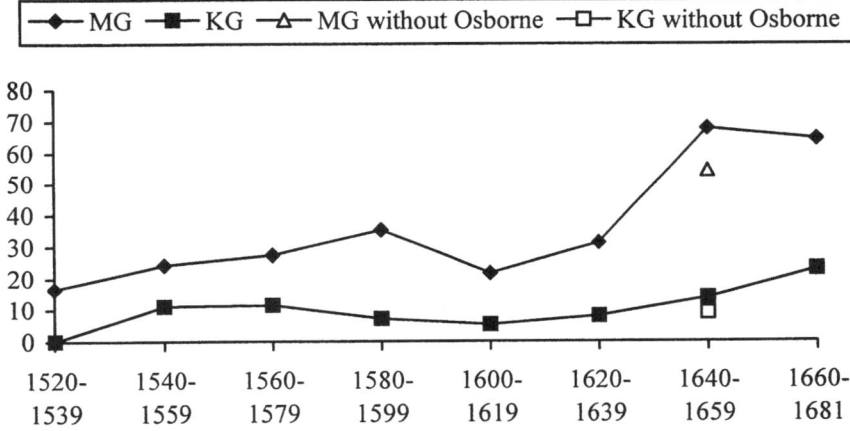

Figure 4. The development of auxiliary *do* in negative declarative sentences 1520-1681 in the *CEEC* (MG = main group, KG = *know* group)

All these different corpora seem to suggest that something happened at the turn of the sixteenth and seventeenth centuries. The change in register indicated by the *Helsinki Corpus* (table 2) gives reason to believe that sociolinguistic variation may shed further light on the development of periphrastic *do* in negative declarative sentences.

5. Sociolinguistic variation and the rise of *do*

According to Tieken-Boon van Ostade (1987: 228), there was clear sociolinguistic variation in the use of (among other things) *do*-less negative sentences in the eighteenth century. Can evidence for such variation be found in the sixteenth century, and does it help to explain the humps in Ellegård's graph and the change between oral and non-oral genres in the *Helsinki Corpus*?

The data from the *CEEC* suggest that the most important sociolinguistic variable in the spread of *do* to negative declarative sentences was gender. Education and social ambition seem to play a somewhat smaller role. Other variables were also investigated, but social stratification, for example, did not offer any significant results. The number of instances in the sixteenth century was too low to allow the study of sociolinguistic variables, although the *know* group was not separated from the rest of the material. Whenever it has been possible to include some pointers from the sixteenth century I have done so, but mostly this section deals with the development of negative declaratives in the seventeenth century. I shall begin by looking at the differences between men and women.

These differences can unfortunately not be studied in the sixteenth century, as the high illiteracy of women provides insufficient amounts of data. If anything, women tend to use the *do*-form less than men, with one exception. Sabine Johnson, a merchant's wife from London (writing in the 1540s and 1550s), uses *do* in 10 of the 15 relevant instances found in her letters. What is more, she uses only the periphrastic form with the 5 instances of *know* group verbs, thus showing a clear preference in the opposite direction from the rest of our informants. However, these numbers are far too small to be anything else than inconclusive pointers. Also the men in Sabine's family show a higher than average frequency of *do*, although in no way as high as hers.

Do men and women differ in their use of *do* in the seventeenth century? This becomes very clear in table 5 and figure 5: women lead almost throughout. Again, the penultimate subperiod has two values, with and without Dorothy Osborne, and again her language makes quite a difference to the development.

Table 5. Gender and the use of *do* in the *CEEC* 1580-1681

	men				women			
	do	simple	total	% *do*	*do*	simple	total	% *do*
1580-1599	107	291	398	26.9	8	42	50	16.0
1600-1619	53	309	362	14.6	18	88	106	17.0
1620-1639	89	419	508	17.5	65	112	177	36.7
1640-1659	142	320	462	30.7	243	106	349	69.6
1660-1681	256	289	545	47.0	98	65	163	60.1
without Dorothy Osborne								
1640-1659					61	50	111	55.0

The difference between men and women becomes statistically highly significant after 1620 (p<0.001). Before that, the figures show no real difference. This may again be connected to the turmoil in the development of the periphrastic construction in the first decades of the seventeenth century.

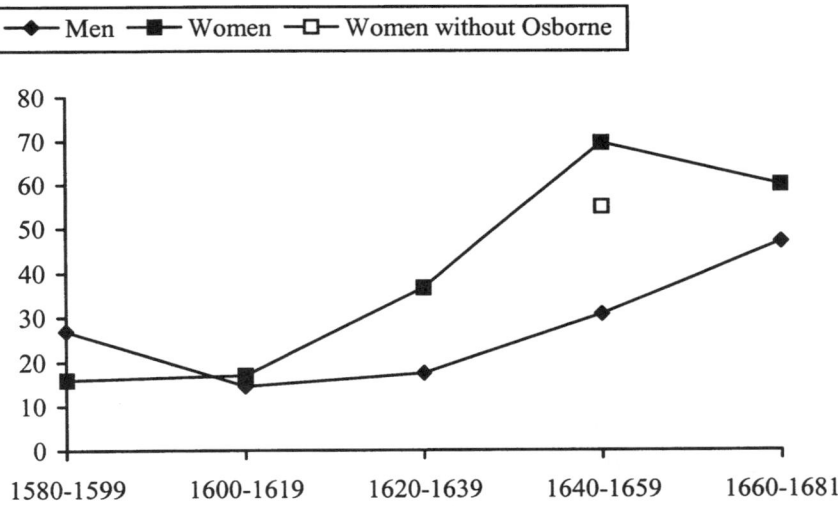

Figure 5. Men versus women 1580-1681 in the *CEEC*

Chambers (1995: 104) argues that separating sex and gender is important in sociolinguistic studies. Gender, according to his definition, is connected with the different roles men and women play and the influence of these roles on linguistic variation. sex, on the other hand, is the determining factor, when differences persist regardless of roles. Chambers (1995: 128) points out that in modern industrial societies women are in fact more mobile than men and therefore most differences are gender differences, explained by mobility. The women of early modern England are not usually described as more mobile than the men, on the contrary most historians lead us to believe that they led far more circumscribed lives. Therefore it is difficult to see how such different roles in society as those between seventeenth-century and late-twentieth-century women still produce the same result: women are pacemakers in linguistic change.

Another point to consider is the fact that many studies in modern sociolinguistics map existing variability rather than change: there is a standard language or a prestige form, and it is towards this form that women tend to lean more than their male counterparts. The spread of the periphrastic construction into Early Modern English negations was a change, which proceeded quite rapidly, and probably produced notable results within a single lifetime.

The results in table 5 are still surprisingly similar to present-day sociolinguistic studies. Cameron and Coates (1988: 13), for example, state that "women on average deviate less from the prestige standard than men ... In modern urban societies it is typically true for every social class." Early modern society differed considerably from the urban societies most sociolinguistic studies are concerned with and accepting this similarity without question might prove dangerous. Women seem to be able to predict what is to become standard, in the case of *do* in negations, as well as in the development of prop-word *one* (Raumolin-Brunberg and Nurmi 1997: 408), and the rise of the third person *-s* (Nevalainen, Raumolin-Brunberg, and Trudgill forthcoming). As the work in the Sociolinguistics and Language History project proceeds, it will be interesting to see how many more changes show women in the vanguard.

One way of explaining this fact is to assume that the new variant was a prestige form; this is to some extent confirmed by results for educated and socially mobile men given below. This assumption is supported by Milroy (1992: 117), who says that "men seem to be principally associated with a change that speakers do not consciously evaluate highly, while women are associated with one adopted by speakers in their more carefully monitored styles". As our informants are mostly literate women, they would have had access to the rising standard language and therefore would have recognised the current prestige forms, and therefore were able to use them. This seems to be the most acceptable hypothesis, although it does not explain why Early Modern women felt the same urge as their present-day counterparts to use more prestige forms. Dorothy Osborne once again increased the percentages of the incoming construction with her very frequent use of *do* in negative declaratives.

Another interesting social variable is education. As women were only rarely well educated, this variable only concerns men.[2] I have divided the informants into two groups, those with high education, and those without one. High education means either university education (Oxford or Cambridge), or Inns of Court (or in several cases both). It has to be remembered that this kind of education was based on Latin, not English; only lawyers needed to be educated in English. Figures for the early sixteenth century cannot be counted, as there are too many cases where we do not have reliable information about the education of our informants.

Table 6. Education and the use of *do* by men in the *CEEC* 1580-1681

	educated				other			
	do	simple	total	% do	do	simple	total	% do
1580-1599	84	238	322	26.1	23	53	76	30.3
1600-1619	36	222	258	14.0	17	87	104	16.3
1620-1639	49	170	219	22.4	40	249	289	13.8
1640-1659	90	193	283	31.8	52	127	179	29.1
1660-1681	164	194	358	45.8	92	95	187	49.2

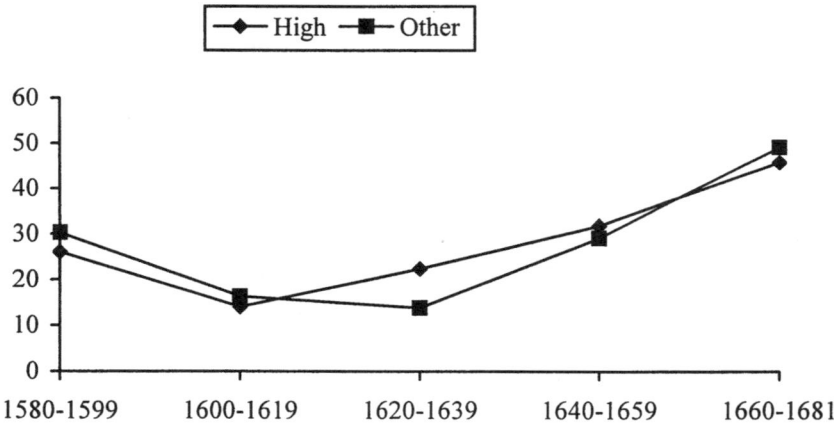

Figure 6. The role of education in the use of *do* (men)

Table 6 and figure 6 show the difference between these two groups of men. The results are statistically significant only in 1620-1639 ($p<0.05$), which is the only time in the seventeenth century when people with high education clearly lead in the use of periphrastic *do*. This ties in with the results obtained by comparing men's and women's uses of the construction: if educated men use the form then it may well be a prestige form which women in turn aim for. The rising trend by educated men is seen only in the second subperiod of the seventeenth century, which is when the difference between the genders also appears. Once again, it seems that around the turn of the sixteenth and seventeenth centuries something happened in the development of both affirmative and negative *do*.

Finally, the role of social aspirers in the development of the periphrastic construction appears to be interesting. Social aspirers means men who moved upwards in the social scale, starting often from quite humble origins and ending up in the top ranks of society.[3] (Again, women have been excluded.) Their role in the rise of *do* in affirmative statements is significant, as they avoided using the construction until the end of the sixteenth century (Nurmi 1998). In negative declaratives, they show no clear pattern in the sixteenth century, but in the seventeenth there is an interesting development shown in table 7 and figure 7.

In the first two subperiods social aspirers lag behind others, but in the last two they reach and overtake others. The difference between the two groups is statistically significant only before 1640 ($p<0.05$), so it is in fact not accurate to mention them overtaking others, although it would be tempting to describe this as hypercorrection, quite typical for the socially ambitious. This connects nicely to the use of *do* by educated people: the aspirers show a 20-year lag in their acceptance of *do*, but once the educated have accepted it, aspirers also begin to see it as a prestige variant and so begin using it. It has to be remembered, of course, that most aspirers were also highly educated: that was their way up the social ladder.

Table 7. Social ambition and the use of *do* by men in the *CEEC* 1600-1681

	aspirers				other			
	do	simple	total	% do	do	simple	total	% do
1600-1619	4	66	70	5.7	49	243	292	16.8
1620-1639	10	93	103	9.7	79	326	405	19.5
1640-1659	18	34	52	34.6	124	286	410	30.2
1660-1681	45	39	84	53.6	211	250	461	45.8

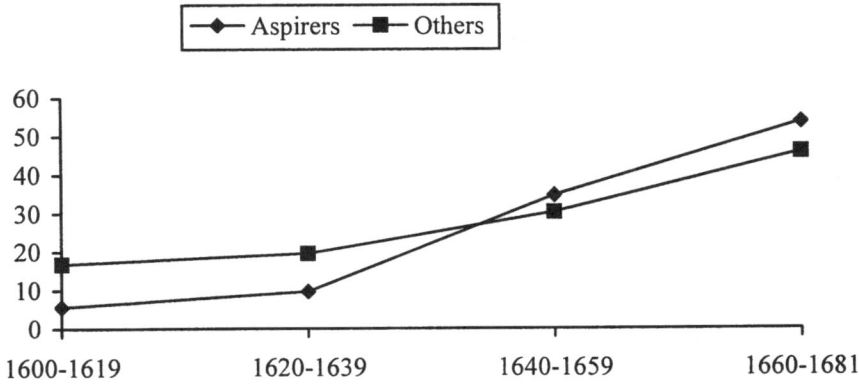

Figure 7. Social aspirers versus others (men)

6. Conclusion

This study has shown that the role of genre may be nearly as important in the development of periphrastic *do* in negative declarative sentences as it is in affirmative sentences. Unlike the results from Ellegård's data, in correspondence the frequency of the periphrastic form increases steadily throughout the sixteenth century, shows a major drop in the beginning of the seventeenth, then continues to rise steadily again. The division into the main group of verbs and the *know* group showed some differences in their respective developments, with more fluctuation in the development of the *know* group, in addition to the well-known reluctance to accept the periphrastic construction. On the whole, however, there seems to be no reason to keep these two groups apart.

Sociolinguistic variation did not provide significant results for the sixteenth century. The most important finding was that the development of *do* in negative declarative sentences differs from that of affirmative statements already in the sixteenth century, as the sociolinguistic patterns of the two changes vary to a considerable extent. While affirmative statements show strong sociolinguistic conditioning in register variation, there was no trace of this in negative declaratives. This might be taken as an indication of a difference in the functions of the two constructions at this early stage, a difference which led later to the regulation of *do* in the NICE-qualities (*N*egation, *I*nversion, *C*ode and *E*mphasis), and to its falling out of use in affirmative statements in the standard written language.

In the seventeenth century, the role of education and social ambition became evident in the use of the periphrastic construction by men. The most important social variable was, however, gender. Women are in the forefront of this change throughout the seventeenth century.

This paper leaves room for further research into the possible connections and differences between the development of *do* in negative and positive declarative sentences. Some further areas to be studied may include the role of social stratification, and the role of other auxiliaries in the spread of the *do*-form to negations. Apparent time has also proved to be a highly descriptive tool in the development of affirmative *do* (Nurmi 1996 and Raumolin-Brunberg and Nurmi 1997). It may yield results in the case of negative declarative sentences as well.

The most interesting question which remains is: what happened at the turn of the sixteenth and seventeenth centuries? Why is there a drop in the use of *do* in both positive and negative declarative statements? Why are sociolinguistic variables only significant after this drop in the development of the *do*-periphrasis in negative sentences? These are some immediate starting points for further research.

Notes

1. Examples taken from the *Corpus of Early English Correspondence* show name of letter collection, year of writing, name of writer and page number. (For bibliographical references see Nevalainen and Raumolin-Brunberg ((eds.) 1996) and Nurmi (1999a).)
2. University education was, of course, not available for women at the time, but there are nevertheless women who must be regarded as highly educated; suitable examples are Queen Elizabeth I and Anne, Viscountess Conway (whose correspondence with the philosopher Henry More is included in the corpus).
3. The social aspirers in 1600-1619 are: Sir Edward Coke (judge), John Holles Earl of Clare (soldier and politician), John Hoskyns (lawyer and wit), Ben Jonson (playwright), Sir Oliver Lambert (soldier and landowner), Thomas Wentworth Earl of Strafford (statesman) and John Whitgift (Archbishop of Canterbury). In 1620-1639, in addition to Holles, Hoskyns, Jonson and Wentworth we have John Cosin (Bishop of Durham) and Sir Arthur Ingram (courtier). In 1640-1659 there are only three aspirers, Cosin, Brian Duppa (Bishop of Winchester) and Sir Richard Haddock (admiral). In the last subperiod, 1660-1681, there are, in addition to Cosin, Duppa and Haddock, Sir Thomas Browne (physician and author), Sir Benjamin Newland (merchant), Sir William Petty (political economist), Sir William Scroggs (lawyer), Gilbert Sheldon (Archbishop of Canterbury) and Sir Joseph Williamson (statesman and diplomatist).

References

Cameron, Deborah and Jennifer Coates
    1988   Some problems in the sociolinguistic explanation of sex differences. In: Deborah Cameron and Jennifer Coates (eds.), 13-26.

Cameron, Deborah and Jennifer Coates (eds.)
    1988   *Women in their speech communities: new perspectives on language and sex.* London/New York: Longman.

Chambers, J. K.
    1995   *Sociolinguistic theory: linguistic variation and its social significance.* Oxford/Cambridge, MA: Blackwell.

Ellegård, Alvar
    1953   *The auxiliary do. The establishment and regulation of its use in English.* Stockholm: Almqvist and Wiksell.

Fisiak, Jacek and Peter Trudgill (eds.)
    forthc.   *History of East Anglian English.* Cambridge: Boydell and Brewer.

Kastovsky, Dieter (ed.)
    1991   *Historical English syntax.* (Topics in English Linguistics 2.) Berlin/New York: Mouton de Gruyter.

Kytö, Merja (ed.)
    1996   *Manual to the diachronic part of the Helsinki Corpus of English Texts: coding conventions and lists of source texts.* (3rd edition.) Helsinki: Department of English, University of Helsinki.

Milroy, James
    1992   *Linguistic variation and change (on the historical sociolinguistics of English).* (Language in Society 19.) Oxford/Cambridge, MA: Blackwell.

Nevalainen, Terttu and Leena Kahlas-Tarkka (eds.)
    1997   *To explain the present: studies in the changing English language in honour of Matti Rissanen.* (Mémoires de la Société Néophilologique de Helsinki 52.) Helsinki: Société Néophilologique.

Nevalainen, Terttu and Helena Raumolin-Brunberg (eds.)
    1996   *Sociolinguistics and language history: studies based on the Corpus of Early English Correspondence.* (Language and Computers: Studies in Practical Linguistics 15.) Amsterdam/Atlanta, GA: Rodopi.

Nevalainen, Terttu, Helena Raumolin-Brunberg, and Peter Trudgill
forthc. Chapters in the social history of East Anglian English: the case of the third person singular. In: Jacek Fisiak and Peter Trudgill (eds.)

Nurmi, Arja
1996 Periphrastic *do* and *be* + *ing*: interconnected developments? In: Terttu Nevalainen and Helena Raumolin-Brunberg (eds.), 151-165.
1998 Periphrastic *do* and the language of social aspirers: evidence from the *Corpus of Early English Correspondence*. In: Antoinette Renouf (ed.), 159-167.
1999a *A social history of periphrastic do.* (Mémoires de la Société Néophilologique de Helsinki 56.) Helsinki: Société Néophilologique.
1999b Auxiliary *do* in fifteenth-century English: dialectal variation and formulaic use. In: Irma Taavitsainen, Gunnel Melchers, and Päivi Pahta (eds.), 225-242.

Quirk, Randolph, Sidney Greenbaum, Geoffrey Leech, and Jan Svartvik
1985 *A comprehensive grammar of the English language.* London/ New York: Longman.

Raumolin-Brunberg, Helena and Leena Kahlas-Tarkka
1997 Indefinite pronouns with singular human reference. In: Matti Rissanen, Merja Kytö, and Kirsi Heikkonen (eds.), 17-85.

Raumolin-Brunberg, Helena and Arja Nurmi
1997 Dummies on the move: prop-*one* and affirmative *do* in the 17th century. In: Terttu Nevalainen and Leena Kahlas-Tarkka (eds.), 395-417.

Renouf, Antoinette (ed.)
1998 *Explorations in corpus linguistics.* (Language and Computers Studies in Practical Linguistics 23.) Amsterdam/Atlanta, GA: Rodopi.

Rissanen, Matti
1991 Spoken language and the history of *do*-periphrasis. In: Dieter Kastovsky (ed.), 321-342.

Rissanen, Matti, Merja Kytö, and Kirsi Heikkonen (eds.)
1997 *Grammaticalization at work: studies of long-term developments in English.* (Topics in English Linguistics 24.) Berlin/New York: Mouton de Gruyter.

Rissanen, Matti, Merja Kytö, and Minna Palander-Collin (eds.)
1993   *Early English in the computer age: explorations through the Helsinki Corpus*. (Topics in English Linguistics 11.) Berlin/New York: Mouton de Gruyter.

Taavitsainen, Irma, Gunnel Melchers, and Päivi Pahta (eds.)
1999   *Writing in nonstandard English*. (Pragmatics and Beyond. New Series 67.) Amsterdam: Benjamins.

Tieken-Boon van Ostade, Ingrid
1987   *The auxiliary* do *in eighteenth-century English: a sociohistorical-linguistic approach*. Dordrecht: Foris.

Shibboleths galore:
the treatment of Irish and Scottish English in histories of the English language

Clausdirk Pollner

Reviewing a number of books of new Scottish fiction in the *Independent* (August 16, 1997: 7), Roger Clarke has this to say:

> It's often said of the Irish that their greatest "revenge" on Britain was to requisition the English language and use it better than the English themselves. The Scots road, according [to the writer Duncan McLean], is to reclaim forms of native "dialect" as a sign of rebellion, nationalism and literary transgression – all rolled into one tartan juggernaut. ...
> Of course, Scots – a language as old as Standard English – has every right not to be called a dialect. Furthermore, it has been a mainstream and acceptable literary tongue north of the Border for centuries. Even the colonial-style flunkies of the 18th century Edinburgh literary scene who were then trying to remove Scots words from their local language had good things to say about Burns's muscular and drubbingly authentic verse.

He is right, of course, in pointing out that Scots is as old as Standard English; whether it has "the right" not to be called a "dialect" is a debatable point – and one that has indeed been debated for a considerable time. We know that terms such as "dialect" or "language" are notoriously difficult to define. One of the more technical ways of defining something as a "language" is to point out that there ought to be a politically independent state involved. In the case of present-day Scotland (as opposed to Eire) that is of course not true. The 1997 referendum, however, may be the beginning of the end of that particular state of affairs. But in historical terms there is no doubt whatsoever that Scots used to have "the right" to be called a language – at least up to 1603 or 1707. It was not so much for linguistic as for political and social reasons that Scots lost prestige and was dropped as a literary written medium by "serious" writers and writers who wanted to be considered "serious", as opposed to merely "entertaining". This then leads us right to the central topic of this conference – the interface of social and historical aspects of English in its various guises.

In what follows I shall look at a selection of histories of English to find out how (and whether) they treat the two "national" varieties of English in Europe that are not English English – i.e. English in Ireland and English in Scotland. Social and indeed attitudinal aspects are particularly relevant here, as Leith (1997: 149) reminds us:

> The opprobrium cast on the regional dialects of England has been visited, on a grander scale, and with far-reaching consequences, on the speech of regions diverse in language and culture, and situated far away from the metropolitan South-East.

For the purpose of this paper I have consulted 25 histories of English, the earliest from 1771, the latest from 1997. My selection is a random one, but it fulfils two conditions: (a) the authors are either British or American; (b) all decades of the twentieth century apart from the fourth (i.e. 1931-1940) are represented by at least one publication. (The majority of titles in my selection are from the eighties and nineties of this century – altogether 11 titles.)

Let me begin with a brief word about the three oldest and non-twentieth century titles: Peyton (1771), Trench ([1855] 1899) and Emerson (1894). Peyton (1771) is not so much a history of English in our modern terms – the Angles, Jutes, and Saxons are confined to a footnote – as an elaborate sort of praise for the English language: "Our tongue is as copious, pithy and significative as any other in Europe" (Peyton 1771: 12). He has one or two remarks on English in Scotland, one being about the "language" vs. "dialect" question. Peyton's opinion here could not be more straightforward: "For that the greatest and best part of Scotland, which call themselves the Lowland men, speak the English tongue varied only in dialect, as being descended from the English-Saxons, nothing is more certain" (Peyton 1771: 6). Peyton has no comments on English in Ireland.

Two of my titles are from the second half of the nineteenth century. Trench (1899) is surprisingly liberal about local varieties of English English. He points out (Trench 1899: 233-234) that they enjoy their own grammars and that there is nothing "barbarous" about them. Scottish English is clearly seen as one of the dialects of English English: "A vulture is not here any more a 'geir' (Holland), nor, except in some local dialects, a rogue a 'skellum' (Urquhart)" (Trench 1899: 55). Since *skellum* is the Scots equivalent of German *Schelm*, "some local dialects" clearly indicates Trench's view of the status of Scottish English/Scots. In fact at another point he expresses this in so many words, when he says: "the northern dialect, or as we call it, the Scotch" (Trench 1899: 101).

Both Irish and Scottish English get a brief mention when he talks about the "same word/different meaning" phenomenon in Southern English vs. its varieties:

> In Scotland a "merchant" is not what we know in England by this name, but a shopkeeper, while in Ireland a "tradesman" is meant not a grocer, butcher, or other engaged in the distribution of commodities, but an artisan (Trench 1855: 56).

He is the first in my selection of histories to take the Middle Scots poets to task for their over-indulgence in Latinisms in their "aureate poetry": "they tore up words from the Latin, which never took root in the language" (Trench 1899: 105). Trench goes on to mention some Scotticisms that have made it into the Southern vocabulary: cf. *gruesome, bonnie, canny, daft, eerie, glamour, lilt, winsome* etc. (Trench 1899: 245). Some of his examples here seem over-generous: words such as *braw, douce, ingle* etc. are still marked "Scottish" in modern dictionaries of English.

Finally, Trench points out that some local dialects – in this case the Scottish regional dialect of Banffshire – find it easier to do certain things, such as the formation of diminutives: "horse, horsie, horsikie, wee horsikie, wee wee horsikie" (Trench 1899: 281).

Emerson (1894) has a sub-chapter entitled "The Scotch Dialect" (Emerson 1894: 100-104). His material is based on Sir James Murray's (1873) *The dialect of the southern counties of Scotland*.

Emerson makes the point that on the one hand, Scotland had – by the middle of the fifteenth century – developed its own "separate literary language" (Emerson 1894: 100); on the other hand he has a dialect map of Britain with "Lowlands" marked between "Northern" and roughly the Highland line – the map is called "*The dialects of England in the 19th century*". This kind of gentle confusion seems to me to sum up the difficulty writers face in the case of "English in Scotland".

Looking now at twentieth-century histories of English – published between 1904 and 1997 – one is aware of a very striking fact: the first ten titles, from Bradley (1904) to Halliday (1975) either have nothing on Irish and Scottish English at all or just a few scattered remarks, the latter being mainly about differences in word meaning. Bradley (1904) is rather typical of this: "In Scotland, where the Old English *hlaford* came ... to be pronounced not *lord* but *laird*, the word has retained a meaning nearer to its original sense, being applied to any owner of landed property" (Bradley 1904: 197).

Lounsbury ([1876] 1906) admits that there is a substantial body of literature in Scots, but still refers to it as a "dialect of English" (Lounsbury 1906: 134). He is rather patronising on Middle Scots literature ("[I]t requires patience to read it, and patriotism to admire it" (Lounsbury 1906: 137).), talks about "the superiority of English literature" (Lounsbury 1906: 138) and refers, astonishingly, to English English as "*the classical tongue*" (Lounsbury 1906: 139) in comparison with Scottish English!

Classen (1919), Wyld (1927), McKnight (1928), Marckwardt (1942), Wrenn (1949), Brook (1958), Bloomfield and Newmark (1963), and Halliday (1975) make it quite clear – either in so many words or indirectly – what they see as their central remit: the treatment of the development of *Standard Southern English*. Wyld (1927) says: "the main object of our solicitude [is] the language of literature and Received Standard Spoken English" (Wyld 1927: 16). He blames the Irish and Scots for the fact that some English speakers differentiate phonetically between words such as *Wales* and *whales* (Wyld 1927: 33) and adds: "Many excellent speakers of Standard English never use the sound at all" (Wyld 1927: 33). He hears glottal stops – now so common in the whole of Britain – in the pronunciation of Danish, German and Scottish speakers.

McKnight (1928) is fairer than some of his predecessors on the topic of Middle Scots literature: "The most distinguished poetry in Great Britain in the fifteenth century was produced by poets in Scotland" (McKnight 1928: 39). Later in his book he re-tells a story that goes back to Boswell's *Life of Johnson* (1772), in which Johnson's biographer talks about a typical eighteenth-century Scottish aristocrat, the Earl of Marchmont, "who had tried to cultivate an English pronunciation" (McKnight 1928: 460). This goes somewhat wrong, for in London he is thought to be an American, with his diction sounding neither particularly English nor Scottish.

Ireland's and Scotland's only appearance in Wrenn (1949) are caused by the Celtic words these countries have contributed to English English; he names examples such as *blarney, colleen, brogue, galore* (from Irish Gælic) and *clan, loch, bog, glen, whisky, claymore* etc. (from Scottish Gælic).

I have commented elsewhere (Pollner 1997) on Wrenn's rather unfortunate and confusing use (at least from today's point of view) of the term "good" English; the following remark is just one example: "There are many types of 'good English' ... outside of England – that of Edinburgh in Scotland, for example, or that of Philadelphia or Boston in America" (Wrenn 1949: 188). He names two varieties of World English, in other words, that are comparatively close to Southern English RP. This, then, is what makes them "good" – albeit in inverted commas.

Brook (1958) is another example of those earlier histories that only mention Scottish and/or Irish English in the context of isolated language facts that differ between the South and the North.

[In Middle English spelling] the letter ʒ was often confused with z, just as y was sometimes used for þ. There are survivals of this confusion in the present-day spelling of some Scottish words and names such as *Menzies, Dalziel*, and *capercailzie*, the pronunciation of which causes trouble to the uninitiated (Brook 1958: 111).

For publications from the last quarter of this century, the picture looks somewhat different. Authors generally devote more space to the treatment of varieties other than Standard Southern English, RP and US English. Irish and Scottish English now play a role in most of them. The majority of my selection from the eighties and nineties treat either or both of them at some length, often devoting subchapters or full chapters to Irish and Scottish English. Exceptions here are Bambas (1980), Wakelin (1988), Bryson (1990), and Blake (1996). Bambas (1980) has nothing on Irish English and is remarkable for a number of misconceptions and some unfortunate phrasings. He talks, e.g., about the "trilled r" heard in Scottish English, which according to him "is referred to as a 'burr'" (Bambas 1980: 50). The term "burr" is, of course, usually reserved for Northumbrian English pronunciation.

To say of Gælic that it has "three living dialects, Irish, Scots and Manx" (Bambas 1980: 27) is a bit unfortunate in the use of the term "Scots", which has been used since the fifteenth century for the Germanic speech of the Scottish Lowlands; and his statement is simply wrong in the case of Manx, the last speaker of which died in 1974. Finally he refers to the Middle Scots poets as the "School of Scottish Chaucerians", again not a very fortunate (or popular) term since it stresses unnecessarily the influence of Chaucer on a group of writers who were poets in their own right – even though they did follow Chaucer in some of their metrical forms, for instance.

Reading Wakelin (1988) – an expert on English local varieties – one is surprised to find nothing of substance on Irish or Scottish English. In his chapter on Middle English he has a selection of texts, including a short excerpt from Barbour's *Bruce* of 1375 (Wakelin 1988: 98-100). He comments: "Middle Scots is, in fact, simply a dialect of northern Middle English, though written in a special system of spelling of a very distinctive kind" (Wakelin 1988: 98). This may be true for Barbour's Early Scots, but not for the peak of Middle Scots writing after 1450; if one wants to class it as having been written in a dialect of Southern English then one should at least – in pedantically chronological terms – class it as early Early Modern English!

Bryson (1990) has very little on Irish English; his main concern here is to mention Irish emigration to the United States (Bryson 1990: 160-161).

He mentions Dunbar as presumably the first writer to use the word *fuck*, in a poem written about 1503; and he mentions the dialect/language issue in the context of Scots:

> Indeed, a case is sometimes made that certain varieties *are* separate languages. A leading contender in this category is Scots, the variety of English used in the Lowlands of Scotland. ... As evidence, its supporters point out that it has its own dictionary, *The Concise Scots Dictionary*, as well as its own body of literature (Bryson 1990: 104).

Bryson sits firmly on the fence on this particular issue; it is puzzling that *CSD* should be named as one of the reasons for calling Scots a "language". The *CSD*'s mother dictionaries – *DOST* (Craigie 1990) and *SND* – might have been better advocates.

This leaves us with those of the more recent histories that devote some space to Irish and Scottish English: Lass (1987), Millward (1989), Claiborne (1990), McCrum, Cran, and MacNeil (1992), Baugh and Cable (1993), Pyles and Algeo (1993), Barber (1993), and Leith (1997).

It is Leith (1997) who expresses the case for at least Scottish English to be treated comprehensively: "Many Scottish people feel justifiably bitter at finding their linguistic inheritance relegated to a paragraph or two in histories of English, and dismissed as just another dialect of English" (Leith 1997: 160). Leith (1997) himself has a chapter on the imposition of English over Scots and Gælic in Scotland, Ireland and Wales and treats the development of Scots and Hiberno-English in some detail (Leith 1997: 153-161, 168-173).

Lass (1987) differs from the other titles of my selection in that he covers both the development of English and its modern structure; he has very comprehensive sub-chapters on the language situation in Ireland and Scotland. He describes the linguistic continuum in Scotland as follows:

The linguistic repertoire in Scotland ranges from local "broad" Scots varieties that may be close to incomprehensible to speakers of other dialects, to "Standard Scottish English" (SSE) – what some writers think is "Standard English spoken with a Scottish accent" – though this is an exaggeration, as any Scot who doesn't speak RP is likely to have Scots lexical and grammatical features (Lass 1987: 257).

In my selection of texts, Lass's book is the first to introduce readers to the Scottish continuum.

In the case of Ireland, Lass distinguishes clearly between Irish English of the North and of the South. He calls Southern Hiberno-English "essentially 17th century Mainland English" (Lass 1987: 263) and expresses his scepticism about a very strong Irish (i.e. Gælic) influence. He prefers to class *she* as "an indigenous and independent development of English" (Lass 1987: 263). Northern Hiberno-English, on the other hand, is seen as "the result of a meeting of Ulster Scots coming down from the North and Southern Hiberno English coming up from the South, and thus [sharing] characteristics of both" (Lass 1987: 270).

Millward (1989) is equally balanced. Under the heading "English around the World", she devotes space to Scotland (Millward 1989: 308-310), Ulster (Millward 1989: 312-313), and Eire (Millward 1989: 313-315). Unlike Lass (1987), however, she does not really make clear what she refers to when she talks about "Scots English". In her list of phonetic characteristics she has the following item: "Although highly educated speakers avoid it, popular speech often has /u/ instead of /au/ in such words as *mouse* and *out*" (Millward 1989: 309). This, it seems, would have been a good moment to introduce the difference between *Scots* and *SSE*. "Highly educated speakers" – i.e. speakers of SSE – do not just "avoid" the monophtong in *house* etc., they do not use it at all. Speakers of rural and urban varieties of Scots, however, use it frequently.

In her "Scottish consonants" section, Millward mentions some characteristics of Highland English – her earlier term "Scots English" obviously means something rather comprehensive: along the lines of "English as used in the Lowlands and Highlands of Scotland."

Baugh and Cable's (1993) short treatment of Scottish English and Irish English is somewhat marred by the fact that they discuss these varieties under the heading of "English dialects". They have a particularly ingenious way of coping with the vexing language vs. dialect problem – namely by having two separate entries in their index that refer readers to the same passage of the book: "Scotland, dialect of: 311-312" and "Scots language: 311-312". A good example of having your Scottish scone and eating it.

Like some of my earlier histories, they are less than fair to the Scottish Makars, when they repeatedly refer to them as "Scottish Chaucerians" (passim). And they rather astonishingly comment: "These authors carry on the tradition of English as a literary medium into the Renaissance" (Baugh and Cable 1993: 153).

Irish English, according to Baugh and Cable (1993), is different from English English for three reasons: (a) the influence of the Irish/Gælic language; (b) the influence of Scots in the Northeast; and (c) the influence of seventeenth-century English that was brought to Ireland and "has remained quite conservative compared with both RP and American English" (Baugh and Cable 1993: 312).

Pyles and Algeo (1993) are unique in my selection in having comments on Irish English but none on Scottish English.

> Towards the northeast of the island, Irish English blends into the variety of Scots brought across the sea by settlers from the Scottish Lowlands, who outnumbered English settlers in that area by six to one. Consequently, in part of the northern counties ... the language popularly used is Ulster Scots, a variety of Southern Scots, rather than Irish English (Pyles and Algeo 1993: 235).

This kind of summary makes it particularly puzzling that the major basis of Ulster Scots – Lowland Scots – is not discussed at all.

Barber (1993) is unique for a different reason: he has very little on Modern Irish English and Modern Scottish English, but a sub-chapter (Barber 1993: 172-174) on Middle Scots, which is treated in the last section of his chapter on Middle English. As was pointed out above, this seems rather unfortunate in terms of the chronology of English and Scots.

Of the 25 histories considered here, three address themselves to non-philologist readers and are written by non-philologists; they are what one might call "popular", "non-technical" treatments of the development of English: Bryson (1990), Claiborne (1990), and McCrum, Cran, and MacNeil (1992). The latter is, in fact, based on a BBC television programme.

Bryson (1990), who is mentioned above, brings a certain lightheartedness to his task – witness throw-away lines such as the following, which "explains" why he quotes a stanza of Burns's "To a Haggis": namely "[to] give some idea of its majestic unfathomability" (Bryson 1990: 104).

Both Claiborne (1990) and McCrum, Cran, and MacNeil (1992) quote the first stanza of Dunbar's "Ane Ballat of our Lady" in order to criticise his use of aureate latinisms. Claiborne (1990) comments quite ludicrously that "[this] glittering vocabulary half conceals its leaden substance" (Claiborne 1990: 136) and goes on to say even more ridiculously: "Readers with a morbid interest in literary monstrosities will find most of the unfamiliar words in the *Oxford English Dictionary*" (Claiborne 1990: 136). A good try – but *DOST* (Craigie 1990) would have been even better.

McCrum, Cran, and MacNeil (1992) mysteriously refer to Dunbar's *Celebrations* and to the fact that he is at least as good as his English contemporaries. English contemporaries?

They are somewhat more restrained than Claiborne in their criticism of what they refer to as "half-chewed Latin" (McCrum, Cran, and MacNeil 1992: 87). Neither they nor Claiborne point out, though, that Dunbar's very conscious choice of this level of vocabulary coincides very closely with his choice of topic – namely "court matter".

Claiborne's section on Scottish English has a number of rather bizarre comments and judgements:

This conservatism [of /u/ in *about* etc.; of /ç/ in *night* etc.] reflects the distance of Scotland from Southern England [and] centuries of Scottish-English hostility (Claiborne 1990: 223).

The Scots vocabulary is also distinctive, and was even more so a century ago, when it included more than five-thousand special words (Claiborne 1990: 223).

Why, one might ask, a century ago? And where does the author get his figure of 5,000 special words? (Incidentally, his very puzzling footnote makes the whole thing even more mysterious. He refers to a dictionary (Claiborne 1990: 302) apparently called "The Old Scots Tongue", printed by Land [sic] Syne Publications, "an undated modern reprint of a dictionary completed in 1857.")

But his most risible comment is this:

> Scots English produced its own literature, but a very modest one. Its only major figure is the magnificient Burns, that hard-drinking "proven fornicator" ... . The poverty of Scots literature reflects the centuries-long poverty of Scotland itself [which induced people to emigrate to England and elsewhere] but in part, perhaps, a certain lack of interest or aptitude (Claiborne 1990: 224).

This is particularly hilarious because of what follows on the same page where we learn that "Ireland, even poorer than Scotland, produced a notable Anglo-Irish literature during the last hundred years" (Claiborne 1990: 224). Poverty in Scotland, in other words, is to be blamed for the poverty of its literature, while even worse poverty in Ireland had the opposite effect.

McCrum, Cran, and MacNeil (1992) are on the whole much more readable and reliable. They do not refrain, however, from expressing judgemental attitudes of the following kind: "Scots is one of the oldest, richest, and most interesting varieties of English" (McCrum, Cran, and MacNeil 1992: 130). They have a rather marvellous example of the type of popular linguistic judgement that is really a social judgement masquerading as a language comment, when they quote the priest of the island of Barra as saying: "I think the English spoken here ... is a beautiful, sweet-sounding, rolling, soft type of English ... It is a very comforting sound compared to the harshness, the whiskied, fast-moving accents you get in the cities and towns" (McCrum, Cran, and MacNeil 1992: 142).

In McCrum, Cran, and MacNeil (1992) the chapter on Scots (McCrum, Cran, and MacNeil 1992: 130-169) is followed by one on English in Ireland (McCrum, Cran, and MacNeil 1992: 170-208), which deals mainly with the anglicisation of Gælic-speaking Ireland. One of the Irish English characteristics they comment on is a tendency to use malapropisms and folk-etymologies, such as *windystool* for *windowsill*, *rosy dandrums* for *rhododendrons* or *piano roses* for *peonies*. Their comment is politically correct:

> Standard English speakers can find this amusing, or charming, or, xenophobically, evidence that the Irish are under-educated. In fact – as we shall see with Black English – malapropism is the linguistic product of British colonialization. These are "mistakes" made by people forced to become fluent in a language that is not theirs (McCrum, Cran, and MacNeil 1992: 179).

We have seen quite a wide range in the treatment of Irish and Scottish English – from complete "ignoral" via scattered remarks to more balanced and comprehensive views. What is striking, above all, is the upsurge of interest seen in publications of the last twenty years. This coincides, of course, with a growing interest in "World Englishes".

Smith (1996), which is both a history of English and a study of language change, sums up this new interest in varieties other than RP, Standard English and Standard American:

> English has become, in the twentieth century, a worldwide language ... . It therefore behoves anyone working in the field of historical study to avoid too anglocentric a focus, since English is no longer the property of just the English. For many years, the historical study of the language was taken to be a study of a steady development towards Standard English as used in the South of England. Since English is now the property of many people a long way from that part of the world, it seems worthwhile to make a conscious effort to overcome this focus (Smith 1996: 165).

References

Bambas, Robert C.
    1980   *The English language: its origin and history.* Norman: University of Oklahoma Press.

Barber, Charles L.
    1993   *The English language: a historical introduction.* Cambridge: Cambridge University Press.

Baugh, Albert C. and Thomas Cable
    1993   *A history of the English language.* (4th edition.) London: Routledge.

Blake, Norman F.
    1996   *A history of the English language.* London: Macmillan.

Bloomfield, Morton W. and Leonard Newmark
    1963   *A linguistic introduction to the history of English.* New York: Knopf.

Bradley, Henry
    1904   *The making of English.* London: Macmillan.

Brook, George L.
    1958   *A history of the English language.* London: Deutsch.

Bryson, Bill
    1990   *Mother tongue: the English language.* London: Penguin.

Claiborne, Robert
    1990   *English: its life and times.* London: Bloomsbury

Clarke, Roger
    1997   Review. *The Independent* (August 16): 7.

Classen, Eugen
    1919   *Outlines of the history of the English language.* London: Macmillan.

Craigie, William A.
    1990   *A dictionary of the Older Scottish Tongue from the 12th century to the end of the 17th.* Aberdeen: Aberdeen University Press.

Emerson, Oliver Farrar
    1894   *The history of the English language.* New York: Macmillan.

Halliday, F. E.
    1975   *The excellency of the English tongue.* London: Gollancz.

Lass, Roger
    1987   *The shape of English: structure and history.* London: Dent.

Leith, Dick
    1997   *A social history of English.* (2nd edition.) London: Routledge.

Lounsbury, Thomas R.
    1906   *History of the English language.* (Rev. edition.) London: George Bell (First edition: 1879).

Marckwardt, Albert H.
    1942   *Introduction to the English language.* Toronto: Oxford University Press.

McCrum, Robert, William Cran, and Robert MacNeil
    1992   *The story of English.* (Rev. edition.) London: Faber and Faber.

McKnight, George H.
    1928   *Modern English in the making.* New York: Appleton.

Millward, Celia M.
    1989   *A biography of the English language.* New York: Holt, Rinehart and Winston.

Peyton, V. John
    1771   *The history of the English language.* (English Linguistics 1500-1800 No. 244.) Menston: The Scolar Press.

Pollner, Clausdirk
    1997   "A breezier idiom": the treatment of varieties in histories of the English language. In: Mechthild Reinhardt and Wolfgang Thiele (eds.), 223-232.

Pyles, Thomas and John Algeo
    1993   *The origins and development of the English language.* (4th edition.) Fort Worth: Harcourt Brace Jovanovich.

Reinhardt, Mechthild and Wolfgang Thiele (eds.)
    1997   *Grammar and text in synchrony and diachrony: in honour of Gottfried Graustein.* Frankfurt: Vervuert.

Smith, Jeremy
    1996   *A historical study of English: Function, form and change.* London: Routledge.

Trench, Richard C.
    1855   *English past and present.* London: Kegan Paul (16th edition: 1899).

Wakelin, Martyn F.
    1988   *The archaeology of English.* London: Batsford.

Wrenn, Charles L.
    1949   *The English language.* London: Methuen (Repr. 1952, 1977).

Wyld, Henry Cecil
    1927   *A short history of English.* (Rev. edition.) London: John Murray (First edition: 1914).

Ethnolinguistic identity as common denominator: a socio-historical investigation of the lexical items for 'people' in South African English

Ute Smit

1. Introduction

Similar to all other British ex-colonies, public life in South Africa today would be unthinkable without English. And this is not a sign of the international status this language holds but of its socio-historical standing. English has become a carrier of societal hierarchies and, at the same time, reflects how dynamically these hierarchies have been changing over time in response to wider socio-political developments. That this social function of English is not only generally true, but also observable in specific linguistic items will be illustrated in this paper. By analysing the lexical items denoting 'people' in South African English I shall focus on the socio-historical implications to be drawn from existing and changing semantic patterns and criteria.

In order to imbed the lexical field study proper, the analysis is preceded by a brief overview of the history of English in South Africa, focusing on extralinguistic events and considering the wider sociolinguistic implications. This will be followed by a discussion of the relevant theoretical and methodological considerations.

2. English in South Africa

2.1. Historical overview[1]

The history of English in South Africa started in 1806 when the English seized the Cape from the Dutch and has continued uninterruptedly until today. Following Lanham (1996: 20) I will categorise these almost 200 years into four periods (see table 1):

Table 1. Periodisation of English in South Africa

	date	event	label	characteristics
1	-1880s	discovery of gold and diamonds around 1870	colonial era	English in rural or small-town communities in the Cape and Natal
2	-1945	end of World War II	era of new society	urbanisation; new social hierarchy, English as upper class language
3	-1990	release of Nelson Mandela	Apartheid era	English politically unimportant, decline in second language use and proficiency
4	ongoing		era of the new South Africa	inversion of political structure; new language policy: multilingualism; privileged position of English

2.1.1. Period 1

From the beginning, English was seen and placed in direct competition with Cape Dutch/Afrikaans and actively supported with the aim to replace the latter. This meant that the first local, South African variety to start developing was a second language amongst the Afrikaans-speaking group or, more precisely, groups, as they comprise white and coloured people.[2] Although, at that stage, their lives must have been fairly intertwined, clear social differentiation on ethnic grounds was already made. With the "1820 settlers" the seeds for the first local first language were sowed in the Eastern Cape and led to a dialect which merged the different features of the imported English varieties (lower-class speech of London and home counties) and incorporated many features from the neighbouring Cape Dutch/Afrikaans-speaking farmers. Another second language variety started to emerge in the various mission schools, where a handful of black Africans were educated (together with white children). Due to their low numbers it is, however, a bit difficult to speak of a fully-fledged Black South African English variety at that time already. A second first-language variety developed in Natal where, between 1848 and 1862, middle- and upper-class families from predominantly Northern England settled. This socio-linguistically very different group had little contact with Afrikaans speakers. Their original English dialects, social standing, continuing contact with England, and local connections led, not unexpectedly, to a very different variety of first language South African English than the earlier one in the Eastern Cape. For manual labour they relied on Indian indentured labourers from 1860 onwards, who subsequently formed a further second-language-speaking group. At the time of the discovery of gold and diamonds, one can thus speak of two first languages and three (or four) second languages differently developing varieties of English reaching into all South African social groups.

2.1.2. Period 2

The discovery of gold and diamonds led to intensive industrialisation and urbanisation in until then internationally unattractive parts of the Boer Republics. Sociolinguistically, this meant that, on the one hand, English became firmly established as the only language of economic and social advancement and, on the other, that its varieties started to stratify socially. This continued into the twentieth century despite, and partly because of, changing political constellations. A linguistically very interesting development in this period is the language shift that took place in the Indian community, from their various Indian first languages to English.[3]

2.1.3. Period 3

With apartheid, Afrikaans was installed and pushed as the main political and administrative language. This had immediate effects on English. Together with the strict separation of the "racial groups" (i.e. no first language teachers in non-white second language classrooms), it led to remarkable drops in standards in second language proficiency, but, as a counter-reaction to the enforced use of Afrikaans, an almost more fervent support for English amongst second language speakers (with the exception of the ruling white minority, of course). Besides very positive attitudes to English, this also meant a wide-spread use of English in these communities.

2.1.4. Period 4

The 1990s have brought unprecedented socio-political changes, which on the "language front" have led to the first multilingual language policy for the nation. While this seems to point to a more even distribution of functions amongst the 11 now official languages in the future, at present English still holds an unassailable, yet not uncontroversial, position as major political, economic, public, and also educational language (e.g. Branford 1996).

Due to its history, South African English displays typical features of a transplanted and nativised language and, furthermore, shows clear variational differences between speakers of the different (originally) first language and second language groups. One area which displays the high degree of localisation of South African English is the lexicon, as simple etymological investigations already reveal: the common South African English words contained in *The South African Pocket Oxford Dictionary* (Bradford 1987) consist of loanwords from Dutch/Afrikaans (52%), calques and independent coinages in English (18%), and loans from Bantu languages (11%) (summarised in Görlach 1996: 429).

2.2. South African English dictionaries

Since new words generally tend to attract a lot of attention, it is not surprising that South African English lexicography has a long tradition in the country (for an overview cf. Silva 1996: 196-208). The pioneering work, undertaken by Charles Pettman, was published as early as 1913 and still provides a useful source of South African English in the nineteenth century. This dictionary was extended in the 1930s and then again in the 1960s. South African English was also considered in prescriptive dictionaries (in the 1970s and 1980s). Without a doubt the most important South African English dictionary-making has been done at the Dictionary Unit for South African English at Rhodes University, Grahamstown. This unit has compiled a number of dictionaries since its initiation in 1970. All of them follow the *OED* in style, i.e. give etymologies and citations reflecting the definitions and sense distinctions. They furthermore indicate connections to international or other varieties of English, where applicable. The first edition appeared in 1978, and was revised three times (1980, 1987, 1991).

In 1996 the unit published a new dictionary of a much more comprehensive nature, paying special attention to reliable citations and definitions (Silva (ed.) 1996, from here on *DSAE: Hist*). Its aim is "to map and illustrate the complex landscape of that variety of English which is particular to South Africans" (*DSAE: Hist*, preface). This has to be seen in connection with the editors' basic understanding that

> South African English is the property not only of South Africa's relatively small number of English-speakers (about 10% of the population), but also of the much greater number of people who use English as a second or third language. All varieties of English are represented in this dictionary, and the provenance of regional or "group" vocabulary is provided wherever a word is not widely familiar to South Africans (*DSAE: Hist*, preface).

Based on an extensive collection of written and spoken texts, the ca. 8500 entries were researched in great detail and only fully included when a reliable amount of citations was found. When less clear-cut cases were included, they are marked as not fully integrated ("||"). In sum, this dictionary adheres to theoretically sound and strictly applied criteria, which guarantee reliability.

2.3. Ethnolinguistic groups

Next to describing the language's history, this brief overview of the development of South African English should have had a second effect, namely to illustrate that the South African social history is deeply marked by century-old social divisions. For the last 200 years at least, South Africans were born and raised in a society whose main structuring principle was "race". Since racial differences "should be understood as physical variations singled out by the members of a community or society as socially significant" (Giddens 1997: 212), it does not come unexpectedly that this fairly rigid compartmentalisation of society has gone hand-in-hand with an equally distinct differentiation of ethnic groups. Ethnicity, here,

> refers to the cultural practices and outlooks of a given community of people that set them apart from others. Members of ethnic groups see themselves as culturally distinct from other groups in a society, and are seen by those other groups to be so in return. Different characteristics may serve to distinguish ethnic groups from one another, but the most usual are language, history or ancestry (real or imagined), religion and styles of dress or adornment (Giddens 1997: 210).

In other words, your ethnic group does not only define who you are or where you stand in comparison with your compatriots, but it also pre-selects and -determines your beliefs, attitudes and actions. To put it in a nutshell, it plays a major role in what people identify with – it marks their social identity. Language, as indicated in Giddens's definition, is very often seen as a distinctive characteristic of an ethnic group; in South Africa, however, it was installed as the major defining characteristic next to skin colour. I would therefore like to argue that, when analysing sociolinguistic questions in this country, the link between social identity and language is particularly important.

Before I can support this claim with my research as a case in point, a few preliminary words on my project are due.

3. The project

3.1. Research aim

The aim of this study is to establish the criteria for group differentiation as found in the South African English lexicon and, if possible, to trace the development of these criteria during the language's 200-year history. The ulterior motive – and final goal – is then to find out in which ways the lexical realisations of South African social groupings reveal people's conceptualisations of their societal structure and dynamics.

Seeing that South African English is so diverse and constantly developing in various communities, my endeavour has been to focus on that part of the entirety of the South African English lexicon which is established enough to be recorded in a major and generally accepted dictionary. This should ensure that it is shared by a high percentage of South African English speakers and results based on it reflect generally held structuring categories. The most useful dictionary of South African English for such purposes is presently the *DSAE: Hist*.

In my study I have therefore collected all the lexemes recorded in the *DSAE: Hist* which describe people (individuals and groups) originating from or living in South Africa.

3.2. Theoretical frame

My idea to collect lexical items referring to a specific semantic category is nothing new in itself, but falls into the fairly well established area of semantic or lexical field studies. This means that I can rely on an abundance of literature describing relevant studies and theories, most of which are in the structuralist tradition following

Coseriu (e.g. 1970). This approach has brought forth a well-founded theory and also a clearly applicable methodology (e.g. Coseriu and Geckeler 1981; Kastovsky 1982), provided that one's semantic field belongs to the "functional language", i.e. it does not show any diachronic, diaphasic, diastratic, or diatopic variation (Dupuy-Engelhardt 1993: 24). Resulting from this prerequisite, it is not recommendable to concentrate on fields that are structured extralinguistically (Dupuy-Engelhardt 1993: 25-26).

When comparing these considerations with my research interest and also my source of data, two basic differences — or, maybe, (de)limitations on my part — become apparent. The first refers to the underlying theory of meaning and concept.[4] Here the traditional structuralist approach to semantic field analysis draws a very clear distinction between concept and meaning, the former as extralinguistically and the latter as linguistically defined. In contrast to this my study is built on the understanding of a close connection between language and ethnic group relations, i.e. the extralinguistic and the linguistic lastingly influencing each other; if not for any other reasons than because of the psychological reality both entities share.

An approach that comes to my rescue here is that of prototype semantics, which regards language as a cognitive entity.[5] When speakers use language in its function of reference, they can only do this successfully when they call upon the relevant concepts and categories. So, referring to an object (i.e. relating it to a word) also always means referring to the position of this object within the category, i.e. to its concept. This position, together with the (fuzzy) demarcation between categories, then leads to the semantic content (i.e. meaning) of the word. Therefore, concept/category and meaning are seen as closely related, but not identical: the meaning of a word depends on its similarity with the prototype.

The second (de)limitation of my study is a result of the research aim formulated for this study. My concern is for that part of the South African English vocabulary that is typical of South Africa, and not of English in general. In other words, I want to look at the part of the South African English lexicon that has been established in and is unique to South Africa, and not the one it shares with other varieties of English world-wide.

This entails, however, that I exclude items used in every-day language simply because they are not particular to South Africa. While this could be interpreted as an artificial restriction weakening the study, it is less unmotivated when considering the specific field – "people living in or originating from South Africa" –, which, by definition, falls into the South African part of South African English rather than the general one.

Within this South African part of the lexicon, my interests are again wider than possible within the "functional language", as I wish to cover all lexical terms, irrespective of their diachronic, -phasic, -stratic, and -topic status. This structuralist prerequisite thus cannot be complied with.

A further, more practical consideration for choosing this specific language sector lies in the unique possibility of data collection based on the *DSAE: Hist*. On the one hand, a dictionary undoubtedly holds a number of methodological weaknesses: it presents de-contextualised, "pre-digested" information. This means that the procedure of collecting instances (in texts), selecting, and deciding on those to include, and of analysing their meaning has already been undertaken. While this might sound quite helpful (as it cuts down on time), it also means that the researcher has to take over the dictionary editors' denotations, sense differentiations, and general categorising without being in the position to question or evaluate them. This is the more problematic if one keeps in mind that the original intention of the dictionary makers might have been quite different from that of a specific study.

Looked at positively, however, the dictionary as source is promising. The entries represent a selection of texts much wider than what could ever be collected for a study like the present one, and thus allow a good insight into the lexical breadth of South African English. *DSAE: Hist* in particular was collated with the explicit idea to represent all varieties of South African English, but only by those lexemes sufficiently substantiated in usage. So, the items extracted from it seem to be particularly well placed for an initial description of the field. Then these preliminary findings could be checked in "real" field studies, i.e. by elicitation from respondents and/or observation in actual language use.

To sum up, while the dictionary as source does not allow a fully-fledged description of the word field "citizens or inhabitants of South Africa", it offers a good overview of the lexical range, on the basis of which the research aim of this study can be tackled.

4. Analysis

The first step in such an analysis is to define the core of the field – the archisememe or prototype, depending on one's theory –, which in my case is 'people (individuals and groups) originating from, or living in, South Africa'. That this rather convoluted description is more appropriate than the simple 'South African' becomes apparent when checking the *DSAE: Hist* entry:

> South African
> 1. before 1910: an inhabitant of Southern Africa
>   qu(otations): 1867-1903 (only white)
> 2. between 1910 and 1961: a citizen or inhabitant of the Union of South Africa
>   qu: 1912-1957 (when referring to other than white, then clearly specified by adj.)
> 3. since 1961: a citizen or inhabitant of the Republic of South Africa
>   qu: 1963-1991 (all groups – but again, specifications)

The three senses given in the dictionary make clear that the exact definition of who can be called "South African" has changed over time, either ex- or including various groups at various times. It could therefore not be used as core description of the field.

4.1. Data

The field based on 'people (individuals and groups) originating from, or living in, South Africa' is obviously very broad and subsumes a number of more specific fields, such as
- individuals vs. groups,
- groups vs. categories,
- general vs. specified terms (e.g. by type of work; family status),
- functional differentiation (e.g. terms of address and reference vs. terms of reference).

But, in accordance with my study aim, I have decided to cast my net as widely as possible. This gives me a broad foundation of specifically South African terms for people, which, so my arguing, will allow me to describe generally applicable attributes and, finally, maybe to uncover an underlying "principle", or, in accordance with the title of this paper, a "common denominator".

So, I went through the dictionary, excerpting all entries referring to people in South Africa, with the exclusion of political parties or church denominations. That resulted in 510 types. My next step was to divide this rather unmanageable amount into broad categories, which resulted in the following list:

broad category	N (ca.)
"tribal & areal" names	88
"general" terms	102
terms of address & reference	103
"job" terms (e.g. military, medicine)	114
terms referring to specific personality traits or circumstances	107
total	510

Of these categories, I excluded the tribal names as proper names because they are referentially unambiguous. On similar grounds, I wanted to exclude "areal" names (e.g. *Capetonian, Transvaler*; i.e. 'people resident in X'), but the data turned out differently, as I will explain below (see section 4.3.). All of the other four categories are relevant for my research question, but, due to restrictions of space, I will focus on the central category in the following, viz. "general" terms.

4.2. "General" terms

In this category I have included all those words (headwords and occasionally other entries, also composites) which, according to the dictionary definition, denote a person/people living in, or originating from, South Africa (male and/or female) without giving further sociological and psychological specifications as to age, family status, social status (including economic, professional or educational status), personality traits, psychological states, and social circumstances.
This has led to 102 items (see table 2).

When looking at them briefly, two obvious observations can be made: Firstly, they blend into South African English from an etymological perspective: 30% from Dutch/Afrikaans, 40% of English origin, 13% from Sintu languages. Secondly, from a pragmatic or language use point of view, the labels used in the dictionary show that there is a lot of diachronic, -phasic and -topic heterogeneity, which divides the items into three groups: the ones without any labels; those marked as connoting offense ("derog.", "off."); and the rest marked as no longer in "normal" use ("hist.", "obs.").

Based on these preliminary findings, the next and main step could be taken, namely to compare the definitions (and quotations) given in the *DSAE: Hist* with the aim to extract the more general criteria of semantic differentiation. Due to the large number of items, I cannot present all of them in detail, but have to restrict myself to a general description. After that, I shall focus on a few, select cases (see section 4.3.). The general categorisation of the words is to be found in table 3 and reflects the criteria established in this study: two basic ones, namely RACE (i.e. skin colour and a few other selected features, e.g. hair) and LANGUAGE, and one more comprehensive one resulting out of those two, namely WHITE – NON-WHITE. The subdivision in table 3 into eight lists reflects the intersection of the three criteria found: the ethnolinguistic criteria (RACE and LANGUAGE) result in white English first language speakers, Afrikaners, Coloureds, (Khoisan), Blacks, and Indians. The third criterion is apparent in the white vs. non-white groups.

Table 2. "General" terms, in alphabetic order (102 items)

abalumbi || *obs?*	crunchie *slang, derog, off*	Maburu || *rare*
African	Dutch *hist*	Malay
Afrikander *obs*	Dutchman *obs, then derog*	Mardyker *hist*
Afrikaner	Engels	Masarwa *derog*
amabhulu || *derog*	Engelsman	mealie (-muncher) *derog, rare*
amabhunu || *derog*	English	
amakula || *derog*	Englishman	Meraai *derog, off*
amangesi || *obs*	Eurafrican *obs?*	mlungu
anderskleuriges ||	European *obs*	munt *derog, off, slang*
Arab	free black *hist*	muntu
Asian *hist*	g/Gammat *derog, off*	national unit *hist*
Asiatic *off, hist*	gattes || *derog*	native *obs, off*
Bantu *(off)*	geelbek *obs*	nie-blanke ||
bastard *hist*	goffel *derog, off, slang*	non-black *obs?*
black	hairy-back *slang, derog, off*	non-European *obs*
blanke ||	Hindoo *obs*	non-white
boer	Hoggenheimer *derog, off*	other coloured
boerevolk	Hotnot *obs derog (for coloured)*	outlander || *hist*
Boesman || *derog, off*		pekkie *derog, off*
Boschman Hottentot *obs*	Hottentot	Peruvian *derog, hist*
	Hottie *off?, colloq*	redneck *obs, derog*
British Indian *hist*	igxagxa ||	rooinek *derog*
brown	Indian	sammy *off*
Bushman *hist*	japie *derog*	San
bushy *derog, off*	Jim *obs, off*	South African Dutch *hist?*
C/Kockney	John *off*	soutie *derog*
Cape Coloured	kaffermeid || *off*	soutpiel *derog*
Cape Dutch *obs*	kaffir *off, derog*	Strandloper
Cape Malay	khaki *hist, then derog*	tottie *obs, off, colloq*
Capeboy *obs, off*	Khoi(khoi)	uitlander
Capey *colloq*	Khoisan	Vaalpens *colloq, derog*
Chinese (Hottentot) *hist*	Kleurling ||	Van der Merwe
	knobnose *obs, off?*	white
Christenmensch || *hist*	kroeskop *off, obs?*	wit ou *coll*
coloured	Lekgoa ||	witmense *coll*
coolie *off, derog*		

Labels: *hist*(orical), *obs*(olete), *off*(ensive), *derog*(atory), *coll*(oquial), *slang*, *rare*; \|\| = not fully integrated

Table 3. "General" terms (in ethnolinguistic groups)

WHITE		
abalumbi ‖ *obs?*	WHITE – ENGLISH	WHITE – AFRIKAANS
blanke ‖	amangesi ‖ *obs*	Afrikander *obs*
Christenmensch ‖ *hist*	Engels	Afrikaner
European *obs*	Engelsman	amabhulu ‖ *derog*
igxagxa ‖ *derog*	English	amabhunu ‖ *derog*
Lekgoa ‖	Englishman	boer
mlungu	Hoggenheimer *derog, off*	boerevolk
non-black *obs?*	khaki *hist, then derog*	Cape Dutch *obs*
white	outlander ‖ *hist*	crunchie *slang*, *derog, off*
wit ou *coll*	Peruvian *derog, hist*	Dutch *hist*
witmense *coll*	redneck *obs, derog*	Dutchman *obs, then derog*
	rooinek *derog*	gattes ‖ *derog*
	soutie *derog*	hairy-back *slang, derog, off*
	soutpiel *derog*	japie *derog*
	uitlander	Maburu ‖ *rare*
		mealie (-muncher) *derog, rare*
		South African Dutch *hist?*
		Vaalpens *coll, derog*
		Van der Merwe

NON-WHITE		
anderskleuriges ‖	KHOISAN	BLACK AFRICAN
kroeskop *off, obs?*	Boschman Hottentot *obs*	African
nie-blanke ‖	Bushman *hist*	Bantu (*off*)
non-European *obs*	bushy *derog, off*	black
non-white	Chinese (Hottentot) *hist*	free black *hist*
	Hotnot *obs, derog*	Jim *obs, off*
COLOURED	Hottentot	John *off*
bastard hist	Hottie *off?, coll*	kaffermeid ‖ *off*
Boesman ‖ *derog, off*	Khoi(khoi)	kaffir *off, derog*
brown	Khoisan	knobnose *obs, off?*
Cape Coloured	Masarwa *derog*	Mardyker *hist*
Cape Malay	South African	munt *derog, off, slang*
Capeboy *obs, off*	Strandloper *hist*	muntu
Capey *coll*	tottie *obs, off, coll*	national unit *hist*
coloured		native *obs, off*
Eurafrican *obs?*	INDIAN	pekkie *derog, off*
g/Gammat *derog, off*	amakula ‖ *derog*	
geelbek *obs*	Arab	
goffel *derog, off, slang*	Asian *hist*	
Kleurling ‖	Asiatic *off, hist*	
Malay	British Indian *hist*	

Meraai *derog, off* other coloured	C/Kockney coolie *off, derog* Hindoo *obs* Indian sammy *off*

The lists of table 3 are, however, a bit too simplistic: historical, obsolete and presently used words are treated indiscriminately. Furthermore, each word is neatly assigned to one category, including those that have been used for a long time. So, possible semantic shifts are not made apparent.

As a next step I have thus done two things: to divide the terms into "historical" and "now" – again a simplification! – and to place them in "space" so as to allow for overlaps. The results can be seen in figures 1 and 2.

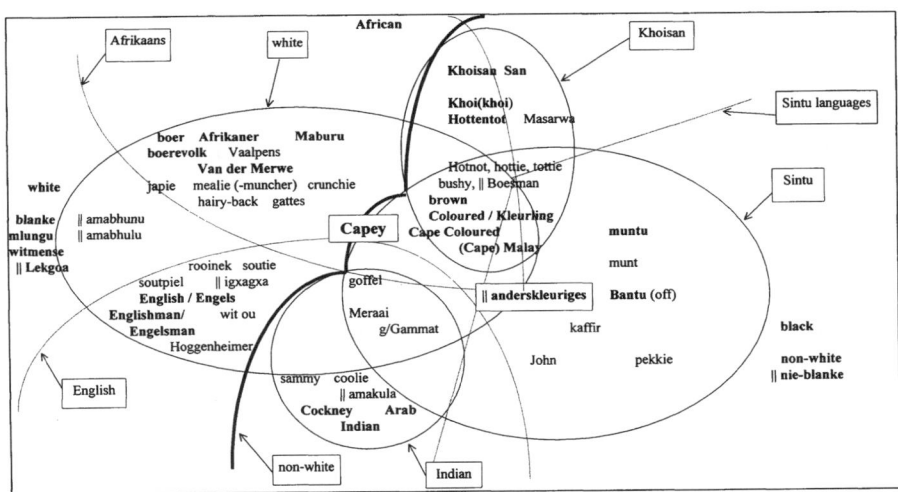

Figure 1. "General" terms, excluding "obs." and "hist." (attitudinally neutral terms in bold print)

Figure 1 tries to depict the "now" situation and figure 2 the "historical/obsolete" one. Figure 1 illustrates, on the one hand, the fairly clear semantic distinctions and lacking overlaps between "white" and "non-white"; "white", "black African" and "Indian". At the same time, it draws attention to the much more complex situation of the "coloured", made visible in lexical overlaps: in individual terms with the black Africans and the Afrikaners (white Afrikaans first language speakers) and in multiple ways with the Khoisan. This is a good point at which to turn to figure 2. This figure presents an attempt at placing chronologically the terms marked "hist." or "obs.". The difficulty being that such a placement can only reflect the date of first recording and not how long and in which respects the term has existed in South African English since. And secondly, this type of presentation along a type of "isogloss" obviously complicates the indication of overlap, especially over more than two categories. Thirdly, this selection of "hist." terms is highly artificial because it excludes many other equally old terms, simply because they are not yet obsolete. So unfortunately, this figure cannot be regarded as an accurate representation of the historical development of the terms. What it does show, however, – and that is why it is included here – is, firstly, the categorisation of the "hist." terms along the 2 (3) criteria RACE and LANGUAGE (and EUROPEAN – NON-EUROPEAN).[6]

Secondly, the figure also points to an interesting overlap, which, similar to figure 1, also includes one term denoting Afrikaans-speakers of different ethnicities (*Afrikander* in figure 1 and *Capey* in figure 2). This means that here we find a case where the criterion LANGUAGE overrides the one of RACE.

In sum, the results have supported the hunch I have had from the start: each of the lexical items clearly denotes a specific ethnic group. So, ethnicity, constituted by RACE and LANGUAGE, has emerged as the underlying denominator. In general, these two interact to create an "ethnolinguistic" grid of classification. A further, more specific interpretation of these two criteria makes up a third one, the in South Africa infamous WHITE – NON-WHITE distinction. While the first two criteria seem to have been relevant to South African English in all of its 200 years, the third, I will show in the following, is a more recent one, a twentieth-century "invention".

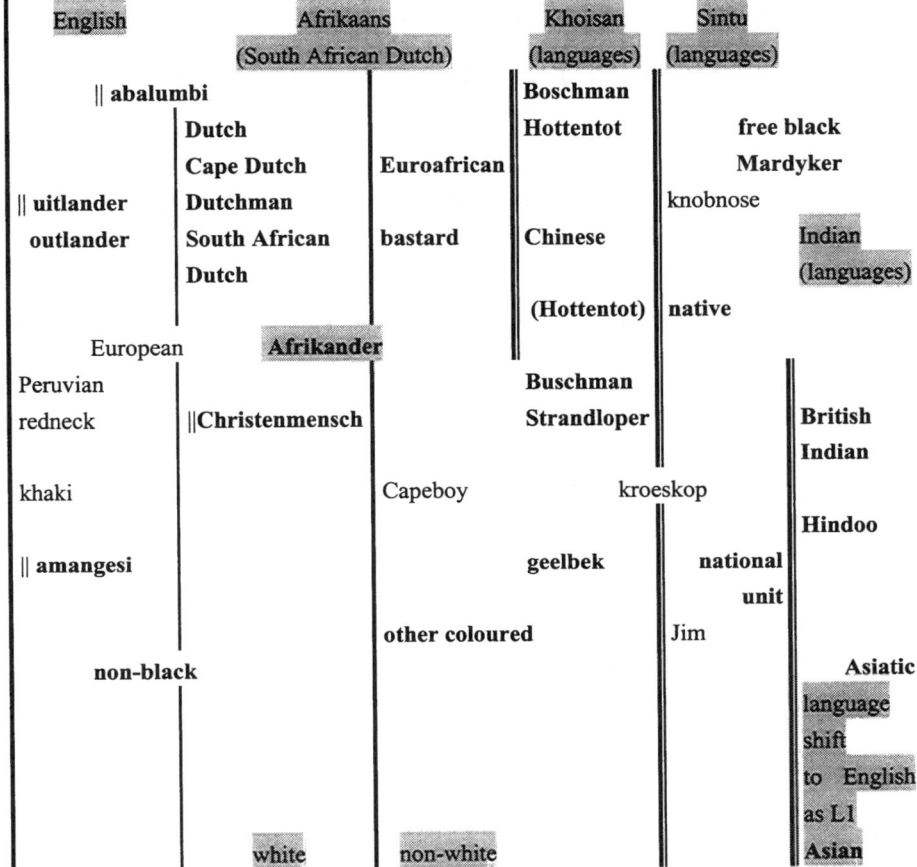

Figure 2. "General" terms, only "obs." and "hist." (attitudinally neutral terms in bold print)

4.3. Specific aspects and items

After this more general description, I would now like to turn to a few select aspects:
(a) terms relevant to the third criterion (entries taken from the *DSAE: Hist*, "qu" = quotations)

European (obs) a white person; for a period, the official term used for a white person.
qu: 1696-1960s (qu. from 1964 and 1980 questioning the use of "European" for South Africans)

non-European (obs) non-white
qu: 1925 (1918 for adj) - late 1960s (later qu seem to be hist.)

white (hist) one of European descent, during apartheid: one classified as belonging to the white group
qu: 1966 (1950 for adj.) - 1970 (late 1980s for adj)

non-white (obs, off) one whose racial ancestry is not predominantly European
[term was used extensively in the past as a blanket term referring to those groups disadvantaged under apartheid]
qu: 1934-1991 (last non-hist. qu: 1970s)

black
1. a member of any of the darker-skinned peoples of South Africa
   qu: 1616-1915 (last non-hist. one in 1852)
2. a dark-skinned person of African origin, belonging to a people whose home language is of the Sintu group; during apartheid: one classified as a "black"
[Black has replaced African as the presently most widely accepted term]
   qu: 1696-1983
3. a member of a people or group which was disadvantaged by apartheid laws, i.e. of any but the white group
   qu: 1953-1989

(b) the "clash" of the two criteria RACE and LANGUAGE (*Afrikander* and *Capey*)

Afrikander
1. obs. variant of "Afrikaner" (a Dutch/Afrikaans speaking white inhabitant of South Africa)
2. obs. of mixed ethnic origin
   qu: 1823-1917 (last qu: taken from a Coloured writer)

Capey *coll.*
1. Cape Coloured
   qu: 1940-1990
2. an inhabitant of the Western Cape or the city of Cape Town
   qu: 1970-1989 (1994)

(c) the relevance of another criterion in this context, namely AREA

"areal" terms[7]			
Transvaler	*highvelder*	*Freestater/Vrystater*	*Bayonian*
Vaalie	*Natalian*	*Transkeian*	*Kaapenaar*
Johannesburger	*Durbanite*	*Ciskeian*	*Capetonian*
Sowetan	*banana boy/girl*	*Albanian*	*Capey*

4.3.1. The white – non-white dichotomy

From the definitions for *non-European*, *non-white*, and *black* I conclude that the South African English ethnic-group terminology underwent a fundamental change around the turn of the century: a new, superordinate distinction becomes apparent, namely the one between white and the others (i.e. coloured, Khoisan, black and Indian), creating such dichotomies as *European* vs. *non-European* and later *white* vs. *non-white*. While *European* and *white* are older terms, their negations are not. The most inclusive term in that time seems to have been *black*.[8] According to the quotations given in the *DSAE: Hist*, it was used for Khoisan and black Africans, but not for coloureds.[9] The fundamental distinction of the apartheid era into *(slegs vir) blankes* and *nie-blankes* was thus already lexicalised in the 1910s.

4.3.2. Two entries: *Afrikander* and *Capey*

With the acceptance of *non-European* as a cover term for 'other than white' as underlying distinction for ethnic terms, I would argue that terms referring jointly to white and non-white groups were unlikely in the major part of this century. The entries for *Afrikander* and *Capey* are a case in point.

The definitions of both words – the only ones with such race-overarching meaning – show that their meaning extends over white and non-white (to stick to these labels). So, how does this support my claim (and not question it)? For *Afrikander* this overarching meaning was relevant in the nineteenth century when it could be used for Afrikaans speakers irrespective of their ethnicity. This could be seen as evidence of the, then still, joint identity of Afrikaans speakers (maybe in opposition to the English-speaking ruling class?). *Capey*, again denoting Afrikaans speakers, started off as designating Cape Coloureds (i.e. Christian Coloureds from the Western Cape). It started then, most likely in the late 1960s, to undergo meaning extension to include all inhabitants of that area. It seems, thus, that a new criterion has started to become active, namely the one of place/area of residence or of origin. For simplicity's sake, I will call it "area" in the following brief discussion.

4.3.3. The relevance of another criterion: AREA

Since *Capey* throws doubt on my initial decision to exclude all areal terms because of their encyclopedic nature, I revised it and looked at all the terms included in the *DSAE: Hist* referring to a person originating from a specific area of the country. This resulted in the 17 terms given in the list above. While it was quite straightforward to place these terms on a map of South Africa with the old, i.e. pre-1994 provincial boundaries, the interesting point was that these terms conjured up clearly racially defined stereotypes in my mind – except for *Sowetan*, *Ciskeian*, *Transkeian* (and *Capey*) all of them "white" actually. So, I compared my introspection with the *DSAE: Hist* citations and found it confirmed. All the quotations before 1990 describe white people (those for *Sowetan*, *Ciskeian*, *Transkeian* blacks). It might of course be that these specific instances were chosen exactly because the dictionary editors (having similar social experience to mine) used their own intuition as basis for their decision with regard to which examples would explain the terms "correctly". So, it could very well be that black, coloured or Indian South Africans used the area terms for other than whites too. But, and this is revealing, some citations after 1990 reveal an all-inclusive understanding – especially *Durbanite* (1992), *Kaapenaar* (1991) and *Capey*. This, it needs to be stressed, pre-dates the scrapping of the Group Areas Act (the act designating specific living areas to specific racial groups).

The area names, I would suggest, are in the process of undergoing meaning extension in "standard" South African English, losing their ethnic denotation. In this context, *Capey* seems to have been the pioneer or, to use a South African English term, *voorloper*.

5. Results and discussion

With regard to the research aim to establish the (development of the) criteria for group differentiation as found in the South African English lexicon, the analysis of the "general" terms has led to the following three results:

5.1. The lexical set 'people in South Africa' (consisting of 102 items) could be clearly subdivided along "ethnolinguistic identity" as represented by "race" and "language". In other words, "ethnolinguistic identity" is the common denominator.

5.2. A superordinate, i.e. more general, classification into WHITE – NON-WHITE could be established for the twentieth century (at least up to 1994).

5.3. The all-inclusive classification of people according to ethnolinguistic identity seems to be coming to an end, as indicated by the fledgling independence of the criterion AREA.

The outcome of this research lends itself to an interpretation of the established criteria with regard to the development of the South African understanding of essential group distinctions of its society. While the criteria as such illustrate very clearly how deeply ingrained ethnolinguistic groupings have been in that nation, the distinction into WHITE – NON-WHITE allows diachronic, developmental observations.

Let us look at the relevant terms once more: *European* and *white* had been part of South African English for a long time when their negations came in use. It is these I want to look at now: *non-European* was replaced by *non-white* (and, of course, *nie-blanke*), and later joined by *black* (see sense 3, given above). Why so? Let us first consider the nature of this category and then turn to the meaning extension of *black*. In contrast to the previously used group labels, this one refers to a group of people by what they are not, namely European or white. This group is thus not described by what the members share, but by what makes them different when looked at from outside, from an outgroup perspective. Therefore, I would argue that this group label did not develop because of an ingroup need (i.e. by those identifying with this group), but because of an outgroup necessity. In other words, I would claim that it was a white creation. It seems to me to express the white *laager* mentality (to use a South African English term): us against them, them being all the others. And the only thing all these others share is that they are different from us. So, from a white perspective, these "others" had a clearly uniting attribute, namely they were "non-white". But this is only uniting from a white perspective, not from an "other" perspective since they had differing ways of categorisation and attribution. For instance, coloureds seem to have seen themselves as *Afrikanders* – as Afrikaans speakers. "*Natives*" might rather have identified with their own tribes than with this white-imposed notion. So, for the whites to successfully impose their understanding of group distinction, it was not enough to simply label it. It was necessary for the "others" to also start feeling like one group, at least on a certain level. It asked for socio-political action. In South Africa, legislation to this end was put into place at the same time as *non-European* emerged, at the beginning of this century – the time of Mahatma Gandhi's experiences in South Africa – and brought to its peak in the apartheid era (especially 1950s-1970s) when there was a very real distinction between whites and the others. It is thus no surprise that those oppressed by the system also started to take on this uniting group identity. The meaning extension of *black* to denote 'a member of a people or group which was disadvantaged by apartheid laws, i.e. a member of any but the white group' gives credit to that. Recent developments of lifting the discriminatory legislation will most likely have its impact on the terminology as well – not yet recorded, though.

This category I would thus claim is an outgroup "invention" and, due to socio-historical and -psychological developments gained ingroup relevance (revealed in *black*), which might, now that the social setup has turned around, already be changing again.

6. Conclusion

The study presented in this paper has clearly illustrated the changing nature of the South African English lexicon, which, in its 200-year history, seems to have responded extremely sensitively to ongoing inner- but also extralinguistic changes. To gain more security about the wider impact of the results, however, they would need to be substantiated by further studies of, on the one hand, different lexical fields to be found in the *DSAE: Hist* and, on the other, the same lexical field with different corpora and research methods. An investigation of lexical items used for 'people living in, or originating from, South Africa' in naturally occurring written and spoken texts will surely throw a new, but hopefully supporting, view on the nature of the lexical field and its ongoing dynamic development.

Notes

1. For more detailed accounts cf. e.g. de Klerk ((ed.) 1996), the many publications by Lanham, e.g. (1985); Lass (1985); or Mesthrie (1992).
2. In South Africa "coloured" refers to people of racially mixed descent. Similar to all other racial terms, it is not uncontroversial. While some reject it for its discriminatory usage during apartheid times, others accept it since it reflects an actual social situation.

3. For a detailed description of the language shift in this community cf. Mesthrie (1992); for the South African Indian English lexis cf. Mesthrie (1990).
4. For more detailed discussions of the lexical-field research and its recent developments cf. e.g. Dörschner (1996), Lutzeier ((ed.) 1993).
5. As evidenced in other studies undertaken from a prototypical point of view, I was not the first to have problems applying the structuralist theory to my lexical field. Next to differing theoretical opinions, one fairly pragmatic reason for this lies in the type of lexical field to be investigated. The structuralist approach excludes a great part of the lexicon from the pool of potential objects of enquiry on grounds of it being of an encyclopedic nature (cf. Dörschner (1996: 21-22)). This part of the lexicon is, of course, exactly that one which displays a close connection to the extralinguistic world, but is nonetheless of interest from a lexical-field point of view (as also mentioned by Kastovsky, September 1997; comment to the presentation).
6. The two exceptions *free black* and *Mardyker* refer to the Malaysian slaves brought to the Cape when that was all what South Africa was.
7. The eighteenth term, *Stellalander* hist, I want to exclude as it refers to an inhabitant of a Republic that existed in what is now the Northern Cape for a few years in the nineteenth century only.
8. *Native* referred to either speakers of a Sintu language or, more generally, black Africans only (*DSAE: Hist*).
9. A rather difficult decision as "Hottentot" was the standard term used for Khoisan at that time, but could also be applied to coloureds. If I interpret the citations correctly (for "black", "Hottentot", etc.), however, then it was more usual to refer to coloureds by either qualifying "Hottentot" or by using one of the other terms (e.g. "Bastard").

References

Bolinger, Dwight
    1980   *Language – the loaded weapon: the use and abuse of language today*. London/New York: Longman.
Branford, Jean and William Branford
    1991   *The dictionary of South African English*. (4th edition.) Cape Town: Oxford University Press.
Branford, William
    1987   *The South African pocket Oxford dictionary*. Cape Town: Oxford University Press.
    1996   English in South African society: a preliminary overview. In: Vivian de Klerk (ed.), 35-51.

Coseriu, Eugenio
1970   *Einführung in die strukturelle Betrachtung des Wortschatzes* (Tübinger Beiträge zur Linguistik 14.) Tübingen: Narr.
Coseriu, Eugenio and Horst Geckeler
1981   *Trends in structural semantics.* (Tübinger Beiträge zur Linguistik 158.) Tübingen: Narr.
De Klerk, Vivian (ed.)
1996   *Focus on South Africa.* Amsterdam/Philadelphia: Benjamins.
Dörschner, Norbert
1996   *Lexikalische Strukturen: Wortfeldkonzeption und Theorie der Prototypen im Vergleich.* Münster: Nodus Publikationen.
DSAE: Hist = Silva, Penny (ed.)
1996   *The dictionary of South African English on historical principles.* Oxford: Oxford University Press.
Dupuy-Engelhardt, Hiltraud
1993   Wortfeldpraxis nach den Prinzipien der Lexematik. In: Peter Rolf Lutzeier (ed.), 23-34.
Fishman, Joshua A.
1995   Dictionaries as culturally constructed and as culture-constructing artifacts: the reciprocity view as seen from Yiddish sources. In: Braj B. Kachru and Henry Kahane (eds.), 29-34.
Geckeler, Horst
1993   Strukturelle Wortfeldforschung heute. In: Peter Rolf Lutzeier (ed.), 11-22.
Giddens, Anthony
1997   *Sociology.* (3rd edition.) Cambridge: Polity Press.
Görlach, Manfred
1996   English – the language of a new nation: the present-day linguistic setup of South Africa. In: Jürgen Klein and Dirk Vanderbeke (eds.), 419-434.
Green, Georgia M.
1989   *Pragmatics and natural language understanding.* Hillsdale, NJ: Erlbaum.
Greenbaum, Sidney (ed.)
1985   *The English language today.* Oxford: Pergamon Press.
Hewstone, Miles, Wolfgang Stroebe, Jean-Paul Codol, and Geoffrey M. Stephenson (eds.)
1988   *Introduction to social psychology.* Oxford: Blackwell.
Hogg, Michael A. and Dominic Abrams
1988   *Social identification.* London/New York: Routledge.

Kachru, Braj B. and Henry Kahane (eds.)
1995 *Cultures, ideologies and the dictionary: studies in honour of Ladislav Zgusta.* Tübingen: Niemeyer.

Kastovsky, Dieter
1982 *Wortbildung und Semantik.* (Studienreihe Englisch 14.) Düsseldorf: Schwann-Bagel.

Klein, Jürgen and Dirk Vanderbeke (eds.)
1996 *Anglistentag 1995 Greifswald: proceedings.* Tübingen: Niemeyer.

Konerding, Klaus-Peter
1993 Wortfeld und das Problem einer sprachwissenschaftlichen Fundierung der Frametheorie. In: Peter Rolf Lutzeier (ed.), 163-174.

Lanham, Len
1985 The perception and evaluation of varieties of English in South African society. In: Sidney Greenbaum (ed.), 149-162.
1996 A history of English in South Africa. In: Vivian de Klerk (ed.), 19-34.

Lass, Roger
1985 South African English. In: Raj Mesthrie (ed.), 89-106.

Lehrer, Adrienne
1993 Semantic fields and frames: are they alternatives? In: Peter Rolf Lutzeier (ed.), 149-162.

Lutzeier, Peter Rolf
1993 Wortfelder als kognitive Orientierungspunkte? In: Peter Rolf Lutzeier (ed.), 203-214.

Lutzeier, Peter Rolf (ed.)
1993 *Studien zur Wortfeldtheorie. Studies in lexical field theory.* Tübingen: Niemeyer.

Mesthrie, Raj
1990 *Lexicon of South African Indian English.* Leeds: Peepal Tree Press.
1992 *English in language shift: the history, structure and sociolinguistics of South African Indian English.* Cambridge: Cambridge University Press.

Mesthrie, Raj (ed.)
1985 *Language and social history: studies in South African sociolinguistics.* Cape Town/Johannesburg: David Philip.

Müller, Robert
1993 Wortfeldtheorie und kognitive Psychologie. In: Peter Rolf Lutzeier (ed.), 215-228.

Peeters, Bert
1991 More about axiological fields. *Canadian Journal of Linguistics* 36 (2): 113-136.
1993 Conceptual axiology and axiological fields. In: Peter Rolf Lutzeier (ed.), 175-183.

Sansome, R.
1986 Connotation and lexical field analysis. *Cahiers de Lexicologie* 49: 13-33.

Schmid, Hans-Jörg
1993 Cottage and co.: can the theory of word-fields do the job? In: Peter Rolf Lutzeier (ed.), 107-120.

Schwarze, Christoph
1985 Léxique et compréhension textuelle, *Sonderforschungsbereich* 99 No. 12, University of Constance.

Silva, Penny
1996 Lexicography in South African English. In: Vivian De Klerk (ed.), 191-210.

Wotjak, Gerd
1993 Semantische Makrostrukturbeschreibung (lexikalisch-semantische Felder) und (enzyklopädische) Wissensrepräsentation. In: Peter Rolf Lutzeier (ed.), 121-136.

Perceived and real differences between men's and women's spellings of the early to mid-seventeenth century[1]

Margaret J.-M. Sönmez

1. Introduction

The main argument of this paper is that, in English at least, where there is variation in spelling there is also markedness, and this markedness by definition affects judgements. Both at the time and in our century commentators have remarked that seventeenth-century women's spelling performance is worse than men's, and a comparison of the spellings of a man and a woman are here used as a way of investigating what this "worse" means linguistically.

From an introductory survey of the sort of comments made about women's spellings, the discussion moves to an investigation of the methodological issues involved in comparing different texts of different lengths by different people. The results of a comparison of the spellings of Lady Brilliana Harley and of the Duke of Newcastle are then presented, followed by a look at what conclusions may be drawn from these issues, both in detail and in more general terms. Two main points of equal importance are emphasised: firstly that methodological rigor is of particular importance when we are dealing with complex material and testing received knowledge, and secondly that we should not base our investigations of perceptions of writing on the same models of language that are used in investigations of the production of writing. The results of the comparison combined with these warnings may be taken as preliminary suggestions for a theory of markedness in spelling.

2. Earlier comments about the spellings of seventeenth-century women

Seventeenth-century spellings show a great deal of variation. This has been commented upon by a number of scholars, and comments indicating that females spelt more erratically than males seem to have been unquestioningly accepted. Zachrisson (1913), for instance, stated that "Ladies are generally worse spellers than men, and also use more dialectal forms" (Zachrisson 1913: 43), where by "dialectal" he generally means non-standard (he uses this word very loosely throughout the book); and Wrenn ([1943] 1967) says he rejects "much of the curious spelling of Lady Margaret Hoby as merely the sort of thing one expects in a woman of good birth at the end of Elizabeth's reign" (Wrenn 1967: 147). Editors of women's letters and diaries from the Early Modern period often comment on their "bad" or even "terrible" spelling but usually add that this was normal for the female writers of the day.

There is plenty of evidence that Early Modern readers judged women's spellings in much the same way. As early as 1596, Coote undertakes

> to teach all my scholers ... the true orthography of any word truly pronounced ... and the same profit doe I offer vnto all other ... that now for want hereof are ashamed to write vnto their best friends: for which I haue heard many gentlewomen suffer much (Coote [1596] 1968).

And the first English Dictionary, Cawdrey's *A Table Alphabeticall* ([1604] 1976), places "ladies" and "gentlewomen" in the same category as "other unskillfull persons" (although perhaps more in terms of their vocabulary than of their spelling). Cockeram apparently wrote his (1623) *English Dictionarie* for "Ladies and Gentlewomen, young schollers, clerks, merchants, as also strangers of any Nation" but not for "gentlemen" (quoted in Görlach 1991: 150); Thomas Blount (1656) says that his *Glossographia* will profit "the more-knowing women and less-knowing men", and the equation of women with relatively uneducated men is continued into the eighteenth century, e.g. with J. K.'s (1702) *A New English Dictionary* designed for "young scholars, Tradesmen, Artificers, and the Female Sex, who would learn to spell truely". Examples of eighteenth century satire on women's lack of writing skills (from Steele and Swift) are given in Scragg (1974: 89).

Present-day scholars agree with the early dictionary and spelling-book writers in assigning these women's spellings to their lack of education (Scragg 1974: 89), although, since men were not taught English spelling either[2], it seems more accurate to talk of a difference in education and social role. Scragg notes that Elizabeth I, "in classical borrowings, where her education gave her an established spelling to follow in Latin, ... spells well" (Scragg 1974: 69)[3].

It should be noted that most women's writings were private and therefore not yet or, at least, less susceptible to standardisation forces. There is growing evidence that spellings could quite sensitively reflect the degree of publicness of their texts, with the more private texts showing less standardised spellings. This is not only the case with, for instance, the spellings of a writer's draft, his secretary's copy, and the printed version of the same text[4], but also within an individual's own productions: Görlach, while stating that by 1700 the spelling was largely fixed, notes that "spelling in private letters, diaries and [a few other texts] remains quite variable until the end of the EModE Period" (Görlach 1991: 46); according to Smith what he calls "colourless", that is, non-standardised but not dialectally distinctive, spellings "survived for a long time, especially in private letters (see for instance, the private as opposed to the public usage of Dr. Johnson in the eighteenth century ...)" (Smith 1996: 76, reporting Osselton's (1984) findings). Work on the *Helsinki Corpus*, for example as reported by Nevalainen (1997)[5], provides further evidence of this type of variation in spelling styles. So we should not be surprised if women's spellings look less standardised than men's when we are most frequently exposed to comparisons between female private writings and male public writings. This is not only the case generally with what is available in print, but more explicitly what is found in handbooks. In Freeborn's (1992) course book, for instance, sections from a woman's letters

(Parry (ed.) n.d.) to her fiancé are shown sandwiched between sections of John Evelyn's *Diary* (remember that Evelyn wrote a proposal for spelling reform in 1664), and Milton's *Paradise Lost* (with "activities" concerning Early Modern spelling based on one of Dryden's essays)[6]. Things are not much fairer in Burnley's "source book", where a letter of Brilliana Harley's is placed between some of Donne's poems and *Meditation* 17 and, again, *Paradise Lost*. We should also note that these passages are all taken from printed sources, of very different dates (Burnley takes the Harley letter from Lewis's (1854) edition, Donne's *Meditation* from the (1627) edition of *Devotions*, and the Milton is given in a facsimile of a seventeenth-century printing, but from which edition we are not told). In brief, since there are very few public writings written by women during this period, we are almost bound to be comparing very different types of texts when we compare women's and men's Early Modern English writings.

It is possible, then, that what has been labelled a difference between men and women's spelling habits is more a difference between text types. Indeed, detailed investigation of the manuscripts of male writers from this period repeatedly reveal more irregular spellings than we are led to expect by our first impressions and by the assertions of earlier commentators. This, too, has a long history, with William Camden in 1605 replying to a Welsh critic of English spelling practices that

> it hath beene seene where tenne English writing the same sentence, have all so concurred, that among them all there hath beene no other difference, than the adding, or omiting once or twice of our silent E, in the end of some wordes (*Remaines Concerning Britain*, quoted in Bolton (1966: 33), Scragg (1974: 70)).

This is, of course, a completely inaccurate claim.

As for present-day scholars, I can recognise the men's spellings I have studied neither in Scragg's statement that spelling was finally fixed around 1650 nor in Görlach's descriptions of seventeenth-century spellings, although this may be in part due to their concentration on printed or "professional" spellings, even when these are not specified, and I am not the only one to have been surprised by the realities of men's spellings from the period, as the comments of numerous editors evince[7].

It may be thought that our present-day conventions which, on the whole, demand a single spelling only for each word, lead all other spellings to look equally wrong in our eyes. Some, however, undoubtedly look more wrong than others. It seems that there is some sort of scale of markedness in our perceptions of non-standard spellings.

In many cases, the spellings found in the writings of women from the seventeenth century seem to be examples of the more wrong ones, whereas those found in their male contemporaries' writings seem more normal. Whether this is due to some social or educational differences between men and women cannot easily be ascertained, but given the different types of texts we are exposed to, as explained above, it seems that the subject needs considerably more research before we can make the sort of confident assertions that our predecessors put forth. We may also question whether these women's spellings are really worse than those of the men, or whether we are too readily accepting received knowledge without scrutiny: it is possible that women's spellings from this period are seen as worse than men's largely because we have so often been told that they are, and we tend to find only what we are looking for. Furthermore, precisely in what way these spellings are worse has never been specified: if there is a difference between the spellings of the two sexes, what sort of a difference is it?

A comparison between the spellings of a "bad" female speller and those of a "normal" male speller from the same period may, then, tell us if there are any substantial differences between them and also take us some way into a theory of markedness in spelling. From our own present-day and post-standardised viewpoints it may indicate a level of the standardisation process which, for spelling[8], has hardly been examined at all – again, that of markedness, but here the idea that development of a scale of markedness is concomitant with development of a doctrine of correctness (Early Modern writers also thought that women spelt worse than men). It should also explain why expectations of seventeenth-century spellings can be so frequently and so far off the mark.

3. The comparison

3.1. Materials

A comparison between the spellings found in manuscript writings of Lady Brilliana Harley (1600-1643) and of William Cavendish, 1st Duke of Newcastle (1592-1676) is here reported. The Harley manuscripts are 115 autograph letters to family members (letters from Lady Brilliana Harley in other hands are not included here), dating between 1623 and 1643[9]. The Newcastle manuscripts are draft writings about horsemanship, dated between 1659 and 1660, and later printed (1667 as *A New Method and Extraordinary Invention to Dress Horses*). Parts of these manuscripts in the hand of an amanuensis have been ignored in this comparison.

The text types here are not strictly comparable, although both come from the "informal" end of a formality scale[10]. Socially, however, the subjects are well suited. Although the Harley letters were written between 30 and 15 years before the Newcastle manuscripts, the fact that the writers were born within 8 years of each other means that they probably developed their spelling habits at almost the same time[11], and both writers are aristocrats from a court background. They are both well known to historians of the period, and Lady Brilliana Harley is also known to historians of the language, amongst whom she has the reputation of being a particularly "wild" speller (Roger Lass, personal communication). As we have seen, her spellings have been used as examples of "naive" spellings from the period, although other women writers of the period seem to display similar numbers and varieties of spellings (see e.g. the *Memoirs of the Verney Family* (1925) (especially the spellings of Lady Rich), the letters of Mrs. Basire (in Basire 1831), and *The Private Diarie of Elizabeth Viscountess Mordaunt 1656-1678* (Mordaunt 1856)). The Newcastle manuscripts are not known to linguists, and checking his spellings against other male writers of the period leads me to believe that his spellings are no more irregular than those of many of his contemporaries (e.g. Isaac Basire, born 1607, Sir William Petty[12], contemporary of John Evelyn 1620-1706, Henry Teonge ?-1679)[13], although it seems that Needham (a medievalist) was struck by Newcastle's "peculiar spellings and graphic habits" when he transcribed "A Pleasant & Merrye Humor off a Roge" for his Welbeck Miscellany in 1933 (see Malone Society (1996: xiv, note 20).).

3.2. Methodological introduction to comparisons

There are many different ways in which one could carry out this comparison along quantitative lines, and examples of a variety of them will be given here in order to investigate which are the most revealing. The paper then moves on to the analyses themselves, which are organised qualitatively in terms of various linguistically representative aspects of spelling, and quantitatively analysed within these categories. Mostly items which fit into already existing discussions on Early Modern English spellings have been selected for analysis. As most of this existing material concentrates on what are called the phonetic aspects of spelling, some examples of this will be examined before analysing the spellings from a morphological and etymological point of view and finally from the less-investigated angle of the appearance of the non-Present-day English spellings. In this way the roles of ear, mind (lexicon) and eye in marked and unmarked spellings will have been examined, albeit briefly. The results will then be summarised before attempting to draw conclusions. An adequate explanation, even of these few sample comparisons, will include a fair amount of overlapping between these categories and other factors.

Throughout this paper the term "non-Present-day English" spellings is used in preference to "non-standard" spellings since what was or was not perceived as standard in the seventeenth century has not been ascertained and was different from our views now.

The Newcastle text (Cavendish 1667) is more than four times the length of the Harley text (Harley 1623-1643)[14], and with such a discrepancy of size it is possible to compare the texts in ways which might yield misleading results. Clearly we should choose one method of comparison and stick to it.

3.2.1. The simplest method is to ask who shows the greatest number of irregular spellings. This can be done either on a word-by-word basis, or on the basis of total vocabulary divided by number of words. The first method is advocated by Görlach as a way of dating texts. In this case, where "the number of alternative spellings for the same words" (Görlach 1991: 49) are counted, difficulties in comparisons may arise over the selection of appropriate words (not only appropriate, but equally represented in both texts), and the resulting figures do not lead to any very precise conclusions.

The second way of counting non-Present-day English spellings leads us to more numerically precise conclusions which may easily be compared, but tells us nothing about the distribution of such spellings. That is, out of two texts showing similar averages, one may show very many spellings for some words but have fixed spellings for the rest, whereas the other may show a small number of alternative spellings for all words. Applying these types of comparison to sample words from our texts gives results which cannot be usefully interpreted, as shown in figure 1.

Choosing frequent words (somewhat arbitrarily defined here as more than 25 occurrences in both texts), so that each text has equal opportunity for showing as many spellings of the words as it may contain, and just looking at words beginning in A, we see that Harley has more irregular spellings than Newcastle in the words *about* (Harley 5 different spellings, Newcastle 3), *are* (Harley 3, Newcastle 2), and *as* (Harley 2, Newcastle 1); that the words *all* (1 spelling each) and *am* (2 spellings each) show the man and the woman to be equally irregular spellers, whereas *again* (Harley 2, Newcastle 9), *an* (Harley 1, Newcastle 2), *and* (Harley 1, Newcastle 5), and *at* (Harley 1, Newcastle 2) show Newcastle as having more irregular spellings than Harley. Overall, Newcastle with 18 different spellings shows more words with irregular spellings than Harley with 16. The number of Newcastle's spellings here is 1.125 times greater than that of Harley's, not a very significant difference.

	Harley		Newcastle	
about	about	7	about	1
	a bout	6	aboute	25
	aboute	4	a boute	35
	a boute	10		
	a bowte	1		
are	ar	1	ar	1
	are	215	are	555
	eare	1		
as	aas	1	as	1272
	as	227		
all	all	176	all	815
am	am	102	am	6
	ame	2	ame	24
an	an	38	an	37
and	and	1229	an	2
			an	1
			and	1
			ande	356
at	at	163	at	3
			att	427
Number of frequent <a-> words here		8		8
Number of different spellings		16		18
Average number of spellings per frequent <a-> word		2.0		2.2

Figure 1. Irregular spellings in frequent <a-> words

A further and simple calculation based on the same data can give contrary results: if we divide the number of different spellings (excluding inflectional variants) by the number of vocabulary items the results are: Harley (201 spellings in a vocabulary of 118 =) 1.70 spellings per word on average, Newcastle (279 spellings in a vocabulary of 166 =) 1.68 spellings per word on average. On this calculation, Newcastle comes out as slightly (but only very slightly) the more regular speller (Harley's average is 1.01 times greater than Newcastle's).

3.2.2. Another way of using numbers to compare spellings is to count the number of invariably spelt words, and to declare this as some sort of index of standardisation or, at least, of regularisation. Here, however, we are again faced with problems of selection: clearly, we should ignore words appearing only once in the text, but what about words which occur twice only, or three times? And what about those words spelt invariably 99.6% of the time, as in Harley's spellings of *as* and Newcastle's spellings of *are* – do they not count for something? How can we tell an error from a "genuine" spelling irregularity? More importantly, under this calculation text length and vocabulary range will strongly affect the results. This method should therefore be used only in comparisons of different versions of the same text.

3.2.3. In order to draw linguistically generalisable conclusions from a spelling analysis it is useful to inspect the spellings of certain classes of words, and this may also be done on a comparative basis. Thus, in the research done here, we show spellings of words belonging to certain phonetic or morphological categories and try to discover whether there are more irregularities in the spellings of one text than of the other within this selected population of words. Here we may decide either to calculate the frequency of these non-Present-day English spellings in the whole text, or we may count all spellings of the selected words and calculate the frequency of non-Present-day English spellings within the smaller world of that group of words. These two calculations can provide very different results, again because of discrepancies in text length and vocabulary range; see for instance what happens when we compare the frequencies of non-Present-day English spellings of {-sion} according to the whole text or according to the sub-set (population) of all Present-day English {-sion} words found in the text (figure 2).

This alerts us to the fact that we are not comparing like with like, and should seek some way of standardising the results. Established tests such as chi-square and the calculations made available by SPSS, for instance, are not usable where there is no constant against which to correlate variables; percentages, whether expressed as such or as decimal figures, do not display all the information required, since it is not always obvious which is the greater, X% of a text 36,000 words long or Y% of a text 167,000 words long. Worse still, there may be large discrepancies between percentages based upon number of features per number of words in the text (the universe) and those based upon number of (the same) features per number of words in which a feature could be or was found (the selected population).[15]

	Harley	Newcastle	
number of non-Present-day English spellings	21	10	Harley 2.1 times more non-Present-day English spellings than Newcastle
frequency in universe (whole text)	1 per 1724 words or 0.0588%	1 per 16,717 words or 0.00598%	Harley 9.70 more frequent non-Present-day English spellings than Newcastle
frequency in population (all {-sion} words)	(21 out of 22) 1 per 1.05 words or 95.45%	(10 out of 13) 1 per 1.3 words or 76.92%	Harley 1.24 times more frequent non- Present-day English spellings

Z test (calculated on population figures):
$Z = 1.64$ at $\alpha = 0.05$, $Z_{crit} = 1.65$, i.e. insignificant difference.

Figure 2. Calculating ratios. Sample case; {-sion} spellings

Instead, we may ask whether the difference between the two frequencies (i.e. the difference between two proportions) is significant or not. For this we can apply a fairly simple test known as the Z-test[16]. Going back to our {-sion} words, then, we may ask if there is any significance in the difference between Harley's 21 non-Present-day English spellings out of 22 and Newcastle's 10 out of 13. Z-test calculations here give us a Z value of 1.64 which, compared with the critical Z value of 1.65 ($\alpha = 0.05$) tells us that it is a borderline case which, under most circumstances would be assessed as insignificant. This works well where a moderate to high incidence of the feature under investigation is present, but where either text shows zero, very low, or 100% incidence it is unusable (which facts, unfortunately, frequently rendered it redundant in the work reported here). These limitations, by the way, also encourage us to calculate percentages according to the smaller populations wherever possible, in order to gain higher incidences. The important thing is to be consistent, at least within individual comparisons of particular features, and to have some way of normalising the results so that all the comparisons may be seen together in the final stages of analysis.

Normalising to the nearest figure that gives full numbers (not those misleading decimals) is usually done by expressing incidence per set number of words, e.g. incidence per ten or hundred thousand words, and this is a good way of showing relative frequencies, but often hard to interpret in cases of low or close incidences, and unrevealing in terms of perceptual force (do we really notice a difference between 1 in ten thousand and 10 in ten thousand, or between 1,000 in ten thousand and 1,500 in ten thousand?). Since I am particularly interested in perceptual force, I have normalised the other way round, that is, frequency is expressed in terms of one incident of the spelling feature per X number of words. These figures may be more meaningful to the non-statistician who knows that one word per, say, 300 is equivalent to more than one per normal modern printed page.

As for the first two methods discussed, they show that we should hesitate before accepting the comments of earlier scholars as true indications of spelling irregularity. Their usual methods of calculation rely upon somewhat randomly selected words, pay attention only to the irregular spellings[17], and furthermore include no reference to the size of the sample text. They can provide very useful indications of present-day attitudes to irregular spellings (which non-Present-day English spellings are selected for comment and which are not makes a long study on its own), but are neither precise nor accurate analyses of the spelling habits of any of their subjects.

In the comparisons reported here many of the categories involved are so large that the sub-set to which they belong is almost as large as the whole text, or is open (e.g. the group of words whose non-Present-day English spellings may involve a missing vowel letter), other categories give results where one text shows 100% or 0% non-

Present-day English spellings. This means that the only constant index through which to compare results of the different comparisons is the frequency within the whole text as described earlier.

3.3. The comparisons

3.3.1. The ear: phonetic spellings[18]

Wyld (1914, 1920) uses selected spellings of Lady Brilliana Harley, among those of many other writers from the period, as evidence for pronunciation, and this is very much the way that Burnley uses her writing in his more recent handbook. He says that her "spelling system is rather inconsistent and idiosyncratic, confusing standard forms with the writer's own phonetic spellings" (Burnley 1992: 256). The comparisons which follow are designed to test whether her non-Present-day English spellings are more "phonetic" than Newcastle's, and if so, could these types of spellings account for the perceived differences between men's and women's spellings?

Words or parts of words which have already been much discussed by scholars seeking pronunciation evidence from spellings were selected for these purposes, and the results are set out in figure 3. This shows phonetic spellings being fairly equally distributed between the two texts.

If Harley's spellings provide us with more evidence of rhoticism (or loss of rhoticism?) than Newcastle's, for example in spellings such as <bettr> (*better*), <gareded> (*guarded*), <coutesy> (*courtesy*) [Harley], <disordes> (*disorders*), <Prtia> (*Persia*) [Newcastle], then Newcastle gives us strong evidence that he pronounced Present-day English RP /U/ and /A/ words with the still unchanged Northern long /u/, for example in spellings like <acoustum> (*accustom*), <coume> (*come*), and <roume> (*room*) [Newcastle, there are no examples in Harley], while the Harley spellings tell us little about her pronunciation of such words.[19] In both these cases the differences between frequencies are extreme enough to make further numerical tests unnecessary.

feature	Harley	Newcastle	relative frequency of non-Pres-E spellings
rhoticism	40 spellings, 1 per 905	6 spellings, 1 per 27,862	H 30.8 times more frequent
"northern" /u/	1 sp., 1 per 36,205	262 sps, 1 per 638	N 56.7 times more frequent
<ar> for Present-day English <er>	158 sps, 1 per 229	3 sps, 1 per 55,725	H 243 times more frequent
<er> for Present-day English <ar>	none	68 sps, 1 per 2,458	N only
<i> for Present-day English <e>	69 sps, 1 per 525	116 sps, 1 per 1441	H 2.74 times more frequent
<e> for Present-day English <i>	132 sps, 1 per 274	351 sps, 1 per 476	H 1.73 times more frequent
Present-day English <ea>	46 sps, 1 per 787	312 sps, 1 per 536	N 1.47 times more frequent
word-final dentals	18 sps, 1 per 2011	340 sps, 1 per 492	N 4.09 times more frequent
averages	464 sps, 1 per 78	1,459 sps, 1 per 115	H 1.47 times more frequent

Figure 3. Phonetic spellings

This pattern of one writer but not the other showing phonetically explicable non-Present-day English spellings in one category of words, and the other writer doing the same for another category of words continues: Harley shows a greater tendency towards <ar> spellings of Present-day English stressed <er> words in words like *certain, servant*, towards <i> spellings of certain Present-day English <e> (for example in *employ, despair,* and *pretty*), and towards <e> spellings of Present-day English <i> (as in *cabinet* and *deliver*, for instance), while Newcastle shows a higher frequency of non-Present-day English spellings in words spelt <ea> today (such as *treason*) and in words where his spellings indicate devoicing or loss of final dental sounds (for example <laffte> for *laughed*, <forwar> for *forward* [Newcastle], <papis> (*papist*) [Harley]).

Looking at these in greater detail, Harley displays <ar> spellings in 158 out of 312 Present-day English <er> words (or 1 per 229 words of text) and Newcastle only 3 out of 157 such words (or 1 per 55,725 words). The Z-test shows this to be a significant difference (Z=10.846). As for <i>/<e> alternations, we can see that <i> for Present-day English <e> spellings are nearly 3 times more frequent, and <e> for <i> nearly twice as frequent in Harley than in Newcastle. The opposite is true with Present-day English <ea> spellings, however, where Newcastle shows a significantly greater proportion of non-Present-day English spellings than Harley[20].

Here, both texts show some <e> spellings of Present-day English <ea>, Newcastle many more than Harley, and in some cases also <ee> spellings. Harley shows some reverse spellings of the <ea> for the Present-day English <e> type, but neither of them show significant numbers of <ea> for Present-day English <ee> spellings. Calculated frequencies of non-Present-day English spellings for words which now take <ea> reveal that Newcastle shows 313 non-Present-day English spellings out of 2295, or 13.6%, and Harley shows 46 out of 961, or 4.79%. The Z-test confirms that this difference is significant at $\alpha = 0.05$ (Z = 7.34, Z_{crit} = 1.65)[21].

Finally, in the case of indications of devoicing or loss of word-final dentals, we find that Newcastle shows nearly 19 times as many such non-Present-day English spellings than Harley, but we cannot apply the Z-test because there is no limit to the sizes of the populations from which percentages could be calculated. Frequencies per whole text are one in every 2,011 words in Harley and one in every 492 words in Newcastle, a noticeable difference.

In total we come across these phonetic spellings 1.47 times more frequently in Harley than in Newcastle, which, over such long texts, may not be a significant figure (the Z-test, as explained earlier, is not feasible for these figures) and is at any rate too small to explain a noticeable difference in spelling styles.

These mixed results, then, do not explain why Harley's spellings look less standardised than Newcastle's. Indeed, my impressions are that it is precisely the opposite sort of spellings, the ones which are phonetically hard to interpret, which seem oddest to us. Staying, then, in the realm of the ear, but here in the realm of the confused ear, let us turn to phonetically obscure, non-Present-day English spellings.

3.3.2. The confused ear: phonetically obscure spellings [22]

By this are meant spellings where sections of the most lexically significant part of the word have been left out or spelt in a way very unrelated to that word's pronunciation or Present-day English spelling. Since, on an assumption that I have not the authority to make, I take it that in English stress is connected with perceptual salience[23], I have selected spellings in which stressed sections are obscured. As stress in English is syllabic and largely centred on vowel sounds ("a stressed syllable frequently has a longer vowel" Ladefoged (1982: 104)), I have focused this part of the comparison on spellings of words where the letters related to syllable peaks are missing. The results are shown in figure 4.

Not many such words were found, but more in Harley than in Newcastle. Harley has 52, and Newcastle 9. With such low incidences, the frequencies per whole text are necessarily very low and Z-test calculations virtually impossible; but with a frequency more than 26 times greater Harley's higher proportion of these spellings is almost certainly numerically significant.

The texts also show a number of words where vowel letters from unstressed syllables are missing (Harley 59, Newcastle 32) and again we find a difference in frequency (Harley nearly 9 times more frequent than Newcastle), which must be significant, although the numbers are again very low and one may question the strength of this feature's perceptual effect.

One aspect of Harley's spellings which is quite noticeable is that of vowel letter doubling or clustering where a single vowel is expected both according to Present-day English conventions and according to the general (but not invariable) rule that short vowel sounds are represented in writing by single vowel letters. We find in Harley spellings like <beeg> for *beg*, <geet> for *get*, and <heald> for *held*[24]. Some doubling is also occasionally found in Newcastle

(<doon> for *done*, <eende> for *end*), but more common are the <ou> for Present-day English <o> spellings that were earlier seen as a dialect-related example of his "pronunciation" spellings. The figures for all cases of two vowels where Present-day English has only one representing a short vowel sound are Harley 317, Newcastle 244, which give frequencies within the whole texts of 1 per 114 words in Harley and 1 per 685 words in Newcastle. This, too, is probably a significant difference in frequency, and although one cannot be more than speculative about this it seems likely that there are enough instances in the Harley text (more than 2 per printed page) for the spelling feature to be more noticeable here than in the Newcastle writings (less than 1 per 2 printed pages).

	Harley		Newcastle		relative frequency
	no. of instances	frequency	no. of instances	frequency	
missing stressed syllable peaks	52	1 per 696	9	1 per 18,575	H 26.7 times more frequent
vowel letter doubling/ clustering	317	1 per 114	244	1 per 685	H 6 times more frequent
transposition of letters	194	1 per 187	22 words	1 per 7,599	H 40.6 times more frequent
averages	188	1 per 193	92	1 per 1,817	H 9.4 times more frequent

Figure 4. Phonetically obscured spelling

Transposition of letters can also result in phonetically obscure spellings, and as this is another feature of Harley's spellings that seemed unusual to me I have compared her transposition habits with those of Newcastle with the following results:

Harley 194 (1 per 187 words), Newcastle 22 (1 per 7,599 words).

That is, Harley shows metathesis 41 times more frequently, surely numerically as well as perceptually a significant difference.

3.3.3. The mind: derivational morphology (morphology and etymology)

If we look at the spellings of English derivational suffixes we are able to examine two things at the same time: whether the speller treats smaller-than-word units of meaning in a regular way, thus indicating a morphological level of spelling understanding, and whether the speller shows awareness of etymology (since many of these suffixes come from classical roots). Here one may expect the difference in male and female education to show up, with Newcastle showing more etymologically correct spellings than Harley.

Looking at the spellings of {com-}, {pre-}, {-able}, {-ible}, {-ic}, {-ify}, {-ity}, {-sion} and {-tion} I obtained some very strong results, but again not always as expected. These are set out in figure 5, in 3 groups: affixes where Harley shows more non-Present-day English spellings than Newcastle, affixes where Newcastle shows more non-Present-day English spellings than Harley, and affixes (in fact just one) where the difference is negligible or non-existent.

affix	Harley Pres-E spellings	Harley non-Pres-E spelling and frequ. in whole text	Newcastle Pres-E spellings	Newcastle non-Pres-E spellings and frequ. in whole text	relative frequency of non-Pres-E spellings
Harley more than Newcastle					
{-able}	none	63, 1 per 575	42	none	H more frequent
{-ible}	none	2, 1 per 18,125	98	1, 1 per 16,717	N 1.1 times more frequ.
{pre-}	109	2, 1 per 18,125	61	none	H more frequent
{-sion}	1	21 or 1 per 1,724	3	10 or 1 per 16,717	H 9.7 times more frequ.

Newcastle more than Harley					
{com-}	149	14 or 1 per 2,586	25	18 or 1 per 9,288	H 3.6 times more frequ.
{-ify}	1	none	none	13 or 1 per 12,860	N more frequent
{-ity}	15	2 or 1 per 18,102	none	93 or 1 per 1,798	N 10.1 times more frequ.ent
{-tion}	57	15 or 1 per 2,414	280	215 or 1 per 776	N 3.1 times more frequ.
{-ic}	none	2 or 1 per 18,103	none	7 or 1 per 23,882	H 1.3 times more frequ.

Figure 5. Morphology and etymology – affixes

From those analysed, affixes which were spelt with non-Present-day English spellings significantly more frequently by Harley than by Newcastle included two related indisputable cases: {-able} and the related suffix {-ible}. On their own the figures for {-ible} are not convincing, but they are consistent with the writers' spelling habits in the related {-able}. We may add to these Harley's 2 non-Present-day English spellings of {pre-}, where Newcastle spelt this affix <pre> in all cases, but this is fairly weak evidence.

The spellings of {-sion} have already been seen as an example of the different ways we may make numerical comparisons between the spellings of these texts, and as you will recall the results of these computations were that there is an almost insignificant difference between the proportions of non-Present-day English spellings of this suffix in the texts, with Harley showing only a slightly higher frequency than Newcastle.

Newcastle shows significantly more frequent use of non-Present-day English spellings in the affixes {com-}, {-ify}, {-ity}, and {-tion}. We can see this particularly clearly with Newcastle's 100% use of non-Present-day English spellings of {-ity} (compared with Harley's 17, or 11.76% non-Present-day English spellings of this item), and again with Newcastle's 215 (43.43%) non-Present-day English spellings of {-tion} compared with Harley's 15 (10.83%)[25]. With 18 (41.9%) non-Present-day English spellings as compared to

Harley's 14 (8.6%) the difference in their spellings of {com-} is also very significant (Z=5.238). Newcastle again shows 100% non-Present-day English usage in his spellings of {-ify} (13 occurrences). Harley's spellings here are 100% orthodox, but since this impressive percentage in fact relates to only one word, we cannot use this as evidence on its own.

One affix, {-ic} was spelt with 100% non-Present-day English spellings in both texts, but occurred only rarely (4 times in Harley, 7 times in Newcastle).

Discussions of etymology in Early Modern English spellings more usually involve that group of words which were given, at that period, newly "etymologised" spellings. Consistently "new" (Present-day English) spellings of these words may be seen as evidence of consciously learned spellings. In order to see if this approach provided clearer results than the affixes had done, a list of eight well known such words (*advantage, author, describe, doubt, hospital, merchant, perfect, victual*) was taken from Görlach (1991: 56-57) and checked from both texts. Only the words *advantage, authority* (included as probably analogous to *author*, which is only found in Newcastle), *doubt* and *perfect(ly)* were present in both texts, and (apart from Newcastle's 161 instances of *perfect*) incidences were low. No different tendencies in the spellings of these words was found to exist between the Harley and Newcastle texts, or at least not when the words are treated as a group. Individually it was found that whereas both Harley and Newcastle spelt all occurrences of *advantage* with <ad-> and all *author*-words with <aught-> (the following vowel letter was either <e> or <o>), Harley never included a <b> in *doubt* (eight occurrences of this word in her text), whereas Newcastle usually did (one spelling without <b> and 17 with).

On the other hand, Harley spelt *perfect-* with <c> in all four instances of this word, whereas Newcastle on two occasions used the older, <c>-less form; this finding is not strong, however, because on all of 159 other occasions Newcastle spelt the word with <c>. Looking at the words from Görlach's list as a whole, and not considering whether or not they are found in both texts, it was found that Harley showed three of these words occasionally spelt in unetymologised form (*authority, doubt, victuals*) and Newcastle showed four of these words occasionally spelt in unetymologised form (*author-, doubt, merchant, perfect*). These are very weak and inconclusive results.

3.3.4. The eye: word shape

Both Harley and Newcastle show a number of cases of metanalysis, or reassignment of word boundaries. These often but not always occur where the first letter of the conventionally spelt word is <a>. I have written them all down as illustrations (figure 6 a), because their perceptual effect is, after all, visual and because the range of words thus treated is greater than rare discussions of this phenomenon indicate.

It may be noted, for instance, that Newcastle splits both common native words such as *above* and common but foreign words such as *l'étoile* and *l'endormi*. Apart from Harley's <o bedience>, <sater day>, <Worek sheere> (*Warwickshire*), <yester day> and Newcastle's <Lan Dormye> (*L'endormi*) all these words have been written so that their first parts are identical with an existing word, either in English or in French, but the second parts are frequently non-words. I wonder what the first-time reader of these spellings makes of Harley's <in a bell> (= *enable*) and, harder still, <a schcoler> (= *ash colour*). Adding up the figures tells us that Harley shows 3.4 times more frequent non-Present-day English spellings of this type than Newcastle.

Harley	Newcastle
a bates (1), *a bell* (2), *a biding* (2), *a bout* (6) *a boute* (10) *a bowte* (1), *a brode* (2), *a bundance* (1), *a bused* (1), [*a clooke* (1), *a colke* (1)], *a cording* (5), *a count* (2), *a counte* (1), *a cused* (1), *a fraid* (2) *a fraide* (4) *a fride* (1), *a gaine* (1), *a gainst* (5), *a goo* (1), *a greed* (1), *all most* (3), *all ways* (1), *a lone* (1), *a long* (1), *a Men* (1), *a*	*a bate* (1), *a bou* (1), *a boue* (20), *a boute* (35), *a brode* (1), *a bundance* (6), *a busde* (1), *a doe* (5), *a frayde* (1), *a gainste* (1), *a gaynste* (10), *a gayne* (16), *a gen* (21), *a gainste* (1), *a gaynste* (10), *a gilitye* (1), *a goe* (3), *a juste* (2), *a justs* (1), *a like* (5), *a lone* (5), *a longe* (1), *all wayes* (1), *a miss* (1), *a peece* (6), *a peer* (5), *a*

mongst (2), *a pale* (1), *a peare* (2), *a pease* (1), *apointed* (3), *a prehention* (1), *a proching* (1), *a proue* (1), *a proufe* (3), [*a purpos* (1), *a right* (1)], *a leven* (1), *a schcoler* (1), *a Shamed* (1), *a surance* (1), *a tempte* (1), *a way* (7), *a waye* (1), *be caus* (2), *be come* (1), *for bide* (2), *for bides* (1), *for giue* (1), *for goot* (1), *in abell* (2), *in a bell* (1), *in Cline* (1), *in Closed* (10), *in Conuenience* (1), *in Coragment* (1), *in deede* (2), *in ioy* (1), *in quired* (1), *in to* (1), *in treete* (1), *o bedience* (1), *sater day* (1), *them selfes* (1), *to day* (5), *to geather* (4), *to morowe* (2), *to morrow* (5), *to morrowe* (1), *under goo* (3), *under rwite* (1), *worek sheere*, *wheare of* (1), *whear in* (1), *will coeme* (1), *yester day* (5)

peerde (1), *a peers* (2), *a propriate* (1), *a shurde* (1), *a ssure* (1), *a stride* (2), *a waye* (13), *a pewie* (1), *a pewye* (8), *a puie* (1), *La mie* (1), *La mour* (1), *de dans* (4), *de vant* (2), *Le Toyle* (1), *Lan Dormye* (1)

Total: 150 or 1 per 241 words in text
H shows 3.4 times more frequent metanalysis than N

Total: 202 or 1 per 827 words in text

Figure 6 a. Metanalysis
The following compounds are not included: *another, any/every/someone, any/every/something, everyday, gentleman, workman, any/every/somebody, her/him/my/yourself,* and items shown in square brackets were not included in the totals.

Studies of children learning to read and write and of the reading tactics of fluent adult readers allow the conclusion that the beginnings of words are perceptually more important than the middles or ends (Huxford, Terrell, and Bradley 1992: 160; Beauvillain 1996). Although some studies indicate that they are not favoured by young learners of reading, the very first letter seems to hold a special place, perceptually, for adult readers (Ehri 1980: 333), and prefixes have recently been shown (Beauvillain 1996: 815) to be more salient than suffixes for fluent adult readers. I therefore looked at all the words in which the first letter was not that found in Present-day English spelling and significant results were obtained, with Harley showing this type of non-Present-day English spelling two times more frequently than Newcastle (the details are given in figure 6 b.).

Harley	Newcastle	relative frequency
165 or 1 per 219 words	353 or 1 per 474 words	Harley 2.2 times more frequent

Figure 6 b. "Wrong" first letter of word

As far as prefixes are concerned, we saw that {pre-} showed no significant spelling difference between texts, which is also the case with {em-} and {en-}, and that {com-}, while being more frequently "misspelt" by Newcastle within the subset of all {com-} words, was nevertheless found to have more than three times more frequent non-Present-day English spellings in Harley when calculated according to the whole texts.

4. Results and discussion

4.1. Results

A summary of the numerical results of all the comparisons reported here is presented in figure 7.

feature	Harley more non-pres-E spellings than Newcastle	equal, negligible or not calculable difference	Newcastle more non-pres-E spellings than Harley
1. "ear"			
/r/	30.8 x more freq.		
short /u/			262 x more freq.
<ar> for PresE <er>	243 x more freq.		
<er> for PresE <ar>		N = 68, H = 0	
<i> for PresE <e>	2.74 x more freq.		
<e> for PresE <i>	1.73 x more freq.		
PresE <ea>			1.5 x more freq.
word-final dentals			4.1 x more freq.

2. phonetically obscure			
strong syllable peaks	26.7 x more freq.		
VV for V	6 x more frequent		
transposition	40.6 x more freq.		
3. "mind"			
-able		H = 63, N = 0	
-ible		H = 2, N = 0	
pre-		neg	
-sion	9.7 x more frequent		
-ity	10.1 x more frequent		
-tion (incl. macrons)			3.1 x more frequent
-tion (excl. macrons)	34.6 x more frequent		
com- per universe	3.6 x more frequent		
com- per population			4.6 x more frequent
-ify		neg. figures	
-ic		neg. figures	
etymological spellings		neg. figures	
4. "eye"			
metanalysis	3.4 x more freq.		
first letter	2.2 x more freq.		
Average times more frequent non-pres-E spellings	31.94		55.06

Figure 7. Results

The bottom row shows on average how much more frequent non-Present-day English spellings were in one text than in the other for each time where that text showed the highest frequency: Harley shows on average 32 times more frequent non-Present-day English spellings of some features than Newcastle, but Newcastle shows on average 55 times more frequent non-Present-day English spellings of other features. These figures provide further indication, if any were needed, of the fact that our perceptions of differences between the spelling competencies of the two writers are based upon something more than purely quantitative factors.

Looking at the distribution of categories, however, we see that there are more features showing more frequent non-Present-day English spellings in the Harley column (13) than in the Newcastle column (5) and, more importantly, that these are not evenly spread (this is clearer if you look at the Newcastle column on the right). Looking at it section by section we see that, whereas all occasions in which Newcastle shows more non-Present-day English spellings than Harley fall into the "ear" and "mind" sections, phonetically obscure spellings and those interfering with predominantly visual aspects of reading are all found to occur more frequently in Harley. These results show that this female speller does not use much more phonetic spellings than her male counterpart, and that any difference in their education is not clearly reflected in a difference between their spellings of classically based affixes or other etymological spellings.

4.2. Discussion

Non-Present-day English spellings which cause us most difficulty in reading tend to be those which are not easily decipherable through our usual strategies. Usual strategies for fluent adult readers seem to involve first of all a quick reference to our lexicon from the whole word[26], using context to disambiguate homonyms; if this fails to satisfy, then a closer analysis on the basis of possible phoneme/ grapheme correspondences comes into play; if simple phonetic correspondence does not work, then a more sophisticated approach involving analogy with other irregularly spelt words (either conventional such as *enough* etc., or based on familiarity with the individual text's irregular spellings) is used. At all stages the meaning context is used to narrow down the range of possible interpretations[27]. Most phonetic spellings, then, may be unorthodox, but are relatively simple to read precisely because they are phonetic. Spellings which are neither orthodox nor phonetic, on the other hand, can cause considerable delay in our reading, and even seem indecipherable.

A number of studies by cognitive psychologists and educationalists have concluded that readers develop "an orthographic image for words they have encountered frequently" (Crowder and Wagner 1992: 82) – or at least readers used to our standardised spelling show this. Other studies indicate that readers can learn new orthographic images quickly as they go along, rather as we familiarise ourselves with difficult handwriting (Brooks 1977 as quoted in Crowder and Wagner 1992: 83-85), and may even include their own frequent misspellings in their mental word-gallery, alongside the standard versions that they read in printed books (Campbell 1987 as quoted in Funnell 1992). Furthermore, it seems that reading is significantly disrupted by such purely visual changes as mixed typography (Brooks 1977 as quoted in Crowder and Wagner 1992: 83-85) and, I suggest, metanalysis[28]. These results indicate the importance of word appearance in readers' perceptual processes, but tell us that an altered word appearance found often enough will cease to disturb the reader. All of this fits in well with our results and with a theory of markedness in perceptions of irregular spellings, whereby we have seen that spellings significantly altering word appearance are found more frequently in the ("marked") woman's spellings than in the ("unmarked") man's, but that across all categories of spellings investigated both writers showed more or less equal frequencies of non-Present-day English spellings.

5. Conclusions

For reasons of unreliability of sources (largely the inherited curse of faulty Camden Society transcriptions), difference of text types in the sources, and methodological naiveté (especially the habit of selecting, for unspecified reasons, only certain "occasional" spellings for comment) we must approach accepted statements about spelling habits of the Early Modern English period as unsubstantiated hypotheses.

Quantitative analysis of spelling variables can lead to clear and comparable results, but must be treated with great care, and simple word-by-word or "number of irregular spellings" counts are hard to interpret. Calculating frequencies as ratios of selected spellings to all the spellings in the text, or as ratios of selected spelling to all the spellings in the selected category will give different results and therefore only one of these should be used for comparative purposes. Choice of which will depend on the researcher's material.

Rigorous investigation of earlier statements is useful not only in clarifying a received "truth" but also in telling us a great deal about variation in written language and how it can best be analysed. If, as here, we are to investigate perceptions, then the theories of reading are more important than theories of spelling production. Conversely, if we wished to investigate spellings from the writers' end, we should pay greater attention to theories of spelling production which, while now paying increasing attention to whole-word or lexical look-up aspects, accept phoneme-grapheme correspondence as of equal importance (PDP cleverly combines the two in a convincing way). The earlier theories and their concentration on only the phonological levels of spelling production have lead to perhaps overly confident interpretations of decontextualised spellings as pronunciation evidence[29], and also to this being almost the only way in which irregular spellings were approached. Our results show this as being particularly unfortunate, since it was precisely at the phonological and lexical levels that the two texts showed no significant difference in overall spelling habits.

Finally, it has been shown that our sample "wild" female speller does not spell more phonetically than our sample "normal" male speller, nor does she use more uneducated spellings than him. It is proposed on the basis of this research that unfamiliar spellings which slow down the reading process are more marked than more familiar ones, or those which are phonetically transparent.

Notes

1. This is a revised version of a paper presented to the "Discovering Historical Sociolinguistics" Seminar at the 4th ESSE Conference, Debrecen, Hungary, September 1997.
2. Simon Daines alludes to this when he records that "I have observed many commendable proficients in the Latin Tongue, who, notwithstanding, have been notably to seek in their English orthoepie and orthographie" (Daines [1640] 1966), and Thomas Lye is perhaps referring to the same educational discrepancy when he aims his spelling book at "persons of riper Age; and those such as, from the very breast, have been ever learning, and never yet come to the knowledg of the true spelling of one syllabl. Read, they hope they can; but spell they cannot; and therefore to write either to child, Friend or Servant, they are ashamed" (Lye [1677] 1969).
3. This refers to her letters. Scragg uses a Camden Society edition, and his analysis should therefore be treated with caution, since the transcriptions used in early Camden Society publications were very frequently inaccurate.
4. As in the case of the Duke of Newcastle's manuscript and printed versions of his English book on horsemanship (see Sönmez 1993).
5. Table 2 of her paper indicates that sixteenth-century private letters could be significantly more innovative than diaries in the matter of third person singular -s endings. This table contains information from Kytö (1993).
6. Dryden of all people: Evelyn's colleague in the move to establish an English Academy and reform the spelling, and arch-standardiser of the language! Ker states in the Preface to his edition of Dryden's Essays, that in his own spelling practice Dryden was "absolutely without concern in such matters" (Ker 1926: vi), but this should probably be carefully investigated before being accepted.
7. For instance Robinson and Adams (Hooke 1935) note of Robert Hooke's spelling that it "sometimes appears to have been phonetic, at others quite without method" but I wrote in my notes that his spelling "is mostly regular" – by the time I got round to reading this book I was clearly inured to the vagaries of seventeenth-century manuscript spellings. The comments of Needham about Newcastle's spellings, mentioned below, should therefore be seen as typical of the editor unfamiliar with manuscript spellings of this time, rather than reflecting any genuine peculiarity of Newcastle's.
8. Some attention has been paid to stigmatised forms in speech (see especially Sheldon (1938)) and lexis (Osselton 1958).
9. These are not the same letters as those printed by the Camden Society under the editorship of Thomas Taylor Lewis in 1854: these transcriptions cannot now be trusted, although it is from this book that most handbooks quote when

using these letters as examples of women's spellings from the period, e.g. Wyld (1920), Burnley (1992). A new and more complete edition of Lady Brilliana Harley's letters, including those studied here, has been made by Jacqueline Eales of the University of Kent, and either has, or should soon be, published by the Camden Society. She told me that the printers queried her transcriptions, asking if she really meant to spell words the way she did.

10. Unfortunately there is very little computer-readable manuscript material accurately transcribed down to the details of accidentals, and this paper is based upon my own small corpus which was put together for different purposes. If the results of this study are sufficiently promising, I hope to continue this line of research with more homogeneous material.
11. As Nevalainen and Raumolin-Brunberg (1989: 77) point out, this is important if spelling change, like other forms of language, "proceeds by generation".
12. *The Petty Papers* (1927). Note that not all these papers were in Petty's own hand.
13. (Teonge 1825). Another version (Teonge 1927) edited by G. E. Manwaring exists. Here the editor comments on the previous edition's inaccurate transcriptions and interpolations, and on the writer's "erratic and inconsistent" spelling, which he mostly "modernizes", retaining only words of philological interest or "quaint spelling" (Teonge 1927: ix).
14. There are 36,205 words in Harley and 167,175 in Newcastle.
15. It is worth bearing in mind the warning that "percentages offer a fertile field for confusion. And like the ever-impressive decimal they can lend an aura of precision to the inexact" (Huff 1973: 100).
16. I am grateful to Giray Berbero lu for explaining this test to me.
17. In a way which Wrenn, perhaps a bit meanly, called "a tendency to 'hunt the letter' " (Wrenn [1943] 1967: 147).
18. Almost all alphabetic spellings have origins in phonological correspondence. They are, however, subject to the forces of teaching methods, formation and dissolution of local or temporary standards, importation of foreign words, foreign sounds, foreign spellings, and to interpretations and reinterpretations along phonological, etymological, morphological, analogical and even ideological grounds. For this reason the disentangling of purely phonological or phonetic information from any given spelling is a hazardous enterprise. I have therefore concentrated in this section only on those spellings which seem best and most clearly to be explained with reference to pronunciation.
19. If it was not for the fact that Harley frequently shows transposed letters, I would take the metatheses in words such as <chruch> to indicate pronunciation of a liquid /r/ such as is still found in the West Country (the writer was brought up in Wales and lived in Herefordshire after her marriage). This pronunciation frequently coarticulates with neighbouring vowels to a degree which makes separation of vocalic and consonantal segments

impossible. Similarly, Newcastle belonged to the north-east of England and his spellings of /U/ Middle English short /u/ may therefore reflect a regionalism. In both cases we have here evidence that aristocrats of this generation are still, to some extent at least, speaking with regionally influenced accents.

20. This spelling feature is taken to be related to a confusion resulting from changes in the pronunciation of words with the reflex of ME /ɛ/, further confused by earlier changes in the spellings of long /e/. See Smith (1996: 109).
21. $\alpha = 0.05$, $Z_{crit} = 1.65$ in all Z-tests reported in this paper.
22. In this part of the comparison, because there is no potential limit to the set of possibly phonetically obscure spellings, all calculations were based on the frequency of such items within the texts as wholes.
23. As is indicated on the phonetic level, at least. See Ladefoged (1982: 104) on the motor theory of speech perception.
24. Many of these spellings may be related to the lengthening of stressed vowels cited earlier (Ladefoged 1982: 104).
25. Here Z is significant, being calculated at 3.645, Z_{crit} 1.65.
26. Although Early Modern English spellings have usually been analysed from a phonetic or phonological point of view, as early as 1954 Vallins was saying that "spelling is ... perhaps chiefly a matter of the eye" (Vallins 1954: 16). From the reading point of view we have much more evidence, summarised by Crystal in the following words: "the 'eye' approach [words are read as wholes without being ... sounded out] is certainly needed in order to explain most of what goes on in fluent adult reading" (Crystal 1987: 211).
27. Ordering of events here is supported by experiments which show "word-letter" or "word superiority" effects – i.e., subjects identify full words faster than the time taken to identify a single letter, and identify words quicker than non-words of the same length and containing the same letters. See Reicher (1969: 275-280) as quoted in Crowder and Wagner (1992: 78).
28. Metanalysis in some cases contravenes not only the expected regularity of letter size but also and more importantly the word superiority effect. Consider, e.g., Harley's <a Cused>.
29. Wrenn's criticism again: "a very considerable number of authors and teachers have been permanently influenced by [Zachrisson's (1913) and Wyld's (1914)] implicit tendency to exalt the occasional spelling in all kinds of historical investigations of our language" (Wrenn [1943] 1967: 131).

References

Basire, Isaac
    1831   *The correspondence of Isaac Basire D. D.* Edited by W. N. Darnell. London: John Murray.

Beauvillain, Cécile
    1996   The integration of morphological and whole-word form information during eye fixations on prefixed and suffixed words. *Journal of Memory and Language* 35: 801-820.

Blake, Norman F. and Charles Jones (eds.)
    1984   *English historical linguistics: studies in development.* (CECTAL Conference Papers Series 3.) Sheffield: University of Sheffield.

Blount, Thomas
    1656   *Glossographia.*

Bolton, Whitney F.
    1966   *The English language: essays by English and American men of letters 1490-1839.* (2nd edition.) Cambridge: Cambridge University Press.

Brooks, L.
    1977   Visual pattern in fluent word recognition. In: A. S. Reber and D. C. Scarborough (eds.) [no page references given in Crowder and Wagner (1992)].

Burnley, David
    1992   *The history of the English language: a source book.* London: Longman.

Campbell
    1987   One or two lexicons for reading and writing words: can misspellings shed any light? *Philosophical Transactions of the Royal Society of London* B295, 397-410.

Cavendish, William, 1st Duke of Newcastle
    1658-1660   Portland Collection, Cavendish Holles Section MSS PwV21, Hallward Library, Nottingham University.
    1660-1667   Portland Collection, Cavendish Holles Section MSS PwV22, Hallward Library, Nottingham University.
    1667   *A new method and extraordinary invention, to dress horses, ...* London: Thomas Milbourn.

Cawdrey, Robert
    [1604] 1976 *A table alphabeticall of hard usual English words.* New York: Scholar's Facsimile Reprints, 1976.

Coote, Edmund
[1596] 1968 *The English Schoole-Maister.* Menston: Scolar Press.
Crowder, Robert G. and Richard K. Wagner
    1992 *The psychology of reading: an introduction.* (2nd edition.) New York: Oxford University Press.
Crystal, David
    1987 *The Cambridge encyclopedia of language.* Cambridge: Cambridge University Press.
Daines, Simon
[1640] 1966 *Orthoepia Anglicana.* Menston: Scolar Press.
Ehri, Linnea C.
    1980 The development of orthographic images. In: Uta Frith (ed.), 311-338.
Freeborn, Dennis
    1992 *From Old English to Standard English: a course book in language variation across time.* Houndmills: Macmillan.
Frith, Uta (ed.)
    1980 *Cognitive processes in spelling.* London: Academic Press.
Funnell, Elaine
    1992 On recognising misspelled words. In: Chris M. Sterling and Cliff Robson (eds.), 87-99.
Görlach, Manfred
    1991 *Introduction to Early Modern English.* Cambridge: Cambridge University Press.
Harley, Lady Brilliana
    1623-1643 BM Add. MSS 7001/4. 70035. 70087. 700105. 70110.
Hooke, Robert
    1935 *Diary of Robert Hooke 1672-1680.* Edited by Henry W. Robinson and Walter Adams. London: Taylor and Francis.
Huff, Darrell
    1973 *How to lie with statistics.* London: Penguin.
Huxford, Laura, Colin Terrell and Lynette Bradley
    1992 "Invented spelling" and learning to read. In: Chris M. Sterling and Cliff Robson (eds.), 159-167.
J. K. (John Kersey)
    1702 *A new English dictionary.*
Ker, W. P.
    1926 *Essays of John Dryden.* Volume 1. Oxford: Oxford University Press.
Kytö, Merja
    1993 Third-person present singular verb inflection in early British and American English. *Language Variation and Change* 5: 113-139.

Ladefoged, Peter
    1982   *A course in phonetics.* (2nd edition.) San Diago: Harcourt, Brace, Jovanovich.
Lewis, Thomas Taylor (ed.)
    1854   *Letters of the Lady Brilliana Harley.* London: Camden Society.
Lye, Thomas
    [1677] 1969 *A new spelling book.* Menston: Scolar Press
Malone Society
    1996   *Dramatic works by William Cavendish.* (The Malone Society Reprints 158.) Oxford: Oxford University Press.
Mordaunt, Elizabeth
    1856   *The Private Diarie of Elizabeth, Viscountess Mordaunt 1656-1678.* Transcribed by Edward Macrory. Duncairn [no publisher.].
Nevalainen, Terttu
    1997   Historical sociolinguistics. Lecture presented at the ESSE/4 conference, Debrecen, Hungary, September 4-9 1997.
Nevalainen, Terttu and Helena Raumolin-Brunberg
    1989   A corpus of Early Modern Standard English in a socio-historical perspective. *Neuphilologische Mitteilungen* 90: 67-110
Osselton, Noel E.
    1958   *Branded words in English dictionaries before Johnson.* (Groningen Studies in English VII.) Groningen: Wolters.
    1984   Informal spelling systems in Early Modern English: 1500-1800. In: Norman F. Blake and Charles Jones (eds.), 123-137.
Parry, E. A. (ed.)
    n.d.   *Letters from Dorothy Osborne to Sir William Temple.* Dent.
Petty, Sir William
    1927   *The Petty Papers.* Edited by the Marquis of Lansdowne. 2 volumes. London: Constable and Co.
Reber, A. S. and D. C. Scarborough (eds.)
    1977   *Toward a psychology of reading.* Hillsdale, NJ: Lawrence Erlbaum.
Reicher, G. M.
    1969   Perceptual recognition as a function of the meaningfulness of the stimulus material. *Journal of Experimental Psychology* 81: 275-280.

Scragg, Donald G.
1974 *A history of English spelling*. Manchester: Manchester University Press.

Sheldon, Esther Keck
1938 *Standards of English pronunciation according to the grammarians and orthoepists of the 16th, 17th and 18th centuries*. Unpublished Ph.D. thesis, University of Wisconsin.

Smith, Jeremy
1996 *An historical study of English: function, form and change*. London: Routledge.

Sönmez, Margaret J.-M.
1993 English spelling in the seventeenth century: a study of the nature of standardisation as seen through the MS and printed versions of the Duke of Newcastle's *A New Method* .... 2 vols. Unpublished Ph.D. dissertation, University of Durham.

Sterling, Chris M. and Cliff Robson (eds.)
1992 *Psychology, spelling and education*. Clevedon: Multilingual Matters.

Teonge, Henry
1825 *The Diary of Henry Teong*. 1675 to 1679. [no editor.] London: Charles Knight.
1927 *The Diary of Henry Teong*. 1675 to 1679. (Edited by G. E. Manwaring.) London: George Routledge and Sons.

Vallins, George Henry
1954 *Spelling*. London: Deutsch.

Verney
1925 *Memoirs of the Verney Family*. Privately printed by F. P. and M. M. Verney.

Wrenn, Charles L.
[1943] 1967 The value of spelling as evidence. In: Charles L. Wrenn, 129-149.
1967 *Word and symbol: studies in English language*. London: Longman.

Wyld, Henry Cecil
    1914   *A short history of English*. London: John Murray.
    1920   *A history of modern colloquial English*. London: T. Fisher Unwin.
Zachrisson, Robert Eugen
    1913   *Pronunciation of English vowels, 1400-1700*. Göteborg: Ward Zachrisson [private printing].

Sociohistorical linguistics and the observer's paradox

Ingrid Tieken-Boon van Ostade

1. Introduction[1]

One of the alleged advantages of applying methods from modern sociolinguistics when studying the language of the past is that we do not need to reckon with the observer's paradox (e.g. Keränen 1998: 30; Nurmi 1998: 163), in that the data for analysis were evidently produced without any stylistic interference due to the presence of an interviewer or a taperecorder. Thus Keränen (1998: 30), for example, argues that "The informants may be conscious of their register, but not because they are aware that their language will be used for research purposes". In my opinion, the question as to whether or not the informant was aware of the fact that his or her language was being researched is irrelevant from the point of view of historical studies; more to the point is the problem of their register consciousness, which must be dealt with by modern and historical researchers alike. Register consciousness presents a conflict with the fact that, as Chambers (1995: 18) puts it, "the style most desired for sociolinguistic purposes is completely unmonitored". In the present article I therefore want to argue that in looking for language which comes as closely as possible to unmonitored language, whether written or spoken, we do have to take account of the observer's paradox, but that the observer's paradox takes a different form from what we would normally expect to find on the basis of our knowledge of present-day interview situations. In other words, it is precisely the register consciousness which creates the problem in doing historical sociolinguistic research, because, as I will proceed to show, we have very little evidence of spontaneous utterances in the literal sense of the term. This is especially true when we are dealing with the written language, but also when we are looking at whatever evidence there is of the spoken language. In arguing my case I will draw on evidence (linguistic and otherwise) from the eighteenth century because that is the period most familiar to me from my research; for all that, I believe that my argument will be of some validity for periods in the history of English other than the eighteenth century.

While it is the primary aim of modern sociolinguists to try and get access to a speaker's vernacular language (see for example Milroy (1987: 23) and Chambers (1995: 18)), in my opinion the historical sociolinguist should – primarily, at any rate – strive after the same objective as much as possible, both for the same reasons[2] and in order to have a common field of reference. Identifying the spoken vernacular for earlier stages of the language is obviously a difficult matter. However, we need not only look for evidence in the spoken registers: I believe that even the written medium contains evidence of the vernacular. If the term "vernacular" is defined as "a relaxed style in which the least conscious attention is being paid to the language of the utterance" (adapted from Wardhaugh (1992: 19)),[3] while being characterised by its own regularity which differs from that of more formal registers (cf. Labov (1981) as quoted by Milroy (1987: 23)), it is indeed possible to identify a written vernacular for the eighteenth century. In Tieken-Boon van Ostade (1996: 328) I have argued that the language of James Boswell's letters to his friend John Johnston of Grange seems a clear instance of vernacular language: the style of the letters is relaxed and informal, and in any case the spelling of the letters is subject to a clear set of rules which are different from and independent of the spelling of published books from the period. Boswell was not unique in using a written vernacular, and in Tieken-Boon van Ostade (in prep.) I intend to show where more evidence can be found.

Studying the written vernacular in relation to more standard registers can, I believe, help us obtain insight into a speaker's sociolinguistic competence which may also be relevant to his or her command of the spoken language, so that even when we will not have enough evidence of the spoken vernacular for a particular period we may still be able to draw up a hypothetical reconstruction of it on the basis of our findings for the written vernacular. In what follows, then, I will proceed from the assumption that in the eighteenth century there existed a written vernacular alongside a spoken one. First, I will discuss the observer's paradox in relation to eighteenth-century spoken language and subsequently to the written language. I will then discuss the extent to which the observer's paradox affects our expectations as to what we will find when applying one present-day sociolinguistic research model to the study of eighteenth-century English, i.e. social network analysis (Milroy 1987).

2. The observer's paradox and eighteenth-century speech

The observer's paradox is defined by Labov (1972: 256) as "the problem of observing how people speak when they are not being observed" (see also Chambers 1995: 18-19). Obtaining first-hand information on how people spoke in the eighteenth century is an obvious problem; at best we have recorded dialogues, such as Swift's *Complete Collection of Genteel and Ingenious Conversation* (1738, ed. by Eric Partridge 1963), which he claims to have based on actual conversations. But we can never be sure to what extent this claim is indeed true, and an analysis of the language of the conversations indicates that the speech of the dialogues is far from naturalistic (Strang 1967: 1965; Tieken-Boon van Ostade 1987: 21). There are, moreover, at least two eighteenth-century authors who were in the habit of recording the conversations they witnessed: James Boswell (1740-1795) and Fanny Burney (1752-1840). Boswell, according to Baldwin (1952: 504), apparently recorded Dr. Johnson's speech – that is, his conversational, not his literary style (Baldwin (1952: 492) – quite accurately in his *Life of Johnson*: "Johnson's conversation in the *Life* sounds very much like the real thing [as] is amply supported by contemporary testimony". His usage of periphrastic *do* in negative sentences and questions in any case comes very close to the other evidence I found in direct speech from the second half of the eighteenth century (cf. Tieken-Boon van Ostade 1987: 180, 1991a: 151). Despite the many editorial changes Boswell made to the text of the *Life* before it was published, a comparison with the notebooks which have been preserved shows that he never changed the wording of the dialogues; probably, according to Baldwin (1952: 503), he "transcribed them from the original notes".[4] As for Fanny Burney, according to Hemlow (1958: 31, 96) she had been recording dialogue since she was fifteen, and over the years had evidently acquired great skill in doing so. An analysis of the occurrence of "vulgar" language in her own writing compared with that in the recorded dialogues carried out by Beljaars (1998) suggests that she apparently recorded what she heard quite literally: Fanny hardly swore herself, but did record others, real people in her diaries and fictional ones in her novel *Evelina* (1778), as using coarse language. Beljaars discovered a social distinction in the use of swear words as well as one according to gender, which suggests that Fanny Burney may well have given quite an accurate rendering of what she heard.

Boswell, according to Baldwin, was in the habit of carrying around a notebook into which he could record the words of the famous lexicographer (Baldwin 1952: 498), and so apparently was Fanny Burney: "You must know," she writes in the first pages of her journal, "I always have the last sheet of my Journal in my pocket, & when I have wrote it half full – I join it to the rest, & take another sheet" (Troide et al. (ed.) 1988-,1: 18-19). Once it became evident that Fanny Burney was in the habit of recording meetings and the conversations that occurred in the course of them and that there was the danger that she might make use of them for her novels, her presence produced a certain amount of discomfort among the rest of the company (Waddell 1980: 260). The following entry in her journal illustrates this: " 'O Miss Burney, continued Dr. Delap, how I wish You were to see him! – you'd put him in a Book directly' " (Troide et al. (eds.) 1988-, 3: 390). One may easily imagine that, once Fanny Burney's identity as the author of *Evelina* (1778) was established, people would be on their guard whenever she was present, and that they would refrain from expressing themselves quite spontaneously, both with respect to what they said and to how they said it. This is as clear an instance of the observer's paradox as one may get. In Boswell's case, it must have worked similarly: the presence of a man following around the object of his admiration with a notebook always ready at hand must have acted as a constraint on the spontaneity of any gathering at which he was present. Johnson also, according to Baldwin (1952: 494), even regularly dictated his words to Boswell, because (rightly or wrongly) he "did not have much respect for his memory". The sentences in such passages, Baldwin notes (1952: 493), "are short, the style clipped, and the general effect almost staccato". Some care therefore must be taken whenever the dialogues in the *Life of Johnson* and Fanny Burney's journals are studied as evidence of the spoken language: with the exception of the passages dictated to Boswell, they are probably very close to the real thing – I even doubt if there is anything better available – but a certain amount of lack of true spontaneity must be reckoned with, which is due to the presence of the acknowledged recorder of the dialogues.

There is, however, another less obvious instance of the observer's paradox which we need to take into consideration when looking for eighteenth-century spontaneous speech; our ability to identify the observer's paradox here depends, I would argue, on our interpretation of the person of the observer metaphorically. The eighteenth century, according to Coleman (1944: 444), "placed a high value upon the conversational art", which means that "conversational ability" was considered an important skill and that good conversations were subject to a number of unwritten but well-defined rules. It is such rules that are ridiculed by Swift in his *Polite Conversations*. Because the conversations that were recorded by authors such as Boswell and Fanny Burney took place in public, they must have been subject to the same conventions. The possibility should therefore be reckoned with that these conversations do not contain much truly informal, "unmonitored" dialogue, which, as I have argued, is after all the object of the sociohistorical linguist's research. Only if the recorded dialogue can be shown to be free from the constraints imposed upon it by the conversational medium can we expect to find evidence of the spoken vernacular.

There must however be a lot of eighteenth-century material which has, as far as I know, never been explored yet, from a sociolinguistic or any other angle. Hope (1993) argues that there is lot of evidence of the spoken vernacular in court records from the sixteenth century, and his analysis shows that there are significant differences between the literary representation of pronoun usage (e.g. in Shakespeare's plays) and that found in non-fictional speech. Such records must exist for the eighteenth century as well, containing depositions from people from all levels of society. An analysis of such records would throw interesting light on how people really spoke as compared to the formalised conversations of the time – though it would seem that a double observer's paradox in the sense as defined above applies here, as the speakers are obviously constrained by the courtroom situation, while their words may not have been entered in the records exactly as they were spoken. Even so, an analysis of such records would help us to get a fuller picture of the stylistic range available to speakers from the period.

3. The observer's paradox and the written language

While the recognition of the observer's paradox with respect to the analysis of the spoken language may not be so much of a problem, especially when an observer was actually present on the scene of the conversation in question, identifying its presence with respect to the written vernacular is a different matter, though it exists there, too. As the observer's paradox takes different forms depending on the nature of the text type, I will make a distinction in the following discussion between epistolary writings and journals.

3.1. Letters

For eighteenth-century letters the observer's paradox likewise takes two forms, firstly in the knowledge on the part of the letter-writer that the letter might not solely be read by the addressee, and secondly in the fact that letters had to be written in accordance with a number of well-defined rules. The first of these is a rather more obvious form of the observer's paradox than the second, which is comparable to that discussed for the spoken language in that the observer's role must be interpreted metaphorically rather than literally. The first type may be illustrated with an example from the biography of the Lennox sisters, Stella Tillyard's *Aristocrats* (1994). The book is based on a voluminous, as yet unpublished correspondence between all the members of the Lennox family, including their servants. The example comes from a note written by Emily Lennox to Henry Fox, her sister Caroline's husband:

> What a creature you are! I receive your letter before a thousand people. "A letter from Mr. Fox, oh we shall have some news." Everybody waits with impatience till I have read it. I open it with an important face and then behold it's full of nonsense and indeed such stuff as is not decent to shew to any creature (as quoted by Tillyard 1994: 94).

Emily is here scolding her brother-in-law for putting her into an awkward position: at the time, personal letters were generally considered to be public property and were expected to be read aloud to the entertainment of all those present (Davis 1966: 9). The knowledge that a letter would not be read by the recipient alone put a constraint on the writer, who could not raise any matters of a truly private nature in the letters. Mrs. Thrale (1741-1821) clearly experienced the effects of this constraint when reading Johnson's letters, for she observes in her private diary that his books "please me more than even his Letters; for in them he is often scrupulous of opening his heart & has an Idea they will be seen sometime, perhaps published" (Balderston (ed.) 1951: 446).[5] The Lennox sisters had a way of circumventing this problem: "Thoughts that were exclusive to writer and reader would often be included on a separate sheet of paper that could be removed before the rest did its round of the drawing-room" (Tillyard 1994: 94). The most extreme form of the kind of public exposure referred to here is the publication of a collection of letters, a fear which evidently worried Johnson but which also presented itself some time previously to Lady Elizabeth Germaine when she realised, upon the publication of Swift's *Works* in Dublin in 1735, that the recipient of her letters "was famous enough for his correspondence to be in danger of getting printed" (Davis 1966: 9). Some authors, Pope for one, revised their letters for this very purpose, thus also presumably pruning them from whatever evidence of the vernacular they might have had in the process. Others wrote their letters for this very purpose, such as Lady Mary Wortley Montagu (Halsband (ed.) 1965-1967), whose *Turkish Embassy Letters* were expressly meant to distribute the news of her stay in Turkey to as wide a group of friends as possible. Consequently, they are not real letters, and Halsband refers to them as "pseudo-letters" (1965-1967, 1: xiv). Even in the case of business letters (though these are less likely to contain much vernacular language) the author had to reckon with the possibility that they might be read by someone other than the intended recipient: as Anderson and Ehrenpreis (Anderson, Daghlian, and Ehrenpreis (eds.) 1966: 270) put it, "there was always the danger that letters of interest to the government might be opened in London".

The second form the observer's paradox takes in eighteenth-century letters is the requirement that letters were written according to a set of fixed rules. Like eighteenth-century conversation, letter-writing was considered an "art" in its own right, and even the most spontaneous letter had to be carefully laboured at to put across that spontaneity in exactly the right way. According to Anderson and Ehrenpreis (Anderson, Daghlian, and Ehrenpreis (eds.) 1966: 272), "throughout the century, epistolary theory subordinated 'art' to 'nature', the composed to the unplanned". An example may again be taken from the biography of the Lennox sisters:

> Emily and Caroline saw themselves as self-conscious letter writers with "formed" styles ... as Caroline revealed when she told Emily how ashamed she was that Ste Fox [her son] still wrote like a child at the age of seventeen. "His letters are quite a schoolboy's. He is well, hopes we are, and compliments to everybody. Adieu. Yours Most Sincerely." Emily's daughter, in contrast, received Caroline's praise for epistolary skill. I wrote

to your daughter Emily ... She is a delightful correspondent, her style quite formed" (Tillyard 1994: 93).

Another example is Mrs. Thrale, who, according to E. Bloom and L. Bloom ((eds.) 1989-1993: 16), "even as she 'scribbled' her letters, ... saw them as literary and historical documents which had to be preserved and published". If letters were not intended as spontaneous documents in the present-day sense of the word, their language must have been subject to the same constraint. Instead of informal, unpremeditated language, we must therefore expect to find carefully constructed and polished sentences. The awareness that letter-writing constituted an art and that the language of letters represented a medium which was characterised by rules independent of those of the spoken language was general and widespread: authors apologised when they did not write and rewrite their letters, such as Betsy Sheridan, when observing in a journal letter to her sister: "But as I scribble a great deal I am forced to write the first word that occurs, so that of course I must write pretty nearly as I should speak" (Lefanu (ed.) 1960: 57). Walpole wrote similarly: "if you have a mind I should write you news, don't make me think about it; I shall be so long in turning my periods, that what I tell you will cease to be news" (Lewis and Brown (ed.) 1941: 29-30). The same awareness is evident among letter-writers with very little education. Expecting to find a reflex of the spoken language in the Clift family correspondence, a late-eighteenth-century collection of letters written by members of a lower-working-class family from Cornwall, Austin (1994: 285) discovered that the situation was more complicated: "as soon as these people took up a pen they framed their minds to a formal mode of thinking". Even the letters of such uneducated letter-writers as the Clift family are characterised by a kind of formality which is imposed on their language by the nature of the medium.

Letters that are less likely to be subject to the constraints discussed here are private letters, such as Steele's letters to his wife Prue which deal with family affairs and which are therefore not of the least interest to anyone else (Anderson, Daghlian, and Ehrenpreis (eds.) 1966: 275-276) and the letters which Lady Mary Wortley

Montagu wrote before her marriage to Edward Montagu in which they discuss the possibility of an elopement (Tieken-Boon van Ostade 1985: 134). In addition, the letters that contain apologies from the author for not adhering to the letter-writing conventions are more likely to contain truly spontaneous material, both as to their contents and as to their language.

3.2. Journals

Private journals are different from letters in that they are usually written for private consumption only, i.e. by the author of the journal in question. As a result, one might expect their contents as well as their language to be completely free from any of the external constraints discussed in section 3.1.: unlike in the case of letters, the author feels unobserved by an addressee when keeping his or her journal. As Ponsonby (1923: 2) puts it, in writing a diary, "no attention need be given to form, even grammar can go to the winds" because the author need not take a recipient into account. Furthermore, the absence of an addressee sets the author free from the obligation of writing within a well-defined convention, as in the case of the eighteenth-century letter. Ostensibly, then, the observer's paradox would be completely absent here. Some journal writers, however, feel that they cannot do without a recipient, as a result of which they invent one. Thus Fanny Burney creates a fictional recipient called Nobody: "I will suppose you, then, to be my best friend; ... my dearest companion – & a romantick Girl ... more tender than if you were a friend [in] propria personæ [*sic*]" (Troide et al. (eds.) 1988, 1: 2). To enable herself to write her journal, Fanny Burney puts herself into the guise of a letterwriter – and eventually the journals take the form of journal letters written to her closest sister Susan. Moreover, despite her resolution to write a journal "in which I must confess my *every* thought, must open my whole Heart!" (Troide et al. (eds.) 1988, 1: 1), Fanny Burney apparently never felt completely free to do so. The main reason for her inhibition in this respect was the fear that the journal might accidentally be read by someone else (Tieken-Boon van Ostade 1991a: 152-157). Neither in its contents nor in its language therefore can the journal be taken as completely unpremeditated. While in Fanny Burney's case it may have been prudence – or prudishness – which thus constrained her, literary authors writing a diary may have been affected by the constraint of their profession, for according to Ponsonby (1923: 1), "literary talent may be a barrier to complete sincerity". In either type of case, we have to do not merely with a subjective representation of affairs but with an edited version of them, whether resulting from personal inhibitions to open one's mind freely on paper or from literary inclinations. In either type of case the language should be taken to represent this process as well; the observer's paradox exists in the self-consciousness of the author when confronted with the medium of the private journal – in this respect, eighteenth-century journals may be quite comparable to the letters from the period.

The best journals from the present perspective are those which are free from the kind of self-consciousness described here, and a good example are Johnson's *Diaries, Prayers, and Annals* (McAdam, D. Hyde, and M. Hyde (eds.) 1958). Daghlian (1966: 109), in discussing the emergence of the man Johnson from his letters, dismisses the diaries as being "too intimate to be used as evidence for what has to be a kind of public portrait". Yet it is this very aspect of intimacy in the diaries which allows us to observe Johnson as he must have been in his most unguarded moments. Another example is Mrs. Thrale and her diaries known as *Thraliana* (Balderston (ed.) 1951). Unlike her letters, which she believed might eventually be published (see section 3.1.), she apparently felt she could express herself freely in this journal, unrestrained by the self-consciousness resulting from the possibility that her writings might be read by other people. While Fanny Burney in her old age edited her journals and letters to make them fit to be read by others after her death, Mrs. Thrale was of a different mind: "stranger still that a Woman [i.e. Mrs. Thrale herself] should write such a Book as this; put down every Occurrence of her Life, every Emotion of her Heart & call it a Thraliana forsooth – but then I mean to destroy it" (Balderston (ed.) 1951: 464). In journals such as these, we can observe the authors as it were secure in the knowledge that they were not being observed; in other words, the observer's paradox does not apply here. It is diaries such as these that even make us slightly uncomfortable, making us wonder, along with Ponsonby (1923: 80), whether we have a right to pry into someone's private affairs. At the same time, there are diaries such as Boswell's *London Journal* which contain highly intimate details but which were indeed meant to be read by others. Boswell sent instalments of the journal to his friend John Johnston of Grange for safekeeping but also so they might read the journal together later. Boswell's writing of the journal, according to its editors Brady and Pottle (1956: xv), resulted from his "yearning for ... exhibitionism", and it is diaries such as these in addition to the ones discussed above which may yield what we are looking for when aiming at analysing the eighteenth-century vernacular.[6]

4. Social network analysis and the observer's paradox

When setting out to study the language of the past, historical sociolinguists are obviously at a disadvantage in comparison with modern sociolinguists in that they cannot, for example, monitor the interview situation in such a way that different speech styles are produced which can be analysed and compared; for historical linguists there is no "danger-of-death" question (Labov 1966: 107-109) to make the speaker forget that he or she is in an interview situation, so that the observer's paradox can be bypassed. The historical linguist has to make do with ready-made material that needs to be taken as it comes. What the historical sociolinguist can do, however, is to start at the other end (as I have argued in Tieken-Boon van Ostade (1994)) and to scan the available material for evidence that might have been produced as if in response to a danger-of-death or similar question (Boswell's description in the *London Journal* of his meeting with a prostitute is a good example), or to apply other criteria according to which the closest equivalent to vernacular speech styles may be identified. The best material for analysis consists of personal letters written solely to be read by the addressee, which are not written under the constraint of the art of letter-writing (Steele's letters to his wife, Lady Mary Wortley Montagu's letters to her husband-to-be, the private sheets in the Lennox correspondence). Apologies for not conforming to the conventions of the medium such as those quoted in section 3.1. above are good indications of the usefulness of the material in this respect. It is interesting to see that the apologies may also be interpreted differently, more positively, as signalling a greater degree of intimacy when the writer frees himself or herself from the yoke of the convention. Betsy Sheridan, for example, writes to her sister, "To you my dear Love I write as I talk in all modes and tempers" (Lefanu (ed.) 1960: 123), and Coleridge does likewise in a letter to Mrs. Evans (5 February 1793): "My pen writes to others, but it *talks* to you" (Jackson (ed.) 1987: viii). According to the editors of his letters, Hainsworth and Walker (1990), Lord Fitzwilliam of Milton "was a magnificent letter writer: always spontaneous, down-to-earth, and, despite occasional errors of sentence structure, syntax or grammar as his fertile mind ran ahead of his scratching quill, he displays a natural mastery of the English language" (1990: x). What the words "natural mastery of the English language" mean has to be further investigated, but the observation that Lord Fitzwilliam "wrote as he thought" is clearly of interest here.

The language of a letter or a journal itself – and this seems equally true of a recorded conversation – can likewise give an indication as to its vernacular character: if the text in question contains one instance of what was then considered to be non-standard language, there are likely to be more. As a criterion to decide what was regarded unacceptable at the time may be used the extent to which a particular form or construction called for comment on the part of the legislators of the language, the eighteenth-century grammarians and schoolmasters. Leonard (1929) contains an appendix in which he provides a list of constructions which were then subject to debate, and Sundby, Bjørge, and Haugland (1991) provides an inventory of all negative usage comments in the normative grammars of the eighteenth century. One example of a non-standard construction is Lady Mary Wortley Montagu's use of *them* as a demonstrative pronoun, as in *Them admirers you speak of* (Halsband (ed.) 1965-1967, 1: 61). The construction is non-standard today and the comments quoted by Sundby, Bjørge, and Haugland (1991) suggest that it was so in the eighteenth century, too.

As for the contents of the letters and journals, which are of immense value in determining the nature of a social network (i.e. open or closed, dense or multiplex, see Milroy ([1987] 1989)), here too the observer's paradox plays a role, for authors might not wish to risk disclosing information that could be harmful to themselves or to others if they felt they were unable to make such observations freely. Fanny Burney's editing of her journals towards the end of her life is a good instance of this; it is just as well for our purpose that the editors of the journals have managed to recover much of the material that was not meant by the author to go down to posterity. Also, an author might present a view of their relationship with someone which might not agree with the other person's perception of the nature of the tie between them: again Fanny Burney is a good illustration of this. In her diary entries from around the time when her novel *Evelina* (1778) was first published (upon which she was introduced into the Streatham circle), she describes the intimate relationship which developed between herself and Mrs. Thrale. Presenting her side of this may have been based on a misconception of the true nature of the relationship;[7] on the other hand, Fanny Burney may have wished to make more of the relationship in her diary in order to present herself in a better light – in her own eyes, in the eyes of a possible reading public? Like her father, who was what might be called a social climber (see various descriptions in Lonsdale's biography of Charles Burney ([1965] 1989)), she may have been very keen on being friends with the leading members of polite society of the day. In reality, however, as Troide et al. observe twice in a footnote ((eds.) 1988-: 247n, 345n), the relationship between the Burneys and Mrs. Thrale was what Bax (forthcoming) would call an asymmetrical one, for the Burneys were less well liked by Mrs. Thrale than Fanny Burney appeared to think. In order to describe social networks of the period it is therefore never enough to base oneself on the information of a single person only. The reverse is found as well, as in the case of Betsy Sheridan, who claims in her journal letters to her sister not to have any social aspirations, unlike her brother, who did; her language, however, shows that she must have shared the same aspirations with her brother (Tieken-Boon van Ostade 1991b). It is the possible desire to pass oneself off in one's own eyes or in those of others at slightly greater or to slightly less advantage which may also be seen as an instance of the observer's paradox. False modesty, as in the case of Betsy Sheridan, is thus a factor that needs to be reckoned with as well.

5. Conclusion

In this article I have tried to show that the observer's paradox exists for eighteenth-century English as much as it does for the language of today. Both for the spoken and for the written language it exists in essentially two forms, in the literal sense in that an observer is actually present, for instance when acknowledged reporters of social gatherings and conversations are present, as well as when there is the fear, principally among letter writers but also among writers of journals, that the text may be read by others than the addressee, either because the text in question is read aloud in company or because it is printed. The latter consideration later leads authors – such as Pope and Fanny Burney – to revise their text to clean it up, both as far as the contents and as far as the language is concerned. The identification of the second form of the observer's paradox rests on what I have called the metaphorical interpretation of the role of the observer: because conversation as well as letter-writing constituted an art in the eighteenth century, the language that is used never comes as it were straight from the heart but is filtered through a set of well-defined rules to give it a seemingly spontaneous, but at the same time polished form. This form of the observer's paradox affects the language of an utterance as much as its contents, as is clear from the fact that Fanny Burney, for example, never in so many words refers to her stepmother's pregnancy (Tieken-Boon van Ostade 1991a7: 154-155). Though my examples have been drawn from the eighteenth century, there is evidence that the point made here is relevant to earlier periods as well. Raumolin-Brunberg and Nurmi (1997: 404) discuss the case of Dorothy Osborne (1627-1695), who believed that "all Letters mee thinks should bee free and Easy as ones discourse, not studdyed, as an Oration, nor made up of hard words like a Charme". This quotation from a letter written in 1653 places the language of her letters in the same category as those by Betsy Sheridan and Walpole discussed in section 3.1. above. The historical sociolinguist thus has to reckon with the observer's paradox as much as the modern sociolinguist does, and I have listed a number of ways by which styles can be identified which are probably closer to the vernacular than those which are found in texts meant for a more public consumption. Even the passages dictated by Johnson to Boswell are not entirely useless – they are comparable to Labov's Reading Style (Labov 1966: 92-96) and may be analysed as such in comparison with his other styles. Far from being useless, then, even the most unspontaneous speech or writing styles can be used for analysis of a speaker/writer's sociolinguistic competence, as long as their relative formality is assessed accurately.

Notes

1. I am grateful to Catherine Belsey for her comments on an earlier version of this article.
2. Milroy (1987: 23), quoting Labov (1981: 3), argues that the study of the vernacular is to be preferred because other styles or varieties of language are acquired later in life and are as it were "superposed" on the vernacular. The vernacular may as much as possible be regarded as a speaker's "own" language.
3. Or, in Chambers's terms, language which is "completely unmonitored" (1995: 18).
4. Mizuno (1991: 155-156) also found that there are generally very few differences between the representation of Johnson's speech in the *London Journal 1762-1763* and the *Life*. Changes mostly involve the kind of alterations that resulted from the transformation of indirect into direct speech.

5. I owe this example, as well as those relating to Mrs. Thrale discussed in section 3.2., to Randy Bax.
6. An updated version of Ponsonby's inventory of eighteenth-century journals seems called for; cf. Tieken-Boon van Ostade (in prep.), which aims at providing an inventory of modern editions of eighteenth-century correspondences.
7. An example of this may be found in the correspondence between Fanny Burney and Mrs. Thrale. Upon Mrs. Thrale's announcement that she was going to marry Piozzi, a decision which created a great stir among her friends, Fanny Burney expressed her disapproval of the forthcoming marriage, upon which Mrs. Thrale responded to the extent that she hoped that they would continue to be friends. Fanny Burney, however, misinterpreted the uncharacteristically short reply she received as an indication that all was well again between her and Mrs. Thrale, but there were never any further letters between them (see E. Bloom and L. Bloom 1989: 108n).

References

Anderson, Howard, Philip B. Daghlian, and Irvin Ehrenpreis
    1966   *The familiar letter in the eighteenth century.* Lawrence: University of Kansas Press.

Austin, Frances
    1994   The effect of exposure to standard English: the language of William Clift. In: Dieter Stein and Ingrid Tieken-Boon van Ostade (eds.), 285-313.

Balderston, Katherine (ed.)
    1951   *Thraliana: the diary of Mrs. Hester Lynch Thrale (Later Piozzi),* Volume 1. *1776-1784.* (2nd edition.) Oxford: Clarendon Press.

Baldwin, Louis
    1952   The conversation in Boswell's *Life of Johnson. The Journal of English and Germanic Philology* 51: 492-506.

Bax, Randy
    forthc.   A network strength scale for the study of eighteenth-century English. *European Journal of English Studies* 4 (3).

Beljaars, Ellen Bernice
    1998   "Miss Slyboots": Fanny Burney's use of vulgar language in her novel *Evelina* and her early diary (1778-1779). Unpublished M.A. thesis, English Department, University of Leiden.

Bloom, Edward A. and Lillian D. Bloom (eds.)
1989-1993 *The Piozzi letters: correspondence of Hester Lynch Piozzi, 1784-1821 (formerly Mrs. Thrale)*. Newark: University of Delaware Press; London/Toronto: Associated University Press.

Brady, Frank and Frederick A. Pottle (eds.)
1956 *Boswell in search of a wife*. New York/Toronto/London: McGraw-Hill.

Britton, Derek (ed.)
1996 *English historical linguistics 1994*. (Current Issues in Linguistic Theory 135.) Amsterdam/Philadelphia: Benjamins.

Chambers, J. K.
1995 *Sociolinguistic theory: linguistic variation and its social significance*. Oxford/Cambridge, MA: Blackwell.

Coleman, William H.
1944 The Johnsonian conversational formula. *The Quarterly Review* 282: 432-445.

Daghlian, Philip B.
1966 Dr. Johnson in his letters: the public guise of private matter. In: Howard Anderson, Philip B. Daghlian and Irvin Ehrenpreis (eds.), 108-129.

Davis, Herbert
1966 The correspondence of the Augustans. In: Howard Anderson, Philip B. Daghlian and Irvin Ehrenpreis (eds.), 1-13.

Hainsworth, D. R. and Cherry Walker (eds.)
1990 *The correspondence of Lord Fitzwilliam of Milton and Francis Guybon, his steward. 1697-1709*. Northampton: Northampton Record Society.

Halsband, Robert
1965-1967 *The complete letters of Lady Mary Wortley Montagu*. 3 Volumes. Oxford: Clarendon Press.

Hemlow, Joyce
1958 *The history of Fanny Burney*. Oxford: Clarendon Press.

Hope, Jonathan
1993 Second person singular pronouns in records of Early Modern "spoken" English. *Neuphilologische Mitteilungen* 94: 83-100.

Jackson, H. J. (ed.)
1987 *Samuel Taylor Coleridge: selected letters*. Oxford: Clarendon Press.

[Jakobson, Roman]
1967 *To Honor Roman Jakobson*. Volume 3. The Hague: Mouton.

Keränen, Jukka
1998 The corpus of Early English Correspondence: progress report. In: Antoinette Renouf (ed.), 29-37.

Labov, William
1966   *The social stratification of English in New York City.* Washington, DC: Centre for Applied Linguistics.
1972   *Language in the Inner City: studies in the Black English Vernacular.* Philadelphia, PA: University of Pennsylvania Press.
1981   *Field methods used by the project on linguistic change and variation.* (Sociolinguistic working paper 81.) Austin, Texas: South Western Educational Development Laboratory.

Lefanu, William (ed.)
1960   *Betsy Sheridan's journal: letters from Sheridan's sister 1784-1786 and 1788-1790.* (2nd edition.) Oxford: Oxford University Press.

Leonard, S. A.
1929   *A doctrine of Correctness in English usage 1700-1800.* Madison: University of Wisconsin.

Lewis, W. S. and Ralph S. Brown
1941   *Horace Walpole's correspondence with George Montagu.* Volume 9. New Haven: Yale University Press.

Lonsdale, Roger
[1965] 1986   *Dr. Charles Burney: a literary bibliography.* [Reprint.] Oxford: Clarendon Press.

McAdam, E. L., Donald Hyde, and Mary Hyde (eds.)
1958   *Samuel Johnson, diaries, prayers, and annals.* New Haven: Yale University Press.

Milroy, Lesley
[1987] 1989   *Language and social networks.* (2nd edition.) [Reprint.] (Language in Society 2.) Oxford: Blackwell.

Mizuno, Kazuho
1992   Variations in Boswell's English. *The Hiroshima University Studies* 50: 150-174.

Nevalainen, Terttu, and Leena Kahlas-Tarkka (eds.)
1997   *To explain the present: studies in the changing English language in honour of Matti Rissanen.* (Mémoires de la Société Néophilologique de Helsinki 52.) Helsinki: Société Néophilologique.

Nurmi, Arja
1998   Periphrastic *do* and the language of social aspirers: evidence from the *Corpus of Early English Correspondence.* In: Antoinette Renouf (ed.), 159-167.

Partridge, Eric (ed.)
1963   *Swift's polite conversation.* London: Deutsch.

Ponsonby, Arthur
1923 *English diaries: a review of English diaries from the sixteenth to the twentieth century with an introduction on diary writing.* London: Methuen.

Raumolin-Brunberg, Helena and Arja Nurmi
1997 Dummies on the move: prop-*one* and affirmative *do* in the 17th century. In: Terttu Nevalainen and Leena Kahlas-Tarkka (eds.), 395-417.

Renouf, Antoinette (ed.)
1998 *Explorations in corpus linguistics.* (Language and Computers Studies in Practical Linguistics 23.) Amsterdam/Atlanta, GA: Rodopi.

Sell, Roger D. and Peter Verdonk (eds.)
1994 *Literature and the new interdisciplinarity. Poetics, linguistics, history.* Amsterdam/Atlanta, GA: Rodopi.

Stein, Dieter and Ingrid Tieken-Boon van Ostade (eds.)
1994 *Towards a standard English 1600-1800.* (Topics in English Linguistics 12.) Berlin: Mouton de Gruyter.

Strang, Barbara M. H.
1967 Swift and the English language: a study in principles and practice. In: [Roman Jakobson] 3: 1947-1959.

Sundby, Bertil, A. K. Bjørge and K. E. Haugland
1991 *A dictionary of English normative grammar 1700-1800.* Amsterdam/Philadelphia: Benjamins.

Tieken-Boon van Ostade, Ingrid
1985 *Do*-support in the writings of Lady Mary Wortley Montagu: a Change in Progress. *Folia Linguistica Historica* 6: 127-151.
1987 *The auxiliary do in eighteenth-century English: a sociohistorical linguistic approach.* Dordrecht: Foris.
1991a Dr. Johnson and the auxiliary *do. Folia Linguistica Historica* 10: 145-162.
1991b Social ambition reflected in the language of Betsy and Richard Sheridan. *Neuphilologische Mitteilungen* 92: 237-246.
1994 Eighteenth-century letters and journals as evidence: studying society through the individual. In: Roger D. Sell and Peter Verdonk (eds.), 179-191.
1996 Social network theory and eighteenth-century English: the case of Boswell. In: Derek Britton (ed.), 327-337.
(in prep.) *In search of the vernacular: the language of eighteenth-century letters.*

Tillyard, Stella
   1994   *Aristocrats: Caroline, Emily, Louisa and Sarah Lennox 1740-1832.* London: Chatto and Windus.

Troide, Lars E. et al. (eds.)
   1988-   *The early journals and letters of Fanny Burney.* Oxford: Clarendon Press.

Waddell, J. N.
   1980   Fanny Burney's contribution to English vocabulary. *Neuphilologische Mitteilungen* 81: 260-263.

Wardhaugh, Ronald
   1992   *An introduction to sociolinguistics.* (2nd edition.) Oxford: Blackwell.

Index of subjects

accent 175
address
~ *"in absentia"* 138, 165
~ pronoun ix, 25-51
form of ~ vi, ix, 29, 32
generic ~ form 155
intimate ~ 44
term of ~ 25, 29, 30, 32, 33, 43-45
adjacency pair 45
affection 151
affirmative sentence xi
affixation 98
Afrikaans 378-380, 388, 390, 392-394, 396, 398
agreement
pronoun ~ xii
subject-verb ~ viii
agriculture 170
Alford, Henry 119, 123
alternation 166
American English vi, 54, 94, 96, 115, 368, 371
amplifier 68
analogy
morphological ~ 96
analytic language 281, 287
anger 35
Anglicisms 178
antedating 199, 202-207, 209, 210, 215, 216, 221, 223
antepenult principle 100, 105
antepenult stress 103
apodosis 127, 128
apprentice 292, 293, 295
Arabic 100
archisememe 386
area xii, 397
area name 397

areal name 387, 396
areal term 395
assignment
Romance stress ~ x
attitude 42
auxiliary vi, xi, 115-133, 339-362

Bantu 380
bisexual pronouns 268
Black South African English 379
booster 68, 69, 72, 73, 84
British English vi, 54, 94, 96

calque 212, 217, 220
Cape Dutch 378, 379
case distinctions 286
case function 31
category 384
category names 150
Celtic 367
Central Scots 230
centralisation 292
centre 279
Chancery 280, 292, 307, 308, 311
change
~ from above 311
~ from below 311
typological ~ viii
Chartism 171
Church of Scotland 171
citation 219
first ~ 199-202, 205, 208-210, 217
closed question 63, 66
closeness 29
clustering
occupational ~ 297
wealth ~ 297
code-switching 34, 175

464 *Index of subjects*

cognition 109
cognitive
 ~ linguistics 109
 ~ strategy 103
collocational constraint 45
colloquial field 21
colloquial speech 284
command 63, 64, 117
communications manuals 260, 263
communicative behaviour 109
compounding 289
concept 384
conditional clause 128
conservative spelling 250
constructionist 56
 ~ approach 58
contempt 35
context 7
contraction 82
convention
 stylistic ~ vii
conversation vii
 ~ analysis 53
 face-to-face ~ vii
 reported ~ vii
conversational
 ~ ability 445
 ~ repair 57
 ~ role 43, 67
core text 252
correspondence
 personal ~ 54
countryside vernacular 229
court records 446
courting 140, 150, 151
courtly behaviour 166
courtroom situation 446
couthiness 191, 193
co-variation 238, 240, 244, 248, 249
crime narrative 64, 65, 68, 73, 76, 79, 81
critical linguistics 111

cross-examination 60, 61, 66, 67, 73, 76, 81
cultural
 ~ community 176
 ~ perception 260

Danish 367
declarative
 negative ~ sentence xi
deference 27, 144
deixis
 person ~ 44
demographic development 290
demonstrative pronoun 27, 454
deontic meaning 128
deontic value 122
depositions 446
dialect
 ~ contact 279, 281, 290, 297, 299, 300, 312, 319
 ~ continuum 298
 ~ mixture viii, 299
dialectology
 historical ~ 227
diaphasic variation xiii
diary writing 450, 457
 ~ conventions 455
diastratic variation xiii
diatopic variation xiii
dictionary word 221
diffusion 249, 251, 279, 297, 300, 301, 304, 306, 310, 327
 site-to-site ~ 310
diglossia 174, 175
diminutives 365
diphthongisation 236
direct speech 73
direction 117
disability 262-264, 271 *See also* physical condition, mental condition
discourse v, 62, 68, 74, 108

~ act 58
~ analysis 53
~ level 79
~ marker 68
~ mode 161
~ situation 108
~ strategy 161, 165
field of ~ 105, 106, 108
discrimination
social ~ 119
distance 44, 46, 164, 231
social ~ 35
distribution 30
donor principle 99, 100
downtoner 68, 69, 71, 73, 83
drift viii, 281, 285-287, 289
Dutch 380, 388
Cape ~ 378, 379

Early Middle English 286
Early Modern English vi, vii, 25, 26, 53, 135, 283, 284, 304, 312, 341, 354, 368, 406-409, 411, 424, 430, 434
Early Scots 234, 368
East Anglia 295
economic distance 229
economy 290
Edinburgh Standard 230, 251
education 45, 96, 97, 106, 123, 233, 344, 352, 356, 358, 422, 429
elicitation 62, 63, 75, 83
emotion 27, 35, 36, 38, 43, 45, 141
emotional
~ attitude 28
~ proximity 27
~ value 135
emphasis 135
emphatic 68
endearment 150
English 96, 289

American ~ vi, 94, 96, 115, 368, 371
Black South African ~ 379
British ~ vi, 54, 94, 96
Early American ~ 54
Early Middle ~ 286
Early Modern ~ vi, vii, 25, 26, 53-89, 135, 283, 284, 304, 312, 341, 354, 368, 406-409, 411, 424, 430, 434
English ~ 364-367, 371
Hiberno-~ 369
Irish ~ 115, 126, 130, 363-376
Late Middle ~ 102, 117, 259, 312, 320
London ~ 279, 280, 295
Middle ~ vi, vii, x, 31, 101, 117, 135-168, 283, 285, 304, 321, 368, 371
Modern ~ vi, x, 31
Northern Hiberno-~ 370
Old ~ 117, 289
Present-day ~ 340, 341
Scottish ~ 54, 115, 363-376
South African ~ vi, xii
South African Indian ~ 400
Southern ~ 367, 368
Southern Hiberno-~ 370
Standard ~ 280, 311, 316, 320, 322, 363, 374
Standard Southern ~ 366, 368
ethnic
~ community 176
~ group 257, 382, 395
ethnicity 257, 382, 396
ethnolinguistic identity xii, 377-403
etymological prototype 100
"etymologised" spelling 424
etymology
spelling and ~ 411, 422, 429
euphemism xii, 259, 265, 270

expletive 21, 53

face-to-face conversation vii
face-to-face interaction 299
face-work ix, 135, 161, 163
familiarity 27, 35
family relation 141, 143
farming techniques 170
fashion 17
fashionable usage 213, 216
field of discourse 105, 106, 108
first citation 199-202, 205, 208-210, 217, 223
first person
 ~ singular 283
 ~ subject 118, 121, 123, 127, 128, 130
folk-etymology 374
form of address vi, ix, 29, 32, 135-168
formal register 33, 96, 97
formality
 degree of ~ vii
 ~ scale 410
free variation 248
French x, 99, 100, 136, 236
frequency 108
functional language 384, 385
future contingency 124
future shock 187
futurity 115, 117, 121-123, 125, 127-129

Gælic 176, 177, 368-371, 374
 Irish ~ 367
 Scottish ~ 367
gender v, vii, viii, x, xi, 53-89, 257, 258, 259, 263, 290, 316, 322, 352-356, 358, 405-439
 ~ shift 287
 ~ stereotype 55
 ~-neutral usage 259

grammatical ~ 289
social ~ 289
generalisation of -*s* 284
generic *he* 259-261, 268, 269, 271
generic masculine 258
generic *they* 269
genitive 286
 ~ forms 284
 ~ inflection 328
genre xi, 227, 228, 344-347, 358
 ~ variation 299
gentry 296
geographical
 ~ distance 227-255, 326
German 107, 365, 367
 Modern ~ 107
Germanic x, 98, 281, 283
glottal stops 367
grammar
 ~ book 118
 ~ rule 131
 prescriptive ~ xi
grammatical
 ~ change 257-277
 ~ gender 286
 ~ word 289
grammaticalisation 289
grapheme-sound relation 227-255
graphemic
 ~ "attraction" 102
 ~ form 96
 ~ image 102
Greek 100
 Ancient ~ 102
 Modern ~ 101

hapax legomenon 208
Harley, Lady Brilliana x
hearer 27
heavy syllable principle 106, 111
hedge 53, 56, 58, 68-71, 73-75, 83, 84

Helsinki Corpus 54
Hiberno-English 369
   Northern ~ 370
   Southern ~ 370
historical
   ~ dialectology 227
   ~ sociolinguistics v, vi, 57
hypercorrect grammar 82
hypercorrection 317, 357

identity 196
i-digraphs 234, 249, 250
idiolect 228, 233
idiolectal usage 200, 207-209
if-clause 124
impersonal form 136
impersonal *it* 261
indefinite
   ~ compound pronoun viii, 282
   ~ pronoun 280, 288, 289, 324, 325, 330
Indian English
   South African ~ 400
indicative 283
   ~ present 283
   ~ subject-verb agreement 311
indifference 35
indirect speech 73
Industrial Revolution 170, 290
inflection 76, 79
   third person singular ~ 54
inflectional ending 235
innovator 55
   linguistic ~ 57, 76, 84
insult 150, 151
intensifier 2, 16, 84
intensive 83
interaction 54, 59, 61, 81, 135, 143, 300
   conversational ~ 53
interview situation 441

intimacy 35, 38, 40, 154, 162-164, 231
intimate address 44
intonation 82
Irish 180
   ~ English 115, 126, 130, 363-376
   ~ Gælic 367
   ~ Question xi, 116, 121, 127
   ~ usage xi
irony 33
Italian 100, 101

journal writing 450, 457
   ~ conventions 455

kinship term 141

land-ownership 296
language 388
   class-influenced ~ choice 172
   covert ~ attitudes 186, 195
   ~ acquisition 98
   ~ as a marker 189
   ~ as a marker of older times 195
   ~ attitude vi, xi, xii, 169-198, 303, 363-376, 377-403
   ~ contact 181, 186, 233, 251, 289
   ~ death 169
   ~ maintenance 300
   ~ mixing 172-174, 176, 178-180, 228
   ~ mixture 279
   ~ shift 169
   ~ variation 227-255
   ~ variety 176
   lesser-used ~s 169
   overt ~ attitudes 172, 186
   "vulgar" ~ 444
Late Middle English 102, 117, 259, 312, 320
Latin x, 99, 100, 117, 355, 365, 407

Neo-~ 102
legalese 228
lesser-used languages 169
letter-writing 230
   conventions of ~ 446, 453, 455
   types of ~ 230
level of education xi
lexical
   ~ change 257-277
   ~ diffusion 299
   ~ fashion 208
   ~ field 377, 383, 399, 400
   ~ retrieval 105
   ~ word 289
lexicographers 201, 212, 215, 217, 220
lexicon xii, 199, 208, 264, 377-403
lexis vi
linguistic
   ~ innovation 299
   ~ innovator 57, 76, 84
linguistics
   cognitive ~ 109
   critical ~ 111
   sociohistorical ~ 441-461
literacy 106, 227-229
loan-word 99
local colour 186, 189
local speech 193
localisation 228, 233
   ~ of texts 228
London English 279, 280, 295
Lowland Scots 371

malapropism 201, 207, 374
manual labour 296
Manx 368
marked construction 283
markedness ix, 25-51, 405, 409, 430, 431
   ~ reversal 26, 38, 39, 43, 44
   ~ value 30

Martin, B. 93
masculine anaphoric pronouns 259
matrix-clause antecedent 285
maxim 155, 159
meaning 384
medical terminology ix, 199
medical texts 210
mental condition 263, 264
message-oriented
   ~ discourse 57
   ~ function 57
metanalysis 425, 426
metaphor 265
meter 45
Middle English vi, vii, x, 31, 101, 117, 135-168, 283, 285, 289, 304, 321, 368, 371
   Early ~ 286
   Late ~ 117, 259, 312, 320
Middle Scots 234, 238, 365-368, 371
migration 279, 290-292, 295, 300, 306, 314, 319, 326
   "betterment" ~ 292
minority 271, 303
   ~ group 257
mobility 228, 229, 233, 354
modal verb xi, 115-133, 341
   marginal ~ 341
Modern English vi, x, 31
   Early ~ 135, 283, 284, 304, 312, 341, 354, 368, 406-409, 411, 424, 430, 434
Modern German 107
Modern Greek 101
Modern Scots 234
morphological
   ~ analogy 96
   ~ parsing 96, 99, 105
   ~ simplification 281, 283, 284, 289
   ~ stress assignment 98

morphology 281
  spelling and ~ 411, 414, 415, 422, 429, 431
morphophonemic
  ~ alternations 284
  ~ restructuring 284
Mulcaster 100
multiculturalism 264
multiple negation 82

naming conventions 83
narrative style 78
nearness 44
necessity 117
negation
  multiple ~ 82
negative
  ~ declarative sentence xi
  ~ prefix ix, 199-225
Neo-Latin 102
network 233
  individual ~ 202
  social ~ 202
neutralisation 30
neutrality 35
Newcastle, Duke of x
nominal inflection 287
nominal plural 284
nominative 286
non-gentry 296
non-personal reference 285
norm 118, 228, 252, 303
North 295
Northern Hiberno-English 370
Northern Present-Tense Rule 311, 312, 318, 319, 326
Northumbrian 304
noun modification 270
noun phrase 289
  ~ structure xii, 270, 288
number 27

object territory 286
objective 285, 286
obligation 117, 125, 155
oblique 286
observer's paradox v, vii, 175, 441-461
occupational clustering 297
occupations 257
Old English 117, 289
on-line word-stress assignment 96, 101, 107
open question 63, 65
Optimality Theory 111
outgroup perspective 398

paraphrase 53
parole 110
parsing
  morphological ~ 96, 99, 105
participant relationship 231
partitive construction 328
past indicative plural 283
past participle 284
past subjunctive plural 283
pattern recognition 102, 104, 105, 108
penultimate 103
perception
  spelling and ~ 425, 429-431
perceptual force 416, 425
performance 110
peripheral pronoun 289
periphery 279
periphrastic *do* xi, 58, 80, 339-362, 443
periphrastic *of*-phrase 286
person 27
  ~ deixis 44
  second ~ pronoun 27, 28, 82
  third ~ pronoun 43
  third ~ singular inflection 54

personal
  ~ correspondence 54
  ~ pronoun 27, 135, 286
  ~ reference 285, 287
  ~ relationship 26, 44
phonetic spelling x, 231, 241, 250, 417
phonetics
  spelling and ~ 411, 414, 417, 429, 431, 433, 434
phonological
  ~ representation 102
  ~ variable 53
physical condition 263-265
physical features 257
"plural-as-singular" address 136
pluralis maiestatis 43
politeness 32, 33, 38, 53, 73, 136, 143, 144, 149
  ~ strategy ix, 165
political correctness xi, xii, 257-277
Portuguese 101
possessive 45
  ~ determiner 324
  ~ determiner *its* 282, 286
  third person singular ~ pronoun 280
postdating 202
postmodification 270, 287
postposed modifier 270
postpositional modification xii
Potato Famine 180
power 27, 62, 72, 81
powerless language 71
pragmatic particle 68
pragmatics 2, 5, 8, 15, 19-21, 25
Prague school 30
prediction 117, 125, 128
prefix
  negative ~ ix, 199-225
premodification 270, 287
preposed modifier 270

prepositional phrase 270
prescriptivism 115-133, 257, 259, 260, 263, 264, 269, 272
present indicative 283
  ~ paradigm 311, 312, 330
present tense inflection 283
present tense marker 319
Present-day English 340, 341
prestige 231
  ~ form 354-356
  ~ spelling x
preterite 284
private writing 407
problem-solving 105
profession 258
progressive form 82
prompter 63, 64, 65, 74
pronoun ix, 26, 27, 31, 33, 34, 40, 44, 45, 135, 322
  address ~ ix, 29, 30, 136
  bisexual ~ 268
  demonstrative ~ 27, 453
  indefinite ~ 280, 289, 324, 325, 330
  indefinite compound ~ 282
  personal ~ 27, 135, 286
  ~ agreement xii
  ~ alternation *See* ~ switch
  ~ fluctuation *See* ~ switch
  ~ of address 135
  ~ retractability 146
  ~ selection 34
  ~ switch ix, 25, 27-29, 33, 34, 36, 38, 39, 43, 135, 137-139, 141, 146, 151, 153, 155, 156, 161-166
  ~ usage 446
  ~ use 149
  reflexive ~ 27
  relative ~ viii, 82, 250, 280, 282, 284-286, 289, 320, 321, 326
  second person ~ 27, 28, 82

Index of subjects 471

subject ~ viii, 280, 282
third person ~ 43
pronunciation vi, 82, 92, 229
   spelling and ~ 417, 433
propriety 173
prop-word *one* viii, 280, 282, 288, 324, 325, 354
prototype 386
   ~ semantics xii, 384
   etymological ~ 100
proverb 155
proximity 28
pseudo-gentry 296
psychological reality 109
public writing 407, 408
publicness 407
purification 173

question 66, 67
   "yes/no" ~ 66
   closed ~ 63, 66
   open ~ 63, 65
   rhetorical ~ 63, 67
questioning 62
quotation 53

race xii, 263, 388, 394, 397
racial difference 382
rank 295, 296, 316
   social ~ 35
reading 426, 429, 430, 431
Reading Style 456
reference 384
   non-personal ~ 320
   personal ~ 320
reflexive pronoun 27
regional variation 290
register 28, 102, 351, 441, 442
   formal ~ 33
   ~ consciousness 441
   ~ variation 329, 358
relation

social ~ 144
relationship
   personal ~ 26
   social ~ ix
relative
   ~ adverb 285
   ~ clause 270
   ~ pronoun viii, 82, 250, 280, 282, 284-286, 289, 320, 321, 326
   non-restrictive ~ clause 320
   restrictive ~ clause 320
religion 257, 263
remoteness 29
reported conversation vii
reported speech 79
research 324
respect 138, 140, 144, 149, 150
response 62, 65, 83
rhetorical question 63, 67
rhoticity v
ritual formula 29
Rogers, Samuel 93
role vii, viii
Romance x, 100
   ~ stress assignment x
root stress
   initial ~ 98, 99, 105
runrig 170
rural 190
   ~ speech 186

Sargeaunt, J. 93
Scots vi, 54, 169-198, 178, 227-255, 363-376
   Central ~ 230
   Early ~ 234, 368
   Lowland ~ 371
   Middle ~ 234, 238, 365-368, 371
   Modern ~ 234
   Southern ~ 371
   Ulster ~ 371
Scotticism 365

Scottish
    ~ English 54, 115, 363-376
    ~ English Standard 234, 251
    ~ Gælic 367
S-curve 300, 306, 310
second and third person subjects 130
second person
    ~ pronoun 25, 27, 28, 82, 136
    ~ subject 118, 121, 123, 127, 129, 130, 326
    ~ subject pronoun 286, 322
segmental variation 91
semantics
    prototype ~ xii, 384
    structural ~ xii, 383
sender database 301
sentence
    affirmative ~ xi
    negative declarative ~ xi
sex 56, 58, 82, 353
sexism 82
sexual orientation 257
Shakespeare, William ix, 1-23, 25-51, 117, 123, 135
shortening of long vowels 231
Sidney family ix
singular *they* 259, 269, 271
Sintu 388, 394, 400
"snowball effect" 301, 310
"snowball pattern" 322
social
    ~ accelerator 46
    ~ affectation 216
    ~ aspirer 352, 356-359, 455
    ~ attitude 45
    ~ awareness 311
    ~ context 169
    ~ continuity 306
    ~ discrimination 119
    ~ distance x, 27, 35, 36, 38, 43, 45, 144, 149, 193, 227-255
    ~ embedding 307
    ~ evaluation 307
    ~ hierarchy 295
    ~ identity 382
    ~ interaction 26
    ~ markedness 309
    ~ meaning 27, 45
    ~ mobility 296, 297, 303
    ~ network 54, 296, 300, 301, 454
    ~ network analysis 443, 452
    ~ rank 26, 35, 45
    ~ relation ix, 135-168, 144, 295
    ~ relationship ix, 27, 165
    ~ standing 27
    ~ status 28, 34, 135, 149, 151, 233, 237, 250, 297, 303, 310
    ~ stratification 279, 352, 358
    ~ structure 290, 295, 296
Socialism 171
sociohistorical
    ~ linguistics 441-461
    ~ status 377
sociolinguistic
    ~ methods 301
    ~ variation 351
sociolinguistics v, xi, 57, 58
    historical ~ v, vi, 57
sociological
    ~ development 290
socio-pragmatic role 159
solidarity 27, 44, 73
sound
    spelling variation and ~ change 227
South African English vi, xii
    Black ~ 379
South African Indian English 400
Southern English 367, 368
    Standard ~ 366, 368
Southern Hiberno-English 370
Southern Scots 371
Southern Standard 251

Index of subjects   473

Spanish 101
speaker 27
   ~ innovation 58
   ~ interaction 57
   ~ types 69
   ~'s vernacular language 442
speech 53, 82
   ~ community 303
   ~ event 59
   ~ formula 155
   ~ situation vii
   ~ style viii, 55, 56, 81, 82, 229, 303, 452
   direct ~ 73
   indirect ~ 73
   reported ~ 79
spelling vi, x, 54, 231, 235, 238, 368, 405-439, 442
   conservative ~ 250
   "etymologised" ~ 424
   phonetic ~ x, 229, 231, 241, 250, 433
   prestige ~ x
   ~ and etymology 411, 422, 429
   ~ and morphology 411, 414, 415, 422, 429, 431
   ~ and perception 405, 425, 429-431
   ~ and phonetics 411, 414, 417, 429, 431, 434
   ~ and pronunciation 417, 433
   ~ practice 228
   ~ production 431
   ~ variant x, 235, 251
   ~ variation and sound change 227-255
spoken interaction vii
spontaneous utterances 441
standard 57, 92, 96, 110, 173, 175, 178, 179, 230, 251, 280, 298, 303, 306, 312, 314, 322, 326, 355, 358, 411

   ~ forms 55
   Edinburgh S~ 230
   S~ English 280, 311, 316, 320, 322, 363, 374
   S~ Southern English 366, 368
   Scottish English S~ 234, 251
   Southern S~ 251
   supraregional ~ 279
standardisation x, 283, 285, 286, 289, 314, 407, 409
status vii, 56, 123, 140, 147, 150, 161, 295, 296, 316
   social ~ 34
   sociohistorical ~ 377
stem-variability 284
stereotype
   gender ~ 55
storage 107, 108
strategy
   cognitive ~ 103
stress x, 91-113
   left-handed ~ assignment 111
   morphological ~ assignment 98
   right-handed ~ assignment 111
   Romance ~ assignment x
   ~ assignment xi, 97, 101, 103, 105, 106
   ~ pattern 103
   ~ retraction 99, 100
   ~ variation x, 91, 92-95, 97
Stress Rule
   Germanic ~ 98, 99
structural semantics xii, 383
structure
   vocabulary ~ 103
style 28
style-shifting 34
stylistic convention vii
subject
   indicative ~-verb agreement 311
   ~ case 31
   ~ function 323

~ marker 283
~ matter v
~ pronoun viii, 280, 282
~ territory 286
~-verb agreement 280, 281, 304
subjective case 285
subjunctive 124, 283
subordinate clause
   conditional ~ 123
   temporal ~ 123, 127
subsistence 292
supraregional standard 279
suprasegmentals 91
swear word 444
Swedish 283
syllable weight x, 107
syncretism 30
synthetic language 281, 287

tag question 53
temporal clause 124
temporal subordinator 124
term of address 25, 29, 30, 32, 33, 43-45, 136, 137, 141, 144, 149, 150
text frequency 34
text type v, x, xi, 54, 59, 344, 408-410, 430, 446
third person
   ~ endings 329
   ~ pronoun 43
   ~ singular 58, 77, 282, 299
   ~ singular ending 76, 79
   ~ singular inflection 54, 77, 280, 284, 298, 304, 305, 308, 309, 311, 322, 326, 327, 354, 432
   ~ singular *it* 286
   ~ singular morphological marking 58
   ~ singular present-tense inflection 284

~ subject 118, 121, 123, 125, 129, 130
thou/you alternation 25
town vernacular 229
transcription 59
trial vii, viii, 53-89, 446
   ~ proceedings 54, 59, 72, 228
   ~ records 83
tribal name 387
turn 36, 60, 63, 65, 67, 71
typological change viii
typology 281, 283, 284, 287

Ulster Scots 371
universal implication law 30
urban 190
   ~ society 354
   ~ speech 186

variation x, xi, 45, 55, 303
   co-~ 238, 240, 244, 248, 249
   diaphasic ~ v, xiii
   diastratic ~ v, xiii
   diatopic ~ v, xiii
   free ~ 248
   regional ~ 228
   stress ~ x
   synchronic ~ v
variational space 238, 250
variationist vii, 55-58, 81, 82, 91
   ~ theory vi
variety vi, xi, xii, 169
verbal agreement 283
vernacular 442, 452, 453, 456
   spoken ~ 442, 443, 446
   written ~ 442, 446
vocabulary 1-23, 175
   ~ development 98
   ~ structure 103
vogue word 16, 21
volition 126

vowel deletion 284
vowel length 234, 238
vowel shift v
"vulgar" language 444

wave model viii, 297, 298, 300, 306, 310
wave theory 280, 327
wealth clustering 297
white – non-white 388
witness deposition 72, 83
women's language 53, 55, 58, 68, 70, 72, 84
word order 281

word shape 425
word-based
 ~ morphology 284
word-coinage 216
word-formation 99, 266
 fashion 201, 208, 212
word-stress x, 91-113
 ~ assignment 105, 110, 111
 ~ variation *See* stress-variation
Wyld's dilemma 298

"yes/no" question 66

zero expression 30

Index of authors

Abbott, Edwin A. 25, 46
Abrams, Dominic 401
Adaktylos, Anna-Maria xiii
Adams, Walter 432, 436
Aitchinson, Jean 101, 111
Aitken, Adam J. 169, 172, 197, 234, 235, 238, 239, 253
Alford, Henry 131
Algeo, John 369, 371, 376
Allen, Irving L. 258, 274
Amis, Kingsley 93, 111
Amussen, Susan D. 62, 84
Anderson, Howard 448, 449, 457, 458
Anderson, Laurie 43, 46
Arnovick, Leslie K. 130, 131
Atkins, Bowman K. 58, 69-71, 87
Austin, Frances 449, 457

Baayen, Harald R. 105, 111
Bailey, Charles-James N. 233, 274
Bailey, Guy 330
Bailey, Richard W. 206, 224
Balderston, Katherine 447, 451, 457
Baldi, Philip 222, 224
Baldwin, Louis 443-445, 457
Bambas, Robert C. 368, 375
Barber, Charles L. 25, 28, 33, 34, 45, 46, 299, 330, 369, 371, 375
Barisone, Ermanno 253, 254
Barlow, Michael 108, 111
Baron, Dennis 268, 274
Baugh, Albert C. 46, 369, 371, 375
Baugh, John 332
Bax, Randy 454, 457
Bazzanella, Carla 46, 49
Beard, Henry 259, 274
Beaugrande, Robert de 111
Beauvillain, Cécile 426, 435

Beier, A. L. 291, 292, 296, 297, 331, 332, 334, 336
Beljaars, Ellen Bernice 444, 457
Belsey, Catherine 456
Bennet, Dina 86, 88
Benson, Larry D. 166, 167
Berberoğlu, Giray 433
Berg, Thomas 111
Bermúdez-Otero, Ricardo 253, 254, 331, 335
Berndt, Rolf 304, 331
Bernini, Giuliano 47, 48
Bertuccelli Papi, Marcella 47, 51
Biber, Douglas 73, 84
Bjørge, A. K. 453, 454, 460
Blake, Norman F. vi, ix, 1-23, 26, 46, 112, 113, 144, 149, 167, 280, 303, 331, 334, 368, 375, 435, 437
Bloom, Edward A. 449, 457, 458
Bloom, Lillian D. 449, 457, 458
Bloomfield, Morton W. 366, 375
Blount, Thomas 406, 435
Bolinger, Dwight 400
Bolton, Whitney F. 408, 435
Borker, Ruth 87, 88
Boulton, Jeremy 291, 303, 328, 331
Bradley Beach, Cornelius 117, 131
Bradley, Henry 276, 366, 375
Bradley, Lynette 426, 436
Brady, Frank 452, 458
Branford, Jean 400
Branford, William 380, 400
Britton, Derek 331, 336, 337, 458, 461
Brockride, Wayne 268, 275
Broderick, Victor 222, 224
Brook, George L. 26, 46, 366, 367, 375
Brooks, L. 430, 435

Brown, Penelope 46
Brown, Ralph S. 449, 459
Brown, Roger 25, 27-29, 45, 46
Bruti, Silvia vi, ix, 25-51
Bryson, Bill 368, 369, 372, 375
Bucholtz, Mary 56, 85
Burchfield, Robert W. 22
Burness, Edwina 46, 47, 49, 50
Burney, Charles 454
Burnley, David 408, 417, 433, 435
Burzio, Luigi 109, 110, 112
Bush, Harold K. 258, 259, 275
Buxton, John 213, 224

Cable, Thomas 369, 371, 375
Caliumi, Grazia 46
Camden, William 408
Cameron, Annie I. 252
Cameron, Deborah 53, 55, 56, 69, 84, 85, 259, 275, 354, 360
Carrol, J. B. 277
Carruba, Onofrio 47, 48
Cawdrey, Robert 406, 435
Chafe, Wallace 74, 84
Chambers, J. K. 353, 354, 360, 441-443, 456, 458
Cheshire, Jenny 55, 84, 131, 259, 275, 283, 331
Chomsky, Noam 109, 110
Claiborne, Robert 369, 372, 373, 375
Clark, Herbert H. 43, 47
Clarkson, Iain 198
Classen, Eugen 366, 375
Clifton, Kay A. 87
Coates, Jennifer 53, 55, 58, 84, 354, 360
Codol, Jean-Paul 401
Coleman, David 291, 331
Coleman, William H. 445, 458
Colen, Alexandra 222, 224
Converse, Charles C. 268, 275

Cooper, William E. 55, 88
Coote, Edmund 406, 435
Corrigan, Roberta 111, 113
Coseriu, Eugenio xiii, xiv, 384, 401
Craigie, William A. 276, 375
Cran, William 369, 372-374, 376
Crawford, Mary 53, 56, 57, 85
Crosby, Faye 55, 68, 85
Crouch, Isabel 55, 85
Crowder, Robert G. 430, 434-436
Crystal, David 93, 259, 275, 434, 436
Cukor-Avila, Patricia 330
Culpeper, Jonathan vi, vii, 53-89

Daghlian, Philip B. 448, 449, 451, 457, 458
Daines, Simon 432, 436
Dalton-Puffer, Christiane vi, x, 91-113
Damper, R. I. 111, 112
Danchev, Andrei 281, 331
Danielsson, Bror 93, 98-100, 104, 111, 112, 280, 328, 331
Darnell, Donald 268, 275
Darnell, W. N. 435
Davies, Andrew 275
Davis, Herbert 447, 448, 458
De Klerk, Vivian 399, 401-403
Denison, David 253, 328, 331
Densmore, Dana 268, 275
Devitt, Amy J. 230, 253
Dijkstra, Ton 105, 111
Dobson, Eric J. 280, 328, 331
Dörschner, Norbert 400, 401
Drew, Paul 47, 48
Dubois, Betty Lou 55, 85
Dunkling, Leslie 31, 47
Dupuy-Engelhardt, Hiltraud 384, 401
Durkacz, Victor Edward 176, 197
Dyer, Alan 290, 332

Eagleson, Robert D. 3, 22, 25, 28, 29, 47
Eales, Jacqueline 433
Eastmond, J. F. G. 111, 112
Eckhardt, E. 112
Ehrenpreis, Irvin 448, 449, 457, 458
Ehri, Linnea C. 436
Elam, Keir 43, 47
Ellegård, Alvar 341, 343-347, 349, 350, 352, 358, 360
Emerson, Oliver Farrar 364, 365, 375
Ervin-Tripp, Susan 47
Everitt, Alan 296, 332

Facchinetti, Roberta vi, vii, xi, 115-133
Fain, Margaret A. vii, xii, 257-277
Feagin, Crawford 332
Ferguson, Charles A. 281, 283, 285, 289, 332
Fillmore, Charles 108, 112
Finkenstaedt, Thomas 25, 29, 43, 45, 47, 136, 137, 140, 144, 146, 151, 154, 165-167
Finlay, Roger 291, 292, 296, 297, 328, 331, 332, 334, 336
Fisher, Jane L. 280, 307, 332
Fisher, John H. 280, 292, 307, 332
Fishman, Joshua A. 401
Fisiak, Jacek 224, 332, 335, 336, 360, 361
Fludernik, Monika 73, 85
Frank, Thomas 25, 47
Freeborn, Dennis 407, 436
Fries, Charles C. 118, 130, 131
Frith, Uta 436
Fritz, Gerd 85, 86
Funk, Peter 222, 224
Funnell, Elaine 430, 436
Furman, Nelly 87, 88

Gale, Wanda 87
Geckeler, Horst xiii, xiv, 384, 401
Giacalone Ramat, Anna 47, 48
Giddens, Anthony 382, 401
Giegerich, Heinz 109, 110, 112
Gillet, Peter J. 47
Gilman, Albert 25, 27-29, 45, 46
Glauser, Beat 178, 180, 197
Gómez-Soliño, José S. 329, 332
Görlach, Manfred 31, 45, 47, 118, 131, 380, 401, 406-408, 412, 424, 436
Gowers, Ernest 119, 126, 132
Gray, Douglas 332, 334
Green, Georgia M. 401
Greenbaum, Sidney 132, 335, 361, 401, 402
Greenberg, Joseph H. 30, 31, 47, 48
Gumperz, John J. 47
Guy, Gregory R. 332

Hainsworth, D. R. 453, 458
Hall, Kira 56, 85
Halliday, F. E. 366, 375
Halsband, Robert 448, 454, 458
Hannay, Margaret P. 212, 213, 221, 224
Hargrave, Francis 83, 85
Harris, Sandra 62, 85
Haugen, Einar 197
Haugland, K. E. 453, 454, 460
Head, Brian F. 27, 31, 43, 48
Heikkonen, Kirsi 336, 361
Hemlow, Joyce 444, 458
Henley, Nancy 61, 88
Hewstone, Miles 401
Hickey, Raymond 48-50, 253, 254
Hogg, Michael A. 401
Hogg, Richard M. xiv, 112, 113, 253, 331, 332
Holmes, Janet 61, 69, 72, 73, 83, 85

Holmqvist, Erik 76, 86, 298, 299, 304, 306, 309, 314, 329, 333
Hope, Jonathan 446, 458
Hopper, Paul 289, 333
Hopper, Robert 269, 271, 276
Horsbroch, Dauvit 169-198
Huff, Darrell 433, 436
Hulbert, James Root 130, 132
Humphreys, Arthur Raleigh 48
Hussey, S. S. 26, 48
Huxford, Laura 426, 436
Hyde, Donald 451, 459
Hyde, Mary 451, 459
Hymes, Dell 47

Ihalainen, Ossi 88, 338
Iverson, Gregory 111, 113

J. K. 407, 436
Jackson, H. J. 453, 458
Jakobson, Roman 30, 48, 458
Jardine, David 83, 86
Jespersen, Otto 76, 84, 86, 259, 275
Johannesson, Nils-Lennart 334
Johnson, Sally A. 82, 86
Johnston, Paul 227, 229, 230, 253
Jones, Charles 169, 197, 198, 253, 254, 435, 437
Jones, Daniel 92, 112
Jones, Deborah 56, 86
Jucker, Andreas H. 48, 50, 85, 86

Kachru, Braj B. 401, 402
Kahane, Henry 401, 402
Kahlas-Tarkka, Leena 254, 289, 325, 331, 335, 336, 345, 360, 361, 459, 460
Kakietek, Piotr 118, 123, 132
Kaltenböck, Gunther xiii
Kastovsky, Dieter v-xv, 86, 88, 224, 284, 328, 333, 336, 360, 361, 384, 400, 402

Katamba, Francis 109, 110, 112
Kay, P. 108, 112
Keenan, Elinor O. 86, 88
Kellermann, Günter xiv, 333
Kelly, Edward H. 82, 86
Kemmer, Suzanne 108, 111
Kennedy, Arthur G. 48
Ker, W. P. 432, 436
Keränen, Jukka 329, 441, 458
Kerkhof, Jelle 140, 151, 155, 166, 167
Kersey, John See J. K.
Kerswill, Paul 303, 333
Kielkiewicz-Janowiak, Agnieszka 45, 48
Kilpatrick, James 271, 275
Kitch, M. J. 292, 293, 295, 333
Klein, Jürgen 401, 402
Klemola, Juhani 328, 333, 335, 337
Konerding, Klaus-Peter 402
Kopytko, Roman 33, 48
Kramarae, Chris 61, 86, 88
Kristensson, Gillis 279, 333
Krygier, Marcin 332, 336
Kurath, Hans 22
Kurthen, Hermann 258, 275
Kytö, Merja vi, vii, 48, 53-89, 215, 224, 253, 299, 304, 333, 335, 336, 337, 340, 360-362, 432, 437

Labov, William v, xiv, 53, 55, 76, 86, 280, 328, 334, 442, 443, 452, 456, 459
Ladefoged, Peter 420, 434, 437
Lakoff, George 68, 87
Lakoff, Robin 53, 55, 56, 58, 68, 69-72, 82, 84, 87
Lancashire, Ian 48, 253
Langacker, Ronald 111, 112
Lanham, Len 378, 399, 402
Lansdowne, Marquis of 437
Laslett, Peter 295, 334

Lass, Roger 109, 111, 112, 283, 332, 334, 369, 370, 375, 399, 402, 410
Lebsanft, Franz 85, 86
Leech, Geoffrey 335, 361
Lefanu, William 449, 453, 459
Lehrer, Adrienne 402
Leith, Dick 280, 334, 364, 369, 375
Leonard, S. A. 453, 459
Levinson, Stephen 46, 48
Lewis, Thomas Taylor 408, 433, 437
Lewis, W. S. 449, 459
Lima, Susan 111, 113
Lonsdale, Roger 459
Losey, Kay M. 258, 275
Lounsbury, Thomas R. 366, 376
Lowth, Robert 118, 132
Luick, Karl 284, 334
Lutzeier, Peter Rolf 400-403
Lye, Thomas 432, 437

Macafee, Caroline 179, 180, 197
MacAulay, Ronald K. S. 193, 197
Machan, Tim William 48, 51
MacNeil, Robert 369, 372-374, 376
Maggio, Rosalie 259, 275
Malsch, Derry L. 48
Manwaring, G. E. 433, 438
Marckwardt, Albert H. 366, 376
Mason, George 118, 132
Mathesius, Walter 92, 113
Mausch, Hanna 31, 48
Maynor, Natalie 330, 331
Mazzon, Gabriella vi, vii, ix, 25, 45, 49, 135-168
McAdam, E. L. 451, 459
McArthur, Tom 197
McClure, J. Derrick 175, 197, 198
McColl Millar, Robert vi, vii, xi, 169-198, 252

McConchie, Roderick W. vi, ix, 199-225
McConnell-Ginet, Sally 87, 88
McCrum, Robert 369, 372-374, 376
McCully, Charles B. 253, 331
McDiarmid, Matthew P. 253
McGrath, Diane 87
McIntosh, Angus 28, 49, 230, 232, 253, 312, 334
McKnight, George H. 366, 367, 376
McMillan, Julie R. 69, 87
Meinhof, Ulrike 82, 86
Melchers, Gunnel 254, 255, 334, 361, 362
Meredith, Mamie 82, 87
Merlini Barbaresi, Lavinia 38, 49
Mesthrie, Raj 399, 400, 402, 403
Mettinger, Arthur v-xv
Meurman-Solin, Anneli vi, x, 54, 87, 227-255
Michael, Ian 118, 132
Miles, Jack 258, 275
Miller, Casey 259, 268, 275
Millward, Celia M. 49, 369, 370, 376
Milroy, James 35, 49, 57, 87, 297, 300, 334, 354, 360
Milroy, Lesley 55, 87, 297, 300, 334, 442, 443, 454, 456, 459
Minkova, Donka 92, 111, 113
Mitchison, Rosalind 170, 198
Mizuno, Kazuho 456, 459
Monsarrat, G. D. 223, 224
Moody, Patricia A. 130, 132
Morgan, Chris 187, 198
Mørk, Endre xiv, xv
Morrissey, Michael D. xiv, 333
Muir, Kenneth 49, 50
Mulholland, Joan 25, 28, 45, 49
Müller, Robert 402
Murray, James A. H. 22, 276, 365

Murray, Lindley 124, 132
Mustanoja, Tauno F. 322, 334

Nagle, Stephen J. vi, vii, xii, 257-277
Nevala, Minna 29, 49, 329
Nevalainen, Terttu vi, viii, xi, 29, 44, 46, 48, 49, 54, 76, 82, 87, 229, 234, 254, 279-337, 339, 354, 359-361, 407, 433, 437, 459, 460
Nevanlinna, Saara 329, 335
Newmark, Leonard 366, 375
Nikula, Tarja 83, 87
Nocera Avila, Carmela 49, 50, 167
Nurmi, Arja vi, xi, 288, 324, 325, 329, 336, 339-362, 441, 456, 459
Nyquist, Linda 55, 68, 85

Ó Baoill, Colin 178, 198
O'Barr, William M. 58, 69-71, 88
O'Connor, Mary Catherine 108, 112
O'Donnell, W. R. 31, 50
Ogura, Mieko 299, 300, 310, 322, 329, 335
Oizumi, Akio 166, 168
Oliver, Harold James 50
Onions, Charles T. 3, 22, 276
Orovan, Mary 268, 276
Osselton, Noel E. 407, 432, 437

Pahta, Päivi 254, 255, 337, 361, 362
Palander-Collin, Minna 329, 340, 362
Palermo, Davis S. 222, 224
Pálsson, Hermann 253
Pantaleo, Nicola 49, 50, 167
Parry, E. A. 408, 437
Partridge, Eric 443, 459
Pater, J. 111, 113
Patten, John 291, 295, 335
Pawley, A. 108, 113
Peeters, Bert 403

Peyton, V. John 364, 376
Pezzini, Domenico 49, 50, 167
Pollner, Clausdirk vi, vii, xii, 363-376
Ponsonby, Arthur 450-452, 457, 460
Pottle, Frederick A. 452, 458
Poutsma, Hendrik 130, 132
Power, M. J. 297, 335
Prögler-Rössler, Karin 269, 271, 276
Pyles, Thomas 369, 371, 376

Quirk, Randolph 25, 28, 45, 50, 330, 335, 340, 361

Ramisch, Heinrich 85, 88
Rappaport, Steve 291, 293, 295, 328, 335
Raumolin-Brunberg, Helena vi, viii, xi, 29, 46, 49, 54, 87, 229, 234, 254, 279-337, 339, 345, 347, 349, 354, 359-361, 433, 437, 456, 460
Reber, A. S. 435, 437
Rees, Nigel 257, 259, 267, 268, 276
Reicher, G. M. 434, 437
Reinhardt, Mechthild 376
Renouf, Antoinette 49, 50, 361, 459, 460
Reploge, Carol 25, 29, 50
Richards, J. C. 113
Richardson, Malcolm 280, 307, 332
Rissanen, Matti v, 48, 80, 87, 88, 253, 288, 325, 332, 333, 335, 336, 340, 344, 361, 362
Robinson, Henry W. 432, 436
Robson, Cliff 436, 438
Romaine, Suzanne 54, 88, 230, 231, 232, 233, 254
Ronneberger-Siebold, Elke 107, 111, 113
Rudza-Ostyn, Brygida 112, 113

Safire, William 259, 270, 276
Salmon, Vivian 25, 28, 46, 47, 49, 50
Salt, John 291, 331
Samuels, Michael L. 298, 336
Sanders, Sara L. vii, xii, 257-277
Sansome, R. 403
Sapir, Edward viii, xv, 281, 285-287, 336
Sarrazin, Gregor 3, 23
Saussure, Ferdinand de 109, 110
Scarborough, D. C. 435, 437
Schäfer, Jürgen 205, 223, 225
Schendl, Herbert 311, 312, 319, 336
Schiffrin, Deborah 332
Schmid, Hans-Jörg 403
Schmidt, Alexander 3, 23
Schmidt, R. W. 113
Schoenbaum, Samuel 49, 50
Schofield, Roger C. 291, 337
Schreuder, Robert 105, 111
Schwarze, Christoph 403
Scott, Charles T. 48, 51
Scragg, Donald G. 407, 408, 432, 438
Sebeok, Thomas A. 46, 50
Sell, Roger D. 460, 461
Semino, Elena 73, 88
Shapiro, Michael 26, 30, 38, 50
Shearer, Beatrice 291, 292, 328, 332
Sheldon, Esther Keck 432, 438
Shimanoff, Susan B. 55, 88
Short, Mick 73, 88
Siegenthaler, John 268, 276
Silva, Penny 381, 401, 403
Smit, Ute vi, vii, xii, 377-403
Smith, Jeremy 374, 376, 407, 434, 438
Smout, Thomas Christopher 198
Sönmez, Margaret J.-M. vi, x, 405-439
Spencer-Oatey, Helen 44, 51

Stamenov, Maxim 111, 113
Stanley, Eric G. 332, 334
Stannard, Una 82, 88
Steckler, Nicole A. 55, 88
Stein, Dieter 76, 88, 131, 284, 299, 335, 337, 457, 460
Stephenson, Geoffrey M. 401
Sterling, Chris M. 436, 438
Stoffel, Cornelius 83, 88
Stone, Lawrence 296, 337
Strang, Barbara M. H. 137, 144, 168, 443, 460
Stringer, Jeffrey L. 269, 271, 276
Stroebe, Wolfgang 401
Sundby, Bertil 453, 454, 460
Sunderland, Jane 82
Sutcliffe, Thomas 107, 113
Svartvik, Jan 335, 361
Swan, Toril xiv, xv
Swanson, Anne 272
Swift, Kate 259, 268, 275
Syder, F. H. 108, 113
Szwedek, Aleksander 224

Taavitsainen, Irma 88, 254, 255, 336, 361, 362
Taglicht, Josef 130, 132
Tannen, Deborah 73, 88
Taubitz, Ronald 118, 130, 132
Taylor, Gary 6, 7, 15, 18, 22, 23
Terrell, Colin 426, 436
Thiele, Wolfgang 376
Thomson, Derick S. 197, 253
Thorne, Barrie 61, 88
Tieken-Boon van Ostade, Ingrid v, vi, vii, xi, 115, 132, 335, 337, 344, 350, 351, 362, 441-461
Tillyard, Stella 447, 449, 461
Timm, Lenora A. 268, 272, 276
Todd, Loreto 31, 50
Traugott, Elizabeth 289, 333
Trench, Richard C. 364, 365, 376

Troide, Lars E. 444, 450, 454, 461
Trudgill, Peter 53, 55, 57, 89, 275, 276, 280, 299, 300, 310, 316, 332, 335, 337, 354, 360, 361
Tulloch, Graham 198
Tyler, Lisa 270, 276

Ureland, P. Sture 198

Vachek, Josef 113
Vallins, George Henry 434, 438
van Bergen, Linda xiv, 332
Vanderbeke, Dirk 401, 402
Verdonk, Peter 460, 461
Verschueren, Jef 47, 51
Visser, F. Th. 117, 133

Waddell, J. N. 444, 461
Wagner, Richard K. 430, 434-436
Wakelin, Martyn F. 368, 376
Wales, Kathleen 29, 31, 34, 44, 51, 259, 276
Walker, Cherry 453, 458
Wallis, John 118, 133
Walter, John H. 51
Wang, William S.-Y. 299, 300, 310, 322, 329, 335
Ward, William 115, 118, 133
Wardhaugh, Ronald 442, 461

Wareing, John 292, 295, 337
Wells, John C. 92, 113
Wells, Stanley 6, 7, 15, 18, 22, 23
Wescott, Roger W. 82, 89
Westvik, Olaf Janson xiv, xv
Whitcut, Janet 132
White, Richard Grant 119, 133
Whorf, Benjamin L. 260, 277
Wicker, Tom 272, 277
Williams, Joseph M. 51
Williamson, Colin 28, 49
Williamson, Keith 227, 229, 255
Winchester, Barbara 307, 338
Winter, Werner xiii
Wood, Anthony 225
Wooton, Anthony 47, 48
Wotjak, Gerd 403
Wrenn, Charles L. 366, 367, 376, 406, 433, 434, 438
Wright, Joseph 299, 337
Wright, Laura 254, 255
Wrigley, E. A. 290-292, 297, 328, 337
Wyld, Henry Cecil 298, 306, 337, 366, 376, 417, 433, 434, 439
Wynne, Kenneth 85, 88

Zachrisson, Robert Eugen 406, 434, 439

Trends in Linguistics. Studies and Monographs

Edited by Werner Winter

Mouton de Gruyter · Berlin · New York

87 Peter Harder, *Functional Semantics. A Theory of Meaning, Structure and Tense in English.* 1996.
88 *Language Contact in the Arctic. Northern Pidgins and Contact Languages.* Edited by Ernst Håkon Jahr and Ingvild Broch. 1996.
89 *A Bibliography on Writing and Written Language.* Edited by Konrad Ehlich, Florian Coulmas and Gabriele Graefen. Compiled by Gabriele Graefen and Carl W. Wendland, in collaboration with Georg F. Meier and Reinhard Wenk. 1996.
90 *Historical, Indo-European, and Lexicographical Studies. A Festschrift for Ladislav Zgusta on the Occasion of his 70th Birthday.* Edited by Hans H. Hock. 1997.
91 Henning Andersen, *Reconstructing Prehistorical Dialects. Initial Vowels in Slavic and Baltic.* 1996.
92 *Natural Phonology. The State of the Art.* Edited by Bernhard Hurch and Richard A. Rhodes. 1996.
93 Hans H. Hock and Brian D. Joseph, *Language History, Language Change, and Language Relationship. An Introduction to Historical and Comparative Linguistics.* 1996.
94 *Insights in Germanic Linguistics II: Classic and Contemporary.* Edited by Irmengard Rauch and Gerald F. Carr. 1997.
95 Seiichi Suzuki, *The Metrical Organization of* Beowulf. *Prototype and Isomorphism.* 1996.
96 *Linguistic Reconstruction and Typology.* Edited by Jacek Fisiak. 1997.
97 *Advances in Morphology.* Edited by Wolfgang U. Dressler, Martin Prinzhorn and John R. Rennison. 1997.
98 *Language Change and Functional Explanations.* Edited by Jadranka Gvozdanović. 1997.
99 *Modality in Germanic Languages. Historical and Comparative Perspectives.* Edited by Toril Swan and Olaf J. Westvik. 1997.
100 *Language and its Ecology. Essays in Memory of Einar Haugen.* Edited by Stig Eliasson and Ernst Håkon Jahr. 1997.
101 *Language History and Linguistic Modelling. A Festschrift for Jacek Fisiak on his 60th Birthday.* Edited by Raymond Hickey and Stanisław Puppel. 1997.
102 Robert S. Bauer and Paul K. Benedict, *Modern Cantonese Phonology.* 1997.
103 *Studies in Middle English Linguistics.* Edited by Jacek Fisiak. 1997.
104 *Culture and Styles of Academic Discourse.* Edited by Anna Duszak. 1997.

105 *New Approaches to Chinese Word Formation. Morphology, Phonology and the Lexicon in Modern and Ancient Chinese.* Edited by Jerome L. Packard. 1997.
106 *Codeswitching Worldwide.* Edited by Rodolfo Jacobson. 1997.
107 *Salish Languages and Linguistics.* Edited by Ewa Czaykowska-Higgins and M. Dale Kinkade. 1997.
108 *The Life of Language. Papers in Linguistics in Honor of William Bright.* Edited by Jane H. Hill, P. J. Mistry and Lyle Campbell. 1997.
109 *English Historical Linguistics and Philology in Japan.* Edited by Jacek Fisiak and Akio Oizumi. 1998.
110 Marta Harasowska, *Morphophonemic Variability, Productivity, and Change. The Case of Rusyn.* 1998.
111 James Dickins, *Extended Axiomatic Linguistics.* 1998.
112 *Advances in English Historical Linguistics.* Edited by Jacek Fisiak and Marcin Krygier. 1998.
113 *Fragments of the Tocharian A Maitreyasamiti-Nāṭaka of the Xinjiang Museum, China.* Transliterated, translated and annotated by Ji Xianlin, in collaboration with Werner Winter and Georges-Jean Pinault. 1998.
114 *Language Change. Advances in Historical Sociolinguistics.* Edited by Ernst Håkon Jahr. 1998.
115 Jacob L. Mey, *When Voices Clash. A Study in Literary Pragmatics.* 1998.
116 *Productivity and Creativity. Studies in General and Descriptive Linguistics in Honor of E. M. Uhlenbeck.* Edited by Mark Janse with the assistance of An Verlinden.
117 Philip Baldi, *The Foundations of Latin.* 1998.
118 *Numeral Types and Changes Worldwide.* Edited by Jadranka Gvozdanović. 1999.
119 Birgit Anette Olsen, *The Noun in Biblical Armenian. Origin and Word Formation – with special emphasis on the Indo-European heritage.* 1999.
120 Bob Morris Jones, *The Welsh Answering System.* 1999.
121 Eva Koktova, *Word-Order Based Grammar.* 1999.
122 Nancy A. Niedzielski and Dennis R. Preston, *Folk Linguistics.* 2000.
123 David Prager Branner, *Problems in Comparative Chinese Dialectology. The Classification of Miin and Hakka.* 2000.
124 *Gender in Grammar and Cognition.* I: *Approaches to Gender.* II: *Manifestations of Gender.* Edited by Barbara Unterbeck, Matti Rissanen, Terttu Nevalainen, and Mirja Saari. 2000.
125 Brigitte Bauer, *Archaic Syntax in Indo-European. The Spread of Transitivity in Latin and French.* 2000.
126 *Codeswitching Worldwide II.* Edited by Rodolfo Jacobson. 2000.
127 *Analogy, Levelling, Markedness. Principles of Change in Phonology and Morphology.* Edited by Aditi Lahiri. 2000.
128 *Textualization of Oral Epics.* Edited by Lauri Honko. 2000.